Situating Globalization.
Views from Egypt

CYNTHIA NELSON
SHAHNAZ ROUSE (EDS.)
SITUATING GLOBALIZATION
Views from Egypt

[transcript]

All rights reserved. No part of this book may be reprinted or reproduced or utilized in any form or by any electronic, mechanical, or other means, now known or hereafter invented, including photocopying and recording, or in any information storage or retrieval system, without permission in writing from the publisher.

Die Deutsche Bibliothek – CIP-Einheitsaufnahme
Situating Globalization : Views from Egypt /
Cynthia Nelson ; Shahnaz Rouse (eds.). –
Bielefeld : transcript Verl., 2000
ISBN 3-933127-61-0

© 2000 transcript Verlag, Bielefeld
Typeset by: digitron GmbH, Bielefeld
**Printed and bound in Great Britain by
Marston Book Services Ltd, Oxfordshire**
ISBN 3-933127-61-0

Contents

Preface — 7
Cynthia Nelson and Shahnaz Rouse

Prologue — 9
Cynthia Nelson and Shahnaz Rouse

Globalization, Islam and the Indigenization of Knowledge — 15
Philip Marfleet

The Islamization of Knowledge between Particularism and Globalization: Malaysia and Egypt — 53
Mona Abaza

Gendering Globalization: Alternative Languages of Modernity — 97
Cynthia Nelson and Shahnaz Rouse

Struggling and Surviving: The Trajectory of Sheikh Moubarak Abdu Fadl. A Historical Figure of the Egyptian Left — 159
Didier Monciaud

Al-daght: Pressures of Modern Life in Cairo   203
MOHAMMED TABISHAT

Creating Bodies, Organizing Selves:
Planning the Family in Egypt   231
KAMRAN ASDAR ALI

Death of a Midwife   255
PETRA KUPPINGER

Problematizing Marriage: Minding My Manners
in My Husband's Community   283
ANITA HÄUSERMANN FÁBOS

A Tale of Two Contracts: Towards a Situated
Understanding of "Women Interests" in Egypt   301
HEBA EL-KHOLY

"We Are Not Feminists!"
Egyptian Women Activists on Feminism   337
NADJE AL-ALI

The Contributors   359

Preface

Cynthia Nelson and Shahnaz Rouse

The idea of this book came into being following a panel on the theme: *Gender Discourse and the Indigenization of Knowledge Debate*, that Nelson organized for the Sixth Congress of the International Association of Middle Eastern Studies held at Bayt al-Ayn University, Mafraq, Jordan April 10-14, 1996. We broadened the theme to encompass issues of globalization and the indigenization of knowledge debates and, in addition to the five original panelists who presented at that conference (Nelson, Rouse, Abaza, Al-Ali, El-Kholy), we invited six additional scholars (Didier, Marfleet, Asdar Ali, Häusermann Fábos, Kuppinger, Tabishat) all with theoretical interest in and research experience on issues of globalization/localization in Egypt. The title *Situating Globalization: Views from Egypt* was chosen precisely to reflect the fact that not only did we all meet each other in Egypt but also because the many dialogues and debates we engaged in with each other catalyzed much of the original research reflected in this book. All authors have written original papers each of which explores a particular dimension of the indigenization of knowledge debate emerging from the intersection of local experience with the broader processes of globalization – one of the most timely and relevant issues that is being debated in both the North and South.

The range of perspectives and original materials dealt with by each author highlights the renewed urgency of the struggle for cultural autonomy and voice within the context of the globalization process. In other words each paper explores how the various processes at both the local and global level intersect to create new discourses and debates around the "indigenization of knowledge". If a new wind of cultural decolonization is blowing through the Arab Middle East, which is having profound impact on the lives of men and women, then we should expect a new scholarship to emerge in order to grasp and understand it. This book is a contribution in that direction.

However, we would not have been able to complete this project without the support and commitment of a number of individuals and institutions. First, we would like to acknowledge the generosity of the Social Science Research Council, the Council of American Overseas Research Centers which helped fund the research of Professor Rouse, and Sarah Lawrence College for providing the leave of absence that enabled her to spend the necessary time in Egypt to undertake this project. Second, we would like to extend our deep appreciation to the American University in Cairo for its support to Professor Nelson in the form of conference grants to assemble the first panel in Jordan, research assistence for seminars and open forums and continuous academic encouragement. Thirdly, we would like to offer our special thanks to Rania al-Malky and Nelly El-Zayat, Graduate Merit Fellows, for their many hours of library reference work, editing and typing of first drafts and their continuous communication with all the participants. Last but by no means least, goes our deepest gratitude to Roseline Matalanis and Yvette Fayez Isaac, loyal staff in the office of the Dean of the School of Humanities and Social Sciences of the American University in Cairo, whose constant readiness and ideal of perfection, were generously devoted to many extra hours assisting the editors in the final preparation of the manuscript.

Prologue

Cynthia Nelson and Shahnaz Rouse

One of the key dimensions of this volume concerns the issue of borders and boundaries. These are both real and imaginary (i.e. symbolic and metaphoric), hegemonic and counter hegemonic. Among those real borders are spatial ones that determine individuals' and communities' everyday location and place in the world – these include borders/boundaries of class, gender, territory, and language(s). Each of these separations in turn has embedded in it, and rests on constructions of 'imaginary' borders and boundaries – for instance the roles ascribed to women, the permissions and opportunities that stem from class and spatial/territorial location. In other words the real and imaginary do not exist as two disparate entities but are inextricably linked to each other in a dialectical move that simultaneously enables and disables movement and action. And it is this circular yet not tautological relation that defines the dilemmas and the promise of globalization.

Until recently, three elements dominated thinking and writing on globalization: first, the *newness* of the phenomenon. Globalization was thus represented as a radical departure from the colonial and early post-colonial period. Second and in relation to the first, globalization was envisioned as *a homogenizing process*, one which threatened to engulf the local and overcome it. Implicit in such thinking is the notion that movement emanates from the north to the south; and furthermore, that the south is helpless in the face of the overwhelming power that still accrues and rests in the advanced capitalist world. The turning point in the view of many progressives and conservatives alike, was the decline and collapse of the Soviet Union, and the emergence of a 'new' world order. Finally, the global was *represented as 'foreign'*, external (to the local). The struggle therefore was posited as consisting of a dialectic encounter between hegemonic forces of globalization and 'indigenous' forces of resistance.

Current re-visioning of globalization challenges all these suppositions. For those of us born in the 'South', globalization is nothing new. It is a new form of an on-going process that took inception during the heyday of colonialism. It might serve as a descriptive term to articulate the current historical period, but it remains theoretically problematic and imprecise. While theoretically globalization is often explained in terms of time-space compression, we feel bound to reiterate, borrowing from Doreen Massey's *Space, Place and Gender* (1994: 147), the extent to which such a conceptualization represents the coming home of capital's outward spread on localities in the core. She states:

> The sense of dislocation which some might feel at the sight of a once well-known local street now lined with a succession of cultural imports ... must have been felt for centuries, though from a very different point of view, by colonized peoples all over the world as they watched the importation, maybe even used, the products of, first, European colonization, maybe British ..., later U.S., as they learned to eat wheat instead of rice or corn, to drink Coca Cola, just as today we try out enchiladas.

Moreover, as well as querying the enthnocentricity of the idea of time-space compression and its current acceleration, we also need to ask about its causes: what is it that determines our degrees of mobility, that influences the sense we have of space and place? Time-space compression refers to movement and communication across space, to the geographical stretching out of social relations, and to our experience of all of this. The usual interpretation is that it results overwhelmingly from the action of capital, and from its currently increasing internationalization ... . But surely this is insufficient. Among the many other things which clearly influence that experience, there are, for instance, 'race' and gender ... . In other words, and most broadly, time-space compression needs differentiating socially. This is not just a moral or political point about inequality; it is also a conceptual point.

The close of this quotation slides into our second point: globalization is *not* a homogenous process, nor is it straightforwardly homogenizing. It affects different localities and peoples within them differentially. The very term 'people' conceals as much as it reveals: are we talking about men, women, the educated or those without education, the rich or the poor, those culturally dominant in a particular context or those culturally marginalized? Should we not re-think globalization as a struggle between dominant groups in different arenas – the economic, the cultural, and/or in terms of gender and/or race, ethnicity, as opposed to those marginalized? Reconsidered in these ways, maybe it might be more useful to think of globalization as a multiplicity of flows in a variety of terrains, bearing witness to the emergence of new political realities and accompanying shifts in power, as well as struggles around these transformations.

Our volume picks up on these problematics of power and its dispersal and concentration. Thus both Philip Marfleet's and Mona Abaza's papers point to the manner in which cultural idioms travel across borders; and these borders are not the traditionally antagonistic ones of 'east' and 'west' but constituted by means of a flow from south to (other parts of) the south. However, the bearers of these cultural flows seek legitimacy from their potential constituency by positing their language – cultural and religious – as local and therefore inherently in opposition to the hegemonic cultural knowledge that has seeped in from 'outside' and led to disempowerment of local 'peoples' and 'knowledges'. No mention is made by bearers to this Islamist knowledge, of the 'foreignness' of this idiom to many *within* the societies in question. Any attempt to contest their positioning and bearers of the indigenous results in charges of either betrayal or brain washing. This mode of articulation, in other words, which masks its own attempts at hegemony and control over all other local languages, represents itself instead as egalitarian – a furthering of democracy, albeit democracy in a new form. Regardless of the self-representation by its proponents, such a positioning disregards multiple cultural languages, knowledges and experiences that are 'authentic' to individuals who live them on a daily basis.

The majority of the papers in this volume address this multiplicity: Heba El-Kholy's article speaks of the manner in which working class women use customary practices as a means of empowering themselves within a marital arrangement and the obliviousness of secular, middle class feminists to such arrangements; Mohammed Tabishat's article shows that both health professionals and men and women of the popular classes rely on a mixture of modern and alternative medical and spiritual remedies in the treatment of *al-daght* i.e. hypertension. Rather than invoke a clear distinction of medical and other languages between professionals and 'the people', this work demonstrates the interpenetration at all levels of various languages and remedies.

But this interpenetration of language can also lead to the dominance of certain discourses over others. For example, in their papers Kamran Asdar Ali and Petra Kuppinger focus on the hegemonic role that the discourse of development and public health play in constructing what constitutes 'healthy behaviors' defined basically as those that affect the economy. Asdar Ali specifically emphasizes how women-sensitive development agendas in Egypt are linked to the larger historical debates on how to control women's bodies in particular and create responsible citizens in general. Kuppinger on the other hand shows how the loss of midwifery skills and eventual control of female bodies by state medicine is part of larger developments in both colonial and post-colonial Egypt. By moving back and forth between the lives and work of midwives within a local community and the larger state policies of order, control and domination we come to understand the hegemonic power of medical/development discourse.

In their piece *Gendering Globalization: Alternative Languages of Modernity* Nelson and Rouse point out how the period of modernity can be seen as transitional, during which individuals are cast into particular identities by their particular location in time and place.

The instance of Doria Shafik speaks to the multiplicity of languages not across peoples but in the same person. Her persona exemplifies the manner in which these are not contradictory impulses but integrated practices consequent to a person's particular existence at a given historical moment. Nonetheless, Doria Shafik suffered at the hands of her peers, both secular and religious, in being denied both as a woman (the Dean of Cairo University refused to give her a job on these grounds) and as a supposedly 'westernized' woman (by the mufti of al-Azhar for her feminist stances). Her ultimate flight from active politics, ironically, resulted not from her religious adversaries but from the left, some among whom condemned her for her critique of Nasser's regime and its denial of women's and human rights to Egyptian women.

Doria Shafik's example speaks volumes for the manner in which identities are thrust upon people, what some Indian writers have referred to as 'forced identities'. In other words, identities that one does not assume but that are imposed on a person by others. There are numerous examples of such 'forcing' in the contemporary world: in Sarajevo, in Cyprus, in many parts of contemporary Africa. For our purposes, the need to distinguish between identities one assumes and dons deliberately, and the identities which one is forced to assume is paramount. In the latter case, the most obvious instance is that of people caught in historical crisis points: during the burning of Babri Masjid in India in the nineties, at India's partition in 1947, and following the 1967 Israel conflict in various parts of the Middle East.

Here the issue of the identities one 'chooses' and the identities into which one is 'forced' become complex and knotted. Conventionally, the resolution to this crisis in identities has been sought in placing people caught between worlds – the old and the emergent – as either modern or traditional; and each of these two terms is either valorized or denigrated depending on those doing the labelling. The articles in this volume suggest – and the instance of Jahanara Shahnawaz and Hamida Akhtar Hussein highlights this – that the languages we speak are as often the consequence of our own life histories and experiences as they are deliberate choices we make. And by extension, to take them out of this experiential context, is to render them meaningless and simply the target of ideological accusation and subterfuge.

The articles by Didier Monciaud, Anita Häusermann Fábos and Nadje Al-Ali particularly illustrate this point. Monciaud for example reconstructs the trajectory of a particular historical actor by locating him in the context of the communist movement in Egypt. Through a biographical approach he unveils and reconstructs the underlying meaning of a life as well as the self-representation of this historical actor. As a result of his experience and the place he occupied in this movement, Moubarak Abdu Fadl figures as a living legend, representing in the present the human continuity and political memory of Egypt.

Häusermann Fábos and Al-Ali, on the other hand, choose to situate themselves in the very process of knowledge construction. In her article *Problematizing Marriage: Minding my Manners in my Husband's Community* Häusermann Fábos considers the dialectical projects of negotiating the roles of spouse and researcher in relation to changing gender ideology for a northern Sudanese immigrant community in Cairo. Her personal understanding of Sudanese norms of propriety, developed through marriage to a man from her research community, led her along an epistemological path towards a hypothesis on the role of manners for Sudanese in marking ethnic boundaries in relation to Egyptian society. Through this process of negotiation, Häusermann Fabos came face to face with the challenge of authenticity and the ethical implications of the research process itself.

Al-Ali appropriately concludes our series of essays by challenging assumptions about western as opposed to indigenous scholarship within the context of the author's research among secular oriented women activists in Egypt. The author's own positionality vis-à-vis the women she interviewed is explored in order to reveal the complexities and ambiguities inherent in the research enterprise. The experience of shifting boundaries between self and other, between the researcher's identity and those of her informants became central to this inquiry. While occasionally presenting a source of self-knowledge, mediation and bridging, the experience of 'being here and there' may pose great dilemmas and conflicts for the researcher who cannot be clearly positioned inside or outside her research community.

This brings us to a final point: might not a better way to approach treatment of globalization be through a more thorough going empirical investigation into the multiple dimensions of the process and its related social relations through the lens of experience and life histories? While recognizing that experience itself does not exist outside representation, can we not simultaneously interrogate people's lives even as we probe the languages in which these lives are explained and made sense of? What we are suggesting is a return to a feminist framework. Not as a way to study women's histories alone, but as *a perspective* that permits us to better understand the lives of the marginalized and their desire for a genuinely egalitarian social order rather than one that posits its egalitarianism in discursive terms alone.

Bibliography

Massey, Doreen (1994) *Space, Place and Gender*, Minneapolis/MN: University of Minnesota Press.

Mignolo, Walter D. (1997) *Local Histories/Global Designs*, Princeton/NJ: Princeton University Press.

Oncu, Ayse/Weyland, Petra (1994) *Space, Culture and Power*, London: Zed Books.

Globalization, Islam and the Indigenization of Knowledge

Philip Marfleet

The rise of theories of globalization has brought increased interest in the idea of indigenous knowledge. As notions of the world as "a single place" have become more influential, there has been greater interest in movements which are said to be expressive of the new global condition. Among these, the current which seeks "Islamization" of knowledge has attracted particular attention. For its leading ideologues, Islamic approaches alone are adequate to understand the contemporary world and to advance a new universal morality. This essay looks at their claims, especially at the idea that Muslim intellectuals are uniquely equipped to contest dominant Western discourses. It argues that rather than contesting such ideas Islamization has complemented them.

Islamic traditions have long developed within a complex of inter-cultural flows and exchanges. This essay therefore also looks at some of the diverse influences that have shaped modern Islamic movements. It argues that by minimizing or even ignoring such experiences, theories of globalization and of Islamization greatly distort the processes at work within contemporary society.

Islamization

For its proponents the movement for Islamization of knowledge aims at salvation of the world community of Muslims – the *umma* – and by extension the whole of humanity. Al 'Alwani, a leading figure within the movement, views Islamization as "the most important issue before the Ummah" (1994: x). It is, he comments, "the Ummah's future, its destiny, its objective, the means of its emergence from its crisis, and the way to building a new civilisation and a new renaissance" (Al-Alwani 1994: x).

The movement's energies are directed overwhelmingly into intellectual activity that aims to provide a suitable framework for Muslims to examine the contemporary world in terms of Islamic belief and practice. This is to be achieved by the identification of foundational religious principles in all areas of life: to assert what Turner calls "a claim about the authenticity of tradition over inherited, imported or alien knowledge" (Turner 1994: 7). The development of a comprehensive Islamic perspective, it is argued, will allow Muslims to challenge dominant models which have emerged within Western academia and which are viewed by the Islamizers as false.

Sardar, who is a leading contributor to the Islamization literature, comments that much of the Western academic tradition requires radical revision. The social sciences are a matter of special concern, he argues, being "cultural constructions of Western civilization [which] have virtually no meaning or relevance for Muslim societies" (Sardar 1997: 47). Muslim intellectuals are therefore required to engage in a new academic practice:

[t]o generate disciplines that are a natural product of the world view and civilization of Islam; [to] use Islamic categories and notions to describe goals and aspirations, thought and behaviour and problems and solutions of Muslim societies.

(Sardar 1997: 7)

To this end, a considerable literature has been produced by Muslim scholars, especially those associated with a series of specialist institutes and study centres established since the early 1980s. They have succeeded in generating debates which challenge Muslim academics to reconsider orthodox attitudes towards scientific thought. Stenberg (1996b: 273) suggests they have had a significant impact, not least because of the implications for the whole Islamic tradition. In effect, the Islamizers have nominated themselves as interpreters of the religious tradition, making claims which define a "true" Islam.

Religion and Globalism

For the Islamization movement the notion of a "global" order is of special significance. On the one hand, it is seen as highly problematic: thus Sardar (1997: 41) identifies the difficulties presented by globalizing processes associated with Western capitalism and what he calls "disciplinary imperialism". On the other hand, the global context is seen to offer opportunities. El-Affendi (1991: 3) comments: "It is time we Muslims realize that we live in a global community, and that our ideas and beliefs are under scrutiny from the whole of humanity". Such scrutiny, he argues, allows Muslims to display fully the qualities of Islam. Abul-Fadl (1992: 10) argues similarly that Islamization "entails reshaping the future of the global order". What is required, she maintains, is nothing less than development of "a new global consciousness which is inclusive" (Abul-Fadl 1992: 9), one in which Islamization will play a key role in "renegotiating the terms of the global encounter" (Abul-Fadl 1992: 11). In promoting Islamic goals, committed Muslims will be "appropriating global interdependence" – in effect, Muslims will seize the opportunities presented by the global condition (Abul-Fadl 1992: 34).

Such references to globalism and to its significance for Islam in the modern world are striking features of the Islamization literature. They might be seen as consistent with the views of non-Muslim theorists of globalization, who suggest that contemporary religious movements in general express a "global calling". In this view, such movements are intimately involved in the generation of a singular world, what Robertson (1992: 6) calls a "global unicity". This development, it is argued, is a function of socio-cultural changes associated with world integration. But what is the "global" condition and what processes can be identified as "globalizing" influences?

Theories of globalization have developed a pervasive influence. According to Waters (1995: 1), "globalization may be *the* concept of the 1990s, a key idea by which we understand the transition of human society into the millennium". Although notions of the global are often diffuse and sometimes elusive, they hold in common the idea of a unifying or integrating world. Among organisation theorists such as Ohmae (1990), who have dominated discussions about the global, the world is best understood as a series of interlocking networks. Here globalism meets conservative economic theory in the shape of neo-liberalism. The global entity is the market, a structure within which entrepreneurial activities sweep over old boundaries such as national frontiers to make a "borderless world". Tensions arise only to the extent that outdated state structures attempt to intervene in rational decision-making processes among transnational corporations and a vast mass of individual consumers. Such notions have had an impact across the spectrum within Western social science, so that writers such as Desai and Harris, once fierce critics of global market models, can also identify the transforming power of capital. For Harris (1995: 228), for example, transnational economic changes are now so profound that they serve "world interest and a universal morality".

Social and cultural theories of the global elaborate a similar theme. Writers such as Giddens (1990; 1991), Harvey (1989) and Hall (1992) emphasize the interconnectedness of the contemporary order, especially the "compression" of time and space which results from technological innovation associated with transnational economic changes. More and more, it is argued, notions of physical distance are challenged by the possibilities of electronic communication. The global system therefore unifies but is also one in which all are affected by the proximity of "elsewhere", producing a new consciousness of Self and Other.

Some currents within this discourse have attempted to use a global framework to criticize dominant models of world culture and especially of historical change, with positive outcomes. Focusing on the long record of interaction between socio-cultural and political formations, they have challenged modern nation-centred perspectives and the associated cultural determinisms which celebrate European "civilizational" values.[1] The mainstream of globalization theory which examines social and cultural matters has, however, suggested a "stronger" theory which has proved more problematic.

Globalization is said to bring rapid change, social and cultural flux, ambivalence and uncertainty – conditions often associated with the "postmodern condition" of fragmentation and diversity. Here, globalization is not merely marketization or mass consumerism but is in Featherstone's words, a "generative frame of unity within which diversity can take place" (Featherstone 1990: 2). The result may be an engagement of large numbers of people in efforts to discover secure locations in a fluid and sometimes disturbing world. Globalization is said to speak both of integration and of dislocation: it is the context within which the attempt to discover authentic socio-cultural locations is pursued. As part of this quest, Robertson argues, a "search for fundamentals" – for certainties or foundational values – is increasingly significant (Robertson 1992: 170).

For Robertson, perhaps the most influential theorist of the socio-cultural dimensions of globalization, world integration is best understood as a series of processes which have brought into being a "globality" or "unicity". This is a systemic condition: all effective social units are shaped by global integration and at the same time play a part in shaping it. In this context the search for fundamentals is highly significant. Robertson (1992: 166) observes: "Defining globalization in its basic sense as involving the compression of the world, one must insist that it is the globality of the 'search for fundamentals' which is its most interesting feature."

The "search" is part of a general quest for particularisms which are simultaneously universal claims. Borrowing from Wallerstein's world systems theory, Robertson argues that by the late 20th century a twofold process was under way, "involving the *interpenetration of the universalization of particularism and the particularization of universalism*" (Beyer 1994: 28; original emphasis). The effect is to constrain "civilisations and societies" to be increasingly explicit about their "global callings (their unique geocultural or geo-moral contributions to world history)" (Robertson 1992: 130).

Such developments are said to have special significance for religion. Increased interconnectedness at the global level is viewed as heightening awareness of the diversity of human experience, challenging local belief systems and the worldviews they sustain. The retreat into isolation sometimes associated with particularism is less and less feasible. At the same time, global pressures become more demanding, requiring interpretation and explanation, and encouraging the reworking of worldviews – promoting the search for fundamentals. Localisms not only discover new elaborations of the universal but also have access to novel means of projecting them, both through innovative technologies and in terms of the heightened receptivity to universal perspectives which is an aspect of the global condition.

As world views, religions are said to have special significance within the globalizing process: of all complexes of ideas they are best equipped to prosper within a "unicity". Waters (1995: 125) refers to the "globalizing sense of mission" of major world religions such as Christianity, Islam and Hinduism, which have now, he suggests, discovered a highly congenial environment. Turner (1994: 83) argues similarly, noting that the changes associated with modernity bring closer the possibility that such belief systems might "realize" themselves.

In this context the search for fundamentals can produce religious movements which, according to Robertson (1992: 170) are nothing less than "a product of globality". Modern religious movements, he argues, are both an expression of the global condition and a force for its consolidation. Beyer (1994: 3) elaborates: "religion can be a proactive force in the sense that it is instrumental in the elaboration and development of globalization: the central thrust is to make [believers] more determinative in the world system." Here even "antisystemic" religious movements – those formally committed to contesting dominant ideas and structures – complement globalizing processes. Religion becomes a positive force in the making of the global condition.

"Islamic Science"

Archer (1990: 1) argues that globalization is pervasive:

Globalization affects everyone since it presents them with a world context which influences them in some of their doings ... we all become global agents because reactions to a single context produce powerful aggregate effects which act back on the world environment.

Within this context, some theorists of globalization also maintain that certain collectivities are more expressive of the global condition than others; most important, that those operating within a universalizing framework may seek more energetically to assert their mission in an integrating world. Here the Islamization movement can be viewed, in Beyer's terms, as one of the "proactive forces" for globalization. Its proponents maintain that Islamization challenges dominant values at a world level, in particular that it contests what AbuSulayman (1993b: xvi) calls the "excess and desecration" characteristic of Western society and which is said to have become a pervasive influence worldwide.

Islamization, he maintains, "must not stop at any physical borders, but must be extended to every corner of the earth and contemporary civilization" (AbuSulayman 1993b: xvi).

For the Islamizers, mainstream Islamic discourse is judged inadequate to this task. Manzoor (1989: 59) argues that contemporary Islamic thought is largely irrelevant to the Muslim reality, being nostalgic, rhetorical, abstract and ineffective in contesting the West. These gross shortcomings require to be confronted:

Obviously ... for Muslim thought, the problem of relevance is a problem of history; indeed it is a problem of the West's power and ascendancy. It is a problem that forces the Muslim thinker to relate his Islamic self to the outside world, which is a creation of Western man, in a spirit of accommodation and compromise, if not downright capitulation. Little wonder, then, that nearly all Islamic discourse is a pathetic exercise in apology: it has arisen after all, as a response to the Western attack ... if Islamic thought is to end its courtship with irrelevance, it must end its debilitating fascination with the West and make a genuine rediscovery of its authentic self.

(Manzoor 1989: 60)

This profound crisis can only be solved by directing new energies towards a strategic goal: "The ultimate focus of Islamic discourse," Manzoor argues, "is the problem of world order" (Manzoor 1989: 60). It is by confronting this global challenge that Muslims will reassert the universal mission at the heart of Islamic belief.

The initiative for Islamization as a project – a collective effort directed to specific goals – came in the mid-1960s. Among the movement's first formal statements was that of Al-Attas, who set out an agenda for "the liberation of man first from magical, mythological, animistic, national-cultural tradition, then from secular control over his reason and language" (Sardar 1989: 30). The project was to be intimately linked with "de-Westernization of knowledge", in particular with contestation of the dualism identified in a separation of value and knowledge in modern European thought. Among co-thinkers, Idris argued that this was integral to the invigoration of Islam, nothing less than "an organized and gradual effort which will culminate in the realisation of an (Islamic) society" (Sardar 1989: 30).

In the mid-1970s a formal initiative was launched. This was the result of an appeal by Idris to Muslim social scientists to elaborate systematically a range of philosophical positions and working perspectives based upon "an ideology of Islam" (Sardar 1989: 30). He maintained that Muslim scholars' belief was to differentiate their work from that of other academics by providing a frame of reference for construction of "Islamic social sciences". These might make use of Western science but would correct its "faulty" ideology (Sardar 1989: 30). Idris argued:

It is true that there are discoverable laws of nature and society and it is true that the behaviour of large scale material things is influenced by the behaviour of their constituent elements, but it is not true that these constituent elements are all there is; and it is not true that the so-called laws of nature are laid down by nature for nature.

(Sardar 1989: 30)

An Islamic science based in the notion of *tawhid* – oneness or unity of God – would identify systemic faults in the Western approach; Muslims might then reveal a knowledge free of the distortions introduced by the West.

The project began to attract a number of prominent Muslim academics, especially in North America. By the late 1970s one influential group had taken a decision to formalize the movement and at an international conference in Switzerland agreed to develop an institutional structure, setting up the International Institute of Islamic Thought (IIIT) in Washington D.C. in 1981. The IIIT has since established a network of offices in South and South-East Asia, North America, Europe and the Middle East, and related groups have developed centres such as the Centre for Studies on Science at Aligarh, India. From the early 1980s, the movement also began to attract academics based in Europe, who have since contributed extensively to the Islamization literature. These have included Sardar, Maurice Bucaille and Roger Garaudy. A number of Muslim political leaders have also endorsed the movement, notably Malaysian Prime Minister Mahathir Mohamed.

Following a further international conference held in Pakistan in 1982, the IIIT published its *General Principles and Workplan*, inviting Muslim scholars in all disciplinary fields "to develop Islamic thought and methodology, the contents of the Islamic vision, and the goals, values and basic principles of Islamization" (IIIT 1984: 1). Within the *Workplan* was an essay by Ismael Raji al-Faruqi which has become particularly influential within the Islamization current. Faruqi attacked Western social science, which he saw as a means of obscuring the realities of the modern world. Its disciplines, he argued, had been developed instrumentally within Western cultures bent upon world domination. He was especially hostile towards their political agendas:

> The Western social sciences – history, geography, economics, political science, sociology and anthropology – were all developed under the impetus provided by romanticism. All of them, each in its own way, are based upon the ethnocentric view that nation, or ethnic identity ... is the ultimate unit of analysis and value. When they speak of 'society' or 'social order', they mean their own national entity or order ... . Sociology boldly affirms the ethnocentric thesis because it deals directly with society and social order. Political science follows. Western geography and history can conceive of the world only as a satellite of the West, the world revolving around England, America, France, Germany or Italy as its heart and core.
> (IIIT 1982: 37-38)

Western economics has been "impertinent enough to claim for itself the status of a universal science", while anthropology is "the boldest of all": in its view, "'humanity' means ethnicity and is logically equivalent to and convertible with it" (IIIT 1982: 38).

Faruqi concluded that full awareness of the conflict between these distorting perspectives and the truths held by Islam had become evident only under contemporary conditions: "it is our present generation that first discovered the conflict as we lived it in our own intellectual lives" (Sardar 1989: 31). This discovery, comments Abul-Fadl (1992: 53), amounted to new consciousness of a need to prioritize the "cultural imperative" within Islamic practice, dictating a common Muslim effort to contest the whole framework of the social sciences. She observes (with a strangely inappropriate allusion to the words of Karl Marx) that Faruqi and his co-thinkers "may have lamented the situation of the Muslim ummah; its intention however was not to bemoan its fate but to act to change it" (Abul-Fadl 1992: 106).

For almost two decades the Islamizers have produced works in the fields of history, philosophy, scientific method, law, economics, philology, sociology, politics, international relations, anthropology and psychology. Their objective, in Abul-Fadl's words, has been that of "reformulating and representing modern social thought from an Islamic perspective" (Abul-Fadl 1992: 99). The impact has been considerable. Stenberg comments that the challenge to mainstream theories of knowledge has affected many Muslim intellectuals, generating debates in which "[A]t stake is the right to define the relation between the Islamic tradition and science and, in the end, the function of the Islamic tradition in general ... to display the 'true' and 'authentic' form of 'Islam'" (Stenberg 1996a: 273).

Indigenization and Globalism

Ghamari-Tabrizi (1996: 317) comments that in approaching the question of "Islamic science" we should be guided by the particular sociohistorical conditions within which it has emerged: "What counts as Islamic is not some transhistorical notion of moral values, but rather a socio-historical position that is the direct consequence of the colonial encounter and its subsequent local oppositional political and intellectual movements."

For over 200 years European states have dominated most Islamic regions. Orientalism has provided rationales for the subordination of their populations by arguing that Muslims ("the Muslim mind") is perverse, unreceptive to rationalist approaches, to "science" and to modernity in general. On this view, Muslims are incapable of positive thought and action: they remain inert, subordinate to those whose rational actions demonstrate the advanced character of European culture. For decades such views were pervasive within Western academia. As Said and others have pointed out (Said 1978; Hussain/Olson/Qureshi 1984), they have been the basis for establishment of specialist disciplines and institutions concerned primarily with imagined differences between Europe and "other" traditions, principally Islam. It is against this background that the Islamizers set out to describe an Islamic perspective as the basis for assertion of Muslim identity. What is striking about their claims, however, is the *embrace* of contemporary circumstances: the assertion that a world marked by the expansion from Europe of industrial capitalism, and by the latter's social, political and cultural expressions, is an especially appropriate condition for the elaboration of an Islamic worldview.

Recent changes in the world order are said to be particularly significant. Ibrahim (1989: 17) observes:

> It is a truism to say that world is changing and shrinking. What is not so well appreciated, however, is that the world is changing and shrinking at a faster and faster pace. Today the rate of change is itself changing and accelerating. Moreover, there have been other fundamental alterations in the nature of change. Contemporary changes are characterized by their global nature, swift interpenetration, increased feedback, irreversibility, complexity and interdependence of one group of changes upon another.

Although the West has long distorted understandings of the world, he argues, it is this *new* order which has compelled a specific Muslim reaction: "the nature of contemporary change forces us to institutionalize an holistic, integrative, collective interactive and continuous process of [Islamic] planning" (Ibrahim 1989: 22). The *umma* is appropriately placed to meet this challenge, Ibrahim argues, because although it is diverse culturally and ethnically it is integrated globally on the basis of commitment to foundational values. Such values embrace all human experience: "There are no new values out there waiting to be discovered. There is complete consensus of the ummah on this issue ..." (Ibrahim 1989: 19). As one in shared belief, Muslims are in fact uniquely situated to respond to the modern world.

AbuSulayman, one of the architects of the Islamization project, concurs. The modern world, he argues, offers no place of retreat: "In today's global village and market, isolationism is no longer a viable choice. Rather, there must be a common degree of principles, values and considerations that allow world society to function and maintain human existence" (AbuSulayman 1993b: xvi). It is in this context that Islamization must extend "to every corner of the earth" (ibid.: xvi).

The notion of globalization appears repeatedly in strategic documents of the Islamization movement, where it is associated with a growing sense that the new state of affairs offers possibilities of realization or fulfillment of foundational Islamic values. Abul-Fadl, for example, writes of a global context in which "a century's technological accomplishments have dissipated the physical distances between communities and cultures" (Abul-Fadl 1992: 106). She comments that: "Isolation and withdrawal are no longer a feasible alternative in a global village where interdependence is the order of the times" (ibid.: 81-82). It is now, she maintains, that the historic unity of Islam can claim its full relevance, providing an answer to the key question: "how to evolve a global architectonics of a community that [is] both free and moral?" (ibid.: 106).

Anees echoes this conclusion, emphasizing that contemporary circumstances have a special significance for Muslims, for "history has come full circle" (Anees 1993: 61). Today's *umma* – "the global Muslim community" – inhabits a world which offers possibilities to recall the early Islamic era of territorial expansion when "the creative Muslim impulse spread its liberating influence far and wide" (ibid.: 61). Now Muslims are challenged by the possibility of renaissance: "Will the Muslim intellect rise to the challenge?" (ibid.: 61).

Such self-conscious identification of the global setting and of its implications for a universal mission might be seen to reinforce the notion that "globality" *is* playing a determinative role in the emergence of Islamization. This is the conclusion reached by Stenberg (1996b: 336), who comments that, "the [Islamization] discourse can be seen as a form of localization of Islam, a construction of locality based on the possibilities of modernity and globalization". Such a view echoes Robertson's observation that indigenization programs in general are "entrapped in, are indeed largely a product of modernity and, particularly, of globality" (Robertson 1992: 168). Such conclusions are misleading, however. Islamization is less an expression of an integrated world than a perspective which wishes to invoke such a world. Like globalization theory, Islamization sets aside the asymmetries and contradictions which characterize the world system. Both currents impose an imagined unicity upon a volatile and disordered world: neither is appropriate as a means of understanding contemporary conditions, including the condition of the mass of Muslims.

Globalism in Question

Theories of globalization have a pervasive influence. In the early 1980s they began to affect the social sciences; within a decade they had taken hold in other disciples and in much of the Western media. Only recently has a counter-current emerged. This focuses on core areas of globalization theory, notably in the fields of economics and political economy. Hirst and Thompson (1996), Harman (1996), Kiely (1996), and Hoogvelt (1997) have examined recent patterns of transnational economic activity. None suggest that these are unchanged or that changes are insignificant; each argues, however, that the notion of world economic integration is far from new, that such patterns have been misread and that the notion of a "borderless world" disregards the impacts of national and regional structures to the point of perversity. I have also argued elsewhere that much of globalization theory is inappropriate for the study of social movements, especially religious movements relating to the Third World (Marfleet 1998a).

These critiques suggest that globalist theories *impose* unicity upon structures which show extreme unevenness and contradiction rather than coherence. In particular, they obscure the disjuncture and conflict characteristic of the modern world. In this sense globalism is consistent with the functionalist traditions of most modern social and political theory: indeed, the notion that "the global circumstance" operates to accommodate anti-systemic movements reinforces the sense that "unicity" is premised upon organicism and a Durkheimian pursuit of social order.

By ignoring structures of the most extreme inequality globalist theory marginalizes most of the non-Western world. Assuming the distributive powers of the market, such perspectives make unproblematic the flows of capital generated by and focused upon traditional centres of accumulation, and the power relations associated with them. World economic activity is still concentrated overwhelmingly with the "Triad" of economic networks in North America, Western Europe and Japan. Most of Africa, Asia and Latin America – home to over 80 percent of humanity – have experienced increased exclusion, to the extent that some regions have recently been identified as zones of crisis all but detached from the world economy – what the United Nations calls the "wastelands" (*The Independent*, 29 December 1996).

In some regions of the Third World economic structures are disintegrating and social and political volatility has increased greatly. Here, comments Cox (1995: 41), even the main global development institutions have abandoned attempts at change "in favour of what can be called global poor relief and riot control". At a world level, inequality has increased dramatically, producing what Cheru (Cox 1995: 41) calls "global apartheid", a vision so much at odds with ideas of a harmonizing world entity as to raise basic questions about the whole globalist paradigm.

Despite the assertion by globalization theory that divisions between "First" and "Third" worlds or "North" and "South" have been rendered meaningless, global theory itself is replete with references to "the West" and to a non-West, sometimes identified as the Third World. The dichotomy is invariably accompanied by homogenization of the two elements and by a focus on exoticized non-European phenomena, especially on anti-systemic movements, with religious movements and especially Islamic currents attracting particular attention. In a recent wide-ranging review of global theory, Waters, for example, is quite consistent with his co-thinkers in identifying "Islamic fundamentalism" as a first example of the cultural impacts of globalism (Waters 1995: 2).

Of the numerous shortcomings of global theory, however, none is more significant than its ahistorical framework. With a few partial exceptions global analyses exclude histories and the making of histories.[2] Together with an overwhelmingly structuralist emphasis this serves to negate the record of human self-activity. The various and changing circumstances under which social agents have attempted to modify their circumstances do not feature in global accounts. The political conflicts and contestations, and the struggles over construction and modification of social and cultural forms, are largely absent. So too with the long experience of interaction between socio-cultural traditions: the record of exchange and diffusion hardly appears within the globalist thesis. Where such ideas are introduced it is to suggest that such exchanges are novel, with the implication that discrete cultural blocs had earlier remained mutually isolated.

At its worst globalism can produce theories of an integrated world which serve as rationales for the aggressive assertion of difference by dominant powers. The most influential of these, Huntington's "clash of civilizations" thesis, combines every weakness of the various globalization currents (Huntington 1993). It offers a picture of homogenized, discrete cultural blocs ("the West", "Islam", "Confucianism") among which past conflicts serve only to warn of traumatic events to come. Predictably, "the West" must prepare to face an aggressive and already blood-stained Orient. It is hardly surprising that more restrained globalist analyses are sensitive to criticisms that such approaches may be viewed as ideological in character. Turner, who is sympathetic to some of the global account, notes the suggestion that the latter can be seen as "evolutionary and teleological ... in fact a new version of Westernisation" (Turner 1994: 108).

Islam and Change

Globalist theory should be approached with great caution; so too with theories of Islamization of knowledge which reproduce much of the globalist account. This is especially important in the areas of history and of cultural exchange.

Abaza and Stauth (1990: 211) comment of those who wish to "indigenize" Islam that they appear unaware of the long history of interaction between Islamic and other traditions and of the implications of their own celebrations of difference:

Those ... who claim authenticity by 'indigenization' might not yet be aware of the fact that the local knowledge, upon which they want to construct an alternative, has long since been part of global structures; or of the fact that they play a part in a global cultural game which itself calls for the 'essentialization' of local truth. The new apologetics for Islamist trends are a derivation of the new Western "essentialism" in inter-cultural studies.

Here it is implicit that those who perceive a "Western knowledge" also view it as constructed "locally". Like all such ideas about discrete "knowledge" of the world, this denies or minimizes the importance of borrowings or appropriations from "other" cultural formations. It is in this sense that the Islamizers' project of de-Westernization focuses upon an imagined coherence which is rooted in European essentialism.

I want to look at one example of the processes of fluidity and change which go to make "knowledge", that of the ideas and movements associated with Islamic activism, often described as "radical" or "political" Islam, or as "Islamism". These movements have been of profound significance but have been largely ignored by the Islamization current. Their histories confirm the idea that socio-political trends within modern Islamic societies have developed within what Abaza and Stauth call "global" structures: that they are elements within complex networks of inter-cultural relations through which ideas have been contested, modified and recast. By looking briefly at a century of Islamist activity I want to demonstrate how inappropriate are the ahistorical approaches shared with globalization theory and with which the Islamizers support a claim to define religious tradition.

Islamism, State and Nation

Islamism has been the most vigorous strategy through which Muslims have been invoked to intervene in the modern world. As a strategy of active engagement it can be contrasted with various quietist currents, with much of "popular Islam" including Sufism, and with orthodoxies usually associated with local power structures and traditional centres of learning.

The central problematic of Islamism has been that of how to direct Muslim energies in relation to ideas and structures associated with Europe and modernism. Since the late 19th century Islamist ideologues and movements have formulated and reformulated a series of perspectives. Sometimes these have remained at the level of abstraction; in other cases they have been directed towards mass activism. They have borrowed from dominant Western models, modified and reshaped them, and adapted them to specific local circumstances. Although these processes have been focused within the Middle East, they have been intimately related to developments in the West and to changes in other regions, notably in South Asia. They have been part of a complex process of cultural exchange in which ideas viewed as distinctively Islamic have been deeply affected by Muslims' interactions with a vast range of "other" traditions.

I want to take one important strand within these processes – that of the strategy to be adopted vis-à-vis the nation state itself, often regarded as the key issue in contention between Islam and perceived hostile Others. Indeed, for the proponents of Islamization this is, Faruqi argues, a crucial issue on which Muslims are obliged to take a stand (IIIT 1983: 37).

Both Muslim and non-Muslim scholars have observed that until the 19th century Islamic tradition did not embrace a formal theory of the state. For over a millennium there was no requirement for *'ulama* (scholars and jurists) to develop such notions. Rulers of the empires which dominated much of the Islamic world, together with local rulers, received endorsement from religious leaders on the basis of a perceived commitment to application of the *shari'a* (the law) rather than to their position vis-à-vis an abstract political structure. The *'ulama* adopted attitudes towards specific polities which they based upon interpretations of the Quran and Sunna (practice of the Prophet), focusing on application of *shari'a* and the extent to which it could be effective. Debates among *'ulama* about the caliphate (*khilafa* – rule of the successors to the Prophet) and the imamate were conducted similarly around questions of legitimacy with respect to the effectiveness of the *shari'a*.

Azmeh (1993: 90) observes that notions of "state" as an organized, continuous structure which can be isolated from a specific exercise of power appears only "as an abstract locus of order and disorder".[3] The "state" is a particular pattern of everyday power relations between ruler and ruled; in Roy's words, "the sovereign reigns in the empirical, the contingent" (Roy 1994: 14).

In the 18th century many predominantly Islamic regions experienced increased social and political instability. One outcome was the emergence of what European scholars have called "pre-modern" reform movements, which undertook new assessments of the Prophetic tradition and initiated discussions about appropriate exercise of power.[4] These developments were greatly accelerated by the colonial encounter with Europe, which prompted a sharp change in approach among Middle Eastern rulers and associated *'ulama*. European penetration of the region was rapid, violent and effective. Within 50 years of the French occupation of Egypt in 1798, almost the whole of North Africa and the Arab East had come under European control or strong European influence. At the political level, the first response of local rulers was that of defensive or "imitative" nationalism, an attempt to develop the same integration of economic, political, social and military structures that had facilitated advance of the European state.

Desire for symmetry with Europe lay behind the attempts of rulers such as Muhammed Ali in Egypt to acquire European states' technique and principles of political and military organisation. Rapporteurs such as Rifa'a al-Tahtawi and Khayr al-Din al-Tunisi returned from missions to Europe to argue for wholesale borrowing by Egyptian and Ottoman rulers. For Tahtawi, who became a prominent figure among the Egyptian 'ulama, it was vital that European approaches in science, industry and even the arts should be adopted, as "their perfection in the European countries is a known and an established fact, and it is right that the right be followed" (Al-Husry 1980: 14). He attempted a synthesis of Islamic political traditions and Enlightenment philosophy which focused on imitation of principles and structures that he believed sustained European advance, above all those associated with the modern state.[5] Khayr al-Din argued similarly, recommending Ottoman rulers to adopt the fundamentals of "political systems" – *al-tanzimat al-siyasiyya* – that he identified in the European states (Al-Husry 1980: 40).

Imitation merely accelerated colonial advance. By the 1860s sustained military, economic and political offensives from Europe had produced anxiety among some sections of the 'ulama that Islamic culture and Muslim identity were under threat. Groups of "proto-Islamists" began efforts to formulate an independent response to the West. By the 1870s they had coalesced around the Iranian scholar and propagandist Jamal al-din al-Afghani, whose pan-Islam, comments Enayat (1982: 56), sought "to release the Muslim mind from the fetters of 'imitation'".

Afghani's vision saw radical reform of the degraded present by organisation of a politics oriented on the faith's unsullied past. Although Afghani was not opposed to European culture as such he formally rejected Western political structures; in particular, he was hostile to the colonizing activities associated with the nation state and the resulting fragmentation of the *umma*. Rather than import the national category, Afghani maintained, Muslims should reassert their own values. In a passage which was to become a guiding principle for Islamic activism over the next 100 years, Afghani asserted that: "Islamic society stands witness to the fact that Muslims do not recognize unity on the basis of tribe, colour or race. It is only the religious brotherhood that counts" (Azmeh 1993: 30). What was required, Afghani argued, was mobilisation around uncorrupted Islamic principle, to be determined by reference to the Prophet's *umma*. He castigated local rulers and 'ulama of the earlier "imitative" generation, calling for a new leadership of right-minded scholars and suitably guided Muslim rulers capable of enforcing the *shari'a*. A first step should be revitalization of the Ottoman caliphate as an act of defence against Western depredation.

What differentiated Afghani from earlier ideologues of Islamic reform was the argument for political action which engaged with the modernist agenda. His pan-Islam emerged as a movement shaped *within* the context of European advance and in which nation states were being established everywhere as the fullest expression of political meaning. To this extent, Afghani's construction of the Islamic past and his vision for the future were both formed with reference to national categories: in responding to the penetration of the national state he reproduced many of its features in his revitalized *umma*, notably its all-embracing political and social character, which imitators such as Tahtawi had already recognized as a European invention.[6]

The vision for change became one of an Islamic polity that could stand against the national category – it was, in effect, an Islam symmetrical to the nation state. Such a direct engagement with the politics of modernism was to have profound consequences for succeeding generations of Islamists. As Roy (1994: 20) comments, "The modernity of Islamist thought is in this quest for the universal state". Yet Afghani's approach to the state did not simply *reproduce* the European model. It was an attempt to seize and manipulate the national category in a way which might make it adequate to the needs of those subordinated by the European colonial venture.

Mass Mobilization

The contradiction inherent in Afghani's approach hardly troubled his supporters. Many were in fact representatives of the modern state – military officers, lawyers and administrators who had emerged from the national structures established in Egypt in the 19th century by Muhammed Ali and his successors. Their hostility was directed less at the idea of the state than at the control exercised through it by the colonial powers. The problem was resolved, in one sense, by those of Afghani's followers who soon extracted the national element from his approach and turned it into the focus of their concerns. During a complex period of interactions between the colonial powers and the religious establishment, notably in Egypt, leading *ʿulama* such as

Muhammed Abduh set out to reinterpret key principles of Islamic legal practice. Hourani (1961: 144-5) comments that in the case of Abduh, founder of "Islamic modernism", the effect was to carry much further the developments seen in the ideas of Tahtawi and Afghani: "opening the door to the flooding of Islamic doctrines and law by all the innovations of the modern world".

Afghani's teachings were an important element in anti-colonial struggles, especially in Egypt and Iran in the 1880s and 1890s. In contrast, the modernists were hardly involved in such movements *as* Islamists: some, such as Abduh, were reconciled with the colonial state; others abandoned Islamism entirely in favour of secular nationalism, founding a series of parties including the Egyptian Wafd. Here, secular nationalism emerged from *within* the Islamist tradition: pan-Islam had in fact stimulated a political current which soon proved far more dynamic.

By the time of the mass anti-colonial struggles which swept the Middle East during and after the First World War, pan-Islam had become a marginal current.[7] The independence movements focused on the demand for *national* self-determination; the notion of Islamic union was hardly raised and that of a revivified, triumphant *umma* was seen as the preoccupation of a small minority of activists. What brought Islamism back onto the agenda was the perceived failure of secular nationalism. Parties such as the Egyptian Wafd had accepted a token role in colonial governments but were soon widely viewed as compromising and ineffectual. In Egypt this set the scene for emergence of the first mass Islamist movement, the Muslim Brotherhood.

The Brotherhood was distinguished from earlier popular movements in being a modern political party, with systematic organization and mass recruitment, and a political programme which Zubaida (1989: 155) describes as "imbued with the assumptions of the modern national political field". From the first it bore the marks of the secular nationalist experience. It was deeply affected by the rise of the mass anti-colonial movement and the (albeit short-lived) successes against colonial occupation. In this sense the Brotherhood was shaped as much within self-consciously secular traditions as within those of the earlier generation of Islamists. Its founder, Hassan al-Banna, saw the movement as standing in the tradition of Afghani, whom he described as "the caller" and "the spiritual father" (Mitchell 1969: 321). But unlike Afghani and his immediate successors, Banna wished to construct a mass organization capable of intervening in mainstream politics with the aim of seizing the national state *for* Islam. To this extent he had further extended the politics of Islamic "modernism", accepting most of the premises of the secularists. Although Banna still argued for pan-Islamic union as a strategic aim, he was focused precisely on the state at the local level, even arguing that, "Nationalism in our minds attains the status of sacredness" (Mitchell 1969: 264). The movement had reformulated Afghani's vision, developing it as a specifically Islamic orientation on the modern state.

Banna presented a vision of Islamic Egypt as a prototype of the unified *umma*. In effect, he fused the nation state with the aspiration to construct a community based in contemporary perceptions of the 7th-century model. An "Islamic" state was seen as realisable; indeed, Banna argued that Muslims had an absolute responsibility to exert themselves in pursuing the project and until it was realized all Muslims would be culpable – "guilty before God Almighty of having failed to install it" (Enayat 1982: 85). Enayat (1982: 85) notes Banna's assertion that such failure constituted a "betrayal, not only of Muslims, but of all humanity".

Formally, the Brotherhood pursued the model of a radically reformed state. Its involvement in national politics, however, was often dictated by pragmatic concerns – in practice it accommodated to the secular state. This led the movement into serious difficulties, especially when in the mid-1940s Egypt entered a series of deep social crises, the anti-colonial movement coming under the influence of radical nationalism and of various Communist currents.[8] One result was that Islamism took a further and innovative turn.

Challenging 'Jahiliyya'

In Egypt and much of the Islamic world the purpose of secular nationalism and of reformist currents such as the Muslim Brotherhood had been to seize and redirect state structures. The actual experience of post-colonial states seemed to place this prospect further from reach. In Egypt from 1952 a highly authoritarian secular regime monopolized power. The local state – the means of "liberation" on which Islamist leaders such as Banna had pinned hopes for reconstituting the *umma* –

seemed to have become an alien force. This experience shaped a new generation of Islamists. In the Arab world their leading ideologue was Sayyid Qutb, once strongly supportive of the independent Egyptian state but who had become hostile to what he saw as its unGodly agenda. Qutb's response was to redirect the Islamic movement away from Banna's reformist perspective into contestation of the whole secular order.

Qutb's project was based upon collective action to reassert the *umma* under conditions in which, he maintained, it had fallen into the deepest crisis. Drawing in particular upon the perspectives of the Indian Muslim activist Abu'l A'la Mawdudi, Qutb asserted that humanity had descended into *jahiliyya* – the "state of ignorance" equated in Islamic tradition with Arabian life before the Prophetic revelation. Under contemporary conditions, he argued, *jahiliyya* was expressed in "rebellion against the sovereignty of God on earth" (Qutb 1988: 49). Muslims must be prepared to liquidate *jahiliyya* and to introduce a Godly and harmonious order under the shari'a, the means being that of uncompromising *jihad* vis-à-vis the secular state. This was to be conducted through "dynamic organisation and active movement" (Qutb 1988: 89). A "vanguard" of committed Muslims should begin the task by leading fellow believers against unGodly rulers.

Qutb acknowledged his debt to Mawdudi, especially in borrowing the notion of a modern *jahiliyya*. Less conscious was his adoption of Mawdudi's frame of reference for change – the nation state. As a young man, Mawdudi had been an active nationalist, supporting the Congress Party's struggle for India's independence from Britain. Like Qutb, he later became disillusioned with the nationalist movement and attacked the idea of the secular state as an imposition upon Muslims and an irruption into the *umma*. He nonetheless maintained that Muslims should struggle for power within the state in order to bring into being a genuinely Islamic polity. After the partition of India in 1947 his Jama'at-i Islami (Islamic Association) argued for radical change of political and legal structures in Pakistan to direct the state towards an Islamic order. Although power should be exercised "in keeping with the Book of God and Sunna of his Prophet" (Engineer 1994: 125) there was no obstacle to Muslim engagement with such structures. Indeed, Mawdudi provided a blueprint for the coming "Islamic state" – giving the first detailed account of a modernist polity legitimized by reference to the Prophetic model, what Engineer (1994: 125) calls "the Islamic theocracy".[9]

Under the Nasserist regime Qutb had found himself in opposition to secular nationalism, communism and the Islamists of the Muslim Brotherhood. He condemned all as part of the *jahiliyya*, especially for their joint participation in the structures of the state, which he deemed the most poisonous invention of secularism. At the same time, he raised expectations of the emergence of a Godly order brought into being by seizing the state itself. This approach gained Qutb posthumous mass appeal when, in 1967, the Egyptian state appeared to collapse in the military conflict with Israel. The deep social crisis which followed brought Qutb's ideas a wider audience. This was drawn by the promise that order, justice and harmony could be retrieved from a corrupt society – not through reform but by bypassing the whole political system, uprooting secular structures and uncovering the Godly core within. For the post-Qutbian generation of Egyptian Islamists the project was, in Roy's words, "to redefine the social bond itself on a political basis, and not simply to apply the *sharia*" (Roy 1994: 38).

During the 1970s, Egypt was in turmoil. Economic crisis, mass migration and urban growth produced rapid social polarization and stimulated a radical mood among young people, among whom Qutb's followers soon discovered a mass audience. They went on to construct an even more assertive form of Islamic modernism. Like Qutb himself, who had earlier been impressed by the "vanguardist" strategies of the secular left, they were influenced by some aspects of the Marxist tradition, notably its focus upon the state as both an agency of repression and potentially one of liberation.[10] Mobilizing the works of the most "militant" jurists and uncompromising political figures of the Islamic tradition, activists such as Faraj shaped a specific interpretation of the past which could be a reference point for contemporary engagement. They spelt out both the necessity of intransigent struggle against the state and the possibility of assertion of an alternative Islamic polity, what Azmeh (1993: 99) calls "the precise and imminent interpretation of the pristine model". This made the *umma* realisable as against the actual presence of the *jahiliyya* – an interpretation, argues Azmeh (1993: 98), for which there was no precedent in Islamic history.

Khomeini's Alternative

The influence of such ideas has since been profound, helping to shape activist strategy throughout the Arab world and making Islamic "radicalism" the main competitor to the gradualist or reformist perspectives still pursued by Banna's successors in the Muslim Brotherhood.

In Iran a related but far more successful approach developed. During the 1960s a network of religious activists emerged among whom a number set out to "retrieve" the notion of political action from a Shi'ite tradition which had encouraged generations of quietism among senior ʿ*ulama*.[11] Some attempted a synthesis of mainstream Shi'i traditions and radical nationalism which they hoped would energize popular opposition to the Pahlavi regime. The most important of these was Ali Shari'ati, whose insistence that "the masses" must change society by making an "Islamic revolution" has been seen as a strategy rooted in the modernist paradigm (Zubaida 1989: 23).

Shari'ati's attempt at fusion of social-democratic and Islamist ideas – sometimes called an Islamic Marxism (Abrahamian 1989: chapter 4) – emphasized that "the people" could recuperate their society by reshaping the nation state. It was echoed by a group of Shi'i ʿ*ulama* associated with Ayatollah Khomeini who had broken from the religious establishment. They maintained that political passivity had become an overriding problem in a country in which "imperialism" was exploiting the masses and that the regime was one which Muslims were now obliged to confront (Khomeini 1981: 50-51).

When Iran moved into revolution in the late 1970s, Khomeini put an ever more urgent emphasis on political action, maintaining that all Muslims had a duty "to put an end to this system of oppression ... to overthrow these oppressive governments and form an Islamic government" (Khomeini 1981: 51). Using a populist rhetoric that placed him alongside Shari'ati and the Left, Khomeini argued that such a government would fulfil "God's promise" to Muslims (Engineer 1994: 181). An "Islamic republic" – an Islamized nation state – was now the focus for discovery of the religious ideal. It was presented in the form of a modernist model complete with social justice and equal rights. This reflected the revolutionary movement's own agenda, for radical social and political change to address growing immiseration and social polarization.[12] Such a rhetoric of revolution was a vital element in efforts by the religious leadership to draw the masses behind Khomeini.

The ayatollah's own specific interpretation of formal Shi'i tradition, of greater significance in his overall political design, received little exposure. Khomeini had already formulated a notion that in place of the "impious" Pahlavi state it was necessary to construct an order based upon rigorous application of the *shari'a* under the supervision of a supreme jurist, the *velayat-i faqih*. It was this approach, implemented by a highly authoritarian regime deeply suspicious of the mass movement, which subsequently shaped the Islamic Republic. Khomeini had in fact produced a dual strategy. On the one hand was a novel Islamic populism; on the other hand was a theory of state structures for which, as in Qutb's model, there was no formal Islamic precedent. The impact of the Iranian experience need hardly be emphasized.

Islamization and History

These observations on Islamism are not intended to narrate a specific history but to draw attention to key developments within religious activism. To the extent that "Europe" (itself a problematic category) absorbed all manner of ideas from "other" cultural complexes, notably from predominantly Islamic societies, self-consciously Islamic currents have absorbed and recast "European" traditions, notably the political structures associated with industrial capitalism, colonialism and the modern nation-state.

Over the course of more than 100 years Islamist currents have responded to the modernist challenge by means of political engagement. Such engagements have often been complex, even apparently contradictory. On the one hand Islamist ideologues have rejected nation, nationalism and the state; on the other hand they have often attempted reformulations of these ideas. They have drawn on ideas often described as "alien" to Islam, making extensive borrowings from liberal and radical nationalism, and from Marxism, in particular from the Stalinized Communism which was influential across the Third World from the 1930s. Even those most hostile to "Western" political traditions have entered discourses of the nation: Mawdudi, for example, who was outspoken in his criticism of the state, made use of the whole range of modernist categories as a means of defining his

Islamic polity. Nasr (1994: 105) comments that Mawdudi's practice of "appropriation of western concepts and ideas to construct an Islamic resistance to the West" amounted to *indiscriminate* borrowing from a tradition that believers were invoked to reject.

Far from developing as a polar opposite to secular currents, Islamism has been intimately associated with them and has indeed been an important stimulus for development of ideas usually viewed as standing outside Islamic tradition. Afghani's pan-Islam, for example, set out a framework for anti-colonial struggle which was an important influence on Arab nationalism, especially upon currents which developed in Egypt, producing the Wafd Party and the first nationalist government. It is in this sense that Islamism energized early forms of secular nationalism. When this current went into decline, Islamism responded by regenerating in the form of the Muslim Brotherhood, a powerful crypto-nationalist movement.

Islamist movements have invariably had a strongly conservative ideological component. They have been elitist and authoritarian and have often accommodated easily to the power structures they set out to contend. At the same time, such movements have expressed aspirations for radical change, sometimes challenging structures of power. When marginalized, they have often retreated to a base within the urban middle class and the junior ʿ*ulama*, which appears to be a stable home. When they have re-emerged, it has often been in circumstances in which popular aspirations play a key role in shaping the agenda. The phenomenon has been one of contradiction, for which an explanation must be sought in the social character of the Islamist leadership. As professionals, functionaries and small capitalists – identified by Mitchell (1969: 329) as "the emergent Muslim middle class" – they have been closely associated with the state. Although they may express intense hostility to secular political currents which have monopolized state power, they are reluctant, in practice, to challenge these structures directly. As in the case of Banna's Brotherhood, Islamist expectations remain unfulfilled.[13]

Despite frequent reverses Islamism has not been static: far from the Orientalist account of a movement restrained by its focus on primordial concerns, Islamism has taken on a host of socio-political identities. Like other religious movements, it has been an idiom for the expression of all manner of ideals and expectations. Its history confirms that, in Turner's words, "[Religious] Beliefs are adopted or rejected because they are relevant or not relevant to everyday needs and concerns" (Turner 1994: 10).

Such an account of Islamist thinking is dismissed by the Islamization current. Sardar (1989: 49) insists that conventional social analysis is *always* inappropriate vis-à-vis Islamic matters, commenting that "sociology was not developed to tackle the problems of Muslim civilization". Such problems can be interpreted only through the embrace of an "Islamic epistemology" – knowledge acquired solely on the basis of principles set out in the Quran and in the Sunna. Early Islamic history is sacred and normative, defining all human experience and making irrelevant efforts at self-assertion by Muslims deemed to violate such principles or to be otherwise imperfect. A century of Islamic activism can therefore be characterized by Sardar (1991: 70) as merely "a form of secularism".

Here the interaction between Islamic societies and cultural "others" can be dismissed, as if it had no implications for the Islamizers' own agenda. But as Abaza and Stauth (1990: 225) comment, Western observers' and Muslim scholars' concern for "authenticities" fails to recognize the latters' histories and formative influences:

the fact [is] that the main 'Islamic' or 'Oriental' appearances in most cases have already been produced in a sphere of inter-cultural exchange between the West and the East: they have largely been a product of global inter-cultural relations.

The Islamization project in fact absorbs an Orientalized practice. Its preoccupations echo those of European scholars who have sought to locate the essential or atavistic qualities of Islam and of Muslims. In developing rationales for relations of domination vis-à-vis "the East", Orientalism depicted an homogenized Islamic culture which induced fatalism and passivity, thereby negating the idea of positive activity among the mass of society. The Islamizers have adopted a strikingly similar perspective, in which generations of struggle for change – including the struggle for an independent Muslim identity – are declared invalid because they are judged to have been imperfectly Islamic. Contemporary Muslims are depicted as inert, awaiting animation by an elite group of rightly-guided scholars.

Despite its commitment to an historic project of de-Westernization, Islamization has also integrated the socio-cultural and political categories associated with modernity. While formally rejecting Islamists' engagement with the state, for example, it has expended enormous energies defining (variously) model Islamic "nations" and "states" based in the Prophetic experience. Here the Islamizers face intense difficulties, with competing and sometimes conflicting interpretations of what is an appropriate contemporary form of the founding, pristine model.[14]

"Capitalist Thought"

Abaza and Stauth (1990: 219) comment that "the 'indigenisation perspective' falls into the very trap of cultural globalisation against which it wants to stand up". There is powerful evidence for this assertion, as when Sardar asserts a form of cultural relativism so extreme that it complements even the views of global determinists such as Huntington. For Sardar (1997: 46), the future offers a "multicivilisational world" of cultural blocs in which "the identity of each civilisation will be shaped by its unique epistemology, historiography and philosophy of life". He suggests (1997: 46) that, "The twenty-first century will thus be shaped by new racial [sic] and cultural forces."[15]

Does Islamization, therefore, merely reproduce the global condition? Are Islamizers, together with other indigenization movements, "entrapped" within globality, as globalization theory suggests? Such a conclusion is inadequate. By imputing determinative powers to an imagined globality, it directs attention away from the specific character of the Islamization movement and the social forces with which it is associated.

Turner (1994: chapter 1) points to the difficulty of considering intellectuals as a "universal category" which can be a source of cultural authority. This is especially important in the case of Islamization: its ideologues are not abstract "intellectuals" but have emerged from specific contexts, largely from universities or dedicated study centres in North America, Europe and South-East Asia. Leading figures who are active primarily in the West are described by Stenberg (1996: 273) as members of a "Muslim elite". He suggests that they have filled spaces opened within Western society, especially within Muslim communities where there is a dearth of senior scholars. This is particularly important because of the character of such communities. Muslims of the West, especially in Europe, are almost invariably marginalized within the wider society, with the result that their communal interactions as believers take on great significance. In a study on migration and religiousness, Schiffauer (1988: 150) observes that here "the religious community often becomes a counterweight to the secular society as well as a place of retreat, a haven". Within such communities there is a special place for those familiar with the complexities of religious tradition and who are able to present worldviews which are relevant to local experience. Islamization, with its emphasis on de-Westernization and assertion of a universal Islamic understanding might seem particularly appropriate: indeed, it might be seen as one expression of what Ahmed and Donnan (1994: 2) call the truly global nature of Muslim society – the contemporary Muslim diaspora.

In fact the Islamizers are not closely associated with such communities but with a narrower layer of Muslim professionals and academics. In a celebratory account of the movement's early history, Abul-Fadl (1992: 53) notes that its "vanguard" included engineers, doctors, educationalists, philosophers and social scientists. Poston (1992: 121) suggests that in the United States the movement has since operated at the college and university level. Stenberg sees its ideologues as a privileged group, their status consisting in social standing and mobility. He observes that they travel widely within academic networks discussing the interpretation, function and future of Islamic tradition (Stenberg 1996: 274). Within such a milieu the pressures of everyday life exerted upon the mass of Muslims, and the latters' struggles to contend them, may seen unimportant as against abstract matters and academic discourses.

Elsewhere, leading Islamizers enjoy a special status through relationships with governments and state bodies which have provided financial support, sponsored study centres and conferences, and helped to establish publishing enterprises. Among the most important mentors of the IIIT, for example, is the Malaysian state. Malaysian Prime Minister Mahathir Mohamed and former Deputy Prime Minister Anwar Ibrahim have vigorously and publicly backed the Institute's initiatives. In 1983, Mahathir drew upon the support of a number of

Islamic governments to establish the International Islamic University in Malaysia (IIUM) as a world centre for studies on Islamization. A founding member of the IIIT, AbdulHamid AbuSulayman (also its chairman and a former president), is Rector of the IIUM. Abu-Sulayman was formerly a senior academic in Saudi Arabia and was secretary of the Saudi Arabian State Planning Committee.[16]

The Islamizers have defined approaches to economic and political affairs which many Islamic governments find congenial. These have emerged mainly from the work of economists who have produced the most extensive literature among the Islamized disciples. Much of their theory, however, has merely put an Islamic gloss on neo-classical economic principles. Even Sardar (1989: 37) has complained that "Most of them [Islamic economists] were, and still are, straight monetarist economists". He argues that their approach to the Western discipline – "with all its assumptions and underlying values, of which they are so critical" – has resulted only in an attempt "to infuse Islamic notions and principles into it". Why, he asks, has there not been a more fundamental analysis – of technology, modes of production, or of land distribution or the elimination of poverty – "a prime disease of Muslim societies" (Sardar 1989: 38). In an unusual (though very superficial) critique from within the Islamization current, Sardar suggests that Islamic economics has served only to complement mainstream ("Western") theory. He concludes:

On the whole, Muslim economists took the Western discipline with all its assumptions and underlying values, of which they are so critical, and tried to infuse Islamic notions and principles into it. Consequently, the charge against Islamic economics that it is little more than capitalist economic thought with an Islamic facade ('capitalism minus interest') has some justification.

Sardar's observation has deeply subversive connotations for Islamization, which here is merely an accommodation of religious tradition to capitalist practice. But such criticisms have not dissuaded leading Islamizers from setting out approaches which celebrate "capitalist economic thought". AbuSulayman (1993b: xvi) asserts the principle that "Social moderation is Islam's objective in the sphere of economics, and the market economy is its means." Such views are well received within many notionally Islamic governments. In Malaysia, for example,

Mahathir Mohamed embraced fully the doctrines of the free market, seeking to thrust the local economy into the mainstream of international capitalist activity. According to Choudhury (1993: 163-166), the strategy has made Malaysia "a model for development", "a unique synthesis of Islam and modernization" and "a near ideal Muslim state" [sic]. Until Mahathir's turn to protectionist policies in the wake of the economic "meltdowns" of 1997 and 1998, this also brought approbation from most Western governments and transnational economic institutions.

The conservative values expressed in Islamic economics reappear in the field of international politics. AbuSulayman (1993b) elaborates an Islamized theory of international relations which directs Muslims to work through existing inter-governmental institutions, especially the Organisation of the Islamic Conference (OIC). The OIC has been a particularly contentious organisation. Established in the early 1950s under the influence of the emerging Gulf states, it was intended to represent formally the interests of the *umma*. It has often been perceived, however, as an instrument of the most assertive Middle Eastern regimes and as an expression of petro-power. Abedin, for example, comments on its "controversial" representation of the *umma*: rather than defending Muslim rights worldwide, he observes, it has been "more interested in maintaining the status quo and representing the commercial interests of Muslim countries" (1994: 31). Moten, a leading political theorist within the Islamization movement, identifies the OIC as "a somewhat [sic] united political front", arguing that it is nonetheless one of the "constituents and continuation of Muslim *nahdah* [reassertion]" (Moten 1994: 132). AbuSulayman (1993b: 161) insists that Muslims should work through the OIC "to protect and serve Islam and Muslim interests and to strengthen Muslim unity".

Conclusion

Abul-Fadl (1992: 53) makes the observation that at any early stage pioneers of the Islamization project chose "the cultural imperative, rather than direct political action". Dismissing collective activity, they opted for the intellectual project. Exertion of an academic community, it was argued, would establish Islamic discourses with the capacity to resolve problems confronting the *umma*. Islamization would operate on behalf of the mass of Muslims, defining an authentic Islam though which the mass of believers could be directed towards appropriate conduct. The task was to be accomplished by a scholarly elite – what the IIIT (n.d.: 1) calls "the Ummah's most enlightened intellects" – which would combat non-Islamic influences on behalf of a mass of Muslims incapable of self-redemption. Intellectual exertion alone could resolve problems of the *umma*: political engagement was largely meaningless, for Muslims were not yet equipped to define their tasks.

The strategy has been elaborated against a background of active political engagement among large numbers of Muslims – a continuation of over a century of struggles which have contested local power structures, including formally Islamic governments. In this context, Islamization is a message of political restraint. The Islamizers have all the appearances of being quietists, holding much in common with clerical establishments which have enjoyed close relations with those in power. Abrahamian (1989: 8) writes, for example, of the role of Shi'i ʿ*ulama* who for generations elaborated a religious orthodoxy which "bolstered the status quo while claiming to keep out of politics." Like the historic quietists, the Islamizers' pronouncements have an ideological character. It may be significant that they received endorsement and material support from notionally Islamic governments at the moment of the latter's most intense anxiety over ideas that political action can be/should be an expression of religious commitment.

For Islamizers, the project of de-Westernization is made necessary and is rendered feasible by the global condition. Like theorists of globalization, they identify a world unified by abstract structures which are seen as expressive of world integration. Human agency and its histories are largely irrelevant: ordinary men and women (including those who declare an Islamic mission) are deemed helpless in the face of forces which have their own logics. Meanwhile, however, the attempts of billions of people to understand their circumstances *and to modify them* continue as before. The scale of inequality and asymmetry at a world level, and the level of disintegration of socio-economic and political structures, suggests that these struggles will intensify. They are certain to be expressed through all manner of worldviews, drawing upon a host of secular and religious traditions from which ideas are appropriated, reshaped, fused and discarded as new notions are pressed into service. Ideas of an abstract globalism and of discrete knowledges will be of assistance primarily to those who wish to negate such activities.

Notes

Thanks to Adrian Budd of South Bank University and to Ashwani Sharma of University of East London for their comments on this article in draft.

1 See, for example, Mazlish/Buultjens (1997).
2 Robertson (1992) attempts briefly to demonstrate a historical dimension to globalization. This is not typical of the body of his work, however, nor of that of most theorists of globalization.
3 Azmeh (1993: 90) comments that the state (*dawla*), "Both lexically and in terms of actual usage until modern times denoted a particular kind of patrimony, the proprietorship of command and authority within a specific line. This abstract *dawla* is constituted of a body politic, in the original sense: a sovereign, his troops, his bureaucrats. What must be stressed is that this concrete body is distinct from a body social and from what later came to be known as civil society."
4 For an analysis of such developments in the Middle East and India, see Brown 1996, chapter 2.
5 In Europe Tahtawi observed a popular identification with the nation-state which he strongly recommended as a principle of political organization facilitating social harmony. Placing the notion of the modern state within Islamic tradition, he introduced the idea of "patriotism" (*wataniyya*), quoting words attributed to the Prophet: "Love of one's country (*watan*, from *watana* [to live/dwell]) is part of the Faith" (see Al-Husry 1980: 14).
6 Keddie (1972: 64) notes that Afghani sought "[a] transition from traditional Islamic ideas to a kind of nationalist appeal, including nationalist reminders of the original glorious age from which the community had declined".
7 Pan-Islamic currents had been confined to the margins of the "Islamic world", notably to Central Asia. For an account of the pan-Islamic Jadid movement in this region, see Carrere d'Encausse 1988.

8 Banna was widely accused of opportunistically developing relationships with the Egyptian government and the king, substituting lobbying, intrigue and compromise for the politics of contestation of the state (Zubaida 1989: chapter 2).
9 For an account of the development of Mawdudi's approach (which bears a striking similarity to the evolution of Qutb's strategy), see Nasr 1994.
10 Islamists of the "Qutbist" movement have used the vocabulary and certain political principles of radical nationalism and of the Communist movement. Roy (1994: 3) suggests that for such "militant" Islamists, the notion of revolution, of the party and its structures, and of the state itself, have been borrowed from the left "and injected with Quranic terminology".
11 Many analyses of Shi'ism have argued that its emphasis upon the imamate and the figure of the *mahdi* have produced a tradition replete with messianic, even "revolutionary" possibilities. Enayat (1982: 25) comments that that Shi'i historicism is indeed "a *potential* tool of radical activism", but adds: "throughout the greater part of Shi'i history, [such expectations] never went beyond the potential state, remaining in practice merely a sanctifying tenet for the submissive acceptance [by the mass of Muslims] of the status quo".
12 Khomeini called on the masses to struggle for an "Islamic republic", in which "there is no oppression and no injustice, there are no rich and poor all the layers of society, all religions, all races and communities will have equal rights" (Engineer 1994: 181).
13 The problem of unfulfilled expectations within the Islamist movements is taken up in Marfleet 1998b.
14 There has been a series of attempts by writers within the Islamization movement to elaborate socio-political models consistent with religious principles and adequate to contemporary conditions. Kurdi (1984), for example, sets out a complex structure which is based, he argues, upon Quranic precedent, with the form of "the early Islamic Nation" dictating principles for the modern state. Here, ideas about "nation", "state", "nationality" and "patriotism" are mobilized unproblematically. Similarly, Moten (1994) sets out principles for an Islamic Political Science, describing in detail the attributes of an Islamic state based upon the early model.

15 In a recent book, Sardar distances himself from Huntington's theories of globalized cultural conflict. Sardar 1998, chapter 2.
16 This information is provided in lengthy biographical notes in works by AbuSulayman published by the IIIT. See AbuSulayman 1993a and 1993b.

Selected Bibliography

Abaza, Mona/Stauth, Georg (1990) "Occidental Reason, Orientalism, Islamic Fundamentalism: A Critique". In Martin Albrow/Elisabeth King (eds.) *Globalization, Knowledge and Society*, London: Sage, pp. 209-230.
Abedin, Syed Z. (1994) "Minority Crises: Majority Options". In Hussein Muttalib/Hashmi Taj ul-Islam (eds.) *Islam, Muslims and the Modern State*, Basingstoke: Macmillan, pp. 31-44.
Abrahamian, Ervand (1989) *Radical Islam*, London: I.B. Tauris.
Abul-Fadl, Mona (1992) *Where East Meets West*, Herndon/VA: International Institute of Islamic Thought.
AbuSulayman, Abdul Hamid A. (1993a) *Crisis in the Muslim Mind*, Herndon/VA: International Islamic Publishing House.
—— (1993b) *Towards an Islamic Theory of International Relations*, Herndon/VA: International Islamic Publishing House.
El-Affendi, Abdelwahhab (1991) *Who Needs an Islamic State?*, London: Grey Seal.
Ahmed, Akbar/Donnan, Hastings (1994) "Islam in the Age of Postmodernity". In Akbar Ahmed/Hastings Donnan (eds.) *Islam, Globalization and Postmodernity*, London: Routledge, pp. 1-20.
Anees, Manawar A. (1993) "Islam and Scientific Fundamentalism: Progress of Faith and Retreat of Reason?". *New Perspectives Quarterly* 10/3, pp. 61-63.
Archer, Margaret (1990) "Foreword". In Martin Albrow/Elisabeth King (eds.) *Globalization, Knowledge and Society*, London: Sage, pp. 1-2.
Ayubi, Nazih (1991) *Political Islam*, London: Routledge.
Azmeh, Aziz (1993) *Islams and Modernities*, London: Zed.
Beyer, Peter (1994) *Religion and Globalization*, London: Sage.
Brown, Daniel (1996) *Rethinking Tradition in Modern Islamic Thought*, Cambridge: Cambridge University Press.

Carrere-d'Encausse, Hélène (1988) *Islam and the Russian Empire*, London: I.B. Tauris.
Choudhury, Golam (1993) *Islam and the Modern Muslim World*, Buckhurst Hill: Scorpion.
Cox, Robert (1995) "Critical Political Economy". In Bjorn Hettne (ed.) *International Political Economy*, London: Zed, pp. 31-45.
Enayat, Hamid (1982) *Modern Islamic Political Thought*, London: Macmillan.
Engineer, Asghar A. (1994) *The Islamic State*, New Delhi: Vikas.
Featherstone, Mike (1990) "Global Culture: An Introduction". *Theory, Culture and Society* 7, pp. 1-14.
Ghamari-Tabrizi, Behrooz (1996) "Is Islamic Science Possible?". *Social Epistemology* 10/3-4, pp. 317-330.
Giddens, Anthony (1990) *The Consequences of Modernity*, Cambridge: Polity.
—— (1991) *Modernity and Self-Identity*. Cambridge: Polity.
Hall, Stuart (1992) "The Question of Identity". In Stuart Hall/ David Held (eds.) *Modernity and Its Futures*, Cambridge: Open University/Polity, pp. 273-325.
Harman, Chris (1996) "Globalization: A Critique of a New Orthodoxy". *International Socialism* 73, pp. 3-33.
Harris, Nigel (1995) *The New Untouchables*, London: I.B. Tauris.
Harvey, David (1989) *The Condition of Postmodernity: An Inquiry into the Conditions of Cultural Change*, Oxford: Blackwell.
Hirst, Paul/Thompson, G. (1996) *Globalization in Question*, Cambridge: Polity.
Hoogvelt, Ankie (1997) *Globalization and the Postcolonial World*, London: Macmillan.
Hourani, Albert (1961) *Arabic Thought in the Liberal Age*, Cambridge: Cambridge University Press.
Huntington, Samuel (1993) "The Clash of Civilizations". *Foreign Affairs* 73, pp. 22-50.
Hussain, Asaf/Olson, R./Qureshi, J. (1984) *Orientalism, Islam and Islamists*, Brattleboro: Amana.
Al-Husry, K.S. (1980) *Origins of Modern Arabic Political Thought*, New York/NY: Caravan.
Ibrahim, Anwar (1989) "From Things Change to Change Things". In

Sardar Ziauddin (ed.) *An Early Crescent: The Future of Knowledge and the Environment in Islam*, London: Mansell, pp. 17-24.

IIIT (International Institute of Islamic Thought) (1982) *Islamization of Knowledge: General Principles and Workplan*, Washington/DC: IIIT.

—— (1984) *Towards Islamization of Disciplines*, Herndon/VA: IIIT.

—— (n.d.) *Background and Objectives of the IIIT*, Herndon/VA: IIIT.

Keddie, Nikkie (1972) *Sayyid Jamal al-Din "al-Afghani": A Political Biography*, Berkeley/CA: University of California Press.

Khomeini, Ruhollah (1981) *Islam and Revolution*, Berkeley/CA: University of California Press.

Kiely, Ray (1996) *Sociology and Development*, London: UCL Press.

Kurdi, Abdulrahman A. (1984) *The Islamic State*, London: Mansell.

Manzoor, S. Parvez (1989) "The Crisis of Muslim Thought and the Future of Ummah". In Ziauddin Sardar (ed.) *An Early Crescent: The Future of Knowledge and the Environment in Islam*, London: Mansell, pp. 57-91.

Marfleet, Philip (1998a) "Globalization and Religious Activism". In Ray Kiely/Philip Marfleet (eds.) *The Third World in the Global Era*, London: Routledge, pp. 185-215.

—— (1998b) "Islamist Political Thought". In Adam Lent (ed.) *New Political Thought*, London: Lawrence & Wishart, pp. 89-111.

Mawdudi, Abu'l A. (1960) *Principles of the Islamic State*, Lahore: Islamic Publications.

Mazlish, Bruce/Buultjens, R. (1997) *Conceptualizing World History*, Boulder/CO: Westview.

Mitchell, Richard (1969) *The Society of the Muslim Brothers*, Oxford: Oxford University Press.

Moazzam, Anwar (1984) *Jamal al-Din al Afghani: A Muslim Intellectual*, New Delhi: Concept.

Moten, Abdel-Rashid (1994) *Political Science: An Islamic Perspective*, Basingstoke: Macmillan.

Nasr, Seyyed V.R. (1994) "Mawdudi and the Jama'at-I Islami: The Origins, Theory and Practice of Islamic Revivalism". In Ali Rahnema (ed.) *Pioneers of Islamic Revival*, London: Zed, pp. 98-124.

Ohmae, Kenichi (1990) *A Borderless World*, London: Collins.
Poston, Larry (1992) *Islamic Da'wah in the West*, New York/NY: Oxford University Press.
Qutb, Sayyid (1988) *Milestones*, Karachi: International Islamic Publishers.
Robertson, Roland (1992) *Globalization: Social Theory and Global Culture*, London: Sage.
Roy, Olivier (1994) *The Failure of Political Islam*, London: I.B. Tauris.
Said, Edward W. (1978) *Orientalism*, New York/NY: Vintage Books.
Sardar, Ziauddin (1989) "Islamization of Knowledge: A State of the Art Report". In Ziauddin Sardar (ed.) *An Early Crescent: The Future of Knowledge and the Environment in Islam*, London: Mansell, pp. 25-27.
—— (1991) "The Postmodern Age". In Manawar A. Anees/A. Abedin/Ziaudin Sardar (eds.) *Muslim-Christian Relations: Yesterday, Today, Tomorrow*, London: Grey Seal, pp. 54-91.
—— (1997) "Beyond Development: An Islamic Perspective". In Vincent Tucker (ed.) *Cultural Perspectives on Development*, London: Frank Cass, pp. 36-55.
—— (1998) *Postmodernism and the Other: The New Imperialism of Western Culture*, London: Pluto.
Schiffauer, Werner (1988) "Migration and Religiousness". In Tomas Gerholm/Y. Lithman (eds.) *The New Islamic Presence in Western Europe*, London: Mansell, pp. 146-158.
Stenberg, Leif (1996a) "The Islamization of Science or the Marginalization of Islam". *Social Epistemology* 10/3-4, pp. 273-287.
—— (1996b) *The Islamization of Science*, Lund: Lund Studies in the History of Religions.
Tucker, Vincent (ed.) (1997) *Cultural Perspectives on Development*, London: Frank Cass.
Turner, Bryan S. (1994) *Orientalist, Postmodernism and Islam*, London: Routledge.
Waters, Malcolm (1995) *Globalization*, London: Routledge.
Zubaida, Sami (1989) *Islam, the People and the State*, London: Routledge.

The Islamization of Knowledge between Particularism and Globalization: Malaysia and Egypt[1]

Mona Abaza

In one world, it is the war of heritage [*turath*] against heritage and the degradation of the heritage with heritage.

(Tarabishi 1993: 15)

National societies are increasingly exposed internally to problems of heterogeneity and diversity and at the same time, are experiencing both external and internal pressures to reconstruct their collective identity along pluralistic lines, individuals are increasingly subject to compelling ethnic, cultural and religious reference points.

(Robertson 1990: 57)

Introduction

Before I proceed to explore the debate on the "Islamization of Knowledge", I would like to point to the inherent ambiguity of the topic. The discourse of Islamization was born out of a reaction to Orientalism yet hardly transcends the problems related to Eurocentrism. The Islamizers of knowledge, similar to other contesting Third world intellectuals, might appear to raise legitimate issues such as decolonizing anthropology nevertheless, the empirical contribution of their writings leaves much to be desired. The problematic of the indigenization of social sciences, "authenticity"[2] and authentic institutions are present in the debate. In relation to this Islamization debate, in recent years, sociologists have raised questions related to the struggle in the sociological field between "local", indigenous and international scholars; whose knowledge counted more and the "bargaining over who knows reality better". The debate over the indigenization of social sciences as a post colonial discourse and the varying competing forces within the sociological field, has already been analyzed by Morsy/Nelson/Saad/Sholkamy (1991). Since the late eighties, a large body of literature, concerned with global versus indigenous knowledge and about the interaction and intricate dialectical relationship between the global and the local, has developed and expanded (see Albrow/King [eds.] 1990; Robertson 1990). Whether the particular emerges against – or is complementary to – the universal and whether the weight of "local truth" may be part and parcel of the global cultural condition, have been themes well elaborated by Roland Robertson (Robertson 1992: 166). Moreover, through globalization, the development of sociology in relation to the modern nation-state, either its integration or disintegration (Featherstone 1990: 1-14) and cultural homogenization versus cultural heterogenization were equally debated (Appadurai 1990: 295-310). The place of culture and culture of resistance/invention of tradition in relation to the wave of Americanization, were issues brought in connection with the technological revolution and mass media. To quote Friedman: "Ethnic and cultural fragmentation and modernist homogenization are not two arguments, two opposing views of what is happening in the world today, but two constitutive trends in global reality" (Friedman 1990: 311).

This paper departs from the issue of indigenization of knowledge to proceed with further empirical details on the debate over the Islamization of knowledge by comparing two different countries: Egypt and Malaysia. Even though the debate appears to be critical of the Western discourse, it seems to be imprisoned in the game of mirrors of "orientalizing orientals" (Said 1978: 325). More precisely, while agreeing with the general critique which Edward Said directed against Orientalism, this paper points to the effects of what Sadeq Jalal Al-ʿAzm expressed as "orientalism in reverse" (Al-ʿAzm 1981: 5-26).

Issues at Stake

To see advocates of Islamization as reacting against the Western paradigms of knowledge makes it appear to be an attractive intellectual exercise for both Western and Muslim intellectuals. This is even more true since the parallel questioning of the paradigms of Western scientific thought stimulated by Kuhn's celebrated work (1962). Feyerabend's conception of the anarchistic enterprise of science, argued for the complexity of history and human change in science where "anything goes" (1975). Equally, there has been in recent years, a growing interest in the magnitude of "local knowledge" in different cultures and times (Turnbull 1993/94: 29-54). Karin Knorr's (1991) constructivism and view of the "fabrication" of knowledge in the laboratory, analyses the context and language of the scientific community. Since then, there has appeared a considerable range of studies arguing that scientific knowledge is socially constructed, emphasizing the relative aspect of knowledge (Murphy 1994). However, the trend of constructivist studies and their affinity with relativism have also faced a dynamic examination for their double standard in exaggerating relativism and thus ignoring whether or not a science is true (ibid.: 960). One major critique was that: "Constructivists ... apply their theory only to the knowledge of others, and resist its application to their own knowledge" (ibid.: 966). Another problem, as Murphy argued, was that constructivists tended to disguise and often exclude the weight of nature and its laws at the expense of the social "fabrication" of science (ibid.: 969). On the other hand, Clifford Geertz's *Local Knowledge* (1993) could be viewed as a poetic work on interpretative sociology and the interaction between the anthropologist's world view with the observed and the various understandings of the observed Self. All these endeavors in the sociology of knowledge, through the search for alternative paradigms, together with the Post-Orientalism debate paved the way, indirectly or directly to self-representation of the voices of the South as "indigenous" and "authentic", local voices.

More than ten years have elapsed since this discourse was taken up by the media and became popularized.[3] In the meantime, (and before I proceed to explain what the claims of the Islamizers are), vibrant criticism has been aimed by secular intellectuals at the empty language of the Islamizers, the rather large quantitative production, reflecting access to ample financing of publications, but the qualitatively poor product or body of writings.[4]

For the Arab scene, one notes the intellectuals who have written various critiques of the "Islamization of knowledge" discourse such as ʿAziz Al-ʿAzmah (1993: 407-414), Burhan Ghaliun (1993: 119-138), Mahmud Gad (1994: 52-59), Mohammed Rida Muharam (1994), Mohammed El-Sayyed Saiʿd (1985: 122-141), Nasr Hamid Abu Zayd[5], the late philosopher Zaki Naguib Mahmud (1987) and Sayyed Yassin (1990; 1992). These critiques of the Islamizers point to their ahistorical vision, and their quest for the authenticating of a mythological past. The critics note the danger of transcendentalism and the imposing of metaphysical interpretations resulting in an inquisition against scientists who are considered political opponents. Put symbolically, the critiques generated within the Arab World pointed to the danger of transferring the priest into the laboratory and giving him the boundless power of the judge and arbiter over the scientific community. The Islamization project, was viewed as rather propagandistic, linked with the growing money of the Arab oil producing countries. The Saudi Arabian, Petro Islam, ideology and the international Islamic networks in financing various conferences, were the main agents disseminating this ideology in Pakistan, Sudan, Egypt and Malaysia. Egyptian sociologist and former director of Al-Ahram Center for Strategic studies, Sayyed Yassin ironically described the Islamization publications as *"kutub tafiha"* (silly books), which were manufactured for opportunist (*intihaziyyah*) purposes. He related the development to the migration of academics to the Arab oil producing countries. Revelation is thus attributed to all forms of scientific enquiry. Akbar Ahmed's *Towards an Islamic Anthropology* (1986: 53-54) was criticized as a shallow work (Yassin 1996: 264).[6] For a critique of the proponents of Islamization of knowledge from a Pakistani perspective and of the negative impact of such discourse on the Pakistani scientific community, it is important to note the work of Pervez A. Hoodbhoy (1991).

Perhaps, instead of just passing harsh judgments on the discourse, we can view this abundance of publications as an expansive form of 'Islamic mass culture' on the level of book production and as the conquering stance of a "new" Islamic public religion. Perhaps also the IIIT[7] publications could be understood as providing a market for the new generation of young Muslims[8] who are searching for publishing outlets in the U.S.A., and other parts of the Muslim world.

This paper will attempt to look at the context and internationalization of the debate. Although the discourse and language of the Islamizers may take a homogeneous shape, and while the debate entails a global dimension, the politics of Islamization locally differ. The rejection of "imported" values and equally, of sociological tools which could be broadly classified under the rubric of "cultural invasion", are the direct consequence of the competitive interaction between East and West. In other words, such a discourse should be contextualized within a West/East dialectical relationship rather than an inherent "oriental" indigenous discourse. I plead here for an interactionionist sociology on the cross-cultural level. The claims of "imported values" are already classificatory terms set by the interaction with the West. In this context Tzvetan Todorov is right in arguing that: "Identity is born through the awareness of difference, moreover, a culture does not develop without its (external) contacts: the intercultural is constitutive of the cultural" (translated from French) (Todorov 1986: 16).

The discourse has been globalized. One can, for instance, purchase in Kuala Lumpur or Cairo the writings of Egyptian, Arab, Pakistani, Malaysian and Arab-American intellectuals, and meet Algerian, Tunisian and Pakistanis working at the International Islamic University in Kuala Lumpur. It is also global in that it was promoted by a Palestinian-American in a Conference in Mecca. This goes hand in hand with a diversification, in the local context, in the pattern of the various governments' maneuvers with the politics of Islamization. These variations could be observed either on the level of co-optation for state construction from "above", or suppression and the use of a reverse Islamic language to fight the underground religious opposition. This paper will attempt to describe the different proponents, each of whom claims to be the "sole" and true advocate of Islam. Yet they all maintain a common denominator in the logic of their argumentation, usually dissociating the history of the Orient from the main stream of universal history. Thus, they refuse to acknowledge the impact of the nearly two hundred years of colonial encounter and the long established process of secularization of the institutions in the Orient. Also, the quality of the writings varies from one context to another. So for instance, the Egyptian intellectual Tariq Al-Bishri[9] recently published an intelligent booklet on the Gulf war, dependency and globalization, Islam and national identity, in the IIIT publications.[10] One might disagree with Al-Bishri's political stand, but the quality of his work is certainly noteworthy in comparison to another book published by the IIIT on Islamizing attitudes and practice in embryology, which twists the Qur'an for instrumental purposes. Through clipping scientific interpretations from the holy book, it unfortunately lends itself to charlatanistic interpretations (Ibrahim 1989). Another paper attempts to apply Islamic beliefs and fundamentals in the areas of mathematics and computer science.[11]

Elsewhere, I have emphasized the specificity of the field of sociology in Malaysia and the impact of the writings and ideas of the Malaysian Syed N. Al-Attas as well as of Isma'il R. Al-Faruqi (Abaza 1993). I also stressed the networks used to build the bridge in sending Malaysian students to study at Temple University, U.S.A. before Al-Faruqi was assassinated under mysterious circumstances (ibid.). The opponents of Islamization attack the whole project for its intellectual poverty and simplistic assumptions. In Southeast Asia some view the key word "Islamization" as mere rhetoric used for a political agenda. That fact which seems to be undeniable, nevertheless ignores the institutional power struggle around who has supremacy to decide upon "knowledge".

Indeed, what we are witnessing today, besides the image of economically deprived, frustrated young anti-government activists, is the expansion of religious institutions constructed by "Islamic states". These institutions are characterized by substantial funding and staffed by academicians who are participating in such ideological state constructions. On the other hand, if we take Europe as an example there is nothing new in the fact that the recession has swept away many Western universities, and consequently many academic positions have been cut down, and funding for research and book acquisition has witnessed a decline. Here Islamization and the creation of alternative channels for academic positions in Muslim countries, could be viewed as reflecting the question of the variation and fluctuation of job markets.

Perhaps one should draw attention to the fact that we are dealing with a new understanding of "Islamic" institutions, which aims to promote alternative educational prospects, to Al-Azhar and Deoband

Universities. For instance, the International Islamic University at Kuala Lumpur[12] has little to do with developing Malay culture or Malay Islam, but rather emphasizes a transformed 'modernized' knowledge. Even if the teaching staff includes traditionally trained Al-Azhar ʿulama, many of them combined their theological training with Western education, long sojourns in the U.S.A. and Europe and call themselves the "New Muslim intellectuals" (Kirmani 1989: 45). For example, the current rector of the International Islamic University at Kuala Lumpur, who was the former president of the International Institute of Islamic Thought in Washington, D.C., ʿAbdel Hamid AbuSulaiman, was born in Saudi Arabia. He obtained his B.A. in 1959 and M.A. in 1963 from Cairo University; he earned a Ph.D. in international relations from the University of Pennsylvania, in Philadelphia in the United States. He also worked at the University of King Saud in Saudi Arabia. He was very active in the Muslim Association in the U.S.A. The biography of the Iraqi born Taha Jaber Al-ʿIlwani one of the founders of the IIIT, reveals that he received his early education in Iraq and then obtained his first degree, M.A. and Ph.D. from Al-Azhar University. We are also told that he was equally active in many Islamic organizations in the U.S.A. Ismaʿil Raji Al-Faruqi, one of the main advocates of Islamization of knowledge spent several years at Al-Azhar which he combined with a secular education.[13] In Egypt, on the other hand, the retired literature professor ʿAbdel Wahab El-Messiri[14] (who is strictly secular trained) by adopting the Islamization discourse, aspires to be the "advisor" and the "intermediary" of the traditional Azharites who lack Western training and are antiquated in their outlook and argumentation.[15]

The Mecca Conference

It was Fu'ad Zakariyya who developed the term "Petro-Islam" phase to designate the Saudi Arabian conservative version of Islam, quite often confused by analysts with revolutionary Islam which aimed at social change (Islam al-Tharwa [wealth] versus Islam al-Thawra [revolution]).[16] The term "Islamization of knowledge" was first devised in Saudi Arabia where the First World Conference on Muslim Education was held at Mecca from March 31 to April 8 in 1977. Three important figures related to this conference are the Palestinian-American Ismaʿil Raji Al-Faruqi, Syed M. N. Al-Attas,[17] and Seyyed Hossein Nasr.[18]

They developed a different understanding of what the Islamization of Knowledge is about. Syed M. N. Al-Attas (1991) presented a paper with the title *Preliminary thoughts on the Nature of Knowledge and the Definition and Aims of Education*. What interests us however, is the impact of such international Islamic organizations, and the successive conferences[19] in spreading the networks and visions of "Islamization of knowledge" all over the Muslim world. In connection with this conference Seyyed Hossein Nasr wrote a paper *On The Teaching of Philosophy in the Muslim World*. It should be noted that Seyyed Hossein Nasr's abundant writings about Islamic philosophy and science and his amalgamation of science with esoteric thinking, date well before the conference.[20] His Sufi vision of Islam seems to have evoked a response in Malaysia.

On the concrete level, the Mecca conference stimulated the creation of two International Islamic Universities of Islamabad and Kuala Lumpur and the different IIIT, in Cairo and Kuala Lumpur (attached to the International Islamic University). In the United States, it led to the creation of the International Institute of Islamic Thought in Washington, the IIIT (Sardar 1988: 98). Furthermore, it is important to note the American Journal of Islamic Social Sciences, published jointly by the Association of Muslim Social Scientists and the International Institute of Islamic Thought. According to these Muslim ideologues, in particular to Al-Faruqi, the intention was to develop "alternative paradigms of knowledge for both natural and social sciences and to conceive and mould disciplines most relevant to the needs of contemporary Muslim societies" (ibid.: 104).

Al-Faruqi proposes a holistic project to Islamize knowledge which is to be taken by his followers and extended to the Islamization of education and science. Al-Faruqi's program advocates that all knowledge must reorder itself under the principle of *Tawhid* (unity with God) (Al-Faruqi 1981: 5). This is because Western social science is "incomplete" and it "violates a crucial requirement of Islamic methodology" (ibid.: 4). Al-Faruqi proceeds by arguing that his project is not a mere spiritual undertaking but he adds an Islamic dimension which he calls Ummatism (ibid.).

In this debate, the clear divide between Islam and the West seems to be centered around the question of faith, which stresses that objective knowledge is the knowledge of God. For the Muslim social scientist, it would seem that knowledge should be interlinked with worship. ʿIlm (which is science and knowledge in its broad sense) becomes according to this modern interpretation a form of ʿibadah (worship), when it is pursued in obedience to God (Sardar, op.cit.: 103).

Parallel to the Mecca Conference, and coinciding with the rising Islamization of Egyptian intellectuals, ʿAdil Hussein, the former Egyptian Marxist economist, presented a paper in the early eighties at the Center for Criminology and Social Studies. The essay entitled *Western Social Theories: Deficient and Hostile* appeared in a volume of collected articles in 1985, entitled *Towards A New Arab Thought: Nasserism, Development and Democracy*. Interestingly ʿAdil Hussein who is an economist and not a sociologist attacks Western social sciences. ʿAdil Hussein's thought was discussed at length by Sami Zubaida (1988), in particular Hussein's paper on social sciences entitled *Western Social Sciences: Deficient and Hostile*. ʿAdil Hussein's stand was also criticized by Morsy/Nelson/Saad/Sholkamy (1991), Tibi (1992) and El-Sayyed Saʿid (1985).

El-Sayyed Saʿid extended his critique to both ʿAdil Hussein and Tariq Al-Bishri's notion of ʿasala' (authenticity). El-Sayyed Saʿid argued that Hussein discarded the already long and well-debated critique in the West concerning the value neutrality of science. He pointed to the fact that Hussein confused the scientific method, as a particular mode of knowledge with the topics of that knowledge (ibid.: 128). Furthermore, El-Sayyed Saʿid expressed a strong scepticism about the end results of developing a metaphysical science that would lead to religious oppression and systematic censorship of topics and ideas. He also expressed strong suspicion about the idea of a metaphysical science and whether losing one's "identity" through interacting with the West is unavoidable. According to Saʿid the notion of identity has been already debated in philosophical and sociological studies, like those of the Frankfurt School, and is in itself an unresolved question. One could extend the notion of "sociology of faith" which Sami Zubaida developed in discussing ʿAdil Hussein's ideas.

In this context, it is also important to point out that the followers of Faruqi such as Akhbar Ahmed, and Ziauddin Sardar, a Pakistani journalist whose writings are published and distributed in Malaysia, have all proclaimed an alternative Islamic world view.

Variations and Perceptions: Contrasts between Egypt and Malaysia

This section will attempt to demonstrate that the unfolding of the debate on Islamization of knowledge has had more serious institutional repercussions in Malaysia than in Egypt. Malaysia is witnessing the construction of a new state discourse on science and Islam which is closely linked to Institutional Islam. The promoters of this discourse could be viewed as attempting to enhance a new bureaucratic elite in Malaysia,[21] the promoters of the "Islamization of knowledge debate" are in the center of power and are spokesmen of the Malaysian government's vision of Islam. They hold significant positions in academic, publishing and government offices.

Although Islam has been the official religion in Malaysia, in recent years the government has been constantly confronted by conflicting *dakwah* or (Arabic) *daʿwah* groups as well as oppositional parties. In an effort to combat the growing influence of Islamic revivalist groups, it has been increasingly borrowing Islamic representations to establish legitimacy vis-à-vis the fundamentalists within the state apparatus. Thus the use of religious symbols has become widespread. In order to counter-attack communism and secular nationalists in many Muslim countries, religious symbols and activities have been employed by diverse regimes in the fight for legitimacy. It is understandable that the political struggle takes the form of a war of religious symbols as Lyon puts it (1983: 112-130). For instance, in Malaysia, the policies of the Mahathir government of the early 1970s were energetically directed towards Islamizing the government machinery, as witnessed by the increase in the number of Islamic programs and policies (Mutalib 1990: 142-143). The state also responded to Islamic resurgence by increasing Islamization procedures in mass media and public life (Muzaffar 1987: 5). Malaysia also witnessed the promotion of a bureaucratized institutional Islam and as a result the Pusat Islam (the Islamic Center that promotes an official version of Islam and counteracts deviants) was upgraded. The official declaration of the 'Islamization of the government machinery' took place in 1984. Islamic judges were promoted to the same status as the civil judiciary in 1988 (Mutalib, op.cit.: 134). Indeed, Southeast Asian intellectuals argue that the state has itself reinforced Islamic resurgence.

The Islamization of the state machinery also occurred in Egypt during Sadat's regime. Nevertheless, there are considerable local and economic differences between these two countries. The first difference is that Malaysia is one of the smaller Muslim countries in Asia, with a population of around seventeen million and yet it is one of the fastest developing Muslim nations. This is why Malaysia has become a fascinating model for some Muslims from the Middle East and in particular from Egypt, which is a heavily populated and economically burdened country on the verge of a serious political crisis and collapse.[22] For those Middle Eastern Muslims like the Egyptian Al-Ahram columnist Fahmi Huwaydi Malaysia, (particularly the northern area of Kelantan, which is led by the opposition party PAS) "imagined" as a different field where Islamic Shari'a, could be paired with economic take off.[23] For instance, Fahmi Huwaydi who advocates the Islamic path and who seems to have directed strong attacks against the secular intellectuals and artists in Egypt, and the former Marxist ʿAdil Hussein who turned to Islam[24], were both invited to Malaysia and wrote a series of articles in *Al-Ahram* the semi-official daily and *Al-Shaʿab* an opposition journal (ʿAdil Hussein) in admiration of the Malaysian economic flowering and its political system[25].

Second, for the sake of speculation, we propose the following hypotheses; the difference between Egypt and Malaysia with regard to the debate over the "Islamization of Knowledge" is that in Malaysia, the debate was mainly concretized by a former militant Muslim student, now the Finance Minister, Anwar Ibrahim. Thus the discourse was promoted and encouraged from above and this has led to the creation of "Islamic institutions" from the top with a large bureaucratic apparatus. The debate is advertised as a state ideology (to counteract the religious opposition in the North of Malaysia, Kelantan). It also seems to carry an institutional importance exemplified in the creation of the International Islamic University (in contrast to the old Egyptian Azhar University in Cairo) as the political card to play for Anwar Ibrahim's credibility.[26] Both governments (in Egypt and Malaysia) faced the problem of Islamizing the state machinery. Both gave an increasing large arena to "official Islam", in order to counteract the growing Islamic opposition exemplified in the student movement and the various Islamic parties. However, Malaysian specialists often complain about the absence of a public culture and the lack of critical intellectuals. Equally, they complain that intellectuals have withered away to be replaced by advisers of the "prince", ghost writers for ministers' speeches, and "think tank" managers of the government. However, whether this is valid or not, one has to acknowledge the oratorical skills and the elaborate and well researched public speeches of Anwar Ibrahim. His attempts to employ a so-called intellectual and scientific jargon in his speeches – even when it is mere rhetoric – deserves attention. Moreover, one has the impression that for many intellectuals in Kuala Lumpur, their dreams and perspectives are to become "better Anwar Ibrahims" through being co-opted by the Mahathir government machinery.[27] The vertiginous Malaysian economic growth,[28] the expansion of the middle classes with growing consumerist attitudes, and the creation of huge "empires of consumption" and shopping malls, attracting large sections of the society,[29] seem to play a role – even if it is a superficial one – in breaking the fear of an Islamic oppositional resurgence.[30] In Kuala Lumpur, it is interesting to see in shopping centers, that the Islamic attire is combined with mobile phones, and with enjoying the food at the "Deli France" Coffee Shops. Telepreaching, in particular for the Muslim community, is done with great sophistication by mass-media professionals. Religious programs constantly emphasize the combining of modern technology with faith. For instance, the breaking of the fast during Ramadan, is represented on TV by showing a scene of a pilot eating dates while he is flying the plane. The revivals of "Malay", "Indian" and "Chinese" cultural artifacts, costumes, and traditions are hybridized with consumer tastes and the Westernization of habits. One could interpret these artifacts as an aspect of "folkorization of culture"[31] which goes hand in hand with the growing etatization in Malaysia. Dances and celebrations of the Chinese New Year take place in the shopping malls and Malay, Indian and Chinese festivities are also celebrated in these super modern settings. In other words, Islamization – in Kuala Lumpur – goes hand in hand with consumerism and the Westernization of habits.[32]

Paradoxically, although Egypt's state machinery has been weakened since the Nasser period, – a shortcoming which went hand in hand with the decline of public services, open door policies (*infitah*), corruption and the growth of an Islamic opposition – one could witness the rise of a public culture in the mid eighties with the increasing significance of journals and magazines.[33] This is not to claim that the Egyptian government is more democratic than the Malaysian one. It is no secret that elections in Egypt have been conducted without respect for democratic principles and procedures. In recent years, observers have pointed out that the government has violently crushed the Islamists.[34] At the same time, the state apparatus has been Islamized and the official Islamic figures have being co-opted by the state.[35] Since Sadat's time the doses of religiosity in mass media and the press have increased to counteract secular forces and to co-opt official Islamic institutions. Human rights in Egyptian jails have been consistently and seriously violated.[36] For that matter the human rights situation is far worse in Egypt than in Malaysia. There now exists in Egypt a wide stratum of literati and secular intellectuals consisting of artists, painters, film makers, novelists, playwrights, journalists, free lance writers, who are currently facing a confrontation with both the Islamists and the state Islamization through the Institution of Al-Azhar. It is difficult however to state that the whole official religious body is entirely under the control of the government.[37] Notwithstanding, Al-Azhar was given extensive powers since Sadat's time and is playing an ambiguous role in promoting an official Islam against the underground Islamists[38] as well as tracking down secular intellectuals.

Secular intellectuals in Egypt are facing strong pressure and are caught in the game of being either co-opted or used as scapegoats by the regime to counter-play the rising religious opposition. One need only to look at the Nasr Hamid Abu Zayd case, the recent attempt against Naguib Mahfouz's life, Farag Foda's assassination and Al-Azhar's constant censorship of literary and political works, to reveal the pressures secular intellectuals are facing. It is possible to argue that they are struggling to shape the culture and debate over Islam, Islamization and secularism in Egypt. In contrast to Malaysia, this group of intellectuals in Egypt is still struggling to revive the period of the liberal age. This stratum[39] might have given a different turn to the entire "Islamization of Knowledge" debate which takes a rather more critical stand towards the question of the official institutionalization and the misuse of religion. Public figures like Hussein Ahmed Amin, Mohammed Sa'id Al-'Ashmawi, Fu'ad Zakariyya, Sayyed Yassin, and the researcher Sayyed Al-Qimni, should be mentioned here, to alert us to their role in this debate. It is perhaps the well being of Malaysia's economy, its rising affluent middle classes[40] that weakens this confrontation between secular intellectuals, the state Islamizing apparatuses and Islamists.⁴¹ But, it might also be the fact that bureaucratic institutions in Malaysia transmit an appearance of "modernity" and "newness",⁴² which is nonexistent in Egypt. Also, although a chaotic and conflictual situation dominates on the institutional level in Egypt, the confrontation between the secularists and Islamists has led to a flourishing of intellectual production. Thus, although public life in Malaysia looks more "ordered" than in Egypt, the debates, as a result of the confrontation, are certainly more stimulating in Egypt.

The Example of ISTAC in Kuala Lumpur

Bassam Tibi, in one of his latest publications had defined the advocates of the Islamization of knowledge as "purist fundamentalists", and Syed Muhammad N. Al-Attas as just another fundamentalist (Tibi 1992: 35, 113). What his analysis misses is the crucial difference in the way local politics affects the Islamization discourse. To only restate Al-Attas's slogan of "de-westernization of knowledge" as an expression of fundamentalism, lends itself to a generalization which clouds the difference between oppositional and institutional Islam. Quite often, Western observers have tended to associate the term fundamentalism with angry, protesting anti-Western social movements. Is this the case with Syed M. N. Al-Attas?

ISTAC, The Institute of Islamic Thought and Civilization, was founded in 1987 by Syed M. N. Al-Attas, who was formerly the Dean of the Arts faculty at the University of Malaysia. Al-Attas began his career as an army officer after studying at Eton Hall, Chester, Wales then at the Royal Military Academy, Sandhurst, England (1952-1955). It is said that he was active in fighting Communism in Malaysia. He then studied at the University of Malaysia and later obtained a fellowship to study at McGill University in Montreal, Canada. Al-Attas earned a Ph.D. from the School of Oriental and African Studies, University of London. His teachers were eminent Orientalists such as Hamilton Gibb, Fazlur Rahman, Tashihiko Izutsu, A.J. Arberry, Sir Mortimer Wheeler of the British Academy and Sir Richard Winstedt (Daud n.d.). No doubt, Al-Attas' philological works reflect traditional orientalism to a great degree. He personally retains a great respect for traditional orientalists like B. Spuler whom he met in Europe.⁴³ Al-Attas' best known books are, *Some Aspects of Sufism as Understood and practised Among the Malays* (1963); *Hamzah al Fansuri. A Sufi Mystic* (1970); *A commentary on Hujjat Al-Siddiq of Nur Al-Din Al-Raniri* (1986); *The Oldest Known Malay Manuscript: A 16th Century Translation of the 'Aqai'd of Al-Nasafi* (1988).

We were told that Al-Attas is a crucial figure in stimulating students to read contemporary revivalist literature. He stimulated the development of the Islamic student movement of the seventies in Malaysia. Al-Attas sponsored a circle of students who met at his house (Anwar 1987: 12-13). For example, Anwar Ibrahim was his former student and is today his friend. Ibrahim is one of the main brains in creating and "generously" financing ISTAC.

ISTAC was originally established as a part of the International Islamic University. Nevertheless, on arrival in Kuala Lumpur, the visitor soon realizes that the two institutions (the International Islamic University and ISTAC) function quite separately. One is also informed that this is due to several factors: (1) the Director's elitist and "hierarchical" understanding of Islamic education; (2) the Institute's policy of limiting the number of students – the exclusivity (only for the *khasah*, the few); (3) the difficulty of access to the library and (4) the basically foreign teaching staff (Iranian, Sudanese, Turkish, American and a few Malays). Al-Attas insists that he has little to do with any of the IIIT activities or conferences in Kuala Lumpur. The emphasis upon the elitist background of Al-Attas as a "Sayyed"[44] of Arab, Hadrami origin, whose ancestors were saints and scholars, his writings on Sufism, together with his military training are all interesting ingredients of elitism, "chivalry" and hierarchy:[45]

There is no doubt, however, that his military training – particularly the Islamic elements of respecting order, discipline and loyalty – continues to influence some of his views and ways as an Islamic scholar and administrator.

(Daud n.d.)

ISTAC was designed personally by Al-Attas, in a moorish style with *mashrabiyyahs* and an invented Islamic architecture. It includes imported Italian pottery, expensive carpets and decorations, ample space and a huge conference room that reminds the foreign visitor of an Italian monastery. It also includes a large Andalusian style courtyard. The library has acquired in the last three years, a large collection of journals, precious old Islamic books and general works, besides the Fazlur Rahman Urdu collection, the Bertold Spuler and the Brunschvig collections. ISTAC publishes works on Islamic sciences and manuscripts. The German orientalist Annemarie Schimmel visited and spoke at the opening of ISTAC.

One could view ISTAC as the symbol of the Malaysian government's vision of 2020, with its intentions to promote economic prosperity as one of the leading Asian tigers, and to cultivate an Islam with money, status and the means to acquire rich collections of books from Europe and various parts of the Western world. ISTAC is the vision of an Islam of power, wealth and lavish institutions. It is no coincidence that ISTAC is located near the Seri Perdana, the Prime Minister's official residence, the Ministry of Education and other Ministries at Pusat Bandar Damansara. Visitors to ISTAC enjoy a view of the hill where the new rich financial class and the foreign embassies are located and where condominiums and villas are blooming. The Beacon on the Crest of a Hill which is the title of one of the publications of ISTAC, refers metaphorically to no one but Al-Attas. Tibi might indeed be missing the point in classifying Al-Attas as a fundamentalist without revealing the social context and nuances differentiating the biography of Al-Attas from that of, for example, Nik Aziz of PAS in Kelantan, Northern Malaysia who opposes the Mahathir government and constantly questions the government's religious credibility.[46]

The Islamization of Knowledge Debate in Egypt: The Cairo Office[47]

Before the attempt on President Mubarak's life in 1995 and the recent government arrests of the established faction of the Islamic movement, and the underground groups, the IIIT office in Zamalek was active in organizing seminars which appeared as working papers.[48] The participants are public, well known, figures like Tariq Al-Bishri, Mohammed 'Immara, the journalist Fahmi Huwaydi, the lawyer Ni'mat Fu'ad. The late Sheikh of Al-Azhar Gad ul Haq was invited, along with Sheikh Abul Wafa Al-Taftazani (Sheikh mashayekh al-turuq al-sufiyya [the Grand Sheikh of Sufi Orders]) and many other Muslim intellectuals. Topics varied from Islamization of knowledge, Islamic sciences, Sufism, contemporary Islamic views, issues related to contemporary Islamic philosophy of sciences to the question of Islamic revivalism. Most probably the paper on *Hisba* (ʿAwad 1990), related to the Nasr Hamid Abu Zayd scandal, was presented at one of these seminars. Not all participants are necessarily advocates of Islamizing knowledge but they are sympathetic to the general policies of Islamization. An exception is the secular philosopher Zaki Naguib Mahmud, who was invited to talk before he passed away. Many of these intellectuals who publish the IIIT are rather spokesmen of various contemporary Islamic trends, which some Western observers, rightly or wrongly, have labelled as Islamic liberals.[49] In the field of political science the writings of Saifaddin ʿAbdel Fattah Ismaʿil and Nasr Mohammed ʿAref are also of significance.[50] It is interesting that Sayyed Yassin, in trying to search for indigenous social and political theories only specified the writings of ʿAbdel Fattah Ismaʿil as genuine attempts to follow up the ideas of the late eminent Egyptian political scientist Hamid Rabiʿ (Yassin 1996: 256-265). According to ʿAbdel Fattah Ismaʿil, western sociological methods, and political concepts are inappropriate for analyzing oriental societies. It also follows from this rationale that concepts such as democracy, nation, the state and elections are inadequate for explaining oriental social and political mechanisms and are thus replaced by Muslim words such as the *umma*, *shura*, and *ijmaʿ*.[51]

I have elsewhere analyzed the discourse of some of the Egyptian proponents of Islamization. Suffice it here to mention that, among the most significant and prolific writers, the late Mohammed ʿImmara is also a known Muslim public figure. In recent years he has written extensively about the Islamization of knowledge.

Along with the thinkers mentioned above, the prominent sociologist Hassan El-Saʿati is an illustrative example of Islamizing knowledge in Egyptian sociology. El-Saʿati has written extensively on industrial sociology, on Ibn Khaldun and sociology and is one of the leading empirical sociologists in Egypt.[52] It is interesting that the language of Islamization appears only in Saʿati's recent works, specifically with respect to the King Faisal award in Islamic Studies.[53] Here our prominent sociologist reproaches Arab youth for cultural westernization (which is a concrete problem). He stresses the need for an Islamization of social science, which should receive support from various educational institutions and advocates also that the Islamic identity should be emphasized. He blames his generation of academics for adopting imported educational methods in social sciences. Their fascination with the West has led to the loss of values according to El-Saʿati. Here, he reminds us of the evilness of the West because it teaches sexuality and encourages youngsters to practice it at a young age which contradicts "our" philosophy. He concludes that cultural colonialism, *al-istiʿmar al-thaqafi*, was the major factor that led to changes in the society.

In a recent study, El-Saʿati recurrently refers to the theme of "Western invasion" and its impact upon youth (El-Saʿati 1992: 59-68). He warns us against the importation of foreign goods, fashions that shape youth and the materialistic invasion. But more importantly, the cultural invasion according to El-Saʿati is also manifested in bookshops which import foreign books and contain "revolutionary", destructive thoughts. Cultural dependency is transmitted from teachers to students. According to him, the spiritual preachers of Western culture constitute the real danger (he nevertheless does not tell us who he really means by that). Here again, consumerism which can be seen as a concrete threat, is interwoven in the language of El-Saʿati with the importation of books and culture. He points to the fact that some of the publications of Arab professors are entirely copied from Western sources (which is not incorrect) (ibid.: 63). Thus the solution for the protection of youngsters would be through the appropriate education of the family, through preachers in the mosques, and better orientation of mass media. Muslim scientists and philosophers should be taught and popularized, since they are ignored at the expense of Western philosophy (ibid.: 66). Here again, that Western philosophy is taught "at the expense" of Muslim philosophy, as if we are dealing with two antagonistic subjects, reveals a great deal about El-Saʿati's recent shift in thought. Unfortunately, El-Saʿati with his major studies in industrial sociology, seems to be compromising himself in this recent stand.

ʿAbdel Wahab Al-Messiri a retired professor of English literature at ʿAin Shams University, and editor of an Encyclopaedia Judaica, is another example of the advocates of Islamization. He adopted the language of "Islamization of Knowledge" in recent years as a participant observer of the American society for eleven years. He earned his doctorate degree in English literature in the U.S.A. In the Faruqi Memorial Lecture he brings up the primary evils of the West which is its sexual decadence:

Let me give you an example of Western man's attitude towards sexuality. This is an area that is always seen as an expression of individual selfhood. But I suggest that it is one of the most fertile areas to see the process of something as social as secularization and to see how it leaves a deep impact on western man. First of all, sex is divorced from guilt, from any moral values, the means for mere pleasure. Then it is divorced from procreation as well, actually it is also divorced from human relationships. I find that casual sex is the ultimate secularization of humans, for two human beings to be engaged in a relationship that is generally supposed in traditional cultures to be an expression of something deeper than the surface.

(Al-Messiri 1993: 8)

Here again we are faced with the dichotomy between a spiritual, pure East versus a materialist, impure, secular, sexually promiscuous West. These dichotomies are used by scientists who are also Islamists as central to their argumentation.

A more important and influential figure for Egypt is Mohammed 'Immara, the editor of the works of Jamal addin Al-Afghani and Mohammed 'Abduh, the two major Muslim reformists. 'Immara's extensive publications on Islamization should be taken into consideration.[54] Regularly over the last ten years, he has written in the newspaper *Al-Wafd* (liberal-right wing), articles on "Islamization of Knowledge" as the alternative to materialist knowledge.[55] 'Immara borrows arguments similar to those promoted by Christian scientists, and by the Greens about the ethical implications of science. Although 'Immara understands that while the laws of biological inheritance are universal, the political implications of genetics may vary; he proceeds to plead for a spiritual and pure East devoid of Western decadence.

'Immara launched a strong attack against the secularists in a paper given at the IIIT in Cairo, in 1993 ('Immara 1993), which appeared in a book in 1995. This is not unconnected to the fact that the government's publishing agency *al-hay'a al-'amma lil-kitab*, embarked on a project of reprinting old works in a series entitled One Hundred Years of Enlightenment (*al-tanwir*), sold at inexpensive prices (25 piastres).[56] The collection entailed historical and intellectual figures such as R. Al-Tahtawi, Al-Afghani, Mohammed 'Abduh, Sheikh 'Ali 'Abdel Raziq, Taha Hussein, Sa'd Zaghlul, Mohammed Hussein Haykal, and Salama Musa. The series was titled "The Age of Taha Hussein". Taha

Hussein is regarded in Egypt today as the symbol of Enlightenment. By undertaking such a project, the government aimed to oppose the obscurantists, i.e. the contemporary Islamists.[57] In this paper, 'Immara seems to attack the entire project of popularizing Taha Hussein and other liberal intellectuals.

The government attempted to popularize the enlightened intellectuals, as *"tanwiris"*, enlightened, but 'Immara wishes to demonstrate that these thinkers are misunderstood and that they were not secularists, but instead rather critical of Western civilization. One could interpret 'Immara's stand as "reactive" against the government "authoritarianism" in imposing its notions of culture, and in this case its revival of a secular heritage, in response to the threat of the Islamists. 'Immara starts with Tahtawi. According to 'Immara, Al-Tahtawi refuted philosophy in Western civilization as misleading. He referred to the atheistic behavior, and the irreligiosity of the French.[58] Furthermore, he argues that Al-Afghani's reformist movement, should not be considered as one of the tanwiris (since 'Immara considers it to be negative). 'Immara points to the fact that Sheikh 'Ali 'Abdel Raziq retreated from reprinting his book[59] in a second edition. At the end of his life the sheikh did not have anything to do with the book, and it was Taha Hussein who apparently, according to 'Immara influenced him negatively.

'Immara's strongest attacks are directed against Taha Hussein, who is regarded as the *"Imam al-mughtaribin wa muqalidin al-gharb"* (the Imam of Westernizers and imitators of the West) ('Immara 1993: 20). According to 'Immara, Taha Hussein's danger for culture was that he argued that the oriental mind is Greek.[60] He insists nevertheless, that Taha Hussein respected religion and advocated that the state should respect religion. 'Immara offers the example that in 1959 as part of the committee of writing the constitution of Egypt, Taha Hussein argued that faith should include the entire holy book instead of just parts of the Qur'an. With this remark, ultimately, 'Immara wishes to rescue Taha Hussein from complete culpability (ibid.: 22).

For 'Immara, Salama Musa is the true symbol of negative secularism.[61] Salama Musa is viewed as a negative "collaborator on the civilizational level" ('Immara 1993: 28). For 'Immara, Salama Musa is portrayed as imitating the West blindly and he argues that Musa advocated that Egyptians should become *"faranjah"* (Westernized, a term also used for foreigners) and to despise anything oriental. He quotes him out of context as follows: "I am a *kafir* [unbeliever] of the Orient, *mu'min* [believer] of the West" ('Immara 1993: 30) in order to attack him on the grounds of Western "collaboration". Salama Musa's symbolic understanding of "Asia" as lagging behind the West is debased and oversimplified here. 'Immara draws a connection between the Orientalists' negative usage of the word "Islam" with the concept of "Asia" to make us believe that Musa is just as guilty as the Orientalists (ibid.: 30). He concludes his criticism with Jabir Al-'Asfuri, the launcher of this series of inexpensive books, because he advocates that Egyptians should cease to search in the past for an identity (ibid.: 31).

'Immara defends Islamism as being the real authentic illuminative project. In so doing, he juxtaposes the advocators of rationalism as imitators of the West.

There is a tendency to see the secular oriented critique of the "Islamization" debate as the reverse side of the same coin. Indeed as Abdallah Laroui appropriately contextualized Salama Musa as "le technophile" (Laroui 1977: 27) who, through the blind adoration of science, is in reality a terrorist who refuses to see that science is not value free. However, it is also true that, as Laroui argued in his introduction, modernity and the relationship between the Arabs has been centered around the question of "who is the other and who I am". Through this question the problematic and clouded understanding emerged that the Occident is an antithesis of the Orient. It might appear antiquated to discuss Salama Musa and Taha Hussein after more than seventy years of the publication of their works, but it seems that they have become the signposts of this confrontation between secular intellectuals and islamists as the attacks on these figures become multiplied in the Islamist milieus. As Al-'Azmah argued the campaign against Taha Hussein and ' Ali 'Abdel Raziq led to various results namely:

… the emaciation of Islamic reformism and its stagnation following its start and the internal degeneration of the stance of the Egyptian secular liberals. These were related with the rise of an irrationalist movement that was anchored in Arabic thought in Egypt; the effects which are still alive in the slogans of *'al'ilm wal iman'* science and faith which was launched by Sadat.

(Al-'Azmah 1992: 235)

The "terrorism" (according to Al-ʿAzmah) practiced against secular intellectuals finds a continuation in ʿImmara's recent writings. In *The Fall of the Secularist Extravagance* (1995b), Mohammed ʿImmara dedicates the entire book to a virulent attack against the Judge Mohammed Saʿid Al-ʿAshamawi. The title in itself implies a strong grudge against secularism. ʿImmara aims to discredit the patriotism of Al-ʿAshamawi, who is accused of collaborating with "Christian" Western and "secular" institutions. ʿImmara discredits Al-ʿAshamawi by arguing that his writings are appreciated by Israeli circles in Cairo. ʿImmara attacks Al-ʿAshamawi's interpretation and raises questions concerning the collection of the Qur'an during ʿUthman and the unification of the reading of the Qur'an; a point which Al-ʿAshamawi raised in common with Nasr Hamid Abu Zayd and earlier Taha Hussein. The attacks proceed to Al-ʿAshamawi's historical interpretations of Hadith, Fiqh and other branches. They crudely discredit Al-ʿAshmawi's ideas and simplify them. Thus Al-ʿAshmawi is viewed as having argued "that the Qur'an contains mistakes", and that Abu Bakr violated the rights of the Prophet. In a another publication, Al-ʿAshamawi is defined as belonging to *talamith al-tanwir-al-gharbi al-ʿilmani*, the students of the Western Secular enlightenment (ʿImmara 1995a: 216).

Such statements appear journalistic and inconsequential but are quite dangerous and seek to incite populist anger. If this curse against secular intellectuals starts with Salama Musa and Taha Hussein,[62] it extends to the contemporary writings of the Egyptian Ambassador Hussein Ahmed Amin (ibid.: 211). Even the Sorbonne trained Egyptian philosopher Hassan Hanafi is not spared this type of criticism (ibid.: 188-197).

Conclusion

This paper attempts to highlight the local differences in the way the Islamization of knowledge was politically directed within the context of globalization. In Malaysia the discourse is closely intertwined with policies of the regime; in Egypt, the discourse of Islamization of knowledge takes a subtle turn in the old and renewed polarization between secular intellectuals and Islamists.

Sadeq Jalal al-ʿAzm argued that one of the major peculiarities of the crisis of the Arab World today is the ascendance of an anti-rationalist movement that stands against progress, science[63] and reason (Al-ʿAzm 1989: 42-58). This trend appears to oppose any objective sociological analysis, and perhaps here the "Islamization of knowledge project" seems to reflect such tendencies, where the battle over rationality becomes a decisive issue. Despite differences in local politics, what the advocates seem to maintain as the end result is a common language, key words and a united way of selecting and retrieving evidence from Islamic heritage and Western philosophy. The Islamizers unite in their aversion to secularism as an imported "Western" notion. If knowledge, according to Al-Attas should be "de-westernized", in Egypt ʿAbdel Wahab El-Missiri's literary analysis of Geoffrey Chaucer's "The Frankeleyn's Tale" and Bertold Brecht's "The exception and the Rule" equally underlies the strong feelings against secularism (El-Missiri 1996: 42-58). The same opinion can be presumed from the writings of ʿAdil Hussein. It is true that El-Missiri might be sophisticated enough in his evaluation of the ritualistic understanding of religion (El-Missiri 1996: 28), but he seems to reproduce the same key words about the materialism of the West[64] and the unlimited Western application of reason (as if an uncritical approach to reason is only restricted to the West). El-Missiri, like Al-Attas, remains silent about the long history of spirituality and metaphysics in Western philosophy which includes Heidegger, and Henry Corbin's important contribution to the Iranian self-consciousness of spiritual Shiʿism. El-Missiri wishes to specify the Green party as the only movement that recognizes the limits of rationalism. He thus denies the historical context and comparisons of the Green movement with the pre-Fascist ideologies in Germany. Both El-Missiri and Al-Attas use the Nietzschean metaphor the "death of God", naively to debase the West as materialistic (El-Messiri 1996: 45). As sophisticated as he might appear, El-Missiri lumps together vulgar social Darwinism with a simplified understanding of Nietzsche's Superhuman, and slogans like the survival of the fittest to designate the crisis of Western civilization (ibid.: 45). Such statements find resonance in the Islamist literature. Where Nasr Hamid Abu Zayd might be right, and where his case is very revealing, is when he denies any political difference in the discourse between moderate Egyptian Islamists, the recognized Islamic figures who are expressing their views in the official channels of religion (on television and newspapers)[65] and banned underground extremists. In fact, he attempts to put their ideological religious discourse into one basket. He sees that the tactics uniting all Islamists is the naming of the political opponents of unbelief (*takfir*).⁶⁶ Abu Zayd also notes the Islamists› reductionist understanding of Marxism being limited to atheism and materialism, and Darwinism which is debased as the "animalization of the human".⁶⁷ This might explain why the Abu Zayd case has taken the shape of a personal Vendetta. It also explains why the fight in the field of social sciences is a faithful mirror of the general political mood in the Islamic World.

Notes

This paper is part of a project financed by the German foundation, the Deutsche Forschungsgemeinschaft. Some points of this paper have been presented at the conference of The International Association of Middle Eastern Studies Sixth Congresses, The Middle East on the Threshold of the 21st Century: Issues and Prospects, April 10-14, Al al-Bayt University, Jordan 1996. I am thankful to Cynthia Nelson and to all who participated in the panel on Gender. I would also like to thank Armando Salvatore for his comments. This paper should be read as an extension of ideas devised in "Some Reflections on the Question of Islam and Social Sciences in The Contemporary Muslim World", Social Compass 40/2, (1993), pp. 301-321.

1 I would like to warn the reader that my field research in Malaysia was undertaken in 1996 and this paper was completed well before the recent financial Asian crisis. No one could foresee such a fast collapse of the stock market in Kuala Lumpur. There was much talk already at the time of my research work about the ideological and political differences between Anwar Ibrahim and Mahathir Mohammed. Anwar was dismissed in 1998 from his position of Finance Minister. The events which resulted in Anwar‹s detention and humiliation through the sexual allegations with which he was charged were unpredictable. Thus, the description I provide here about affluent consumerist middle classes and Muslim intellectuals who are closely linked to power has changed considerably after the crisis.

2 The debate on authenticity stirred vigorous reactions which can-

not be discussed in detail here. Suffice to point to Arab intellectuals like Fu'ad Zakariyya, 'Aziz Al-'Azmeh, Hussein Ahmed Amin, Georges Tarabishi, Nasr Hamid Abu Zayd, the late Mahdi 'Amel (Hassan Himdan), Mohammed Arkoun, Mohammed Sa'id Al-'Ashamawi, Abdallah Laroui, and Sadeq Jalal Al-'Azm. They, all from very different perspectives, dismantled and questioned the binary opposition of "authenticity" versus the imported; the spiritual East versus materialist West and the invoking of a much disputed Islamic heritage for instrumental ideological purposes. It was also observed that class analysis and Marxist discourse was intentionally blurred to be replaced by the "authenticity" discourse. All these intellectuals pointed to the major changes that affected the intellectual field to shift from Arabism and socialism to Islam.

3 For an overview of the recent stand of the islamization of knowledge see Sardar 1989b: 25-27.
4 Tibi proposes that the whole Islamization of knowledge debate is an import from Washington. The proliferation of their publications is due to the heavy financing of the Saudi Petro dollars. See Tibi 1992: 113.
5 Nasr Hamed Abu Zayd is the Cairo University Professor of philosophy who in 1992 was refused the Professorship, an event which resulted in a scandal. He has been attacked for apostasy for pleading hermeneutics of the text. Abu Zayd pleads for historisizing and contextualizing the religious texts. See Kermani 1994: 25-51.
6 Ahmed's book was equally harshly reviewed by Richard Tapper's book review (1988: 568).
7 IIIT stands for International Institute of Islamic Thought.
8 It is interesting to note that the IIIT publishes many M.A. and Ph.D. theses of young academics.
9 Tariq Al-Bishri's ideas about cultural authenticity have been recently analyzed in detail by Leonard Binder 1988.
10 See Al-Bishri 1992: 18. He argues that the Muslim world is facing a great dependency on the West and promoted the idea that there is a fierce intellectual war between the forces of *al-fiqr al-wafid* (the introduced) against the forces of *al-fikr al-mawruth* (the inherited, indigenous thought).

11 See Zahid 1989, for a more recent refutation of such interpretations see Hussein 1983.
12 The International Islamic University at Kuala Lampur was founded in 1983. According to the Modern Oxford Encyclopedia of Islam "[t]he International Islamic University, Malaysia, seeks to permeate the teaching of all knowledges with Islamic values. The university is presently sponsored by the Organization of the Islamic Conference and seven other Muslim countries in addition to Malaysia: Maldives, Bangladesh, Pakistan, Turkey, Libya, Saudi Arabia and Egypt. Its philosophy of the integration of religious knowledge and worldly sciences, together with the vision of Islamization of human knowledge, were inspired by the recommendations of the First World Conference on Muslim Education held in Mecca in 1977." See entry: 'International Islamic University at Kuala Lumpur'. In John Esposito (ed.) (1995) The Oxford Encyclopedia of Islam, vol. 2.
13 Ismaï'il Raji Al-Faruqi was born in Palestine in 1922. He studied in both traditional and religious schools and at the American University in Beirut. He obtained his Ph.D. from Indiana University, U.S.A. He spent four years in Al-Azhar University in Cairo, two years at the School of Divinity at McGill, and then at the Islamic Research Institute in Islamabad, in Pakistan. He later joined the department of Religion in Syracuse University and in 1962 created The Muslim Students Association. In 1968 he joined the Department if Religion at Temple University. See Ba-Yunus 1988: 13-14.
14 ʿAbdel Wahab El-Missiri also signs his name as ʿAbdel Wahab Al-Messiri. This paper will quote his name in the two different ways.
15 Communication with Professor Al-Messiri, Cairo, May 1996.
16 Fu'ad Zakariyya has pointed to the fact that some of the conservative forces utilize the language of Islamic revivalism with a revolutionary rhetoric, to blur the appalling class differences in the Muslim countries. See Zakariyya 1987.
17 There are nevertheless basic differences in orientation between Al-Attas' and Al-Faruqi's views of Islamization of knowledge. Al-Attas stresses strong Sufi inclinations as a form of knowledge, while Al-Faruqi expressed strong sympathy towards Fiqh. In ad-

dition that there were very strong personal anitpathies between Al-Attas and Al-Faruqi.

18 I could not check if Seyyed Hossein Nasr attended the conference. Nevertheless, he published a paper in connection with the conference. See Nasr 1981: 53-72, a paper presented in connection with the First International Conference on Muslim Education, held in Mecca 1977.

19 For further details about the various conferences that took place afterwards, see Abaza 1993.

20 Seyyed Hossein Nasr is of Iranian origin. Nasr was born in 1933 and studied in the U.S.A. After receiving an undergraduate degree in Physics at MIT (Massachusetts Institute of Technology), he wrote his Ph.D. thesis in History at Harvard. See Hoodbhoy 1991: 69.

21 According to the 1980 census there are 6.9 million Muslims in Malyasia out of a population of 13.07 million. The remaining population consists of Buddhists, Hindus, Christians, Sikhs and followers of Confucianism, Taoism and other traditional Chinese religions, followers of various folk religions and others (see Muzaffar 1987: 1). The Malays represent 63.9 percent, the Chinese 25.5 percent while the Indians are around 9.7 percent of the population.

22 Concerning the idea that Egypt is on the verge of collapsing because of relative deprivation and political discontent, see Casandra 1995.

23 Although Northern Malaysia is considered to be among the poorest regions.

24 Who has aligned himself to *Al-Sha'ab* newspaper, which in recent years expresses a growing Islamic tendency, and became its editor-in-chief.

25 See also the recent articles in *Al-Muslimun* (1.11.1993, 26.11.1993 and 3.12.1993), which provide a panorama and equally praise contemporary Malaysian Islamic institutions. The author, a journalist argues for the merits of Islamic revivalism which is coupled with economic stability and welfare.

26 Concerning this point, it is interesting to note that Sardar's *An Early Crescent. The Future of Knowledge and Environment in Islam* was prefaced by Anwar Ibrahim the then Minister of Culture.

27 One can also mention here the case of the Malaysian intellectual Chandra Muzaffar who shifted in recent years from being critical of the regime to a position of strongly supporting the Mahathir regime. This coincided with Muzaffar's strong attacks of the West, in particular after the Iraq-Kuwait conflict.
28 Malyasia has been in the last few years witnessing a vertiginous 9 percent rate of growth. But where is this growth leading to is the question mark raised by many observers. See Gargan 1996.
29 Even if it is a frustrating window-shopping.
30 One often hears in Kuala Lampur that the Malaysian government is delivering the goods.
31 I borrow this term from Zubaida 1989: 117.
32 The phenomenon of shopping malls and expanding consumerism of the new "fat cats" applies globally to many Third World countries. It is not unique to Malaysia or Egypt.
33 For example *Rose Al-Yussef*, *Al-Mussawar*, *al-Sha'ab*, *Al-Ahali*, *Al-Qahira*, *Qadaya Fikriyyah* and *Al-Wafd*, *Al-Ahram Weekly*, and *Al-Ahram Hebdo* and many other popular magazines.
34 For example with brutal arrests of the young Islamists. For instance during 1981-1991, 450 (officers, soldiers, government officials and Islamists) were killed and 1050 wounded in violent skirmishes. From July 1992 to July 1993 there occurred 239 violent incidents, while between 1986 to 1990 only 46 incidents were recorded (see Siyam 1994: 8). In fact, a close look at *Al-Ahram Daily* in the last two years reveals frequent skirmishes as well as the appearance of a kind of an informal civil war taking place in the villages of Upper Egypt between government officers and "terrorists." This exists alongside current court cases against "terrorists." See for instance the current trial of the Jihad group, in which 42 were arrested (*Al-Ahram Weekly* 22.5.1995).
35 Nevertheless, after the recent attempt of assassination of President Mubarak during the month of June, 1995 in Ethiopia, the government undertook massive arrests of the Islamists as well as arresting members of the Muslim Brothers.
36 The assassination of the secular writer Farag Foda in 1992 in Cairo by fundamentalists connected with the *jihad* group indicates the escalation of the polarization in which Farag Foda's killing was utilized by the government. This incident instigated harsh repres-

sive measures against the extremists such as the application of the death sentence and the detaining of prisoners for periods of six months before trial which led to protests from the Egyptian Human Rights Association concerning the deplorable conditions in Egyptian prisons. See Roussillon 1994: 295.

37 For instance during the Population Conference in Cairo 1994, the Sheikh of Al-Azhar expressed views antagonistic to and conflicting with the opinions of the Mufti of Egypt. This reveals that the religious body is not homogenous in its opinions.

38 Nevertheless, observers pointed to the consent of some Al-Azhar 'Ulama to the Islamists underground ideology.

39 I am quite aware that many will disagree on the magnitude and the concrete impact of the secular intellectuals in Egypt today.

40 Not forgetting the particularity of Malaysian ethnic composition with a large Chinese population. In recent years observers pointed to the rising "New Malay" business class that was born out of Mahathir's economic policies and which collaborates closely with Chinese Capitalists.

41 Although Shamsul argues that one of the major consequences of the Islamization in Malaysia has been the sharpening of the "secular" versus the "religious" spheres in the community as a whole. See Shamsul 1994.

42 At least in the form of the construction of huge lavish and modern buildings and architectural complexes.

43 Personal Communication with Syed Muhammad N. Al-Attas, ISTAC, Kuala Lumpur, December 1995.

44 The *sharif* (plural *ashraf*), *sayid* (*sadah*) are titles to call the Hasani branch of the Prophet's offspring. See Serjeant 1957.

45 One is often reminded at ISTAC, hierarchy and ritual, a very Malay feudal trait.

46 Nik Aziz'a PAS, (*Parti Islam SeMalyaisa*), Haji Nik Aziz Nik Mat, the Head of *Parti Islam* in Malaysia, who was born in 1931 in Pulau Meleka, Kelantan. In 1952-1962, he studied at Deoband University (India) and Al-Azhar University in Cairo to obtain his B.A. and M.A. degrees. In 1967 he became MP of *Parti Islam* by election in Kelantan. In 1968, he was elected head of the *Ulamak* ('Ulama) or religious scholars wing of the PAS National Party, *Parti Islam SeMalaysia*. In 1990, he was appointed *Mentri Besar*.

47 It is beyond the scope of this paper to analyze in detail the Egyptian sociological field and the relationship of Arab versus Islamic sociology. For a comprehensive overview of the Egyptian sociological field (Roussillon 1991). Nevertheless Roussillon argues that the two discourses (Arab versus Islamic) in Egypt are structurally homologous. He, in fact, sees no difference between the two stands.
48 A lot of these seminar papers were later published in Egyptian newspapers, or in books as is the case of Mohammed ʿImmara.
49 I am referring here to Leonard Binder's *Islamic Liberalism* who discussed at length the ideas of Tariq Al-Bishri and Mohammed ʿImmara.
50 See ʿAref 1994. The book was a large compilation of Islamic manuscripts dealing with politics in Islam. Through undertaking such an endeavor ʿAref directly criticizes the writings of ʿAli ʿAbdel Raziq, Khaled Mohammed Khaled and others claiming that they did not investigate properly the "*turath*" in order to "authenticate" Muslim political thought.
51 In political science see the works of Saifaddin ʿAbdel Fattah Ismaʿil from Cairo University who sees that concepts such as civil society and democracy are alien to Islamic culture. Ismaʿil uses the term of the Umma to found rights according to *sharīʿa* and conclude that the *ʿulama* are the institutional power of the Umma (ʿAbdel Fattah Ismaʿil 1989: 297).
52 See for example El-Saʿati 1976, 1961.
53 Hassan El-Saʿati "Interview with Hassan El-Saʿati, the Faisal AWARD Recepient in Islamic Studies", *Al-Sharq Al-Awssat*, 15.4.1993.
54 See for instance Mohammed ʿImmara's publications in 1991 (a,b,c).
55 See Mohammed ʿImmara, "Islamization of Knowledge. The Alternative for Materialist Knowledge", *Al-Wafd*: (7.3.1991), (19.3.1991), (20.3.1991), (21.3.1991), (22.3.1991), (23.3.1991), (24.3.1991) (in Arabic).
56 The government's attempt to launch an "enlightenment" movement could be interpreted as the other facet of the monstrous flowering of religious symbols, language and also of a charlatanry which was ironically instigated at earlier times by the government.

The uncontrollable effects of the decaying system of education on the national level and the expansion of "informal" religious institutions, the controversy over wearing the Islamic attire in schools, which was first met with the consent of the government but later when the phenomenon became intractable, harshly and abruptly fought. All these, shaped the dialectics of the game over "enlightenment" versus "obscurantism" between the government and the Islamists.

57 Notice here the paradox of the government counteracting Islamists by claiming a secular stand and ʿImmara's opposition to the government by insisting on Islamism as the alternative.

58 ʿAziz Al-ʿAzmeh argues exactly the contrary of ʿImmara in that the early reformists like Al-Tahtawi recognized their borrowings from Western liberal thought. Al-Tahtawi read Rousseau, Voltaire, Montesquieu and Condillac extensively. See Al-ʿAzmeh 1994.

59 Shaykh ʿAli ʿAbd Al-Raziq published in the twenties *Islam and the Principle of Authority*. He argued that "the Caliphate was neither a basic principle nor a necessary institution," his book cost him the denial of the status of ʿ*Alim* and was strongly attacked by the institution of Al-Azhar.

60 Concerning this point see Albert Hourani's essential analysis of the thinkers of the liberal age. Hourani argued that for Taha Hussein, it was the spiritual geography and not the physical one which was important. Egypt belonged to Western civilization rather than to India. See Hourani 1983, 1962: 330.

61 This is because Salama Musa at the beginning of the century defended modern scientific ideas and was interested in Darwin's theories of evolution.

62 The attack on Taha Hussein and Salama Musa is also found in Sayyed Qutb the martyr and leader of the Muslim Brothers' writings. It became a standard argument among the Islamists. See Abu Zayd 1992: 48.

63 Al-ʿAzm acknowledges that science was never value-free and that politics were always decisive in scientific research.

64 The debate about the spirituality of the East versus the materialism of the West found echoes already in the works of early Egyptian liberal intellectuals. For an overview and a critique of such a position, see Al-ʿAzmeh 1992: 236.

65 Abu Zayd sharply criticizes the position of various Muslim figures. These include Shaykh Muhammad Al-Ghazali, one of the founders of the Muslim Brothers, the political attitude of *Al-Sha'ab* newspaper (Labor party with Islamist tendencies), Shaykh Mohammed Metwali Al-Sha'arawi, the television star preacher, Fahmi Humwaydi, the *Al-Ahram* columnist and Yussef Al-Qaradawi, an Azhari and former Muslim Brother.

66 Nevertheless, it is important to stress that the social actors in the Islamic movement in Egypt are far from being monolithic. The Muslim Brothers for instance are today an established force which plays the rules of the game set by the government (before Mubarak's attempted assassination). The Islamic movement also won a large audience among the middle class through the trade unions such as the medical, the engineers' and lawyers' trade unions. These trade unions have been active socially and have access to institutional legal channels.

67 Abu Zayd (1992) draws a broad critique of Sayyed Qutb's work and his general principles. Qutb namely juxtaposes the Islamic system in a relationship of total opposition with Western culture and mourns the separation between church and science in the West (ibid.: 48).

Selected Bibliography

Arabic Language

'Abdel Fattah, Nabil (1995) *Tqrir al-halah al-diniyya fi misr* (Report of the Religious Situation in Egypt), Cairo: Marquaz al-dirasat al-siyasiyyah wal-stratijiyyah.

'Abdel Fattah Isma'il, Saifaddin (1989) *Al-tajdid al-siyasi wal waqi' al-'arabi al-mu'asir* (Political Renovation and Contemporary Arab Reality), Cairo: Maktabat al-nahda al-misriyyah.

'Abdel Kerim, Khalil (1995) "*Min aafat al-fikr al-'arabi al-islami al-mu'asir mithal tatbiqi: Dirasa naqdiyyah mugmalah likitab al-hall al-islami – faridah wa darura lifadilat al-shaykh yussef al-qaradawi*" (Negative Aspects of Contemporary Arabic-Islamic Thought, a Concrete Example: A Comprehensive Critical Study of Youssef al-Qaradawi's Book "al-hall al-islami faridah wa darura"). *Qadaya Fikriyya*, July, pp. 259-268.

Abu Sulaiman, ʿAbdel Hamid (1991) *ʾAzmat al-ʿaql al-muslim* (The Crisis of Muslim Thought), silsilat al-manhajiyah al-Islamiyah, The International Institute of Islamic Thought (IIIT).

Abu Zayd, Nasr Hamid (1990) *Mafhum an-nass, dirasa fi ʿulum ul-qurʾan* (The Meaning of the Text. A Study in the Sciences of Qurʾan), Beirut: Al-marqaz al-thaqafi al-ʿarabi.

—— (1992) *Al-khitab al-dini, ruʾya naqdiyyah* (The Religious Discourse. A Critical Perspective), Beirut: Dar al-muntakhab al-ʿarabi, 1412.

—— (1996)(ed.) *Al-qaul al-mufid fi qadiyyat abu zayd* (Useful Talk on the Case of Abu Zayd), Cairo: Maktabat madbuli.

ʿAmel, Mahdi (1988/1989) *Naqd al-fikr al-yawmi* (Critique of Everyday Thinking), 2nd edition, Beirut: Dar al-farabi.

ʿAref, Nasr Mohammed (1994) *Fi masader al-turath al-siyassi al-islami* (On the Sources in the Political Islamic Heritage), Cairo: The International Institute of Islamic Thought (IIIT).

ʿAwad, ʿAwad Mohammed (1990) *On the Nature of the Hisba*, Cairo: The International Institute of Islamic Thought (IIIT).

—— (1992) *Nathariyyat al-tanmiyya al-siyasiyya al-muʿasira* (Contemporary Political Development Theories), Cairo: The International Institute of Islamic Thought (IIIT).

Al-ʿAzm, Sadeq Jalal (1989) *"Difaʿ an ʿan al-taqadum"* (In Defense of Progress). In *Al-nathariyyah wal mumarasah fi fikr mahdi ʿamel* (Theory and Practice in the Thought of Mahdi ʿAmel), Beirut: Dar al-farabi, pp. 453-467.

—— (1992) *"Al-ghazw al-thaqafi mugadadan"* (Cultural Invasion Repeatedly). In *Thihniyyatal-tahrim* (The Mental Taboo), London, Cyprus: Riad El Rayyes Books.

Al-ʿAzmah, ʿAziz (1990/1987) *Al-turath baynal sultan wal tarikh* (Heritage between the Sultan and History), Beirut: Dar al-taliʿa.

—— (1992) *Al-ʿilmaniyyah min manthur mukhtalif* (Secularism from a Different Perspective), Beirut: Marquaz al-dirasat lil wahda al-ʿarabiyyah.

—— (1993) "The Islamization of Knowledge and the Obstinacy of Irrationality". *Qadaya Fikriyya* 12, pp. 407-414.

—— (1996) *Dunia al-din fi hadir al-ʿarab* (The World of Religion in Present of Arabs), Beirut: Dar al-taliʿa.

Al-Bishri, Tariq (1992) *Mushkilatan wa qira'a fihima* (Two Problems and Readings), presented by Taha Jabir Al-ʿIlwani, The International Institute of Islamic Thought (IIIT): 1413H.

—— (1996) *Al-hiwar al-islami al-ʿilmani* (The Secular Islamist Dialogue), Cairo: Dar al-shuruq.

Huwaydi, Fahmi (1996) *Al-muftarun, khitab al-tataruf al-ʿilmani fil-mizan* (The Slanderers. The Extremist Secularist Discourse), Cairo: Dar al-shuruq.

Al-ʿIlwani, Taha Gaber (1996/1988) *"Islamiyyat al-maʿrifa"* (The Islamization of Knowledge), unpublished IIIT paper presented at Strasbourg.

ʿImmara, Mohammed (1971) *Al-madiyyah wal mithaliyyah fi falsafat Ibn Rushd* (Materialism and Idealism in the Philosophy of Averroes), Cairo: Dar al-maaref.

—— (1991a) *Islamiyyat al-maʿarifa* (The Islamization of Knowledge) Cairo: Dar al-sharq al-awssat, madinat nasr.

—— (1991b) *Maʿalim al-minhaj al-islami* (Signposts on Islamic Methodology), Al-Azhar al-Sharif jointly with The International Institute of Islamic Thought (IIIT), Cairo: Dar al-shuruq.

—— (1991c) *Fil manhaj al-islami* (Islamic Methodolgy), Herndon/VA: The International Institute of Islamic Thought (IIIT).

—— (1993) *Fikr al-tanwir bayn al-ʿilmaniyyin wal-islamiyyin* (Enlightenment between Secularists and Islamists), Cairo: The International Institute of Islamic Thought (IIIT).

—— (1995a) *Al-islam bayn al-tanwir wal-tazwir* (Islam, between Enlightenment and Falsification), Cairo: Dar al-shuruq.

—— (1995b) *Suqut al-ghuluw al-ʿilmani* (The Fall of the Secularist Extravagance), Cairo: Dar al-shuruq.

—— (n.d.) *Salama musa, ijtihad khati' am ʿimala hadariyyah* (Salama Musa, A False Interpretation or Civilizational Collaboration), Cairo: Gamiyyat al-marqaz al-ʿalami lil-tawthiq wal dirasat wal tarbiyyah al-islamiyya.

The International Institute of Islamic Thought (IIIT) (1990) *Al-manhajiyya al-islamiyyah wal-ʿulum al-sullukiyya wal-tarbawiyyah Islamic* (Methodology and Educational Sciences), Herndon/VA: The International Institute of Islamic Thought (IIIT), 1411/AH.

Al-ʿIraqi, ʿAtef (1995) *Al-ʿaql wal tanwir fil fikr al-ʿarabi al-muʿasir*

(Reason and Enlightenment in Contemporary Arabic Thought), Cairo: Al-mu'assassa al-gaamiyyah lil dirasat wal nashr wal tawzi'.

Al-Jaberi, Mohammed ʿAbid (1986) *Nahnu wal turath* (We and The Heritage), Casablanca, Morocco: Al-markaz al-thaqafi al-ʿarabi (The Arabic Institute of Culture), 5th edition, Cairo: Al-maʿhad al-ʿalami lil-fikr al-islami, The International Institute of Islamic Thought (IIIT).

—— (1988/1984) *Takwin al-ʿaql al-ʿarabi* (The Structure of The Arab Mind), 3rd edition, Beirut: Markaz dirasat al-wahda al-'arabiyyah.

Khalil, Imaduddin (1990) *Islamiyyat al-maʿrifa*, The Islamization of Knowledge, 7, 1411H, The International Institute of Islamic Thought (IIIT).

Mahmud, Zaki Naguib (1987) *Fi-tahdith al- thaqafa al-ʿarabia* (The Modernization of Arabic Culture), Beirut, Cairo: Dar al-shuruq.

Al-Messiri, ʿAbdel Wahab (1995) *"Ishkalliyat al-tahayyuz"* (The Bias Problematique), Cairo: The International Institute of Islamic Thought (IIIT) published with the Syndicate of Engineers.

El-Saʿati, Hassan (1961) *A Sociological Survey of the Bab al-Shaʿriyyah Quarter,* Cairo: Ain Shams University.

—— (1976) *ʿIlm al-ijtamʿa ʿal-sinaʿi* (Industrial Sociology), Cairo: Dar al-maʿarif bimisr.

—— (1992) "Studies on the Islamization of the Family, Crime and Society". Maktabat Saʿid Ra'fat, Cairo: Jamiʿat ʿAin Shams, pp. 59-68.

Saif al-Nasr, Ali (1993) *"Al-sahwa al-islamiyya al-muʿasira wal-ulum al-insaniyyah"* (Contemporary Islamic Revivalism and Social Sciences), al-Mustaqbal al-Arabi, Beirut: Marqaz dirasat al-wahda al-arabiyyah, 4/170.

Siyam, Shahata (1994) *Violence and the Religious Discourse in Egypt* Cairo: Sina lil Nashr.

Tarabishi, Georges (1991) *Al-muthaqafun al-ʿarab wal-turath* (Arab Intellectuals and Their Heritage), London: Riad el-Rayyes Books.

—— (1993) *Mathbahat al-turath fil thaqafa al-ʿarabiyya al-muʿassira* (The Slaughter of the Heritage in Contemporary Arab Culture), London: Dar al-saqi.

Yassin, Sayyed (1996) "The Strategic Discourse and the Political Movement". In Sayyed Yassin (ed.) *Al-kawniyyah wal usuliyya wa ma baʿad al-hadatha* (Globalization, Fundamentalism and Post-Modernity), Cairo: Al-makataba al-akadimiyyah, pp. 256-265.

Zakariyya, Fu' ad (1987) *As-sahwa al-islamiyya fi mizan al-ʿaql* (Islamic Revivalism in the Light of Reason), Cairo: Dar al-fikr al-mu'asir.

Western Languages

Abaza, Mona (1993) "Some Reflections on the Question of Islam and Social Sciences in the Contemporary Muslim World". *Social Compass* 40/2, pp. 301-321.

—— (1994) "Perceptions of the Middle East in Southeast Asia and Islamic Revivalism". *Orient*, March, pp. 107-124.

Ahmed, Akbar S. (1986) *Toward Islamic Anthropology: Definition, Dogma and Direction*, Ann Arbor/MI: New Era Publications.

—— (1988) *Discovering Islam*, London, New York/NY: Routledge and Kegan.

—— /Donnan, Hastings (eds.) (1994) *Islam, Globalization and Postmodernity*, London: Routledge.

Albrow, Martin/King, Elizabeth (eds.) (1990) *Globalization, Knowledge and Society*, London: Sage Publications.

Anwar, Zainah (1987) *Islamic Revivalism in Malaysia*, Kuala Lumpur: Pelanduk Publications.

Appadurai, Arjun (1990) "Disjuncture and Difference in the Global Cultural Economy". *Theory, Culture and Society* 7, pp. 295-310.

Arena (1991) "The Postcolonial Critic – Homi Bhabba Interviewed by David Bennet and Terry Collins". *Arena* 96, pp. 47-63.

Al-Attas, Syed Muhammad N. (1963) *Some Aspects of Sufism as Understood and Practised Among the Malays*, Singapore: Malaysian Sociological Research Institute.

—— (1970) *Al Fansuri. A Sufi Mystic*, Kuala Lumpur: University of Malaysia Press.

—— (1978) *Islam and Secularism*, Kuala Lumpur: Muslim Youth Movement of Malaysia (ABIM).

—— (1985) *Secularism and the Philosophy of the Future*, London, New York/NY: Mansell.

—— (1986) *A Commentary on Hujjat Al-Siddiq of Nur Al-Din Al-Raniri*, Kuala Lumpur: University of Malaysia Press.

—— (1988) *The Oldest Known Malay Manuscript: A 16th Century Translation of the ʿAqai'd of Al-Nasafi*, Kuala Lumpur: Department of Publications University of Malaysia.

—— (1989) *Faces of Islam. Conversation of Contemporary Issues*, Kuala Lumpur: Berita Publishing.

—— (1991) *Concept of Education in Islam. A Framework for an Islamic Philosophy of Education*, Kuala Lumpur: International Institute of Islamic Thought and Civilization.

Al-ʿAzm, Sadeq Jalal (1981) "Orientalism and Orientalism in Reverse". *Khamsin* 8, pp. 5-26.

Al-ʿAzmeh, ʿAziz (1986) *Arabic Thought and Islamic Societies*, London, Sydney: Croom Helm.

—— (1993) *Islams and Modernities*, London: Verso.

—— (1994) "Modernist Muslim Reformism and the Text". Paper presented at a "Conference on Islam and the Challenge of Modernity, Historical and Contemporary Contexts", Kuala Lumpur: The International Institute of Islamic Thought and Civilization, 1-5 August.

Bagader, Abu Bakar A. (1983) *Islamization of Social Sciences. Islam and Sociological Perspectives*, Muslim Youth Movement in Malaysia (ABIM): Kuala Lumpur.

Ba-Yunus, Ilyas (1988) "Al-Faruqi and Beyond: Future Directions in Islamization of Knowledge". *The American Journal of Islamic Social Sciences* 5/1, pp. 13-14.

Binder, Leonard (1988) *Islamic Liberalism: A Critique of Development Ideologies*, Chicago/IL, London: The University of Chicago Press.

Büttner, Friedmann (ed.) (1971) *Reform und Revolution in der islamischen Welt*, München: List.

—— (1991) "Zwischen Politisierung und Säkularisierung – Möglichkeiten und Grenzen einer islamischen Integration der Gesellschaft". In Erhard Forddran (ed.) *Religion und Politik in einer säkularisierten Welt*, Baden-Baden: Nomos.

Casandra (1995) "The Impending Crisis in Egypt". *The Middle East Journal* 1/49, pp. 9-27.

Daud, Wan Moh Nor Wan (n.d.) *Prof. Dr. Syed Muhammad Naquib Al-Attas. An Introduction*, Kuala Lampur: Institute of Islamic Thought and Civilization (ISTAC).

EI (1960) = *Encyclopaedia of Islam*, new edition, Leiden: Brill.

Esposito, John (ed.) (1995) *The Oxford Encyclopedia of Islam*, New York/NY: Oxford University Press.

Al-Faruqi, Isma'il Raji (1978) "Islam and Other Faiths". In Altaf Gauhar (ed.) *The Challenge of Islam*, London: Islamic Council of Europe, pp. 82-113.

—— (1981) "Islamizing the Social Sciences". *Islamika*, Kuala Lumpur: University of Malaysia, pp. 1-8.

—— (1995/1984) *Islam*, 3rd edition, Beltsville/MD: Amana Publications.

—— /Al-Faruqi, Lois-Laniya (1986) *The Cultural Atlas of Islam*, New York/ NY: Macmillan.

Featherstone, Mike (1990) "Global Culture: An Introduction". *Theory, Culture and Society* 7, pp. 1-14.

Feyerabend, Paul (1975) *Against Method*, London: Verso.

Flores, Alexander (1993) "Secularism, Integralism and Political Islam. The Egyptian Debate". *Middle East Report* (July-August), pp. 32-38.

Friedman, Jonathan (1990) "Being in the World: Globalization and Localization". *Theory, Culture and Society* 7, pp. 311-329.

Gargan, Edward A. (1996) "Malaysia's Economy: Will Boom Turn to Bust?". *International Herald Tribune*, 3-4 February.

Geertz, Clifford (1993) *Local Knowledge. Further Essays in Interpretative Anthropology*, New York/NY: Basic Books.

Glick, Thomas F. (ed.) (1974) *The Comparative Reception of Darwinism*, Chicago/IL, London: The University of Chicago Press.

Hoodbhoy, Pervez A. (1985) "Ideological Problems for Science in Pakistan". In Ashgar Khan (ed.) *Islam, Politics and The State. The Pakistan Experience*, London: Zed.

—— (1991) *Islam and Science: Religious Orthodoxy and the Battle for Rationality*, London: Zed.

Hourani, Albert H. (1983/1962) *Arabic Thought in the Liberal Age 1798-1939*, Oxford University Press, 2nd edition, Cambridge: Cambridge University Press.

Hussein, Kamel (1983) "Le commentaire 'scientifique' du coran: une innovation absurde". *Mélanges Institut Dominicain d'Études Orientales du Caire (MIDEO)*16, pp. 293-300.

Ibrahim, Ahmad (1990) "Towards a Contemporary Philosophy of Islamic Science". *The American Journal of Islamic Social Sciences* 7/1, pp. 1-14.

—— /Siddique, Sharon/Hussain, Yasmin (eds.) (1985) *Readings on Islam in Southeast Asia*, Singapore: Institute of Southeast Asian Studies.

Ibrahim, Syed I. (1989) "Islamization of Attitude and Practice in Embryology". In M.A.K. Lodhi (ed.) *Islamization of Attitudes and Practices in Science and Technology*, Islamization of Knowledge Series 9, Herndon/VA, 1409AH: The International Institute of Islamic Thought (IIIT).

IIIT (1982) *Islam: Sources and Purpose of Knowledge*. Proceedings and Selected Papers of the "Second Conference on Islamization of Knowledge", 1402AH/AC, Herndon/VA: The International Institute of Islamic Thought (IIIT).

International Seminar (1995) *Islam and Confucianism. A Civilizational Dialogue*, University of Malaysia, 12-14 March.

Kermani, Navid (1994) "Die Affäre Abu Zayd. Eine Kritik am religiösen Diskurs und ihre Folgen". *Orient* 35/1, pp. 25-51.

Keyes, Charles F./Kendall, Laurel/Hardacre, Helen (eds.) (1994) *Asian Visions of Authority. Religion and the Modern States of East and Southeast Asia*, Honolulu/HI: University of Hawaii Press.

Kirmani, Mohammed Zaki (1989) "Islamic Science". In Ziauddin Sardar (ed.) *An Early Crescent. The Future of Knowledge and Environment in Islam*, New York/NY: Mansell, pp. 140-162.

Knorr-Cetina, Karin (1991) *Die Fabrikation von Erkenntnis. Zur Anthropologie der Naturwissenschaft*, Frankfurt/M.: Suhrkamp.

Kuhn, Thomas (1962) *The Structure of Scientific Revolutions*, Chicago/IL: The University of Chicago Press.

Laroui, Abdallah (1977) *L'idéologie arabe contemporaine*, Paris: François Maspero.

—— (1987) *Islam et modernité*, Paris: Édition la découverte.

Lodhi, M.A.K. (ed.) (1989) *Islamization of Attitudes and Practices in Science and Technology*, The International Institute of Islamic Thought (IIIT), Islamization of Knowledge Series 9, 1409AH.

Lyon, M. L. (1983) "The Dakwah Movement in Malaysia". *Assyahid. Journal of the Muslim Youth Assembly* I/1, pp. 112-130.

MAAS (The Muslim Association for the Advancement of Science) (1991-1993) *Journal of Islamic Science*, Aligarh, India.

Maidin, Zainuddin (1994) *The Other Side of Mahathir*, Kuala Lumpur: Utusan Sdn. Bhd.
El-Missiri, ʿAbdel Wahab (1996) "Parables of Freedom and Necessity: The Rising Levels of Secularization as Manifested in Two Literary Works". *The American Journal of Islamic Social Sciences* 13/1, pp. 42-58.
Morais, Jean Victor (1984) *Anwar Ibrahim: Resolute in Leadership*, Kuala Lumpur: Arenabuku Sdn. Bhd.
Morsy, Soheir/Nelson, Cynthia/Saad, Reem/Sholkamy, Hania (1991) "Anthropology and the Call for Indigenization of Social Science in the Arab World". In Earl T. Sullivan/Jacqueline S. Ismael (eds.) *The Contemporary Study of the Arab World*, Edmonton/AB: University of Alberta Press, pp. 88-111.
Murphy, Raymond (1994) "The Sociological Construction of Science without Nature". *Sociology. The Journal of The British Sociological Association* 28/4, pp. 957-974.
Mutalib, Hussin (1990) *Islam and Ethnicity in Malay Politics*, Singapore: Oxford University Press.
Muzaffar, Chandra (1986) "Islamic Resurgence: A Global View". In Taufik Abdullah/Sharon Siddique (eds.) *Islam and Society in Southeast Asia*, Singapore: Institute of Southeast Asian Studies.
—— (1987) *Islamic Resurgence in Malaysia*, Selangor, Malaysia: Darul Ehsan Penerbit Fajar Bakti Sdn. Bhd.
—— (1995) "Two Approaches of Islam: Revisiting Islamic Resurgence in Malaysia", unpublished paper.
Nagata, Judith (1984) *The Reflowering of Malaysian Islam: Modern Religious Radicals and Their Roots*, Vancouver/BC: University of British Columbia Press.
Nasr, Seyyed Hossein (1966) *Science and Civilization in Islam*, Cambridge: Harvard University Press.
—— (1966) *Ideals and Realities in Islam*, London: George Allen and Unwin.
—— (1981) "On the Teaching of Philosophy in the Muslim World". *Hamdard Islamicus* IV/2, pp. 53-72.
—— (1987, 1988) *Traditional Islam in the Modern World*, 1st edition by KPI Limited, London; Kuala Lumpur: Foundation For Traditional Studies.
—— (1992) "Islamization of Knowledge: A Critical Overview". The

International Institute of Islamic Thought (IIIT), Occasional papers 17.

—— (1993) *The Need for a Sacred Science*, Surrey: Curzon Press.

—— (1995) "The Islamic Philosophers' Views on Education". *Muslim Education Quarterly* 2/4, pp. 5-16.

Rashed, Roland (1993) "La philosophie des mathématiques d'ibn al-haytham: Les connus". *Mélanges Institut Dominicain d'Études Orientales du Caire (MIDEO)* 21, pp. 87-275.

Robertson, Roland (1990) "Nostalgia? Wilful Nostalgia and the Phases of Globalization". In Bryan S. Turner (ed.) *Theories of Modernity and Post Modernity*, London: Sage, pp. 57-74.

—— (1992) *Globalization, Social Theory and Global Culture*, London: Sage Publications.

Roussillon, Alain (1990) "Intellectuels en crise dans l'Égypte contemporaine". In Gilles Kepel/Yann Richard (eds.) *Intellectuels et militants de l'islam contemporain*, Paris: Seuil.

—— (1991) "Sociologie égyptienne, arabe, islamique, l'approfondissement du paradigme réformiste". *Peuples Méditerranéens* 54-55, pp. 111-150.

—— (1994) "Changer La Société par le Jihad: sédition confessionelle et attentats contre le tourisme: rhétoriques de la violence qualifiée d'islamique en Égypte". Dossiers du CEDEJ, Le Phénomène de La Violence Politique: Perspectives Comparatives et Paradigme Égyptien, Le Caire, pp. 295-319.

Said, Edward W. (1978) *Orientalism*, New York/NY: Vintage Books.

Sardar, Ziauddin (1986) "Redefining Science Towards Islam: An Examination of Islamic and Western Approaches to Knowledge and Values". *Hamdard Islamicus* IX/1, pp. 23-34.

—— (1988) *Islamic Futures: The Shape of Ideas to Come*, Selangor, Malaysis: Pelanduk Publications.

—— (1989a) *Explorations in Islamic Science*, London, New York/NY: Mansell.

—— (1989b) "Islamization of Knowledge. A State-of-the-Art Report". In Ziauddin Sardar (ed.) *An Early Crescent. The Future of Knowledge and Environment in Islam*, London, New York/NY: Mansell, pp. 25-27.

—— (ed.) (1989c) *An Early Crescent. The Future of Knowledge and Environment in Islam*, London, New York/NY: Mansell.

—— (1991) *How We Know, Ilm and Revival of Knowledge*, London: Grey Seal.

—— (1995) "Understanding Postmodernism". *Pemikir* (Membangung Minda Berwawasan) Oktober-December, pp. 131-158.

Al-Sayyid, Mustapha Kamel (1993) "A Civil Society in Egypt?". *The Middle East Journal* 47/2, pp. 226-234.

Serjeant, Robert Bertram (1957) *The Saiyids of Hadramawt*, London: Luzac and Co.

Shafiq, Muhammad (1994) *Growth of Islamic Thought in North America. Focus on Isma'il Raji Al-Faruqi*, Brentwood/MA: Amana Publications, 1414.

Shamsul, A. B. (1994) "Religion and Ethic Politics in Malaysia. The Significance of the Islamic Resurgence Phenomenon". In Charles F. Keyes/Laurel Kendall/Helen Hardacre (eds.) *Asian Visions of Authority. Religion and the Modern States of East and Southeast Asia*, Honolulu/HI: University of Hawaii Press, pp. 99-116.

Siddiqui, B. H. (1991) "Knowledge: An Islamic Perspective", The International Institute of Islamic Thought (IIIT), Islamabad, *Pakistan Occasional Papers* 16.

Stauth, Georg (1992) "Leonard Binder and the Hermeneutic of Authenticity – Critical Note". *Arabica*, pp. 85-105.

—— (1993) "Islam and Emerging Non-Western Concepts of Modernity". In Lars Gule/Oddvar Storeboe (eds.) *Development and Modernity. Perspectives on Western Theories of Modernization*, Bergen: Ariadne, pp. 254-272.

—— (1994) "Critical Theory and Pre-Fascist Social Thought". *History of European Ideas* 18/5, pp. 711-727.

Stollorz, Volker (1992) "Mit der Bibel gegen Darwin". *Die Zeit*, 29 January.

Tapper, Richard (1988) "Book Review of Ahmed, Akbar S. Toward Islamic Anthropology: Definition, Dogma and Direction". *MAN* 23/3, p. 567.

Teik, Khoo Boo (1995) *Paradoxes of Mahathirism, an Intellectual Biography of Mahathir Mohamad*, Kuala Lumpur: Oxford University Press.

Tibi, Bassam (1986) "The Interplay Between Cultural and Socio-Economic Change. The Case of Germany and the Arab Region – Cultural Innovation in the Development Process". In Klaus Gottstein (ed.) *Islamic Cultural Identity and Scientific-Technological Development*, Baden-Baden: Nomos, pp. 93-103.

—— (1992) *Islamischer Fundamentalismus, moderne Wissenschaft und Technologie*, Frankfurt/M.: Suhrkamp.

Todorov, Tzvetan (1986) "Le croisement des cultures". *Communications* 43, pp. 5-26.

—— (1993) *On Human Diversity: Nationalism, Racism and Exoticism in French Thought*, Cambridge/MA: Harvard University Press.

Turnbull, David (1993/1994) "Local Knowledge and Comparative Scientific Traditions". *Knowledge and Policy. The International Journal of Knowledge Transfer* 6/3-4, pp. 29-54.

Zahid, Muhammed Ishaq (1986) "Use of Islamic Beliefs in Mathematics and Computer Science Education". In M.A.K. Lodhi (ed.) *Islamization of Attitudes and Practices in Science and Technology*, The International Institute of Islamic Thought (IIIT), Islamization of Knowledge Series 9, 1409AH, pp. 91-101.

Zubaida, Sami (1988) "Islam, Cultural Nationalism and the Left". *Review of The Middle East Studies* 4, pp. 1-33.

—— (1989) *Islam, the People and the State*, London, New York/NY: Routledge.

Gendering Globalization:

Alternative Languages of Modernity

Cynthia Nelson and Shahnaz Rouse

Emerging from globalization and related crises of modernity are debates surrounding the relationship between women and knowledge, and issues of situationality and plurality. Modernity as an historical material process enters the Third World bringing with it its own cultural and linguistic baggage. The issue of "women's/human rights" arises out of this engagement with modernity. The ensuing contestation over the ideals of freedom, justice and equality brought about by the unevenness and incompleteness of the materialist project generates a plurality of voices speaking from individual experiences with this historical encounter. The colonized "other" in her confrontation with modernity generates various forms of struggles and ways of speaking which articulate and grapple with the contradictions that modernity generates (e.g. secularist, Islamist, nationalist).

The problematic we address in this paper explores precisely the contradictions contained within modernity, that not only create a plurality of voices but also generate different languages and idioms through which women's struggles for rights come to be articulated, recognized, suppressed and/or repudiated. We are interested in examining these questions through a shift in focus from an emphasis on discourse to a concern with experience which permits us to incorporate difference without reifying it.

In this paper we examine the plurality of experience and voice of three women – Doria Shafik, an Egyptian; Jahanara Shahnawaz and Hamida Akhtar Hussein, from the Indian subcontinent – whose lives and works traverse the historical transition between colonialism and neo-colonialism spanning the twentieth century. Through a close reading of these women (Nelson on Shafik and Rouse on Shahnawaz and Hussein) we move from a perspective that homogenizes voices to one that locates itself in their multiplicity. This reading also illumines different possibilities and forms of women's struggles.

In looking at their individual biographies we notice stark differences. However, on another level, all three women are engaged in a quest for self-expression and representation. This quest itself is marked by the particular conditions of hybridity that emerge in the subjective experience of each of these women living through this historical transition. As Sangari has described:

The hybrid [individual] is already open to two worlds and is constructed within the national and international, political and cultural systems of colonialism and neo-colonialism. To be hybrid is to understand the question as well as to represent the pressure of such historical placement. [This hybridity] both historical and contradictory, is also the ground for analysis and change.
(Words in parentheses added.)

(Sangari 1993: 264)

In conclusion, we examine how our work informs the larger debate on globalization, gender discourse and indigenization of knowledge.

The Voices of Doria Shafik[1]

Doria Shafik (1908-1975) epitomizes what Emma Goldman described as "the life of the transition stage, the hardest and most difficult for the individual as well as a people" (Falk 1984: ix). On the one hand is the life of the historic society of the Nile Valley responding to the direct confrontation with the expanding society of Great Britain, which first imposed its control over Egypt in 1882 and then tried to maintain it by momentum of its own growth and in accordance with its own beliefs until the Egyptian revolution of 1952. On the other hand is the unfolding consciousness of an Egyptian women, who lived through much of this period of social and political transformation and came to public prominence particularly in the post World War II era when the old order was crumbling in the face of increased discontent over how Egypt should be governed. While Egyptian society struggled to liberate itself from colonial domination, Doria Shafik struggled to awaken a feminist consciousness and forge a new self identity of "The New Woman" so as to awaken Egyptian women to their rights in a world that was rapidly "modernizing". In the face of strong political and religious opposition she challenged and criticized those cultural traditions and Islamic institutions within her own society that she believed not only adversely affected women's lives but also served to strengthen erroneous western/colonial representations of the "oriental Muslim woman". As she attempted to change her society in order to find space for her own feminist project, Shafik found herself caught between the margins of the worlds of the colonizer and the colonized and suffered the human price that is exacted when that project was carried beyond the political tolerance of her own society.

It is this dialectic between a society's national struggle for liberation and a woman's personal quest for human freedom, particularly during the turbulent years between nineteen forty-five and fifty seven that the history of Egypt and the life of Doria Shafik intertwine. To understand how the life of an individual intertwines with the life of a society during a particular moment of "colonial encounter" in which each life comes into a new awareness of itself we need to move from a perspective that homogenizes voice to one that examines the multiplicity of voices even within one person. And in Shafik's case we discover a multiplicity of voices. Before engaging in a closer reading of these "alternative languages of modernity" let us situate Doria Shafik within her historical context.

Shafik's own origins encapsulated social shifts that were occurring in early twentieth century Egypt. She grew up in a very modest and traditional middle class Muslim family in the provincial towns of Tanta and Mansura during a period when Egypt was passing through the throes of great internal turmoil following World War One, and which erupted in the 1919 Revolution. During the 1920s and 1930s educational opportunities for women were slowly beginning to open up and for some young women like Doria Shafik, education became an outlet from constraints of tradition, particularly the pressures for an early arranged marriage, and a chance to discover alternative possibilities to a conventional life. Doria exploited that avenue to the fullest and obtained her *Doctorat d'État* from the Sorbonne in 1940, achieving the highest accolade, *mention très honorable*.[2] Although not the first Egyptian woman to receive such a degree, at twenty-nine she was certainly among the youngest. Education may have been a release for her craving to achieve but her ultimate ambition was to enter the public and political arena and it was within the context of post World War Two Egypt that Doria Shafik catapulted herself into national and international prominence.

During her brief but dramatic appearance onto the public stage of Egypt, she openly challenged every social, cultural and legal barrier she viewed inimical and oppressive to the full equality of women in her society and contributed in constructing an Egyptian feminist discourse surrounding women's rights and Islam. Breaking with the reformers of an earlier generation she represented a radically different model for and also created a different discourse on the women's movement in Egypt. Set against the backdrop of the post war social and political upheaval unfolding in Egypt, Doria Shafik attempted to shape a feminist consciousness on several fronts. First through writing: she was the founder and chief editor of two prominent women's journals – *La Femme Nouvelle* in French and *Bint al-Nil* in Arabic – as well as the author and co-author of several books in Arabic on the history, development and renaissance of the social and political rights of Egyptian women.[3] Second through mobilization: She established a feminist organization, Bint al-Nil Union, through which she challenged the very bastions of male authority under both pre-revolutionary and revolutionary regimes. Finally through a strategy of non-violent confrontation: marching on the Egyptian parliament; attempting to run for parliamentary elections; coordinating a sit-in at Barclay's Bank to protest the British Occupation; and finally staging an eight day hunger strike at the Journalists' Syndicate for women's rights. Throughout her career (1945-1957) she met and spoke openly about "women's rights" not only with the president of her own country, but also with the heads of various states[4] on Arab women's struggles for political equality and human freedom, only to lose her own freedom and civil liberties in 1957 following her dramatic protest against the populist regime of Gamal Abdul Nasser which she believed was eroding democracy in Egypt. Although silenced and virtually secluded from public life from 1957 until her death in 1975, she continued to struggle – only this time it was against the isolation and solitude that this banishment to the world of internal exile imposed.

Alternative Languages of Struggle

As a middle class Muslim woman who grew up within one culture, was educated in another and tried to forge a feminist project through the languages of both (French and Arabic), Doria Shafik embodies what Sangari calls the hybrid individual. Through a close reading[5] of her published writings we can follow the trajectory of her struggle to come to grips with and mediate between these different dimensions of her hybrid self identity during a highly charged anti-colonial nationalist political climate.

As the third child and second daughter of six children (three daughters and three sons), born of parents from different class and cultural backgrounds – her mother from an impoverished but notable Turko-Circassian family; her father from a modest, but educated native Egyptian family of civil servants – Shafik early in her life became aware of difference only for her it was associated with the pain of class difference within her own family:

> There always seemed to be an unspoken feeling of mortification within Mama, who felt diminished compared to her cousins, the majority of whom had married wealthy landowners. And within Papa, a profound hurt. He loved my mother deeply and had achieved a high level of culture through his own efforts, yet he felt irreconcilably outclassed. A great tragedy existed within my own family and they hardly even realized it.
>
> (Shafik 1960: 57)

At about the time of the outbreak of World War I when Doria had reached the age of primary schooling she was sent to live with her grandmother in Tanta, where her parents placed her in the French mission school of Notre Dame des Apôtres. By 1926 she finished her secondary education in Alexandria where she attained the French Bachot achieving the second highest score in the country. Two years later she won a national essay contest, celebrating the 20th anniversary of Qasim Amin's death which brought her to the attention of the prominent Egyptian feminist, Huda Sha'rawi, who invited her to speak at the theater of Ezbakiyya Gardens on May 4, 1928.

Doria Shafik stood before her audience and for the first time publicly proclaimed her feminist vision. It was an extraordinary speech for a girl of nineteen, revealing her charming candor. Paying homage to Qasim Amin,

a name which has been eternally engraved in our hearts. Has he not been our guide in the darkness? I will try to be one of his disciples whose example will teach women to fend for themselves in spite of the necessities of the material world.

She continues by lamenting,

what miseries the depths of the harems have concealed for so long! What experience can one acquire if one has simply made a trip from one part of the house to the other? And in her torpor the woman was not aware of her own captivity, having always led the same life she did not think she could liberate herself.

Then she muses on the question,

why certain men persist in isolating women? Do they believe that age-old traditions cannot be adapted to the current of modern life? Or is it that they do not understand the absolute value of liberty? Perhaps we should lock them up for one or two years for them to get the idea of what they impose on women.

Then she directly challenges,

You men, when you decide to let women out, you cover their faces with lugubrious black veils so that they can't see the world except through a cloud. And when you tire of the first wife, you believe you were wrong in your choice, so you take a second, and a third … .

She concludes her essay by pointing out the benefits to men if women were truly educated:

Would you content yourselves with a heart without any knowledge of life? Do you believe that a woman could truly love you if she did not understand you? And for her to understand you, mustn't she be educated? Young girls of today, are they not the mothers of the future? Does an ignorant mother know how to give her child a clear idea about infinity, duty, justice? ... You men construct walls around your daughters, you multiply the number of gates and guards, but you forget that walls are never high enough for feminine ruse. To enable them to communicate with the outside world, your daughters have an old woman or a domestic servant. You show them the world through the windows of their imagination so they see only illusions. And at the first opportunity they fall into the abyss. Why don't you use religion as your support? Give your daughters a good conscience and let them out into the world!

(Shafik 1928: 12-14)

As if answering Shafik's call, Huda Sha'rawi immediately procured a scholarship from the Ministry of Education for this impassioned young woman to travel to Paris and begin her studies at the Sorbonne.

Voices from the Sorbonne (1929-1932)

In her earliest essays written from the Sorbonne and published in Huda Sha'rawi's *L'Égyptienne*, we hear the voice of a modernist's longing for the freedom to discover the world as well as the loneliness and estrangement of a soul yearning for the familiarity of home. Often during moments of despair and unhappiness Doria escaped to the world of her imagination and expressed her innermost thoughts through the metaphors of Egypt, the desert and her beloved Nile.

Alone next to the waves that pass, no sound reaches you except the heavy roaring of the always majestic Nile, the echo of infinity from the desert, that mysterious silence where the human soul finds a point of contact with Eternity; a sublime and mournful kiss between perfection and the still imperfect human being; between man and Divinity, a kiss that leaves an indelible mark within the silence of the desert.

(Shafik 1929: 25)

Shafik's essay written during her first year in Paris constructs a dialogue between the "Child of the Nile" and the "mighty Sphinx", and is important for what it reveals about her self image and inner feelings as well as her attempt to build and nourish a sense of self confidence:

Child: 'Sphinx, I would like to be like thee, regarding the universe from on high and seeing nothing except infinity that circles everywhere under the multiple forms of mere mortals. The Nile gave birth to me and Madam Sha'rawi Pasha became my protectress.'
Sphinx: 'Poor human being, who are you in comparison to the Past? You who wander in the desert and do not know your way because you do not know yourself.'
Child: 'I am the being that wants to touch true knowledge with her own hand.'
Sphinx: 'Do not despair. You are still young and the truly strong souls are the ones forged by suffering. Above your despair place hope beyond all reach.'
The child of the Nile arose and slowly moved forward keeping the head of the mysterious Sphinx in view. A voice in the distance called out: 'Courage, Child, and I shall answer you.'

(Ibid.: 26-27)

The contrapuntal themes of Doria Shafik's hybrid world seem etched into the metaphors of this essay. The mystical bond between herself and the Nile; the mournful kiss between perfection and the imperfect human being; the reconciliation of dreams merging with infinity, the trauma of being thrown into another culture with its painful obstacles and grievous blows; but then the forging of strong souls by suffering; the despair of this being, who wants to touch true knowledge with her own hand.

In another essay she mused on the question, "Does a Woman Have a Right to Philosophize?" (Shafik 1930: 18-28) In attempting to answer her own query, she articulated what she believed was the great drama bursting forth to which the modern era may bear witness: "The sensitivity of the woman; the intellect of the man – two contradictory aspects within a single being." Through her defense of woman's right to philosophize, Doria Shafik was not merely arguing for the right to study one subject as opposed to another, she was offering us her ideas on the crisis challenging the woman of the modern era:

If it is true that every reality is the truth of the moment, then we are witnessing the great turning point that constitutes the crisis traversed by the woman of today: a passage from one moment to another moment of her history, a substitution of a new reality for another reality. How can we move from a romantic conception of things to a new realism? Woman has confined herself to this world of 'Feeling' of Rousseau to the exclusion of clear knowledge. Being a toy of her own passion she has become the toy of those who want to live love. For a long time woman has adopted this sentimental attitude, which undoubtedly had its charm with you, gentlemen. Now one must consider a new woman very different from the old. It is time that a new realism wipe away the tears, from now on useless and even paradoxical. Realism as I understand it consists of getting rid, as much as possible, of illusions of the imagination and as a condition of this effort to conserve the desire of Being, this cry of the Self. It is from this Self that I set out and ridding it of all hallucination, I introduce it into the world of pure knowledge. I ask for a return from this sentient wandering. I ask for a passage from the complaints of Rousseau to a social adaptation that prepares the return to realism.

(Ibid.: 20)

By the phrase "a return from this sentient wandering" she means a passage from the first stage where woman abounds in sensitivity, to a second stage where woman explains the universe for herself.

This self that is passionate can, by looking back upon itself, study objectively the passionate Being that it was. This Being with a Janus face, is simultaneously both an 'I' and a 'me'. It is this being in all its [indefinable] complexity, which must constitute the proper object of philosophy. Woman must, in so much as she is intuitive, be able by looking back upon her past, regard this intuition objectively. This calm of reason is indispensable to the present feminine epoch.

(Ibid.: 23)

In her attempt to grapple with one of the fundamental issues in philosophy: the relationship between intuition (immediate, spontaneous, subjective knowledge) and reason (distanced, systemic objectified knowledge), she explores the context of the situation facing women, like herself, who are caught between two philosophical moments:

The opposition of the woman of yesterday to the woman of today reflects the great opposition of an intuitive philosophy to a more systematic philosophy. I mean a philosophy of presentiment where mystery reigns, but one in which the harmonious base is glimpsed by the human heart. Perhaps it's there wherein lies great philosophy? Anyway there is another philosophy that is venerated much less than this latter one but has the advantage of being incontestably realistic. It is a philosophy concerned with the multiple problems posed at every moment to the individual to which the only solution is Action.

(Ibid.: 25)

The feminist problematic involved, therefore, an intellectual struggle to unite contradictory modes of knowing – intuition and analysis. Shafik did not intend to leave the argument one of mere opposition between two eras of the woman or two opposed philosophical positions. She wanted nothing less than to find a true synthesis:

How could I explain to myself the synthesis of an intuitive and systematic conception of the universe? As magic has given birth to science [the analogy permits me to say] so the woman of today, daughter of the woman of yesterday, preserves within her that which she was, but she lives with a new life. How can woman, in being artist, pretend to pure knowledge? She is herself a work of art! In this work she is no longer placed as an object of contemplation. Her goal is knowledge. She wants to conceive clearly that which she has produced spontaneously. She wants to introduce the spirit of system into that which, by its essence, defies analysis. She sees the possibility of blending intuition and Concept. And in this, one cannot refuse her the Right to Philosophize!

(Ibid.: 28)

There is a definite "modernity" in the manner in which Doria has structured the crisis posed in the successive moments of feminine history when a new adaptation is substituted for the old. Although in this essay she is not analyzing any particular historical reality where this transition is taking place, she does reveal a certain insight into the problem she is confronting as a woman intellectual who desires to fight to be recognized in this world "where so many authorities (daughters of centuries past) would like to ridicule her." She believed in her right to choose, at the same time conscious of the struggle involved.

In her last essay to appear in *L'Égyptienne*, "*Rêverie d'une femme d'aujourd'hui*", written at a time of emotional ambivalence in her own life – she had just completed her License d'État from the Sorbonne and was returning to an unsure future – Doria muses on the quandary of the modern woman of our time:

Forgetting time and everything that the measure beats, the young woman of today wants to live in wholeness: a sympathy between herself and the universe; a genuine dream that seeks harmony between the storm that overturns the self, and this other storm which never ceases to give existence to the universe: a fight and always a fight. Between lived reality and being: Love! A word that will never die away except with the human being! But today love of whom and love of what?

(Shafik 1932: 15)

In a vein similar to her earlier essay in which she conversed with the Sphinx, Doria writes: "A young heart thinking only of the true, the tragic, the sublime. Youthful and old at the same time, a human being who questions 'who are you?'". As she tries to tries to formulate an answer she reveals her own inner struggle to maintain a sense of autonomy in a world where "objections will be made against the possibility that the woman wishes above everything to be equal to man!" Through her metaphors we grasp something of the meaning of her life:

What can I grasp of myself outside this material and social crust? If one could transpose the formula of Descartes into the order of life and say: 'I fight therefore I am,' then every act would perhaps have a meaning. In this fight, our young dreamer is engaged in contemplation. Yes, but a lived reverie, because the ideas that manipulate her are experienced ideas! It is always the same problem, a solution forcibly suspended, a relentless flight that dies and is reborn: There lies humanity. There is the woman of today.

(Ibid.: 19)

An Awakening Feminist Consciousness

By publishing these essays it is clear that the editors of *L'Égyptienne* were reaffirming to their readers that, "the torch of the Egyptian women's movement has been placed in the hands of the new generation represented by Doria Shafik" (Editors of L'Égyptienne 1928). Shafik gladly accepted this mantle of approval from her idol and protectress as she felt that destiny had presaged a role for her to play in bringing women into the broader national struggle. And upon her return from the Sorbonne, after completing her doctorate, she wrote a treatise, *La Femme Nouvelle en Égypte* (1944), in which she sets out to describe the social situation of Egyptian women. By writing in French she was directing her message to the educated Egyptian elite, the class she wanted to catalyze as the vanguard of social change for the poorer majority of the Egyptian masses. She began by challenging the western orientalist view of Egyptian women:

The social situation of the Egyptian woman is in a general way very little understood in the world. Westerners are still impressed by the writings of those early travellers, who first probed the East. These very unscientific writings might, through a great stretch of the imagination, provide a portrait of the Egyptian woman of an earlier time. But they certainly distort the idea of the Egyptian woman on which the West bases its views today. She has evolved so fast that one can hardly recognize her. Compared with her sister of the beginning of the twentieth century the Egyptian woman of today is a totally different woman with new ideas, different habits and unlimited ambition. It is with the particular goal of clarifying this situation that I have written this book. I focus on the social situation of the Egyptian woman as it was not so long ago, as it is in our day, and as she hopes it will be in the future.
(Shafik 1944: 8)

Through her portrayal of the new woman in Egypt Shafik articulates her own vision of feminist consciousness and self image during this moment of historical transition when Egypt was struggling toward its own national independence:

One of the first questions posed for the [educated] woman is the safeguarding of her femininity; another is the role of woman in public life, and a third is the role of woman in society. Feminism in the true sense of the word is the total comprehension between man and woman, not a perpetual fight between the two sexes. As for the statement that "women normally constituted and not too ugly are not made to be politicians, diplomats, generals or drum majors" I am revolted! You forget Cleopatra, the most beautiful diplomat and politician, and Joan of Arc, the charming warrior. The feminine genius is not necessarily accompanied by ugliness. One finds equally that nearly all exceptional women whose names have come down in history, have been unhappy. That is their affair. One must believe that they preferred an unhappy and meaningful life to a complacent but stupid one. 'Nothing renders us so great as great suffering,' as the poet says.

(Ibid.: 10-12)

For Doria the educated elite woman had a special mission, to bridge the immense gap between the women of the upper classes and those of the poor. She argued that it is the particular responsibility and obligation of this elite to change and transform those traditional socio-cultural and legal barriers inimical to woman's free and full participation in the life of the country. That she should engage in public criticism of customs oppressive to women in her society was due to her conviction that Islam, if properly understood, offered no barrier to women's freedom. An argument she had made in her doctoral thesis:

We are like a huge machine whose cogs fail to mesh. There has been too much progress at the top of society and none at all at the bottom. Yet it is on this basis that the solid foundations of any society, and particularly of female society, are laid, and it is from this layer of society that the majority of mothers come. Here is an issue to which we should devote the greatest attention.

(Ibid.: 75)

Voices of 'La Femme Nouvelle' and 'Bint al-Nil' (1945-1957)

In 1945 shortly after publishing *La Femme Nouvelle en Égypte* Shafik received an offer from the notorious Princess Chevikar[6] asking her to serve as editor-in-chief of Chevikar's French magazine *La Femme Nouvelle*, which led to mounting criticism among certain critics in the broader Egyptian society that Shafik was more French than Egyptian. To counter this criticism she promptly established her own Arabic women's periodical, *Bint al-Nil*. Through the voices coming from the pages of these two magazines we sense the profound transformation of an earlier feminine expression into a critical feminist expression.[7]

Through the pages of *La Femme Nouvelle* Doria portrayed the greatness of Egypt and the capabilities of its woman. By invoking history and cultural heritage she gave dignity to the continuity of woman's self image:

At such an interesting period as our own in which the most diverse spirits tend to come together and establish understanding, I wanted a review capable of reflecting our state of mind, and of putting us in touch with the rest of the world. A review which would be the mirror of our present progress, and the echo of a very old civilization which is being reborn and which will never die.

(Shafik 1947)

This analogy between the rebirth of an old civilization with the emergence of the "new woman" which resonates throughout Doria's editorials on one level was her voice directed to the west with the expressed purpose of countering negative stereotypes of Egypt with a more positive image of its heritage and potentialities:

La Femme Nouvelle reappears today, as if restructured, with a great role to play – that of reflecting our present renaissance, of putting us in touch with other countries, and this serving as a bond between ourselves and the rest of the world. Until now almost all the works produced on Egypt are in foreign languages and written by foreigners, either passing through or living in Egypt. This was Egypt seen from the 'outside' as one might say. But with *La Femme Nouvelle* we offer a description of our Egypt from what may be called the 'inside'. We tell you about her as we would tell you about our mother whose arms have cradled us.

(Ibid.)

It is interesting that Doria does not consider that *La Femme Nouvelle* is foreign, despite its use of the French language, since on another level she was addressing the French speaking native elite whose support she wanted to draw towards the cause of women. The metaphors she used to describe the New Woman is that of message and messenger, bond and bridge.

Our readers will be, so to speak, members of a grand family, that of the New Woman, the one who works without respite. The one who has no other goal but the continued progress of the oriental woman. She will be this new messenger directing herself toward the West and will make it hear her voice. In one immense stride, she will throw a magnificent bridge between the East and the West.

(Shafik 1946)

The New Woman is a message, an unusual message, arising from the distant mists of history and advancing into the future; a message that reveals hidden treasures and relieves Egypt from the burden of so many secrets that she alone has borne for six thousand years! A message that probes freely into the depths of time; a message of those endless and innumerable unknown riches, of hidden treasures. The New Woman is a message of an art that gives life to stone and instills life into the inert. But she is also a messenger that reveals the changing aspect of Egypt and its renaissance.

(Shafik 1948)

She argued that East and West are not hermetically sealed entities but, on the contrary, complete one another, and the new woman enriches herself not only with her own past but with her manifold relations with other civilizations.

There was a time when East and West were two inscrutable worlds, two irreconcilable monads evolving along two parallel roads and never meeting. Through space and time, various civilizations shake hands, understand one another, unite and complement one another. This edition essentially bears witness to this reconciliation, to this rapprochement, often unexpected, and yet so harmonious. *La Femme Nouvelle* will serve as a bond between the intellectual and artistic life of Egypt and the West.

(Shafik 1949)

By focusing on Egyptian culture, Doria was also depicting the renaissance of Egypt. Through its aesthetic heritage, its poetry, painting, theater and music, Doria was also trying to reveal Egypt from the inside.

In contrast to *La Femme Nouvelle*, *Bint al-Nil* had another focus and objective. *La Femme Nouvelle* was Shafik's French aesthetic/cultural voice turned outward to the Occident with the goal of conveying the true image of Egyptian greatness. *Bint al-Nil* was her activist/feminist voice directed inward to the Arabic-speaking world of the emerging middle class not only in Egypt but also throughout the Arab countries of the Levant. Doria wanted to wake up educated men and women to their duty and responsibilities in solving the nation's problems. *Bint al-Nil* was her vehicle for educating men and women –

in the profound meaning of that term – awakening consciousness to women's basic rights and responsibilities:

Women of our generation have as yet not learnt to take control of their lives. They are as yet not ready to enter the arena of politics. It is rare to find women who know the names of our politicians. Moreover they don't know the politicians outside Egypt. All of this is information that one can freely obtain from the newspapers that our fathers, brothers and husbands bring home. Most women, however, only read the obituaries and the social news. I do not ask that women work in politics but I do think that they should be aware of what goes on. We are harming our own children more than anyone if we remain incapable of informing them of the events that take place in public life. In raising our children we should have a comprehensive understanding of political events. Thus the evolution of society begins with its women and *Bint al-Nil* will be an aid in the education and evolution of the Egyptian woman and thus contribute to the Progress of the nation.

(*Bint al-Nil*, 1946)

Despite her denial, the issue of women and politics was always a prominent theme in Doria Shafik's writing. However, in the early years, the conservative influence of her husband and Ibrahim Abdu[8] kept a lid on her volatile ideas. As Abdu admitted,

'Those first editorials of 1946 do not reflect the sentiments and works of Doria Shafik. They are mine! I wrote down those ideas, not Doria!' When pressed to explain the circumstances which necessitated this more cautious approach he responded, 'I had a difficult time toning down Doria's confrontational approach. During this period the Shaykhs of Al-Azhar were strongly and publicly against women going to university with men and entering those professions that were exclusively man's work, such as medicine, law, engineering, and science. So as not to incite the al-Azharites' immediate wrath and violent opposition to *Bint al-Nil*, I thought a better strategy was to go step by step at a more moderate pace. Also as a university professor at that time, I was more in touch with the explosive political situation than Doria.'[9]

The first issue of *Bint al-Nil* appeared during a period when Egyptian society was experiencing dramatic acts of violence, including assassinations and widespread student and worker demonstrations which fanned social unrest. We hear the more conservative voice of Abdu filtering through the editorials of *Bint al-Nil*:

I don't, however, think that our active women should be asking for equality because this will not serve the purpose of our movement ... Nature has created a distinction between men and women which is difficult to negate. Women were created most importantly of all to bear children. If we equate her with men we would be liberating her from her natural responsibilities. This role that nature has cast women in makes equality between men and women not feasible. The religious (Sharia) laws were imposed on men for the sake of women. They were created to guard women and their rights before and after divorce; so how can we ask for equality when all religions have differentiated between the sexes ... Instead of asking for equality, we should be asking for a change in the legislature that has been unfair to women.

(*Bint al-Nil*, Jan 1946)

A comparison of the sentiments expressed above in *Bint al-Nil* with Shafik's statement in a different context, that of her 1944 treatise, reveals the extent of Abdu's control over Doria's Arabic voice.

We must pull the Egyptian woman out of the quandary in which she has suffered for centuries. The attainment of total equality with men is the axis of the Egyptian woman's modern existence and admits no concession however minimal.

(Shafik 1944: 43)

By 1948 the message and tone of *Bint al-Nil* began to change, suggesting that Doria was starting to speak out more distinctly in her own Arabic voice uncensored by Abdu:

Men in Egypt do not want what is best for their country. They fight us in our efforts to develop our country. At times they do this in the name of religion. We have never heard of a religion that stands between women and their right to life. At other times they say that it is in the name of tradition. What tradition stands between women and their ability to do good? In fact it is the inferiority complex from which some Egyptians suffer which makes them behave in this way. Gentlemen make way for us and let the procession take its natural course.

(*Bint al-Nil,* Jan 1948)

And from the end of the forties until she was put under house arrest Doria Shafik engaged in a much more open criticism of society and her storming of Parliament in 1951 and hunger strike in 1954 opened up a public debate on the question of women's rights and human freedom. Given her own interest in reconciling Islam and modernity she argued vehemently that Islam was not in contradiction to her vision of women's legal and political rights. In her view the issue of women's rights was not restricted merely to suffrage. She wanted nothing less than to change the Islamic personal status laws that allowed the husband unlimited polygamy, the unilateral right to repudiate his wife and the right of child custody as well as the civil laws that prohibited women from running for elected office and serving as parliamentarians. She wanted to abolish *Bayt al-ta'a* (House of obedience)[10] and requested that the measures taken by the police to enact the law also be abolished.

Bint al-Nil and *La Femme Nouvelle* not only epitomize Doria Shafik's attempt to fashion a new image of and for the Egyptian and Arab woman during the critical post war period, they also reveal how the aesthetic and the activist, those dual and competing strands in her life, are woven more intimately and profoundly into her lived experience as she seeks to discover her destiny. Both magazines centered around the construction of identity, whether cultural or sexual, evincing not only Doria Shafik's personal struggles but also her disquiet over the general debate in society at large between pan-Islamists and Egyptianists as to the more appropriate ideology for the political future of Egypt.

The tension between the aesthetic and activist within her own persona not only contributed to her enigmatic public image but also reinforced the conservative Muslim belief that Doria Shafik was a tool of western society trying to undermine the society's Islamic values. Her modern ideas about women's role in the life of nation, as well as her own unescorted trip to Europe to affiliate with a western feminist organization, drew harsh criticism from Islamic fundamentalists, who argued that women's participation in public life was a source of *fitna* (or social anarchy). In their view her affiliation with western international women's organizations was just another example of an on-going conspiracy that combined the motivations and battle plans of colonialism with the goals of international Zionism. Only in the guise of the women's movement, it had chosen to launch its attacks against the Islamic family structure, the cornerstone of Muslim society. Thus any demand for women's right to political power or call for restrictions in divorce procedures and polygamy was perceived as an imperialist plot designed to undermine the Egyptian social structure.

In 1944 following her trip to Europe where she had officially registered her Bint al-Nil Union with the International Council of Women, one fundamentalist group, the Flame of Muhammad, launched a stinging public criticism against Shafik accusing her of being an agent for her country's enemies: [11]

Colonialism has many games and tricks. The Egyptian Feminist Movement, in the shadow of Muslim society, needed a dramatic plot that would give its required thrust and achieve its required goals in the shortest time possible. Therefore it needed a personality that would play the role of opposition in the games of agents in this sphere of women. First there was Huda Sha'rawi, who founded The Egyptian Feminist Union; then there was a second one who established the national feminist party and renewed the ways of corruption; the third was the Bint al-Nil Party, which seeks to save the woman from the man and recapture the lost rights of women. Who is this personality playing the role of adventurer? None other than Doria Shafik. In 1949 she established the Bint al-Nil Party and within a month she travelled to England, which at the time had 85,000 troops occupying the motherland. There she was received by heads of states and leaders. The British press received her and shed their light on her and published many talks that depict her a fighter and the first leader in Egypt for the liberation of women from the shackles of Islam – the restraints of the veil; the scourge of divorce and polygamy. A reporter from the Scotsman iterated the goals of the Bint al-Nil Party as expressed by Doria Shafik: (1) to get the vote and enter parliament; (2) to abolish polygamy; and (3) to introduce European divorce laws into Egypt! The ideas of this 'suspect' woman came from colonial instigation and through colonial institutions.

(Al-Gohari 1980: pp. 259-264)

Doria Shafik's quest for self expression represented an indigenous and authentic response to the civilizational encounter that enfolded her. From the moment she established her journals in 1945 until her final defiant act in 1957 protesting against the authoritarian regime headed by Gamal Abdul Nasser, Doria Shafik was engaged in a cultural critique that was simultaneously directed outward to the Other (the West) and inward toward the Self (Egypt and Islam) in a project that was aimed to dismantle the distorted and stereotyped images of the oriental woman as well as the patriarchal frameworks in which these were embedded.

As a genre of intellectual cultural production, Shafik's two journals engage directly in the construction of a public discourse surrounding feminism, Islam and political power. As a style of cultural critique, these journals represent the first stage of a process, which Hisham Sharabi has defined as

the critical movement marking the fundamental shift and cultural crisis of post-modernism. The model of the post-modern critic, then, is the person who occupies a space of critical consciousness ... a criticism that must distance itself from domination and assume an adversarial position.

(Sharabi 1987: 15-16)

I read Doria Shafik's languages of struggle not so much as postmodern but as representing the contestation of Self and Other within the framework of modernity. As a woman intellectual, who straddled two cultures and interrogated her own, Doria Shafik is more representative of the hybrid individual or what Christopher Norris describes as "that modernist colonial figure, the internal exile – half in and half out – homeless and dispossessed."[12]

Voice of the Muse (1949-1957)

At the same time that Doria Shafik was struggling for the political rights of Egyptian women she was also writing and publishing her poetry – revealing yet another dimension of her political and cultural hybridity. The appearance of *La Bonne Aventure* (1948), her first collection of poetry, gave her enormous satisfaction in an otherwise hectic and conflict-laden life.

This need to write poems was as necessary to me as breathing! It is true that I was alive to poetry from my first year of study in Paris – but it is only much later that I was awakened to Poetry – as an expression of the Absolute. The publication of my booklet of poems helped me to discover a certain consistency to this Infinity resonating within me and which I was unable to formulate; to this grand flame, whose moving presence I felt but could never reveal.

(Shafik 1960: 343)

She was thrilled that her work had been recognized by Pierre Seghers, one of France's most distinguished publishers[13] who founded his own publishing house during the war to support the writings of such resistance poets as Louis Aragon, Paul Eluard, Pierre Reverdy and others who were to become among Doria's favorites (Seghers 1978). He not only encouraged young foreign poets like Pablo Neruda, Federico Garcia Lorca, Elsa Triolet, he also authored several books of his own work including poetry, prose anthologies, songs and films. Following his death on November 4, 1987, Jean Orizet eulogized Seghers as follows: "Poetry has lost its most fervent lover, its most active defender. It is still befitting to remember that Seghers was above all the poet of abandon and passion."[14]

If Huda Sha'rawi can be credited for encouraging and supporting Doria's feminist ardor and Princess Chevikar for offering Doria the opportunity to channel her restless search for a mission into journalism, then Pierre Seghers must be singled out as the one person in her life who recognized, appreciated and encouraged the soul of the poet smoldering within her. From the moment they first met in 1947 Seghers became her trusted friend, her literary critic, her publisher, but above all her mentor within the world of modern poetry.

When she came to Paris it was not only to see me. She came for many other reasons. She was busy with her magazines, her publications, her struggle for women's rights. She was extraordinarily active. But I don't think she ever came to Paris without seeing me. And that's another thing. My domain, my sphere of activity, was within the realm of poetry and this is what brought us together, a friendship that became more and more profound.[15]

Through her friendship with Seghers, Doria was encouraged to explore, discover and give expression to her "inner lyricism" as Seghers once described her special style. Over the years Seghers and Shafik exchanged letters and poems. Shafik often sending Seghers samples of her work, asking for his criticism and he, in turn, sending her his published books often inscribed with warm and affectionate dedications. Doria had begun working on a large opus which she first entitled "Christ Rouge" but later changed to "Redemption", metaphors chosen from those childhood memories of the glass stained windows of the nun's schools. "You are very near to Pablo Neruda as well as to the *Épiphanes* of Henri Pichette. In this union of spontaneity and hard work they are a lesson to all."[16]

Poetry was not a frivolous diversion for Doria, it was central to her being and it is through her poetry that we gain an understanding of the interior world of this enigmatic woman. As Seghers commented,

> She was a poet. That's all. With this zeal, passion, ardor. I believe that a man or a woman living passionately is someone who is not calm; there is this demand, this anxiety and this need which are not calm and placid. There is always this ardor; this ardor is like a fire and fire torments itself. She was like that because she was an artist; she was a woman of thought.[17]

This recognition by one of France's *"poètes de l'élan et de la passion"* further encouraged Doria to write and she produced a second collection, *L'Amour Perdu* (1954), the same year that she staged her eight day hunger strike for women's rights. Her final five volumes of poetry appeared in 1979 published posthumously by her daughters with the help of Seghers. In his words the earlier poems are:

> A beginning, an annunciation, a preface to her work. They are more radiant, more silky, more smooth than her later ones. At the same time I think there is a certain strength, a certain vigor, a certain severity, a certain sobriety and a certain subterranean power in her later work that surpasses the first ones. This later poetry goes deeper, much deeper. It is a poetry where thought, reflection and the inner life are, they say, more evident. It is more solemn if you like. The first poetry announces, moreover a temperament like this. It is still the beginning. But afterwards we feel this gravity, this seriousness which endures until death.[18]

Among the poems of *L'Amour Perdu* we listen to a voice that is moving further into the interior landscape exploring the themes of solitude, destiny, the Absolute, struggle and the suffering of the human heart, and where "the profound source of her inner lyricism dominates."

Le Désert

A perte de vue s'étend	As far as the eye can see
le Silence ...	Silence stretches out ...
Las nappes de sable	The sheets of sand
pleurent leur solitude	sobbing their solitude
Et les rares bédouins	And the rare bedouins
passent leur chemin ...	passing on their way ...
Mais	But
là ...	there ...
n'est pas	is not
le vrai Désert	the true Desert
Celui	In the one
que dans mon coeur	that
se creuse	deeply penetrates
en profondeur	my heart ....
le soleil	where the sun
y est	is
interdit ...	forbidden ...

These poems are uniquely grounded in Shafik's Egyptian experience as she delves deeper into her culture and finds familiar motifs to revitalize and be revitalized in her poetry. A Cairo Night, The River Nile, Domes and Minarets, The Flute Player, the "Sakkieh" all became transformed into her lyrical melodies. In an anthology of *Poètes en Égypte* appearing in 1955, the editor writes of Doria Shafik:

Between her two magazines she is a prolific bilingual writer; she also writes poems with an engaging simplicity where interior landscapes and Egyptian impressions are fixed in the most rapid but sure touches.

(Moscatelli 1955: 204)

Such touches we hear in her depiction of a Cairo night:

Le Caire La Nuit

Nuit pétrie d'amour	Night consumed by love
où mon coeur	where my heart
retrouve	discovers
sa première émotion … .	its first emotion … .
Nuit mouillée de lumière	Night drenched in light
où mon âme	where my soul
touche	strokes
à l'enchantement …	enchantment …
Nuit mêlée de pénombre	Night bleeding into dusk
où mon être	where my being
erre	wanders
dans son torment	in its torment

Or through her image of her beloved Nile:

Tantot miroitant	Its crystalline
sex eatix	waters
cristallines … .	Now shimmering … .
Tantot vert	Now green
comme	as
une belle saison	A magnificent spring … .
Tantot rouge	Now red
et fougueux	and fiery
comme le sang … .	as blood … .
Tour à tour	At the same moment
provoquant	challenging
et docile	and docile
Sombre	Somber
et nonchalant	and nonchalant
Perfide	Treacherous
et avenant …	and comely …
Avançant	Advancing
majestueusement	majestically
dans La Valée …	through the Valley …
Défiant	Defying
le monde	the world
et les gens … .	and the people … .

Nil	Nile
bienfaiteur	benefactor
Nil	Nile
autoritaire	domineering
On voudrait	One would like
te comprendre	to understand you
On voudrait	One would like
l'approcher.	To approach you.
Dans ton mystère	In thine mystery
tu restes	Thou rest
là	there
muet	mute
secret ...	secret ...

Through these images and metaphors of Egypt, Doria Shafik not only explores her inner emotions that are both personal and political, individual and universal, but foreshadows the despair that was to overcome her during these long years of house arrest and self imposed seclusion.

The Voice of Interior Music (1957-1975)

On February 6, 1957, Shafik walked into the Indian Embassy, having announced to the international media that she was embarking on a strike,

> to hunger unto death, to protest the two enemies of my freedom – Israel, which is occupying Egyptian land, and the present authoritarian regime which is leading the country into bankruptcy and chaos.

This was her last political exploit and ultimately led to her being placed under house arrest, her journals being confiscated, and her name officially banned from the Egyptian media until her tragic death on September 20, 1975, when her name reappeared on the front pages of the Egyptian press. Ironically, this final defiant act in defence of that single principle of individual liberty resulted in her entering an eighteen year period of near seclusion, in many ways more painful and tortured than the harems she had witnessed as a child growing up in Mansura and Tanta.

Doria's house arrest abruptly ended a public career which had spanned more than thirty years from 1928 when she first stood beside Huda Sha'rawi on the platform of the theater at Ezbakiyyah Gardens and delivered her impassioned and in some ways prophetic, eulogy to Qasim Amin.

Withdrawn from public view, abandoned by former comrades and denounced by her society as a "traitor to the revolution", Doria Shafik was only forty eight years old when she embarked on her final and most difficult battle: the struggle against isolation and solitude that this banishment to the world of internal exile imposed.

From this isolated ambience, where my enemies believe they have driven me back to a slow death, I nevertheless have discovered the most beautiful windfall; my own existence as a human being. At what door can I knock in order to leap over these invisible bars of my prison? Invisible even for those, who up until this point, were near to me and in the habit of seeing clearly. Here I am hunted down on the moving sand, encircled by wolves and vipers. In this indescribable desert, where my optimism at every trial still pushed me to hope, I advance in the void, echoing my own call. I speak to the deaf. Where are the people? I belong to them! I am made of the same stuff! Human! One can be made to do anything but no one can oblige me to go against my conscience. There I affirm myself as Absolute. There I exist in the most elevated sense: I am free. At the end of three years of seclusion, at the end also of my years of struggle, I have discovered you, liberty, essence of my being. Liberty: you give unique meaning to this work. I have dedicated this work to you, and to all those who, like me, have suffered from loss of freedom.

(Shafik 1960: 585)

On the final page of these memoirs written during the first years of her house arrest, she scripts a line of verse in homage to Paul Eluard, to whom she dedicated her work.

> O Liberty
> I make you a gift
> Of my heart

> Without you
> Life
> Means
> Nothing

Shortly after news of her house arrest reached Seghers, he sent her this personal note:

For you, Doria, who will always remain the very image of beauty, the flame and passing of living poetry: for you, who are your country, and to whom I remain so near. With most faithful friendship, Seghers.

For ten years after her house arrest, Seghers faithfully continued writing to his friend and sending her copies of his latest poetry. We find affectionate inscriptions such as: "To Doria, the art of always being able to keep oneself company"; "For Doria Shafik, these stones from the same temple; with my loyal memory"; "For you, Doria, whoever sings his troubles enchants it!" But Doria never responded and Seghers eventually stopped writing.

However it is essentially through her poetry, that "voice of interior music" that we catch a glimpse of what Seghers often referred to as "her most authentic truth". The following poems written during those final years appear in an unpublished volume which she entitled "Hors Temps":

Because they were conceived and written in an atmosphere escaping our perceived time, that eternally narrowly measured time. The setting of these poems is timeless. It is an immediate apperception of our interior life whose essence belongs to infinity, to the unlimited. The profound meaning of these poems is in the expression of interior music that emerges from the depths of our hearts, when our heart is pure, transmitting the echoes of our soul which, when it is elevated to the lofty heights of purity becomes capable of capturing the Absolute.

(Shafik n.d.: 8)

In this brief homage to her favorite resistance poet we sense her pensive mood:

O, Reverdy

quelle résonance!	what resonance!
Le coeur en silence	the heart in silence
se tait	holds its tongue
et laisse parler	and lets the others
les autres.	speak ….
Il n'a plus rien à dire	There's nothing more to say
Il a tout dit	It has all been said
[ce qu'il fallait dire]	[that which one must say]
Et son silence	And its Silence
à travers l'absence	through the absence
de véritable vie	of a genuine life
erre	wanders
dans le désert	in the desert
de la mélancolie	of melancholia
Mais le poids de l'angoisse	But the burden of anguish
tassé	boxed in
en barricade	against a wall
se découvre	discovers itself
soudain	suddenly
et se révolte	and revolts
sans bruit sans vaine	without noise or vain
parade	display
levier inexorable	unyielding lever
des HEURES de matin	HOURS of the morning

Or in this silent lament which was her message to the world outside her prison:

Don't be surprised
That I write to you in verse
When the customary prose is there
It is, you see,
That I have suffered some setbacks
Hemmed in by walls
Not of stones, it is true
But worse – I hope you understand
And only poetry

> Friend of passionate souls
> Should explain to you
> My name begins with D
> and I am a woman …
> Daughter of the Nile
> I have demanded women's rights
> My fight was enlarged
> To human freedom
> In a world of oppression
> I have dared to demand
> this freedom
> And what was the result?
> I have no more friends
> So what?
> Until the end of the road
> I will proceed alone
> Without hesitation, without turning back
> What does loneliness matter?
> Nausea – disheartening torture
> I feel my heart is big
> So big that it overflows
> The barriers of treason
> And rejoins, in the four corners of the world,
> All Souls of Good Will

As Doria withdrew further into herself she struggled against the encroachment of loneliness through the only means left to her. More than ever, she relied upon her trusted muse, who became both her mistress and companion and through whom she could express her anguish.

> How to Live Without Poetry
> How
> Without this rhythm of life
> To endure
> the passing of the days
> empty of content and
> these departures without

> return
> departures of all our hopes?
> How to live without
> this interior music
> which alone permits us
> to bear the heavy burden
> of inexpressible sorrow?
> how to live without
> this profound breathing
> that is poetry
> friend
> of those who suffer
> of those
> with too sensitive a heart
> of those who want
> and insist on wanting
> to make of their life
> a work of art

Unyielding she continued through her poetry to denounce repression, hatred and violence. Under these conditions of separation and loneliness that became more and more difficult for her to endure, she proclaimed her attachment to the absolutes of Freedom, to Good, and to Love. She filled thousands of blank pages with words that gushed forth in a stream of consciousness, revealing the slow process of a self disconnecting from a world of social and family ties drifting slowly towards the ultimate fusion with the Absolute.

Through these voices of inner struggle we follow the trajectory of Shafik's withdrawal from the everyday world and her transformation in time and space reflecting a heightened involvement with the transcendental, foretelling her final act of will which was to throw herself from her sixth floor balcony into the void on September 20, 1975.

The Voices of Jahanara Shahnawaz and Hamida Akhtar Hussein

Jahanara Shahnawaz (1896-1979) and Hamida Akhtar Hussein (1918-) were both born in colonial British India. At independence in August 1948, both came to live in Pakistan. Their lives, like that of Doria

Shafik, represent the lives of the transition. However, their individual trajectories are not identical: their voices and actions bear witness both to the historical times they lived in (at different periods during the passage from coloniality to neo-coloniality), and to the uniqueness of their particular encounters with those times. In this portion of the paper, I examine a single autobiographical text by each of these two women, so as to tease out their respective experiences and voices and their engagement with processes and dilemmas of modernity. Let me start with a brief biographical sketch of each woman.

Jahanara Shahnawaz[19] was born in Baghbanpura, near the city of Lahore, in Punjab Province. Her family belonged to the Arain Muslim community.[20] Her father, Muhammad Shafi, was a well known lawyer and political figure, active in Muslim League[21] politics. As his favorite child, she received her initial political education starting at a very young age, at his hands: [22]

Since the age of twelve, I had become a companion in the house of my father, and he used to talk to me of his political work and would often read his speeches and statements to me. He would discuss the political situation and other topics, welcome comments on the salient points, and while doing so trained me to take part in the political life of the country. It was his greatest wish to prepare me for work in the political sphere.

(Shahnawaz 1971: 36)

Jahanara was initially educated at home, as was customary for Muslim Indian girls of her time. In 1908, she joined Queen Mary's College, a posh girl's school in Lahore organized along lines similar to institutions established by the British to educate boys from elite Indian households. She and her sister, Geti, joined the school the day it started: "There were only eleven girls who attended, and my name was placed first on the register" (ibid.: 33). She continued her studies after an early marriage in 1911 at age fifteen. Though she remained in school for another year after the birth of her first child in the summer of 1912, it was only to study Arabic and learn embroidery.

During the colonial period and after, Jahanara was active in women's and national politics. She entered public life while young, writing articles for papers and women's magazines as early as 1906. A serialized story by her was published in book form in 1915, when she was nineteen. She was an active member in many organizations including the All India Women's Conference[23] (in which she served as provincial branch president for many years, and later as national Vice President in 1932), the Red Cross Society, the Muslim League and the Muslim Educational Conference, including their women's sections. In 1917, she was among the organizers for the annual session of the Muslim Ladies' Conference. At that moot, she proposed a resolution against polygamy "which was passed unanimously and became a standing resolution of the Conference."[24]

Despite this extensive political involvement it was only after 1920 when during a trip to Calcutta, Bengal, she and other women family members came out of seclusion, that Jahanara began to participate in gender-mixed political events. During debates on the enfranchisement of women under the Montague-Chelmsford Reforms, she spoke before a mixed gathering for the first time. Subsequently she was to speak to many such gatherings in different locales on a variety of issues.

She was appointed delegate to several of the Round Table Conferences[25] held in London in the early through mid-thirties. In 1931, she was invited by the Secretary General of the League of Nations to visit their offices as a 'Collaborator'[26] to study the League and its various committees' workings. In 1935, she served as the only Indian delegate appointed to the League of Nations Advisory Committee for the Protection and Welfare of Children. She contested and won provincial elections in 1937, 1946[27] and after independence. She was a member of the Constituent Assembly before independence and continued in this capacity afterwards as well, when she served on four parliamentary committees responsible for drafting the constitution for the new state of Pakistan. In this capacity, she worked for women's rights to be assured under the new constitution. She also helped frame the charter of Women's Rights, which was supported by all women's groups then in existence in Pakistan; and later, campaigned to have this charter accepted by the National Assembly which approved it unanimously in 1954. When the Constituent Assembly was dissolved in 1956, and Martial Law declared, she withdrew from public political life and devoted the rest of her life to reading and writing.

Hamida Akhtar Hussein too was born and raised in British India. Unlike Jahanara Shahnawaz, she grew up in an intellectual rather than a political household environment.[28] Her family was based in central

India, in the then-famous town of Aligarh.[29] Her surroundings reflected the preoccupations of the Muslim literati and intelligentsia, and combined linguistic, literary and political considerations. Because of this her concerns and intellectual pursuits, although revolving around nationalist concerns as well, were distinct from Jahanara's in various respects. Among these differences was a focus on the position and place of the Urdu language in a united Indian anti-colonial movement; an immersion in literature and the world of aesthetics; an awareness of being at the center of the Muslim literary and political renaissance. And because of the geographical location and cultural position of Aligarh, an awareness of the significance of working across sectarian/communal lines with Hindus and other religious communities.

It is noteworthy that for Hamida Akhtar's generation of middle class girls, women's education was now a norm. Hamida studied at the Aligarh Muslim Women's College, a companion institution to Aligarh University, an all male institution at the time. However, despite studying at a segregated school, unlike Jahanara's household, Hamida's family were not strict in observing gender segregation at home. She met young men, friends of her brothers and cousins. It was this social exchange between genders, which led after matriculation to her marriage to Akhtar Hussein, a fledgling writer and journalist, after a lengthy but secret courtship, known only to several of her girlfriends. Hers was a marriage of choice (although formalized through parental channels). After marriage, she moved far away from home to Hyderabad, Deccan, to live in an all male, literary environment. After marriage when outside her marital home, she still did not practice *purdah*, but inside the household there was a strict segregation of the *zenana* from the male quarters.[30] She lived until widowhood, as a close companion to her husband, devoting her life to him. While independent minded, her coming to voice publicly[31] followed the death of her husband. It was then that she began to write.

The two texts one each written by these two women that are read closely here are Jahanara Shahnawaz's *Father and Daughter: A Political Autobiography* (1971) and Hamida Akhtar Hussein Rai Puri's *Hum Safar* (1996). Jahanara's book is by no means her first written text. As mentioned earlier, she started to write in 1906 in Urdu language papers and magazines. Her work *Husn Ara Begum* first serialized in a women's magazine *Khatoon*, was later published as a book under the same title in 1915.³² Like some of Shafik's writings, this work attempts to construct and appeal to "The New Woman". Jahanara wrote extensively for different organizations in which she had membership; she also wrote speeches both for her father and on her own behalf. She used both Urdu and English to write, basing her choice on the context.

Hamida Akhtar Hussein's autobiography, is her first writing attempt, as mentioned earlier. She writes only in Urdu. Since this text came out, she has written and published a children's book, which contains stories she was told by her mother and grandmother; has finished a second autobiographical book as sequel to *Hum Safar*; and is considering a cookbook of recipes from Hyderabadi kitchens. Two of these four texts deal with what are considered "women's subjects" – children and food. In my interview with her, Hamida said these themes allowed her to pay homage to women in her family and surroundings.

Several factors are noteworthy: the fact that each of these women should write autobiographically, a form of self-identification often considered forbidden to women of their generation; that both women wrote their autobiographies at least in part, as homage to significant men in their lives – Jahanara to her father, Hamida to her husband; and that both wrote these texts *after* the death of these men; last, that despite this overarching framing and acknowledgement of men in their lives, there is a clear recognition of the significance of women's contributions not only to this world of men, but also in their own right. The sheer act of writing autobiographically itself serves to bring the authors – these women – themselves to the center, even though this center may be shared. The autobiographical form therefore serves as a vehicle for self representation but not as in *masculinist* autobiographies. I use the term masculinist deliberately to denote a type of writing that constructs the self as autonomous agent, stripped of any historical/experiential baggage which comes into existence precisely by severance from the past and prior connections and influences.

It could be argued that this gesture which includes an acknowledgement of male influences in their lives, reflects the continued hold of patriarchal norms. Alternatively we could posit that such narration celebrates the debts one accumulates in life and recognizes their contribution to, and hence the circularity rather than linearity, and indeed the contradictoriness of self formation rather than celebrating and creating the "heroic" self. Rather than a simple narrative of progress, we thus have a narrative of ambiguity that lies at the heart of this (auto)-biographical style, and which may be more accurately reflective of "lives lived in the transition" especially for those on the margins of that transition. The gendered self here is seen as not born in isolation but in context, therefore always embedded in social relations and history.

Hamida's text remains more faithful to this non-linear narrative than does Jahanara's. It is striking in the latter's work how she comes to stand on her own and stake out her own positions in the aftermath of the deaths of her father and her first husband. This raises the question whether this re-inscribes a masculinist voice, or whether instead, we might see it as a coming to voice of the author precisely because of the removal of patriarchal barriers in her personal life? The latter is as plausible a conclusion as the former.

The actual languages and the idiom in which each of the two women write also deserves mention. Jahanara wrote her autobiography in English, although she was capable of writing it in Urdu. And she writes in a style that is fairly conventional using references to family archives and government records to substantiate her position and assertions. Hamida Akhtar on the other hand, writing in Urdu, writes not in a formal literary Urdu style but in an oral, story telling style. The mode of writing is totally unconventional in terms of Urdu autobiographical writing and gives more weight to her voice, without necessarily giving her an authoritative voice. Thus, while Jahanara attempts to move to the center positing an objectively constructed autobiography relying on "scientific evidence", Hamida remains comfortable on the margins.

Their difference in style perhaps reflects their respective aspirations to power, and different dimensions of power. It also problematizes a simple understanding between the construction of power, and the relationship and struggles surrounding voice and power. Thus Jahanara, through the form she adopts – writing in English, using archives, dates, "scientific" evidence – might be seen to draw closer to a privileged voice and therefore engaged in an attempt to grasp power at its center. Hamida, on the other hand, by her refusal to write in a formal, literary Urdu style, eschews any attempt to gain currency through formalistic literary devices. Instead, by retaining the voice of orality and the vernacular, generally associated with women and other marginals, she continues to stay outside the mainstream, but to enhance for us, the readers, a certainty that what we are listening to is indeed her voice. She demonstrates by her writing, that to gain voice does not necessarily signify the ability or even desire to usurp power in a hegemonic sense.[33]

The use of language reflects each woman's particular biography and experiences. Hamida grew up in an environment where Urdu was a highly regarded form of literary expression, and remained immersed in it all her life, both as a young single woman, after marriage, and even following widowhood. The circle of friends with whom she socialized and continues to do so, are largely literary figures, and have included both Hindus and Muslims, but more often prominent Urdu writers. Her choice of Urdu as the language of her autobiography reflects this history. But it does more than simply mimic it: the fact that she chooses to write in a vernacular style speaks to her desire to retain her own voice rather than simply reproduce the literary voice that reverberated in her home.

Jahanara, on the other hand, studied in a English-medium school. This and her public political experience may have something to do with her desire to write her autobiography in English rather than Urdu. It may also reflect her desire to have a readership that was not simply local. However, the fact that English was still the dominant language institutionally in Pakistan when she wrote, as well as being the language of the elites, definitely suggests a different agenda and readership than that which Hamida Akhtar envisioned.[34]

Struggles over language, linguistic domination and shifts therein are telling: by the time Hamida Akhtar wrote *Hum Safar*, Pakistani society had taken a definitive turn culturally from English to Urdu; and while not suggesting that this was why Hamida Akhtar chose to write in this language, the fact of her doing so gives her both greater access and currency in the nineteen nineties. This suggests a need to problematize the relationship between language, authenticity and hegemony; and the need to see their connection as historically constructed and variable rather than as ahistorical and static. This awareness needs to be held in mind alongside issues of readership and power alluded to earlier.

Another matter of form in the two texts is the play with visual images. Jahanara's book uses none except on the front cover which has a photograph of her and her father taken in London in 1930. She is wearing what looks like a sari, khusas on her feet, a fur trimmed coat, and has her hair covered.³⁵ The spine has a portrait of her alone. On the back cover are newspaper clippings which laud her political contributions. In Hamida Akhtar's book, on the other hand, there are eight pages of photographs, which are like a family album, starting with her husband and his family. She, her family and friends come towards the end of this album. In none of the photographs does she have her hair covered. On the back cover is a striking portrait of her as a young woman.

These visual images demonstrate a mix between convention and crossing of boundaries: in Jahanara's case, a shift from her close attachment to her father (front cover) to the political reception of her own work and contributions (back cover). In Hamida's case no simple reading is possible either. The choice of her portrait as an attractive young woman cannot be simply read as a nostalgia for the past on the part of an elderly woman, but must be seen also as pride in one's looks and singularity. Which of the two women's choices of photographs are more "feminist" and which more "traditional"? There is no straightforward answer, which suggests that perhaps the problem resides with that mode of questioning itself.

Jahanara Shahnawaz's *Father and Daughter* is interesting in both its title and choice by which the author names herself. The book's title suggests her tutelage at her father's hands; and that it is not a complete accounting of her life, only of her political life. Part of her life remains cloistered, secluded from view. The name chosen for the author with the appellation Begum, like the cover photo, posits a relational self: a self named through marriage.

Furthermore, the text itself moves from these relations (in which both husbands play a very marginal role) to an emphasis in the last third of the book, on her apart from these relations. The family remains important but now in the form of her daughter, and the extended 'tribe' of Arains from which Jahanara came.³⁶

The title *Hum Safar* for Hamida's book can be roughly translated as 'fellow traveller' or 'companion'. It is a reference to the closeness between the author and her husband. The title highlights the 'companionate' marriage that Hamida experienced unlike Jahanara, whose marriage was arranged for her by the men of her household.[37] However, the text disallows a straightforwardly 'positive' reading of marriage 'by choice' by pointing to the contradictions in the marital relationship and the coming to awareness of the author of these only as she sits down to write this, her self expression, rather than simply her autobiography. In her introductory chapter she states, "As I started re-living my past I better began to understand Akhtar and my own weaknesses and strengths in depth" (Rai Puri 1996: 11). The writing of the autobiography thus illumines what had been unseen and unremarked upon before.

The chapters in Jahanara's autobiography are in the following sequence: "The early years"; "Towards the emancipation of women and the country's freedom"; "The Lonely Furrow"; "The Constituent Assembly and Democracy"; and the final chapter: "The Philosophic Mind". Throughout Jahanara links her personal life to her political one; the two seem seamless and interwoven. This raises the question: is this the way she experienced her life or is this a deliberate narration accentuating its political rather than personal dimensions? And what does this tell us of her understanding, and construction of the relationship between the two domains of the political and personal?

Her introductory chapter makes a direct link between her life as a child growing up in a very politicized family, the historical times in which she lived (the struggle for freedom from colonialism and also minority rights for Muslims), her desire to see women as active participants in the political process, and her own sense of destiny as a significant public/political figure. She writes (in a voice that is reminscent of Shafik's):

> The annual sessions of the Educational Conference were held in one of the capitals of the provinces ... . Father and other young members of the family would attend them ... . In the early years of the century, as a child of six or seven, I used to dream of the day when women would be allowed to attend such gatherings and even address them, and I would picture the moment when I would have a chance to make my speech to the Conference ...
>
> (Shahnawaz, op. cit.: 5)

In this chapter there is evidence of the contradictory character and influences of modernity on the young Jahanara. She grew up in a segregated but not a cloistered household. In her childhood, only men of her family and class moved freely in public spaces; women relied on them for news of the outside world. But there is mention as well of women in the public domain who served as role models, including Sarojini Naidu, the famous poet and feminist/nationalist activist. The twin influences of Jahanara's mother and father are mentioned in this context, alluding to the fact that her mother was among a new generation of women, active in public life even though in seclusion.

Education is a key motif: Quranic, Urdu, and English. The former two were undertaken under female influence (mothers, aunts), the latter under the guidance of her maternal grandfather. This suggests that women of an earlier generation in her household did not have access to English education, but were trained to read and write Urdu and Arabic; women's education was seen as a social 'good' in their social and class circles; last, a shift was already underway where education in more than the local languages was being impressed on those who could afford it, whether by formal or informal means; and in this effort both men and women participated. It was this emphasis on women's education which led Jahanara to write and publish an article on the topic in 1906, which was published in the journal *Tehzib i Niswan*.[38] This mention of a prior generation of women to whom the young Jahanara looked up to occurs several times in the text. It is revealing that this community of women is multi-religious: Hindu, Muslim, Christian; and also multi-national: British, Indian and even Middle Eastern. Thus, while national politics increasingly turns sectarian in religious terms (with communal riots breaking out and more and more Muslims, including her father, being firmly committed to a Muslim national politics), the women continue to provide a very different example until late into the anti-colonial struggle. As mentioned, the All India Women's Conference to which Jahanara belonged included women from all communities resident in India regardless of race, religion, nationality. Jahanara continued her membership in it until the eve of independence even though her nationalist politics took her towards the Muslim League.

The one area in which the rosy picture of familial life that Jahanara paints breaks down pertains to her marriage. She makes it clear that men (her father and maternal grandfather) made the decisions: following her maternal aunt's death, Jahanara was betrothed to this aunt's widower husband, much older than herself, but approved of by her maternal grandfather and father. This incident, along with the coming out of 'purdah' at the behest of her father, show the experience of modernity and its tensions.[39] The arranged marriage itself is hedged in her favor by her family's insistence that she stay with them until twenty (with her husband) and be able to continue her education as long as possible (which turns out to be until 1913 – a year after the birth of her first daughter).

In the narrative of her early years, Jahanara enacts a silence of sorts – there is mention of her husband's breakdown (alluded to as having been caused by a series of consecutive deaths in his family), and her dedicated (and single handed) nursing him back to health. This breakdown seems to be pivotal in the text but we are given little detail. Does this reluctance to elaborate reflect one of the taboos that exist in writing her life? Is it a concession to patriarchal norms or a deliberate and conscious attempt to maintain privacy?

In her second chapter which links women's emancipation and the country's freedom in its title, little mention is in fact made of women's emancipation. Instead, the chapter elaborates her father's political career, the political twists and turns of anti-colonial politics including the emergence of Muslim separatist politics. The chapter seems to reflect her desire to exonerate her father from charges against him as separatist and sectarian. It ends with mention of his death and her ensuing bereavement.

In this chapter and the next, she takes great pains to demonstrate that Muslim politics did not necessarily mean anti-Hinduism but rather the protection of minority rights. In this regard, she mentions Nahas Pasha of Egypt's assurance to the Copts of their rights (by giving them a blank paper signed by him) as a way of guaranteeing their participation in the nationalist cause:

Nahas Pasha, by working in this manner, won the confidence of the minorities in Egypt and gave them the impetus to fight for the freedom of their motherland side by side with the majority community. Muslims were asking for majority rights in the provinces of the Punjab and Bengal, only which was their due, and were prepared to accept even bare majorities. The Hindus should have said 'by all means, have it' and by so doing they would have won the confidence of the Muslims. Statesmanship meant winning the confidence of each and all by generosity and by the acceptance of their legitimate claims.

(Shahnawaz, op. cit.: 131)

She also stresses that her own work for women and municipal rights for all communities (during her term as Municipal Commissioner) won her support from all religious groups. This issue of minorities continues to inform her politics even after independence.[40]

In this third chapter her statement that she "had to fight a lonely battle throughout the rest of my life" (ibid.: 144) is striking. She suggests that she continued in political life as a gesture towards her father. But ironically it is after the death of her father that she begins to discuss women's representation more systematically and at greater length.

Under the 1935 Constitution, the British Government had conceded provincial autonomy, with a parliamentary system resembling the British system. Entering politics in her own right, and asked what she saw as the aim of her work in the legislatures, she replied:

We women had realized very early in our work of general advancement that, unless women entered the sphere of legislative work, it would not be possible for them to achieve economic independence and emancipation.

(Ibid.: 160-161)

She thus establishes a link, like Doria Shafik, between political representation and women's emancipation. It is also striking that she continues to draw strength from other women, using the collective "we women" as her figure of speech.

There is also an interesting shift in Jahanara's perspective as her exposure to Europe and European social relations deepens. She starts as an admirer of the material advances in European society while commenting on what she sees as their lack of spirituality and reflectiveness. (She tells us that she was always drawn to Islamic mysticism.) Later, as her familiarity with both England and the U.S. intensified, she notes with surprise that most women went to either 'finishing' or vocational schools rather than going on for university education, especially in Britain (ibid.: 170). This remarks indicates the earlier assumption of an existence, in the West, of equality in men and women's education and occupational pursuits. This practice is not critiqued; rather, Jahanara comments on such an educational model as worthy of emulation in the Indian context:

> I remember asking a young girl from a rich family, whose home was at Oxford, which university she would be joining. She had passed the London Matriculation examination rather well, but she looked at me and said: 'I am not a blue stocking, why should I join a college? I have been admitted to a finishing school.' Blue stockings were those who did not have much chance of getting married. The finishing schools were more like the Home Economics Schools and as no institutions of that type existed in our country, I knew that this all-important question had to be taken in hand immediately ... .
>
> In my speeches or otherwise talking to the Minister concerned during 1937-38, I tried my best to draw attention to the forming of a new policy for education, which should be organized like the pattern of a carpet, so that boys and girls belonging to every cadre of society could be fitted into it and there would be no armies of intellectuals roaming about in the streets. I pointed out ... that the weeding out of children should begin from the age of eleven onwards, when the primary course finished.
>
> (Ibid.: 171-172)

Should this recommendation be seen as a form of cultural "borrowing" or in fact a hybrid practice that combines local institutions and interests with forms adopted from outside that reinforce, in this instance, particular notions of meritocracy, class privilege and women's emancipation?

Jahanara's international travels increased after her husband's death in 1938, and brought her not only in contact with the "West" but also other parts of the "East" and "South". These travels brought exchanges with others in Sudan, South Africa, Egypt, and also enabled her later to use the knowledge gained through these travels in her struggle for women's rights. The 'borrowings' or hybridity therefore, did not simply occur in relationship to one part of the world, but represented a broader spectrum of north, south, east and west; and in all instances, the ideas and practices sought to be emulated were selectively appropriated.

Throughout, we witness Jahanara's struggle between three elements: gender (her own brand of feminism), nationalism (Hindu/Muslim unity and/or minority rights), and class/quom distinctions. The latter is the least problematized of the three elements especially before Independence; the other two remain vexed and contradictory both in her discussions of them and in her practical and everyday politics around them. There is also evidence of an increasing "feminist" stance on her part which is reflected in greater outspokenness and independence in political positions and criticisms, greater persistence on behalf of women and lesser compromises being made, and fewer and fewer references to men as influencing her decisions. Thus, in discussing events after the creation of Pakistan, she briefly mentions marrying a relative in 1948. Her comment on this event runs as follows:

> He [her new husband] had been educated at Oxford and was fond of my children. It was mutually agreed that I should retain my earlier name.
> (Ibid.: 236, parantheses added)

This decision to retain her previous name suggests her increasing agency not only in her public/political life, but now also in her private one. And it is an interesting fact that these developments occur only after the deaths of her father and first husband, and the achievement of national independence from colonial rule.

It is also significant that her daughter rather than any male figure comes to inform her post-independence politics. There is continuity here: Jahanara retains her familial loyalties, while simultaneously strengthening her concrete connections with women. Her daughter Tazi's last words to her before she died in a plane crash while still a young thirty were: "Please, mother, remember the new State must be a progressive Muslim State and you must never forget to work for it" (ibid.: 240).

Jahanara took this advice to heart. Her discussion of post partition politics contains severe criticisms of the restrictions on democracy, with respective regimes and political figures making concessions to the

ʿulama. She posits the debates over the Constitution as ones in which the new political leadership compromised opportunistically; whereas she stood her grounds and kept up the demand for a democratic system with adult suffrage for all including minorities and women. She mentions the achievement of adult suffrage soon after independence in 1947, but because of fears stemming from prejudice against women among the (male) electorate, asked for reserved seats until such time as they could become an established part of the elected political system. Throughout the process of Constitution formation, she continued to insist on linking issues of democracy and women's rights and representation. In foreign policy she advocated neutrality vis-à-vis the super powers, arguing that:

> I pointed out that friendship with the neighboring Powers was essential for our very existence. In the world, the two systems were at loggerheads with each other and our ideology, for which we had made such tremendous sacrifices, believed in neither. We had a precious philosophy of our own, therefore it was all the more reason that we should take the best of both other ideologies.
> (Ibid.: 255-256)

Here too, she was to take a more balanced approach towards both India, and the capitalist and socialist blocs, compared to the bulk of her male political counterparts in the liberal mainstream.[41] Not only that, her position stems not from a "western" political philosophy but what she calls "a precious philosophy of our own", alluding to her own interpretation of an Islamic framework which guaranteed democratic rights for all. A "modernist" Islamic philosophy if you will.

On women's rights, she critiques the premier women's organization created after independence – the All Pakistan Women's Association – which she charges with having abandoned its earlier commitment to all women, only to become the stronghold of elite women, especially those connected with officialdom. She also criticizes state sponsored feminism as dangerous given the state's increasingly anti-democratic stance. She felt the top-down control in APWA was a threat to women's abilities to "secure … their rightful place as equal citizens with men" (ibid.: 268). The state was hijacking the women's movement and doing so through infiltrating women's organizations, and corruption of the electoral process (ibid.: 283-295).

There is an increasing pessimism in her writing:

> Did democracy ever function in Pakistan? No, never. A handful of persons had captured power and they were continuing to rule. If one of them was not a success in one office, he was given another … . The unwarranted delay in framing the Constitution, and not letting real democracy come into being in the country had led to all these difficulties … . Had the Constitution been drafted and enforced in 1952, where might the country be today!
>
> (Ibid.: 301)

Upon losing the democratic struggle even before the declaration of Martial law in 1956, she retired from official political life. This is a woman who, with little formal education, rose to participate in parliamentary politics both during the colonial period and after, was a champion of women's rights (in a way that shifted in definition and scope over time), spoke and wrote eloquently on Constitution building, and who finally left politics when she saw the possibilities for democratic rule collapse, living out her days in self imposed political exile. The title of the final chapter bears a reminder: "The Philosophic Mind" – but here this philosophic mind is not devoted, as in Doria Shafik's case, to philosophy or inner reflection but to a musing on the failure of democracy. The text and even her philosophical concerns remain political to the very end of this narrative. We are never permitted to see within.

Hamida Akhtar Hussein provides us a very different model/picture. Born in 1918, she grew up in a very different personal environment from either Doria Shafik or Jahanara Shahnawaz, although all three women shared a similar historical time. Here is a woman who was never active in any form of public politics, feminist or otherwise. Yet her text itself represents voice and a concerted (albeit occasionally masked) journey into (public) self representation. This becomes evident not only in the substance of her autobiography but also in its entirely different mode of expression and self-enunciation. In the discussion that follows of *Hum Safar* more attention will be paid to issues of form, of language and voice, and only secondarily will other substantive themes raised in the text be considered.

Hamida raises issues of form, language and voice herself, at the very outset. Her first chapter, entitled *Dilki Baat* (literally: heart talk; figuratively: inner dialogue) directly discusses her inability to write; but it also suggests that writing for her has to be from the heart: it has to be intuitive, subjective, 'honest'. No claims here to universality, objectivity, or generalization. She links this inability to write to her awe of her (writer) husband, a sentiment that barred her from 'coming to voice': [42]

Spending my life with Akhtar, I kept a lock on my tongue [can also be read 'voice'] because his aura always loomed over me. I always thought myself inferior and looked up to him ... . When Akhtar finished having his life story written and I read it, I wanted to expose what he had left unsaid ... but I didn't dare ... (parantheses added).

When a family friend advises her following her husband's death to write down their life together as a form of solace, narrating it as if she were speaking to a friend, she responds "I don't have pen or paper" (Rai Puri, op.cit.: 9). When informed by the same friend that he will provide both she writes: "I found his innocence amusing as if I could write simply upon his sending me pens; I who had never even written a line and had no courage to" (ibid.).

This dissimulation is frequent and yet countered constantly in this text. Claiming her lack of courage to write, she nonetheless writes – this is after all *her* text. Yet she waits until after her husband's death, to come 'to voice', and this too in a form uniquely her own.

Not surprisingly, it takes a woman friend – a writer herself – to get her past the initial barrier. Upon informing this friend of her promise (to her husband's friend) to write combined with her inability to do so, this friend – a well known Pakistani poet, Fehmida Riaz – prompts her to simply 'speak' the images she sees in her mind's eye; and when Hamida does so, Fehmida writes down her words. This is the inception of writing. The imagery is that of film (a series of images in front of her eyes) and the form that of story telling, that is, orality. The age of the writer when she enters into this journey is seventy two.

Hamida is fully aware of the form and style of her writing. When she receives back comments from the family friend who got her started on this project, she muses over his comments on her language, which he praised "despite" its vernacular form:

> I went into deep thought – on what he had written. In the recesses of my mind was the [idea] that such language was spoken in streets and alleys. [But] ... I would keep writing ... [about] the happiest days of my life.
>
> (Ibid.: 10)

There are numerous transgressions in this text. Among them those already mentioned: writing in the vernacular, in spoken not in literary form; not only writing, but publishing this (auto)biography, and following that up with more writing. But other transgressions abound as well. The first one we are made aware of, is her secret communication and courtship with Akhtar, whom she later married. We are told of the liberal background she grew up in, and her decision, against her mother's explicit desire, to marry Akhtar. She may not be a rebel; but neither is she voiceless.

This person, who tells us that she was always in awe of her husband, makes it clear that from the very beginning of her marriage she transgressed some of the 'rules' of the all-male household into which she moved after marriage, and slowly subverted others. We are made aware of her subjectivity – not as a victim this, but as an active agent – who manages to turn a very difficult situation around through struggle. There is a double-play on agency here: her autobiographical narration of certain contexts which reveal her subjectivity to the reader plus her self consciousness awareness of doing so in this autobiographical project. This mode of representation calls into question her 'lack' of voice that she had alluded to earlier. We, the readers, are made aware, that the writer saw things clearly even when she did not overtly speak/challenge them. And we are informed as well, that the sheer act of writing has opened her gaze even further. This book serves as solace, it honors her husband, and simultaneously it constitutes an expose, an exorcism, a speaking of things that were hitherto unsaid, unspoken and expected to remain so. It is a lifting of taboos – self imposed and/or socially sanctioned. And in a literary ploy which also plays on memory as 'truth' the writer is 'forced' to speak those things that could not (previously) be said, inferring that she is speaking the truth. This is a very different mode of verification than the one adopted by Jahanara: the latter's bases its appeal on scientific values, Hamida's on moral grounds.

This book then, in its subtext, subverts it own explicit narrative: to serve as solace and to honor her husband. Indeed, these two explanations become alibis for Hamida's writing of herself through a focus on the everyday, the local, and the particular, that which only she knows. She is the holder of secrets; it is she who reveals them; and ultimately, it is she who is at the center of this story telling.

Historically Constituted Subjectivities

It is my contention that Jahanara Shahnawaz and Hamida Akhtar Hussein represent their respective times, their socio-economic backgrounds, and individual agency. Hamida, born several decades after Jahanara in a house where seclusion is not practiced strictly, in a literary family and milieu, takes education and its benefits for granted. This does not prevent her, like Jahanara, from leaving her education at an early age, to get married. Unlike Jahanara, however, her marriage represents a new form of arrangement, in which she has an active decision making role.

Oddly though, it may be this very fact that prevents Hamida from taking a public political stand either in the nationalist movement or in women's circles. The very liberalism that is so much a part of her life, may also explain the 'private' nature of her struggles. (These struggles were private in a dual sense: they largely revolved around her familial relationships; and they were kept private until the writing of her autobiography.)

What links the two women is their increased vocality upon finding themselves without the men whom they were closest to. For Jahanara, this means the death of her father first and later that of her husband. For Hamida, it is her husband's death that unlocks her voice and mind publicly. The former, however, links her voice to issues of democracy, human rights and women's struggles. Hamida, on the other hand, is engaged in a very solitary struggle – one that is primarily hers alone.

These experiences and texts call into question any linear reading of modernity and/or its accompanying languages. They suggest that difference, multiplicity, and hybridity reside both within modernity and among its 'discontents', and only a focus on the particular-cum-historical can reveal the full range of possibilities and struggles. They also emphasize the "negotiated" self crossing boundaries of the old and new and in the process itself creating "the modern".

Conclusion

The lives and works of these three women represent the various voices of struggle and its modalities. Women's struggles must be seen and analyzed in terms of their multiplicity and hybridity. In most discussions feminism is represented as if it were constituted of one set of assumptions. The possibilities of different feminists speaking across boundaries to and with each other whether this be across cultural and social boundaries or across cultural, social and historical boundaries are closed off and hence lead theorists to speak of "western" or "eastern" or "Muslim feminism". Thinking in these global categories does not allow the theorizing of the different and various forms of feminism. The criticism that any feminist/women's struggle is a western import (a critique often made against Doria Shafik) eclipses the fact that each of these three women has a particular history that creates her particular feminist struggle.

The processes of globalization do not necessarily lead to homogenization of feminist struggles towards one universal goal or even along a single path to that goal. But on the contrary create particular historical realities and cultural contexts within which women are socialized including their socialization into different languages through which their struggles are articulated. Assia Djebar has presciently understood the process of writing women's lives:

Here, then, is a listening in, by means of which I try to grasp the traces of some ruptures that have reached their term. Where all I could come close to were such voices as are groping with the challenge of beginning solitudes.
(Djebar 1992: 1)

It has been through our focus on the experiential and biographical lives of these three women that we have been able to illuminate how each woman's confrontation with modernity generates different forms of struggle and ways of speaking.

This excursion also calls into question the meaning of the notion of authenticity. What is often proffered as "indigenous" or "authentic" by many writers on the indigenization of knowledge culture is often a fixed, almost naturalized notion of authenticity. Our paper suggests much more complicated, shifting, and multiple meanings to the term. This reading is made possible by our methodological stance which proceeds from the epistemological premise that "the everyday world is problematic" thus enabling us to move beyond formulaic debates based on a priori categories that are assumed to be universal as to what is or is not authentic.

We are talking about the consequences of a silence, an absence, a non presence. What is there – spoken, sung, written, made emblematic in art – and treated as general, universal, unrelated to a particular position or a particular sex as its source and standpoint, is in fact partial, limited, located in a particular position and permeated by special interests and concerns.

(Smith 1987: 20)

The lives of the women who are the focus of this paper together traverse nearly a century of globalization (read modernity), a period that brackets and frames their particular encounters with colonialism, nationalism, and post coloniality. Each life represents a struggle to grapple with the contradictions created by these broader historical transitions. We who read these lives are forced to ask whether the contradictions we note are internal to each self or externally imposed by those others whose vested interests preclude a recognition and tolerance of the multiplicity and hybridity of identities produced by the uneven processes of change brought about by globalization.

Given the issues of partiality and positionality raised above, it is highly problematic to talk about globalization without gendering it and its accompanying processes. This is not to simplistically suggest that women as a category are uniformly positioned in relationship to globalization. We are not replacing one universalizing stance with another. The differences even within women highlighted by the tracing out of the lives of these three women not only demonstrate the centrality of the experiential standpoint but underscore the significance of the local and particular context of those experiences. The differences between Doria Shafik and Jahanara Shahnawaz demonstrate our point. On the one hand they both articulate the necessity of human rights and democracy as essential to women's achieving full equality, albeit each of them used different mechanisms to argue and carve out her position. On the other hand, the reception of their voices within society was vastly different. India was under direct British colonial rule; contrarily, in Egypt, although there was a significant British colonial presence, given its protectorate status, Doria's fight for women's political representation brought her into a direct confrontation not with the British, who operated behind the scenes, but rather with the male native ruling elite. Therefore, Doria's struggle was seen as a form of betrayal of "authentic", local concerns, whereas identical concerns on the part of Jahanara and Indian women activists were seen as entirely legitimate and supported by the majority of Indian male nationalists.

This coming to voice on the part of each of these women takes sharply different forms. Unlike the previous example where the historical times and context effect the way their voices are heard, the actual forms their voices take, reflect much more the particular encounters and responses to the times. The voices of Doria Shafik combine the forms of the political/poetic/philosophical, while Hamida Akhtar Hussein's utilizes the style and the form of the vernacular with an emphasis on detail and the everyday. Jahanara unlike these two women exposes very little of her innermost self in her writing. Her inner subjective self is always subsumed under public/political issues. These differences in form are not arbitrary: their voices reflect the shifting character of their struggles over time. Therefore voice must be seen as intimately related to the trajectories of their lives and not as an abstraction. With Doria Shafik we witness the transformation of the voice of external challenge to the voice of interior music, both reflective of a different struggle. With Jahanara Shahnawaz we see an increasingly self confident voice as she turns from the tutelage and oversight by (male) guardians, to an assertive and self conscious critique of existing power structures and authoritative political figures. For Hamida whose writing comes very late in her life, following the death of her husband, writing becomes a way of coping with solitude and also a form of unveiling. Among all three women there is reflected this real sense of the solitary self brought on by quite different lived experiences. However in their works we detect a common theme that choosing to write is a conscious act of resistance – against silence, taboos, forced incarceration. The very act of writing becomes a mode of self liberation. Writing for each of them is more than more than about a cause, it is also about self definition, self exploration and survival.

We might ask, what then is the relation between coming to voice and power? There is an assumption in the very term globalization that suggests that we are 'one village' and therefore more and more coming to speak with one voice. Such an assumption masks and mutes the different voices not only within individuals but also between them. This is not to conclude that the processes of globalization must end 'in a tower of Babel' but to assume a gendered standpoint that allows us to practice a critical reflexivity along the lines suggested by Assia Djebar when she writes:

Don't claim to 'speak for' or, worse, to 'speak on', barely speaking next to, and if possible very close to: these are the first of the solidarities to be taken on.

(Djebar, op. cit.: 2)

Notes

1 See Nelson (1996) for an in-depth account of Shafik's life.
2 In the French doctoral system, one is required to write two theses. Her primary thesis was *L'Art pour L'Art dans L'Égypte Antique* (Art for Art's Sake in Ancient Egypt) and her secondary thesis was *La Femme et Le Droit Religieux de L'Égypte Contemporaine* (Women and Religious Rights in Contemporary Egypt). Both published by Paul Geuthner, Paris: 1940.
3 *al-Kitab al-Abiyad li Huquq al-Mar'ah al-Siyasiyah*, 1953 (The White Book on the Political Rights of Women); *Rihlati Hawla al-'Alam*, 1955 (My Trip Around the World). Co-authored with Ibrahim Abdu, *Tatawwur al-Nahda al-Nisa'iyah fi Misr*, 1945 (The Development of the Renaissance of Women in Egypt); and *al-Mar'ah al-Misriyah min al-Fara'niah ila al-Yawm*, 1955 (The Egyptian Woman from the Pharaohs Until Today).
4 During her world tour following her 1954 hunger strike she met the Prime Ministers of India, Ceylon, Lebanon and Pakistan; she publicly chastised the president of Pakistan for taking a second

wife; she lectured to audiences in Europe, the United States, South Asia as well as the Middle East on women's issues in the Arab world.

5   For purposes of this paper, I am focusing primarily on her French writings. Those works she did publish in Arabic were co-authored with Ibrahim Abdu and hence it is not clear whose voice is really speaking. All excerpts taken from the French are translated by Nelson.

6   Princess Chevikar (1873-1947) married Fuad in the mid 1890s, long before he had any pretensions to the throne. Spoilt and capricious, Chevikar was as well born as her husband and considerably richer. Their marriage nearly cost Fuad his life. As a young man Fuad was an impoverished playboy who owed money everywhere. His Italian upbringing had given him a taste for gambling and mistresses, but he had very old fashioned ideas about the seclusion of Muslim women, and Chevikar resented deeply being kept in the harem from morning until night. Chevikar gave birth to their only son in 1896, who died in infancy. After the birth of her second child, Princess Fawkieh, she decided she could no longer bear her husband's violent temper and finicky habits, and returned to her family in Constantinople. Her husband got her back, as he was entitled to do under Muslim law; but Chevikar had an elder brother, Prince Sayf al-Din, who swore to deliver her from this tyrant. On 7 May, 1898, Sayf al-Din rushed up the stairs of the Khedival Club, found Fuad in the Silence Room, and shot him several times before anybody could stop him. Fuad was so badly wounded that his doctors decided to operate then and there on the floor. They took a bullet from his ribs and another from his thigh, but one lodged in his throat was too near an artery to be removed. From that day until his death, the future Sultan/King of Egypt was left with a permanent disability in his speech described as a high spasmodic bark. Fuad divorced Chevikar and the criminal court committed her brother to a mental asylum in Ticehurst, Sussex near Tunbridge Wells where he stayed for nearly 20 years. Many years and several husbands later Chevikar, having inherited an enormous fortune, returned to Egypt, where she focused her attention on the young King Farouk. She died in 1947 at which time Doria Shafik took complete control of *La Femme Nouvelle*.

7   The terms "feminine expression" and "feminist expression" are indeed problematic terms. Fenoglio-Abd al-Aal (1988) finesses the dilemma by employing the term feminist "to designate everything that attempts to disengage the woman from behavior that is obliged, defined and imposed from the exterior, that is to say everything that revolves around the woman in whatever way without engaging her in a liberating commitment" (p. 32). In the context of this paper I accept the ambiguity that the Arabic term, *nisa'iyya* conveys. It carries the double meaning of feminist and feminine and its was perhaps this ambiguity that allowed Doria Shafik to define her own position on the terms by stating: "Our feminism is totally feminine."

8   Ibrahim Abdu, a close friend of her husband Nour al-Din Ragai, established the first department of journalism at Cairo University and because of his expertise helped to found, along with Doria and Nour, the *Bint al-Nil* magazine. Because his Arabic was much stronger than Doria's, he often helped her write the editorials. At the beginning, while she was learning the trade so to speak, she often deferred to his more conservative views.

9   Personal communication March 31, 1985. Also see Khalifa, *al-Haraka*, 1973: pp. 173-176.

10 Refers to the right of the husband to force his wife to return to his house through the use of police force if necessary.

11 There is strong evidence that these specific excerpts were taken from an earlier work by Abdal-Wahab (n.d.).

12 From a lecture delivered at a conference on "Images of the Other in Contemporary Literature" held at Cairo University, December 1994.

13 Pierre Seghers published a series he entitled *Poésie*. It also included the poetry of the French surrealists Paul Eluard, Tristan Tzara, Louis Aragon, as well as the short books of verse by Lewis Carroll and Henry Miller.

14 "Adieu à Pierre Seghers", *Le Monde*, November 7, 1987. "La poésie vient de perdre son amoureux le plus fervent, son défenseur le plus actif ... Il convient encore de rappeler que Seghers fut aussi et d'abord poète de l'élan et de la passion."

15 Personal interview, September 10, 1986. Paris, France.

16 Personal letter, October 1956.

17 Personal interview, September 10, 1986.
18 Personal interview, September 10, 1986. These later works to which he refers are *Larmes d'Isis* and the four volumes comprising *Avec Dante Aux Enfers*.
19 This biographical sketch is pieced together from several primary and secondary sources. Primary sources include interviews with family members and friends; secondary sources include Naresh Kumar Jain (1979); Sarfaraz Hussain Mirza (1981); All India Women's Conference, *Reports,* 1930-47.
20 Among Indian Muslims, at the time, there were clear demarcations into different *quoms* of which the *Arain* were one fairly large collectivity. These quoms loosely paralleled the Hindu caste system in that membership within the quom was hereditary; one's quom designation also had a bearing on one's occupation, marital arrangements which occurred, at the time, largely within one's designated quom, etc.
21 The *Muslim League* was the party which, during the colonial period in India, came to be the corporate representative of Indian Muslims, especially those living in the Muslim majority areas, and those who felt marginalized by Hindu dominated political parties, even non-sectarian ones. At the time Jahanara came to political consciousness, many Muslims were members of the Indian National Congress (INC), a non-sectarian political organization made up of Hindus, Muslims and other groups. Jahanara's father, Sir Muhammad Shafi (who was knighted by the British) remained always outside the fold of the INC.
22 It is also noteworthy that her father opted to train her as his protege rather than his elder son, or indeed any one of the male offspring in the family.
23 This organization was formed in 1926. Margaret Cousins, who was a founding member of the Women's Indian Association (WIA) was also the moving force behind AIWC's creation. According to Jahanara, the circular Cousins sent argued for its constitution on the ground that there was a need for an organization that could "achieve and safeguard the rights of women and ... work for their general advancement" (Shahnawaz, 1971: p. 92). Christian, Sikh, Hindu and Muslim women worked together in this organization, long after communal politics became a norm among many

Muslim male political figures including Jinnah, the leader of the Pakistan movement, and head of the Muslim League at the time of independence.

24 Shahnawaz, op.cit.: p. 50. It is noteworthy that this question was on the agenda of Indian Muslim women's groups very early. Though radical as a feminist demand for the time, it was one that was the norm among women activists.

25 These were a series of conferences by the name held in London by the British government to determine the status of India and the question of political representation for Indians, including the issue of decolonization. Jahanara spoke at two of the Round Table Conferences in 1930-31, 1932-33 and to its Joint Select Committee in 1934, on behalf of women and minorities.

26 This was a special designation used by the League of Nations to invite prominent figures to study and become familiar with the League's workings and practices.

27 In 1937, she was elected as member of the Punjab Legislative Assembly, and was appointed Parliamentary Secretary for Education, Medical Relief and Public Health. In 1942, she was expelled from the Muslim League when she refused to abide by its decision on a political matter. However in 1946, she was allowed back in, and was once again elected member of the Punjab Assembly. It was in this capacity that she was elected to the Constituent Assembly in 1946, as a representative to that Assembly from the Punjab. She was one of two Muslim women to serve in this capacity, both before and after independence (Mirza 1981).

28 The intellectual milieu of the time was itself imbricated in nationalist/anti-colonial politics. What I mean to stress by this distinction is not the *absence* of politics in Hamida Akhtar Hussein's household but the literary turn that such politics took.

29 Aligarh was the site of the first Muslim University to be founded in India, and an intellectual renaissance among Muslims which gave priority to education as a way of moral and social "uplift" for the community. Aligarh University produced many prominent Indian Muslim intellectuals, politicians and professionals, many of whom came to play a significant role in anti colonial and nationalist politics including cultural politics. This sketch is based on Ha-

mida Akhtar Hussein's own autobiography, interviews with her, as well as interviews with family friends.

30 *Purdah* is the Urdu term used to signify women's seclusion, segregation and/or the observance of *hijab*. Hamida never observed *purdah* in her dress, but experienced spatial separation of men and women's quarters early on in her marriage. The term *zenana* refers to women's quarters and/or domestic space. The system, as she experienced it, is not similar to the *harem* of the Middle East (also found among upper class families in the Indian subcontinent). Rather, the *zenana* in the household she moved into after marriage consisted of a spatial separation of the domestic quarters from male work places (which were in the compound of the house itself). This arrangement was not entirely dissimilar to the arrangement that existed in her natal home, although in her marital home the lines initially were much more severely drawn and seldom transgressed. In her natal home, the demarcation existed more for visitors who expected it, than for family members and close friends.

31 The term *publicly* is used cautiously here, meaning simply a formal entry into the public arena such as exposes the individual to a wider array of impersonal audiences. While utilizing this term, we remain cognizant of how one's private life may also have *public* implications and manifestations, and therefore the necessity to not reify the division between the two domains into a fixity that does not empirically exist.

32 A copy of this novella, which is primarily exhortatory to young woman, can be found in the India Record Office in London.

33 I am using the term *hegemony* here to refer to the move to domination, centering, or becoming normative.

34 One needs to highlight the times: when Hamida wrote, Urdu had become the official language of Pakistan ousting English from this spot. However, English still continues to be the language of privilege and a class marker. Her use of Urdu therefore cannot be read straightforwardly in terms of linguistic contestations and struggles between dominant/subordinate languages. What is unique of course is the vernacular, spoken style that she adopts: that remains marginalized in publications in both languages.

35 The very hybridity in clothes and style is itself striking: the *sari* is

a dress worn by Muslims and Hindus in pre-partition India; in recent Pakistani history there have been attempts to re-cast it as 'Hindu'; the *khusa* is a typically north Indian/Pakistani shoe style; the coat with fur trimming is 'western'; and the hair covering suggests a departure from purdah but a gesture to modesty.

36 Her daughter Mumtaz, whom Jahanara calls by the diminutive Tazi, was clearly a favorite child, whose early death left a definite lack in Jahanara's life. This daughter was a political activist, staunchly anti-colonialist, secular, and a gifted poet and writer. It is ironic that the second daughter, Nasim, who was also an activist – and belonged to a more left wing tradition – is not given the same recognition by Jahanara. On the issue of 'Arains', Jahanara continued to engage in a type of populist politics that bases itself in the sub-continent on familial connections. Thus her continued connection to her *quom* what she designated as 'tribe' using colonial classificatory terminology, is as much a political move as it is a familial convention.

37 It also shows the generational shift between the two women where new marital forms and possibilities had come to exist partially because of social reforms and the normativizing of the idea of "The New Woman" herself. This shift represents both a radical step and a move towards new and distinct types of gender relations not necessarily resting on liberation.

38 *Tehzib* refers to upbringing; enculturation. *Niswan* simply means women. Together the reference is to 'the new woman'.

39 It is worth considering whether this decision represents patriarchal power and authority solely, or whether it is compounded by a mixture of gender, class and *quom* restrictions. Jahanara's first husband, Shah Nawaz, was an established lawyer and well known political figure. He also belong to the same kinship group as her family. We are told in the autobiography that Jahanara favored a younger man, whom her mother also approved of, but the elder males favored her deceased aunt's widower. Following the sudden death of the younger suitor due to an illness, Jahanara tells us that she no longer cared about whom she married, and decided to let her elders have her way. It is noteworthy here that her mother is the only figure who stands by her in this matter of marital choice: the men are systematically aligned against her. It is also notewor-

thy that Jahanara nowhere acknowledges this stand on her behalf on the part of her mother as being significant, although she does narrate the various positions taken by the different actors involved (Chapter 1: "The Early Years").

40 Jahanara, while recognizing women as numerically equivalent to men, politically used their minority status (in hegemonic terms) as a way to politically ensure representation for them after independence along the same lines that she had supported for Muslims at the Third Round Table Conference in London prior to independence.

41 Jahanara's second child – another daughter – named Nasim, was an active member of the left. She and her husband, General Akbar, were both arrested in the 1951 Rawalpindi case in which several individuals were accused of criminal conspiracy to overthrow the state. It is worth asking to what extent Jahanara's foreign policy position was shared with her two daughters, Mumtaz and Nasim, both of whom espoused left-of-center positions. This question becomes all the more important because it reflects a departure in Jahanara's prior complacency regarding class privilege and its reproduction.

42 Rai Puri, op.cit.: 11. Remarks in parentheses added. The word she uses is *zubaan* which means both tongue and voice. This and all coming translations are by Rouse from the original Urdu text.

Selected Bibliography

Arabic Language

Abdal-Wahab, Muhammad Fahmi (n.d.) *Al-Harakat al-Nisa'iyya fil-Sharq wa-silatuha bi-isti'mar wa-sahyuniyya al-alimiyya* (The Women's Movement in the East and Its Connection to Colonialism and World Zionism), Cairo: Dar al-'itsam.

Al-Gohari, Muhammad Mahmoud (1980) *Al-Ikhwat al-Muslimat wa-bina al-Usrah al-Quranah* (The Muslim Sisters and the Foundation of the Muslim Family), Cairo: Dar al-Dawah, pp. 259-264.

Khalifa (1973) *al-Haraka al-Nisa'iyya al-Haditho fi Misk* (The Modern Women's Movement in Egypt), Cairo: Dar al-KUTTAB, pp. 173-176.

Urdu Language

Rai Puri, Hamida Akhtar Hussein (1996) *Hum Safar*, Karachi: Maktab DANIAL.
Shahnawaz, Jahanara (1915) *Husn ara Begum*, Lahore: Paisa Akhbar.

Western Languages

All India Women's Conference (1930-47) *Reports*.
Djebar, Assia (1992) *Women of Algiers in Their Apartments*, London, Charlottsville/VA: University of Virginia Press.
L'Égyptienne (1928) "Hors Texte". *L'Égyptienne* 52 (December).
Falk, Candace (1984) *Love, Anarchy and Emma Goldman*, New York/NY: Holt, Rinehart and Winston.
Fenoglio-Abd al-Aal, Irene (1988) *Défense et Illustration de L'Égyptienne: Aux Débuts d'une Expression Féminine*, Cairo: CEDEJ Publications.
Jain, Naresh Kumar (1979) *Muslims in India: A Biographical Dictionary* 1, New Delhi: Manohar.
Mirza, Sarfaraz Hussain (1981) *Muslim Women's Role in the Pakistan Movement*, Lahore: Research Society of Pakistan.
Moscatelli, Jean Pierre (1955) *Poètes en Égypte: Anthologie Présentée Par Jean Pierre Moscatelli*, Cairo: Les Éditions de l'Atelier.
Nelson, Cynthia (1996) *Doria Shafik. Egyptian Feminist: A Woman Apart*, Gainesville/FL: University Press of Florida.
Orizet, Jean (1987) "Adieu à Pierre Seghers". *Le Monde*, 7 November.
Sangari, Kumkum (1993) "The Politics of the Possible". In Tejaswini Niranjan/P. Sudhir/Vivek Dharesshwar (eds.) *Interrogating Modernity: Culture and Colonialism in India*, Calcutta: Seagull, pp. 264-272.
Seghers, Pierre (1978) *La Résistance et Ses Poètes*, 2 vols., Paris: Marabout Éditions.
Shafik, Doria (n.d.) *Hors Temps*. Unpublished manuscript.
—— (1928) "Un Petit Mot". *L'Égyptienne* 35 (June), pp. 12-14.
—— (1929) "L'Enfant Du Nil" (The Child of the Nile). *L'Égyptienne* 53 (December), pp. 25-27.
—— (1930) "Une Femme a-t-elle le droit de philosopher?" (Does a

Woman Have a Right to Philosophize?). *L'Égyptienne* 64 (December), pp. 18-28.

―― (1932) "Rêverie d'une Femme d'aujourd'hui" (Dream of a Woman of Today). *L'Égyptienne* 82 (November), pp. 15-19.

―― (1944) *La Femme Nouvelle en Égypte* (The New Woman in Egypt), Cairo: Schindler Press.

―― (1946) "We Want Rights Not Equality". *Bint al-Nil* 2 (January), pp. 2-5.

―― (1946) "Message to the Reader". *La Femme Nouvelle* 1 (June), pp. 3-4.

―― (1946) "Ourselves and Politics". *Bint al-Nil* 12 (November), pp. 1-2.

―― (1947) "The New Woman". *La Femme Nouvelle* 5 (December), pp. 6-8.

―― (1948) "Make Way". *Bint al-Nil* 30 (January), p. 4.

―― (1949) "La Bonne Aventure" (The Pleasant Adventure). *Poésie* 49, Paris: Pierre Seghers.

―― (1954) "L'Amour Perdu" (The Lost Love). *Poésie* 54, Paris: Pierre Seghers.

―― (1960) *French Memoirs*. Unpublished manuscript.

Shahnawaz, Jahanara (1971) *Father and Daughter: A Political Autobiography*, Lahore: Nigarishat.

Sharabi, Hisham (1987) "Cultural Critics of Arab Society". *Arab Studies Quarterly* 9/1, pp. 15-16.

Smith, Dorothy (1987) *The Everyday World as Problematic*, Boston/MA: Northeastern University Press.

Struggling and Surviving[1]:

The Trajectory of Sheikh Moubarak Abdu Fadl.

A Historical Figure of the Egyptian Left

Didier Monciaud

The chronicler who narrates events without distinguishing between big ones and small ones, takes into consideration, by doing so, the following truth: everything that has ever happened should not be considered lost for history.

(Walter Benjamin)

The objective of this study is to reconstruct the path of a particular historical actor and to locate his specific experience in the context of the period and to reflect on what it represents for his generation. Moubarak Abdu Fadl possesses a profile and a trajectory which are both rich and original. Of Nubian origin, he studied at the Islamic university of Al-Azhar, where he became a Marxist and was expelled for his political activities. He was to become a leading member of DMNL[2] until its *self-dissolution*.

Following this, he closely participated in the *invigoration* of the communist movement in Egypt. For a long time, he had served as one of its spokesmen. In 1987 he ran as a candidate for parliamentary elections. Research done on communism has tended to exhibit a preference for intellectuals and labour cadres whose social visibility led to their greater prominence. Moubarak Abdu Fadl, coming from the lowest population strata never became part of the educated middle class and the new administrative and cultural elite as did many of his fellow comrades. Both his uniqueness and his quasi absence from the historical record on the Egyptian left contribute to the fascination he holds for the biographer/historian.

The biographical emphasis helps unveil and reconstruct the underlying meanings of a life as well as the self-representation of the historical actor. Neither over nor under-estimating individual autonomy we take as our point of departure the view:

> that history is basically shaped by social forces. It results precisely from a full understanding of the fact that an infinite number of individual pressures will tend to create random movements which largely cancel each other out to the extent that they are purely individual. In order for a definite movement of history to appear – that is, for history to possess a pattern that is intelligible and not merely a meaningless succession of unconnected accidents – common aspects have to be discovered in individuals' behaviour.
> (Mandel 1986: 61-62)

The critical reinterpretation of Moubarak Abdu Fadl's itinerary is based on four interviews[3] as well as critical readings of the works on the Egyptian communist movement and political history[4]. This relocates *practice-oriented approaches*. The interest in the experience of people can help "not to distort the quality of people's subjective experiences nor isolate their consciousness from the world it perceives" (Morsy/Saad/Nelson/Sholkamy 1991: 106).

The goal here is to choose an exemplar for a particular collectivity. He is a member of a generation of Egyptian communists who can be described as *historic* although they appear on the margins of recorded history. As a result of their experience and the place they occupied in the movement, Moubarak Abdu Fadl and his generation figure as *living legends*, representing at the present time the human continuity and a part of the political memory of Egypt. Moubarak Abdu Fadl posseses characteristics as well as sharing with them a particular historical identity. Such a biography highlights uniqueness and singularity while simultaneously serving as a collective instrument of analysis of a social group. It leads us to tend to understand the subject's 'point of view' constraining a reflection of the multiple interrelations which are the bases of the production of biographical facts, including those of the scholars.

(Pudal 1991: 111-112)

The biographical method is not without certain risks: by emphasizing the individual it tends to separate the subject from the social field in which the action is taking place, while postulating the existence of a subject or a life geared towards accomplishment (Dammame 1994: 183). It also creates the illusion that life has but a single meaning (Pudal 1991: 112). The subject is also the informer. He is asked to recall, describe and discuss his own life. "He becomes the spokesman of his own history, the representative of his past, the informer on his own conduct and action" (Peneff 1994: 27). The subject, therefore, reveals some opinions but these opinions are occasioned by the presence of the interested interviewer, who is not in the least neutral. As Pollak specifies:

The location of the interview itself, like the autobiographic writing, is a point of attestation and reconstruction of identity of the person being interviewed. This shapes the preliminary negotiations of the meetings and the delimitation of the demanded writings.

(Pollak 1986: 12)

The historical time during which the subject recounts his life conditions the interpretation in a decisive manner. Numerous subjects have the tendency to mask their real personality and efface themselves behind the group. It is a matter of recounting his life in the name of a general value.

There also exists a specific discourse of interviews which can be defined as

the will to conform with the presupposed values of the interviewer, when he is himself distant from the narrator, both socially and intellectually because of his status.

(Peneff 1995: 57)

The interview can show "an idealization of the past and an exaltation of moral traditional values, as a reaction to the interviewer" (Peneff 1995: 57-58).

This essay is divided into two main parts. The first will provide a chronological trajectory of Moubarak Abdu Fadl's life. We will then focus on the foundations of such a commitment. We will study the period of the Nasserist regime, followed by a discussion of the course of Fadl's activity after the dissolution of the movement.

The study will attempt to understand the different dimensions which shaped Fadl's path through the Egyptian left. His adherence to Marxism will also be investigated by tracing how his life participates in the formation of what could be identified as a *national communism*. We will conclude with an assessment of his heritage.

Origins of a Commitment

Moubarak Abdu Fadl was born into a poor family on June 23 1927, in the village of Armima located in the Nubian section of Egypt. His father married four times and had fifteen children from two of his wives. He migrated to Cairo to work as a modest employee in the tax Service and lived in the popular neighborhoods of Boulaq, Sabteya and al-Azhar. Towards the age of eleven, Moubarak Abdu Fadl became concerned about his future, a preoccupation he shared with Nubian boys of his age. A common ideal was to remain in the village with one's family. The dream for the majority of youth of this era was to work in a city as domestic servants of rich Egyptians or foreigner families and then return to marry and settle in the village. Most of them lived in Cairo the whole year to return home only for a few weeks.

As he grew older, Fadl wanted to leave the village to work. His father at that time a servant himself thought ill of such a future for his son as he detested his own experience. He made a great effort to dissuade his sons from following the same path explaining to them that education would afford them the chance to escape such a destiny by allowing them to become civil servants.

Towards 1939, however, defective eye sight prevented Fadl from entering government school shattering his father's hopes. He rejoined his father in Cairo where he was obliged to take the only path available for someone coming from so modest a background: the al-Azhar school system. He devoted two years to memorizing the Koran before he could enter al-Azhar in 1942. His professional hopes faded, he contemplated being reduced to the functions of a Sheikh reciting the Koran at funerals. During this interim, the child who had not had the least desire for such a destiny, tried, unsuccessfully to resist his parents' will. Passing the entrance exam he joined the secondary al-Azhar school. He was grouped alongside all other Nubian students with the Sudanese in the *riwaq shamal al-Soudan* (order of north Sudan).

He recalls how much he detested wearing the Azhar uniform during these years. No sooner were the classes ended than he would quickly don his *gallabeya*. After completing the required readings, he frequently went to libraries especially *Dar al Kutub* (National Library) to devour books by contemporary authors, among them Taha Hussein, Mahmoud Abbas al-Aqqad, Tawfiq al-Hakim and also the nationalist historian Abdel Rahman al Rafi'i. In later years this academic background provided him with the title of Sheikh which he kept and by which he is known even in communist ranks.

The Nubian and Sudanese Azhari students of the third year received a monthly stipend of three pounds in addition to a government grant of one pound. Fadl gave all his salary to help his family as his father's income only totaled two pounds a month. This generosity led him to be treated with profound respect at home. Matters of great seriousness were discussed with him. One day when his father lost his salary and that of one of his friends which totaled eight pounds, Fadl helped by collecting money from among his fellow students. He attributes his political commitment to the misery and poverty experienced by him and by the majority of Nubians. His joining of al-Azhar further strengthened his sentiments as the Azharites more so than other students came from poor backgrounds. He also felt patriotic emotions at the vision of English troops in the city. This representation, to be more accurate, is characteristic of autobiographical accounts where

conforming with the telegraphic reconstruction which underlies all accounts of a life labeled as political, it is always presented as the result of a fundamental experience which affected the narrator's youth, determining his values and his cause.

(Neveu 1994: 9)

The combination of experiences within his family, his community and al-Azhar, directed his own self-questioning towards politics. Around 1944-45, he met a Nubian student who aroused his political consciousness asking him what he knew about communism. He answered that all he had heard was that communists defended the poor. The student suggested that Fadl learn more about it. He began to study Marxist theory under the tutelage of a Nubian-Sudanese. The material they used were seven reports which dealt with such topics as the sicknesses of society, development, capitalism, colonialism, socialism, the party, fascism and the war which impressed on Fadl that communism first and foremost is an orientation in favor of the disenfranchised. Eager to learn more he asked for the seven reports but was met with refusal. During the same period, he also frequented Henri Curiel's bookstore *Au Rond Point*[5]. This bookstore was inclined towards francophone and cosmopolitan audiences with progressive and Marxist materials in foreign languages. However the literature became rapidly accessible to Arabic speakers through translation, notably with a series known as the green books, referring to their cover. Fadl plunged into his first Marxist readings. A while later he entered EMNL[6].

We emphasize here that this organization was known for its mild position on the subject of religion, choosing to differentiate it from political questions. One Azharite Abdel Rahman al Thaqafi published two brochures on Islam analyzing it as a religion opposed to exploitation and domination. The issue of faith never constituted a key problem for the future Sheikh Moubarak. What really mattered to him was the point of view of *class* and not philosophical considerations.

With more strength and visibility than the ordinary, it is in the times of crisis in a social system, when the individual is confronted with abrupt social and political change, the transformation of their social conditions and with the disintegration of their identities, that these alternative cultural forms become widespread and take over the dominant forms. Another 'world' provides new ideals with which to identify and that are all gathered in an intellectual and practical scheme, an entire stock of models of action and images of the self, significantly directing the conduct of these candidates, in quest of fame, such Saints of justice, in a position to actualize them.

(Damamme 1994: 185)

The organizational structure of EMNL consisted of a system of sectors based on corporate identities like the Nubians, students and workers. The movement was also present in university faculties as well as in provincial institutes. Each sector was essentially composed of a small number of Sudanese, Nubians and Egyptians. Fadl was dissatisfied with the fact that his comrades were mainly content with discussing general matters. He desired more active intervention. Thus he began to speak out from the top of the *minbar* in the mosque. On King Farouk's birthday, which was an official holiday at al-Azhar, he gave a speech opposing these festivities. He denounced the role of the King as the agent of British colonial domination. Within a few months, he was made the leader of the Azhar sector.

The sector consisting of almost seventy members (Botman 1988: 44). EMNL was the only Marxist group involved among Azharites. The membership of the organization remained very flexible. A Nubian, who was also an Azharite, could belong to the two sections and there developed close relations between Nubians and the Sudanese (al-Amin 1995: 433-54) earning the nickname of "the society of salt and sodium" (al-Sa'id March 1994: 70). These sectors enjoyed a special status with Curiel (Perrault 1987) who decisively supported their action. Sheikh Moubarak smiled as he remembered Curiel wearing shorts at his meetings with Azharites and Nubian students. EMNL analyzed the role of the Azharites as follows:

Men of religion in the country have always played an important part against imperialism – French, Turk, English. At present, Zahra (code name for al-Azhar) is standing at the crossroads between the people and the bourgeoisie. The importance of Zahra is as follows: it is the religious body which assists reaction, its men represent the working classes, they enjoy spiritual confidence among the people, their roots grow deep among many classes of Egyptians – teachers, preachers, Imams, etc. ... As they are so important, we must win them away from reaction and the Palace. Our aims: To make the Azharites join in the national struggle with us. We must not allow the Azharites to be a toy in the hands of reaction.[7]

The young communist Nubians including Zaki Mourad (al-Sa'id April 1992; Zaki 1979: 64), or Mohammad Khalil Qassem (al-Sa'id Feb 1992; Abdu Fadl 1989; Ishaq 1996), to name but a few, participated in the activities of the Egyptian Marxists according it a specific Nubian dimension. The Nubian-Sudanese Abdu Dahab (al-Sa'id March 1994) played a key and pioneering role. He had a great amount of political experience. Co-founder and leader of EMNL, he worked on the paper *Hureyat al Shu'ub* before editing *Omdurman* in 1945-46, for the Sudanese living in Cairo. There were also a number of other Nubian students of al-Azhar. They intervened in the associations and community clubs in Cairo. They were particularly active in the Nubian Club, located at the time behind ʿAbdin court. Created in 1920, it was almost completely under the control of Nubian notables who were far from dynamic. The young militants tried to extend their efforts towards other Nubian community associations.

Mohammad Khalil Qassem, one of the leading organizers, wrote articles and poetry in the club review *al-nuba al-haditha* and organized large social activities especially in Nubian residential areas of Abdin, Boulaq and Imbaba. Actions were not limited to cultural or social fields; there were political battles as well. During this period the Sudanese party *Umma* began propagating the idea of secession among the Nubians of Egypt. As the Nubians were considered to be of Sudanese origin a separatist scheme was advocated. The Nubian Marxists counter-attacked vigorously by asserting their cultural and historical affiliation to Egypt.

The radicalization of these young Nubians was closely linked to their social position as a minority. Sheikh Moubarak recalled that when he was young, a Nubian taking a walk could find himself surrounded by a group of children who would call him *barbarian* and mock him. The solution was not to be found in a fanciful, utopian separation but sustaining their position in a community that fully recognized their rights.

Fadl's activities caused him troubles when his father discovered some hidden pamphlets at home. His commitment became known later. After a heated dispute with his father, he was kicked out of the house.

In 1947, the unification of the two groups, EMNL and ISKRA (meaning spark), resulted in the rise of a new organization called DMNL. Sheikh Moubarak stressed the political differences between these two trends. EMNL was geared more towards mass action, while ISKRA was more interested in theory. ISKRA members came mostly from an upper-class background while members of EMNL were from the lower strata. The DMNL weekly, *al-Gamahir*, was influential[8]. Fadl organized the work of the al-Azhar and Nubian sections until 1948-49[9] when he became a full-timer for the Damanhour-Mahalla region. Arrested in Mahalla in 1948, he was successively interned in Mahalla, Tanta and Hackstep. He was not freed until February 1950. Expelled from al-Azhar for the first time in 1948, he returned in 1950 before being definitively expelled in 1951.

After 1950, Fadl joined the leadership of DMNL serving on the central committee, political bureau and the permanent secretariat. He remained faithful to Henri Curiel and his orientation. The situation at the same time was marked by the imprisonment of key organizers. He had to analyze the burning of Cairo in 1952. He considered the king and the English to be responsible. He was arrested and set free after he denied owning a pamphlet found in his possession. Once, the police pretended he was Sudanese; he successfully overcame an expulsion to Sudan!

The Revolution and the Nasserist Experience: Between Confrontation and Integration

The coup of July, 1952 was no surprise to the DMNL as the latter had a sector in the army and forged strong bonds with the Free Officers. DMNL supplied support in the publication and dissemination of pamphlets. Nasser only accepted the participation of Marxist officers on an individual basis. Fadl speaks of an organic connection.

The political reactions to the coup were very diverse. DMNL, the only group informed about the preparations, supported it, while the other organizations denounced it as a right-wing and pro-American putsch. Beinin made the following estimations: at this moment DMNL numbered two thousand members, the Worker's Avant Garde around three hundred and the ECP-al-Raya[10] around one hundred (Beinin 1987: 575).

The *Kafr al Dawwar* episode in 1952 was the first conflict between communists and the new regime. This worker's strike erupted in a small industrial village located about thirty kilometers from Alexandria. It turned into a violent riot and resulted in the killing of workers and soldiers. The proceedings of the military court resulted in two death sentences. DMNL could only denounce the verdicts deploring the limited vision of a *patriotic* regime[11]. For Fadl, the position of DMNL at the time was to defend the workers *and* avoid a confrontation with the regime. He vigorously repudiated accusations that DMNL supported the anti-worker repression.

During the struggle between Nasser and Naguib in early 1954, the Communists were overtly critical of the regime's contradictions. For them, the decision of 24th of March to return the army to its barracks and re-establish democracy could have become effective only if there had existed a credible alternative. While in prison Sheikh Moubarak and his comrades were surprised by the popular demonstrations hostile to democracy. They understood that the army played a role in these events. DMNL called for the fall of the dictator, sought to make alliances with other tendencies and experimented with the idea of a National Democratic Front (Ramadan 1976) in which Wafdists, Socialists and Communists join together. For Fadl, this line was a grave mistake. It was legitimate to criticize the regime but wrong to call for its overthrow.

During the years 1952-56, while he was at *Rod al-Farag* prison, Sheikh Moubarak conceived an escape plan with his fellow prisoners. The plan appealed to Prince ʿAbbas Halim interned for his labor activities. Finally, five of the prisoners made their escape along with Fadl who was recaptured a month later. At the time of his interrogation, he was literally dying of hunger and asked to eat before confessing. After the meal, he explained that he woke up alone in a cell, found the window wide open and at the spot decided to leave! In 1953 he was condemned to three years of imprisonment.

In 1955 the splinter groups of DMNL unified. The new organization (the United Egyptian Communist Party [*mowahad*]) was now in opposition to the regime. Thus it rapidly changed its orientation with the new Egyptian foreign policy called positive neutrality. Egypt was developing links with Eastern European countries, with the famous arms deal with Czechoslovakia.

After the evacuation treaty, Nasser went to Bandung for a non-alignment conference in April 1955 where he affirmed his leadership on an international level. DMNL provided political support while maintaining its criticism on democracy. It issued a declaration entitled *Imperialism is Our Principle Enemy*. This text can be seen as a subordination of the struggle for democracy to the building of a national front against imperialism (ibid.: 576).

The communists supported the nationalization of the Suez Canal in July 1956. They emphasized an *anti-imperialist* trend while maintaining their critique of authoritarian aspects. Sheikh Moubarak left prison a few months before the 1956 war. DMNL actively participated in the resistance in Port Sa'id (al-Rifi'i/Shatla 1957) and worked with the committee of popular resistance. For Fadl, the other groups mainly issued statements.

A new daily *al-Misa'* run by Khaled Mohi Eddin (Mohieddin 1993) promoted progressive themes. Sheikh Moubarak underlines the importance of this paper in the popularization of leftist ideas. His organization cooperated closely with this evening daily (Beinin 1987).

After the 1956 war, the regime freed many communist prisoners. In November 1957, a merger took place with ECP al-Raya giving birth to the Unified Egyptian Communist Party (*moutahhid*). The Workers and Peasants Communist Party (former Workers' Avant-Garde) joined to form the Egyptian Communist Party in January 1958.

From the very beginning the ECP was divided, firstly over the Egyptian-Syrian unity. DMNL militants supported such a unity while those coming from the other groups stood by the Syrian communists who refused to dissolve themselves. When Syria seceded, HADITU members were against such a break while the others were in favor of it. The split finally materialized over Qassem's independent line towards Nasser in Iraq. The party supported Qassem. Ex-DMNL members left to set up the ECP-DMNL.

In fact the disagreement concerned Egypt. Two tendencies and approaches existed: the first one was in opposition to the Free Officers without calling for its overthrow; the second one characterized the regime as an agent of imperialist forces. The two trends redefined their view: the first one having a positive characterization of the regime as *anti-imperialist* while the second one remained in opposition.

For Fadl, the idea of unifying such trends was immature. There was no serious study of the reasons behind the split. He recalls a *genuine rush* in the unification process. The break-up occurred because, for him, the organization always consisted of two blocs. He remembers a meeting where he was suspended from voting after having criticized the other position. This type of action led to retaliatory measures and paved the way for the split.

The Marxist support for Qassem was considered treason by Nasser. A new wave of repression began on the first of January, 1959. The police launched a massive operation arresting more than 280 people followed by 700 others between January and April. Most of the leaders of ECP-DMNL found themselves interned again. Some prisoners including Fadl nevertheless sent a letter of support for Nasser in September 1959.

Imprisoned successively at the Citadel, in the oasis, then in Cairo, Sheikh Moubarak was sent with his comrades to Alexandria to appear before the military court in 1959 (Labib 1990: 417-27). They opted for a legal defense without any hope of success and also submitted their political agenda. Refusing to admit their membership to the ECP-DMNL, they reaffirmed their agenda and their support to Nasser while maintaining that he had been misled. They were condemned to ten years of hard labor.

These proceedings took place at the time of the nationalization of Misr Bank in February 1960 and continued during that year. Sheikh Moubarak was at Abu Za'bal jail where the discussions were quite fervent among the prisoners. Several tendencies confronted each other. The first one considered the current experience as a way of opening the road to a socialist revolution. The others rejected this hypothesis. Nevertheless all agreed on the patriotic nature of the regime.

A prison conference organized soon before July 1961 elaborated the analysis that came to be known as the *socialist group*. Fadl played a key role in this analysis. For such an approach, the influence of the socialist movement and the patriotic and independent orientation of the Nasser group, led to the existence in Egypt, of non-scientific socialist trends. According to their thought, the Communists should seek the reinforcement of the unity of action with such a trend in favor of the national democratic objectives. Such a process would lead the way to scientific socialism (Labib 1990: 427).

Key members such as Zaki Mourad and Sherif Hatata believed unity was possible with Nasser group. Fadl considered the group to be socialist and its policies to be progressive. It appeared to him possible to envision a unity but the conditions were not yet ripe. It was necessary to preserve their independence until that time, without incurring any hostility. The strategy had to be decided during the congress[12].

Supporting a regime which sent them to jail was based on their political analysis. My question about this apparent strange paradox did not disturb Fadl. The organization gave critical support to the regime. This was the attitude of Shuhdi Atteya who later died of torture. During their trial, Atteya publicly supported the regime while criticizing authoritarianism and internal issues.

In April 1964, the Communists were freed.[13] For them maintaining an autonomous organization was an issue. Some ex-leaders had already joined the regime. Key members such as Zaki Mourad and Sherif Hatata (Hatata 1995) joined the Socialist Avant-Garde (al-Sa'id 1986: 273). In 1963, Nasser had set up a secret organization made up of those with faith in the revolution and in socialism (Selim 1982: 59-227; Hamrouche 1983: 237-76). Former or active communists like Abdel Ma'boud al Gibali, Ahmed Rifa'i or Fouad Morsi were suggested (Anis 1994: 15-17).

The regime also sent envoys like Khaled Mohieddin, Ahmed Fou'ad and Ahmed Hamroush to convince them to disband[14]. At the time of the ECP-DMNL congress, Kamal Abdel Halim, the most famous figure of the party decided to dissolve the organization even though support for the idea to continue still existed. The dissolution was made public in spring 1965 (*Qadaya Fikrya* 1992: 389-403).

Dissolution or Resignation?

In jail the Communists evaluated the economic and social measures positively. DMNL considered it necessary to encourage such a move while ECP-al-Raya was still focusing on the monopolistic nature of the regime. Sheikh Moubarak considers that unity with the regime was a real issue as Nasser was talking about socialism and had set up an avant-garde organization. Abdu Fadl was a supporter of an evolutionary method "like a process which achieves development over a long period of time."

The nationalization of the Bank Misr and other anti-capitalist measures weighed heavily in their conclusion. Our interlocutor recounts how the idea of a unified socialist party had influenced them with the example of Cuba where revolutionaries and Communists had joined together. Their evaluation of the situation was, in his eyes, false. They also believed wrongly that a single organization could be based on socialist thought.

Maintaining a structure was rejected. The Communists never tried to coordinate common work or even a common line within the Arab Socialist Union. They simply joined as individuals as working collectively could have hampered them, and they could have been accused of disloyalty.

Such a decision illustrates their strategy of integrating the movement with the national struggle against imperialism (Beinin, op.cit.: 579). Today, Fadl believes that they rushed. They should have continued discussions even without an organized link. Their decision led to the dismantling of the movement. The state also put pressure: it favored a kind of social integration through jobs and positions.

Their orientation can be grasped in a work entitled "The Egyptian Road Towards Socialism" published by *At-Tail'a*; with contributions by Michel Kamel, Loutfi al-Kholi, Mohamed Sid Ahmed. Fouad Morsy's article expresses the point of view of Tibi and Sabri Abdallah in that it emphasizes that the experience of socialist transformation had started in Egypt. The communists insisted on the organization of an avant-garde to lead this process.

The Nasser group never accepted any communist role despite the content of the National Charter, the nationalizations and the social transformation. A famous joke circulating at this time was revealing. During a visit to *At-Tali'a* magazine, Nasser asked Abou Seif Youssef, the head of the magazine, if he was a candidate for his position as editor. After replying that he was not, Nasser explained: "You're really smart," then he turned towards all those present and said: "Your role is like St. Peter – you're here to do propaganda, but not to lead."

The regime permitted the participation of individuals so as to neutralize them. It contained the Communists, exploited their abilities and talents but destroyed communism as a movement and prevented Marxists from existing as a political force (Botman 1988: 147). As a result, the communists with their agenda contributed in blocking all forms of independent expression of the labor movement, and participated in putting all forms of social expression under strict state control (Beinin 1989: 87).

For a better understanding of such a strategy, we must consider the immense influence of the original Soviet theories of non-capitalist development (Hosseinzadeh 1989) in vogue at the time. This was a key element in the debates and orientations of the movement.

> According to this view, there was certainly a bourgeoisie in every social stratum of the Arab-Muslim world through their integration in the relations of production, and of which the interests coincide with those of the large masses of workers in the cities and in the country – a coincidence resulting at a time when it was necessary to construct an internal national market and, above all, to oppose capitalist imperialism which finds, in these social stratums, obstacles to domination. The social classes being in other respects undeveloped in this kind of social formation, often fall back on the petite-bourgeoisie to play this role; this is how things went with the Nasserist regime yesterday, the Syrian and Algerian today. These regimes, concerning this issue, assure non-capitalist economic development since, by effectively opposing imperialist economic penetration, they create the material conditions for the transition towards socialism by developing national productive forces.
>
> (Naïr 1984: 367)

The return to civil life was carried under the auspices of a committee dealing with the ex-prisoners. Fadl's request to join the Socialist Avant Garde was rejected. After leaving prison in 1964, he was given a job in the consumer co-op of Benzion. He wanted to live in Aswan among Nubians. One engineer from the Kima company offered him a job there. So he left and took the job and began being politically active there. After he was expelled from the Socialist Union, he tried to arrange meetings and political discussions. A year later, his company decided to send him back to Cairo. For him, this was mainly because they wanted to impede any of his political activities.

Returning to the Path after the Disenchantment

The survival of the Communists entailed the disappearance of the movement as an independent force, retaining only small groups or networks. The effective marginalization of the Marxists, reduced to subordinate roles, provoked a profound and serious demoralization (Ismael/al-Sa'id 1988: 127). For them this unity was supposed to be a fusion. It turned into a completely different experience that embittered a significant number of them. It induced a "progressive glide towards disintegration" (Shoukri 1981: 404). Moreover, a large majority of militants were to abandon the ranks following this experience.

However, here and there, some members decided to return to the road of action. The circle's episode (Farrag 1993: 19-24) then began. This process led to the reconstitution of an Egyptian Communist party. Secretly, a set of militants decided to regroup and to restructure. Three main circles played a decisive role. Fadl, with his friends Zaki Mourad and Seif Eddin Saleh slowly began to make contact, discuss and regroup themselves. The group in which Sheikh Moubarak participated included more than a dozen people and was named *al-Sumr* (the blacks) because it was mostly made up of Nubians. A second circle, perhaps the most famous, included Michel Kamel, Adib Dimitri and Nabil al-Hilali. Known as *al-Shorouq*, it carried out its first program in Lebanon in 1972. The third of these historic circles was organized around Mohammad Tawfiq and Sa'ad Kamal. It was called *al-Humr* (the red) with reference to the red hair of one of its main leaders Mokhtar al Sayid (al-Sa'id, April 1993).

This operation started during the Nasser era and accelerated with the defeat in June 1967. The link-ups with members notably came from the Nasserist Youth. They began once more to reflect on their setbacks, their errors. The security issue and the integration of numerous former Communists into the regime forced them to be discreet. They relied initially on personal contact based on mutual confidence. The idea was not to rush to open discussions for clarifications. Three main types of members participated in this process: old Communists, young Nasserist Marxists uncovered during the Nasser experience and young university activists (Ismael/al-Sa'id 1988: 129).

None of these networks dared call themselves a Communist party. Our interlocutor explained that they had first to sort out theoretical questions, to reach a practical agreement. Such an agreement was reached in April 1972 and allowed the beginning of some joint work. The unified group published their documents under the pseudonym of Ahmed Urabi al Misri. During the 1973 Ramadan war, the publication of a journal entitled *al-Intissar* (The Victory) started. The first thesis project was edited in January 1974. A political draft was published in

August 1974. The re-establishment of the Communist party was officially announced on the first of May, 1975.

The first congress was to be held secretly in Egypt in the early eighties. The historic role of these circles was underlined in the theses compiled as *Barnamig al-hizb al-shuyu'i al-misry* (1983: 243-50). The congress also reverted to self- criticism, stating that "the decision of the dissolution of the Egyptian communist organizations was a grave political error" (ibid.: 227). The denunciation of this decision was, according to Fadl, one of the bases for the unification of those circles and was publicly affirmed (ibid.: 237). The text included a particular passage about the "old communists" who took part in the dissolution in order to vindicate them. This dismissed a lot of critics who wanted to oppose them, going as far as making accusations of treason. Fadl publicly refuted his own analysis of the *socialist group* (Abdu Fadl/ Nassar 1991: 289-96).

After the Kima society, Sheikh Moubarak worked in the publishing house of Dar al-Thaqafa al-Gedida around 1967. He left a little later to become a party full-timer. In the seventies and eighties he was one of the public figures of his party.

He was arrested several times: after the workers' strikes and demonstrations in Helwan in 1975 then again on the day following the riots in January 1977. The authorities launched a violent campaign against the left denounced as responsible for the disorder. The different Marxist organizations and the legal *Tagammu'* party were victimized (Soliman 1987: 45-78; 'Abdel Raziq 1984). In 1979 Sheikh Moubarak was jailed for his opposition to the Camp David agreement. He escaped in 1981 when the round-ups took place in September before the assassination of Sadat. In the early eighties, he was one of those accused during the legal proceedings against the Communists (al-Hilali 1989) following which he was sentenced to three years in prison prior to being given amnesty for health reasons.

Sheikh Moubarak was one of the communist public spokesmen from 1980 to 1989. In the 1987 parliamentary elections, he was one of three candidates supported by the ECP (*Al-Ahali* 11., 18., 25.3.87). The latter's objective was not to win, join parliament or to achieve good results. Sheikh Moubarak wanted to seize the opportunity to make people hear their voice and to increase their audience. In East

Cairo, he gained some 428 votes or about 1.15 percent (Morsy 1989: 341-47). The *Al-Ahali* presented him as the "militant, Marxist, Azharite since the forties, independent and supported by the *Tagammu'*" (*Al-Ahali* 11.3.87).

His advanced age and health problems curtailed his activities, but he continued to be active. Lately, he figures among the key Egyptian socialists signatories of a press release entitled "To the Masses of Egypt" (*Al-Ahali* 29.11.95). This text expressed the option of different Marxist trends at the time of the legislative election, mainly critical of the political and economical reforms and of the Oslo agreement. The signatories called for a popular vote in favor of those opposing "the American-Israeli domination and their projects." This obviously drew a positive response from the *Tagammu'*, the Nasserists and some independent left candidates.

Personal Stakes: Being a Leftist on a Daily Basis

A Nubian Communist Commitment

Regarding the path of Sheikh Moubarak, an underlying pattern emerges. His experience was at first that of a Nubian Marxist. The foundations of his activity were closely linked to his condition as a Nubian in Egypt in the thirties and forties. He thus always made sure that he maintained a bond and kept up relations with his original community. He made numerous efforts never to stay too far from his family and the village of his birth. This point is essential and is evidenced by many visits to his village.

After coming out of prison in the sixties he was asked in Cairo to become the president of the association of those originally from his village. He was elected unanimously. The association did not even have an office. A collection allowed them to get an apartment in the district of Abdeen. One day he contacted an official of the ministry of electricity concerning the provision of electricity to his village. A delegation was sent and he obtained an agreement. Fifteen days later, their village had electricity. He refused compensation from the villagers, explaining to them that he had not laid out a penny from his own pocket. They therefore offered to install electricity in his house at their expense. Refusal met their offer.

In this manner he strove to assist his village when it was in need. During the Sadat era, he hid for about a year among Nubians. When he once asked a relative for asylum, the relative answered him "You ask for an extraordinary thing, but if I tell you no I shall be afraid." He stayed for short periods with different families, moving when he felt that he was becoming a burden. It was impossible for him to think that they could work with the security forces.

This Nubian dimension took on a more overt political form. The presence of a leftist Nubian representative for Kum Ombo, Moukhtar Goma'a, at the time of the 1990-95 legislature, was significant. He appeared as the representative of the Nubian population. This was very important in Sheikh Moubarak's eyes. He appreciated and supported this MP who was imprisoned and tortured under Nasser and who struggled against poverty.

Fadl spoke of his family without hesitation but not extensively. He married late, at the age of thirty according to a typically Nubian tradition. For him, a marriage outside his community was difficult signifying an almost automatic break with his roots.

My logic was always to preserve the bond with my relative, my village and the Nubians. Any other choice would not have kept me close; so I married a woman from my village with whom there were parental links.

He was considered to be sensible because he sought to maintain links with his roots. About his children, he explained that living the life of a militant, fraught with imprisonments and escape, he was able to attend only very sporadically to his responsibilities at home. Nevertheless, he believed that he had managed to create and maintain strong links with them. His eldest named after the martyr Shohdy Atteya, studied literary criticism in the ex-U.S.S.R. His second son studied Civil Engineering in Russia. His daughter is an archivist at the *Al-Ahli weekly*. His youngest son is still at school.

Concerning such strong links with his community, let us quote a French veteran evoking his own case.

Like the tree that endures much longer by its roots than by its foliage, I remained faithful to my roots ... at the end of a very long struggle oriented towards the future that only appears through the slow march of men walking with their heads high.

(Tillon 1977: 13)

The Militant Model

Such a path helps us to understand how this kind of engagement represents, according to Jean Chesnaux, an *art of living*, which succeeds in forging an entity that has meaning to those who belong to it. It can be seen here as an example of the enhanced value of personal behavior and ethics. There is a tendency to conceive action quasi-exclusively in terms of example incarnated beyond the strictly political content. In Fadl's own view, the militant must try to become an example in his daily life. He has a responsibility towards others and for others. "The Communist must be with the masses. For that he must be human, having the spirit of sacrifice and an instinctive sense of duty." The advocated values such as humanity, respect, courage and integrity make up this revolutionary virtue, of which the communists must be the symbol. "You cannot always talk, it is necessary always to act in your daily life, to be correct." This invokes what Kriegel analyzed:

> In principle the idea that the Communist is responsible, not only for himself, but also for the others for whom he must behave as a little sun. Lighting, warming and leading in his course, a circle of satellites: his neighbors, his friends at work or at play and generally, his companions in misery and hope.
>
> (Kriegel 1985: 140)

Fadl has been living in the very popular neighborhood of Dar El Salam on the outskirts of Southern Cairo. He was astonished at a question asked of him concerning the influence of political affiliations in his daily relationships. For him, the accusations of atheism or his actions never had the slightest influence on his relationships with those around him. People know he is a Communist. With his neighbors, he always played a role of support and solidarity. The determining factor remains in his eyes that he is always able to help them. According to him, there were two ways of convincing people: through discussion or concrete action.

The adherence to Communism, while awarding a supplement of justification, of meaning, of dignity to acts, even the most ordinary ones, and to say so while sanctifying them, gives the feeling of harmony and bliss. All committed lives are penetrated by this.

(Kriegel 1985: 142)

His commitment also generated strong friendships. His best friends were those who shared ideas and prison with him. His real friends were Zaki Mourad, Mohamed Khalil Qassim and Rifa't al-Sa'id, general secretary of the *Tagammu'* party. He maintained solid links with *common* people.

The Experience in Prison

In the course of our interviews, Sheikh Moubarak did not spontaneously evoke his imprisonment. This experience had two functions for him:

for those who are weak or hesitant, this break made them even weaker, for the others, prison reinforced their strength and made them more determined.

This notion was widespread among militants for whom prison experience was a personal litmus test. It was more moral and physical than political and represented an educational phase. It displayed an almost infallible optimism which held out even in prison. He believed that

bad times always pass nonetheless early experiences played a role in my intellectual formation. There is no place for despair when one is a political militant. The participation in the struggle gave us confidence and the militants who abandoned it were already either 'tired' or 'weak'. The optimism was not only political. After the torture my family cried. I smiled and told them not to cry, that this was nothing.

Tortured many times in prison, he suffered the same cruelty which lead to the death of Shuhdi Atteya ('Issa 1990-1991; al-Sa'id 1982). An investigation had established the facts and gathered testimonies on the case (al-Sa'id 1982: 61, 69-70). After the proceedings of 1959, he was transported with many of his comrades to Abu Za'bal. At first they thought the sentence was ending. Yet no sooner had they arrived when once more they became the victims of bad treatment and other cruelties. He recalls that the police modified their treatment according to their evaluation of their action and responsibilities in the organization. Shuhdi Atteya was the first to be accused and he himself was the second. Other than him, there were five more who were tortured. Shuhdi Atteya died there, even though he was strong. He lost consciousness quickly. At the death of Shohdy, the other five were immediately isolated and placed in what they called the "hospital", a simple place managed by a few doctors. Parents and close relatives led a vigorous campaign in court against the police and the authorities out of anger and fear for their wellbeing. Nasser was then on a visit to Yugoslavia. In order to keep up the good relations with Tito, the Egyptian president ordered an investigation, the immediate suspension of the implicated soldiers and the transfer of the prisoners to Qanater. This was the last case of torture against Marxists in Abu Za'abal. Sheikh Moubarak explains his attitude towards the torture:

> In difficulties and catastrophes you can't cry, even under torture. When a friend dies, you cry. This is a belief ('*aqida*), the tears are not weakness, but on the contrary, become an enemy.

The prison also signified for him a collective human and political experience. He found himself with other political prisoners. Together, they went through this tough experiment which also was an intense period of politicization, with meetings, discussions and reflection. It was also his first contact with other Marxist groups. They continued to act through letters sent to acquaintances. The Communist spirit was upheld daily thanks to the solidarity of the community. It was truly a micro-society.

Specific Dimensions of a Struggle

The Founding Act

The adherence to Marxism generated a militant commitment. This theoretic affiliation is deeply rooted in an event or a set of events. In the present case, it was Fadl's condition as a poor Nubian at the time when the rapid development of a national movement and of a progressive utopia were taking place. This was a key element at the end of World War II. The coherence, the logic, and the world vision ensuing from this commitment took shape.

> It is in similar experiences, when the militant ... feels inducted by history, where he feels the course of his existence is being carried and oriented by the wind of history, which solidly and durably weaves the feeling of belonging to a camp, to a world which upholds the notions of fidelity, loyalty and legitimacy, that constitutes the base of the [communist] conscience.
>
> (Brossat 1991: 88)

This is a logic of protest springing from his immediate real life. Here is analogy with Charles Tillon through his work *La révolte vient de loin* (Tillon 1972) with a feeling of revolt "reigned the flower of a confused hope" (Tillon 1977: 15).

A Certain Understanding of Marxism

Here the basic principle is that Communism is on the side of the oppressed layers. For Fadl the decisive factor lay in the miserable condition of his family and the Nubian community. Kriegel distinguishes between three types of commitment: political, existential and ideological. Fadl's example can be counted as an existential one.

> The situation of those for whom belonging to the Communist party constitutes a state of nature and are part of it 'by birth': not necessarily because they are born in Communist families, but rather because the Communist option is derived unequivocally from their national, social, professional and cultural character.
>
> (Kriegel 1985: 170-171)

The adherence to Marxism represents more than a simple move to political action. It offers a global alternative vision of the world. It also provides a theoretical framework that could pave the way for radical and effective changes. Man can get the conscious mastering of history with huge potentials to the building of a new society. Science, knowledge and competence altogether provide for humanity the means of liberating itself through understanding and control of the world.

This ideology gives explanations and solutions to all questions and symbolizes this *"redemptive utopia"* of the present time because it is

> intensely democratic, by opposing the ancient hierarchies; and denying the necessity of existing again, encouraging the spread of knowledge, which was judged to be in natural agreement with the doctrine, exalting the technical and moral and intellectual resources latent in all of us, denying all the facilities, the new theory opened the large doors of the future.
>
> (Rodinson 1972: 303)

This intellectual framework provides a global alternative vision to the existing world.

> It implicitly, but vigorously proposes an ethic which gives each member a lot of moral satisfaction from his engagement. The proletariat must overturn the unjust social order, condemned by science and man in general for universal moral reasons, which must be in favor of the inversion; the individual will not have a clear conscience when he collaborates with what is bad. Engaged in this way, every act, even in private life, in agreement with ideology, is a step towards the realization of myth.
>
> (Rodinson 1972: 249)

It is convenient to highlight that such an example corresponds to a radicalization of the educated class. It appeared in the categories of some *small intellectuals*, a term used by Daniel Hémery in its non-pejorative sense – "small concerning their perspective of social rise but not concerning their intellectual capacity," proletarized, they denied themselves access to the classic functions of the intellectuals (Hémery 1984: 306). The educated strata occupies a particular *intermediary* place. As they are blocked in the exercise of their essential social functions, they opted for an opposition to the existing social and political order (Hémery 1984: 304).

A Certain Ideological Profile

The adherence to Marxism equally procured a confidence and a certitude about a definite sense of history.

The impassioned feelings about the movement of history hindered by immense obstacles and by its variants, the feelings of a besieged stronghold, are essential in the full deployment of the Stalinist conscience.

(Brossat 1991: 85)

The militant does not learn history in books but in life and action.

Contrary to the great majority of men, he lives in the feeling of the presence of history, in the conscience of history. This immersion and his personal existence in history, this feeling of proximity with history, the conviction that it is the work of humans, and that he himself is such an actor, pave the way to ineradicable subjective intensity.

(Brossat 1991: 90)

This type of certainty is based on deep conviction of being in the same phase with the course of history, which is what gives the militant an almost unshakable sense of confidence. This mixture of optimism and hope (Brossat 1991: 90, 121, 199) is a decisive factor in Sheikh Moubarak's *Stalinist Communist* consciousness.

A Type of National Communism

A Nationalist-Marxist Synthesis

In the case of Vietnam, Hémery underlined the production of specific Marxisms as responses to the crises of non-western societies. This approach is most relevant to the Egyptian case. The tight link with nationalism is inescapable. Marxist ideology is used as a global system offering a substitute to ancient forms of thought and projects according to a perspective of national and social *change*. "Marxism is going to come forward, in the context of historic impossibilities, as an alternative solution to the policy of nationalism and as reactualization/overtaking of the problematique which is its own" (Hémery 1984: 301).

Marxism produces a more coherent and rational outcome of the nationalist project with its scientific dimension. Its project is to build a society that has to get rid of any colonial influence. It offers an "alternative solution to political nationalism as the reactualisation/bypassing of the problematic" (Hémery 1984: 310). This syncretism means the rise of a *National Marxism*.

Patriotic and reformist at the same time, such a project cannot be reduced to the fight for independence. It also implies a deep social transformation. The continuity with the patriotic tradition is an attempt to insert the Marxist element into the national culture. We can therefore speak of an extension of the revolutionary nationalist commitment. In its *soviet* form, it provides the theory of imperialism, the vanguard party and other tools and structures, new political practices and the potential to wage a new type of struggle.

The Founding Matrix: Stalinism

Most researches on the Communist movement in Egypt have paid little attention to its Stalinist matrix despite the latter's impact on its political strategy and the practices.[15] Stalinist hegemony meant the borrowing of themes, theoretical works and strategical approaches from Moscow and its international current (Lowy 1987: 392-400). The Communist development, was above all, determined by national and quasi-nationalist imperatives.

Although the U.S.S.R. was looked upon as the fatherland of socialism, Fadl's perception of it remains strictly Egyptian. As a patriot, the U.S.S.R. appeared to him as the only international power supporting his country's claims, thus making it a natural ally. The Soviet Union was to become the supreme example as well as the concrete reference to the possibility of achieving profound social transformation. This was nothing unique at the time, especially in Cairo.

Soviet planning was literally a utopia for them. It incarnated an incredible and fascinating experience of rapid transformation, economic growth, industrialization and agricultural collectivization where the state was the agent of social transformation. There was never any mention of the authoritarian side of the Soviet experience. The essential strength of this Marxism is the demonstration of its historic viability offered by the U.S.S.R. The Soviet model is seen as evidence that it is possible to escape from the historic fatality of colonialism.

Stalinist U.S.S.R. drew a precise model of revolution, a path of historical development, which represents the only chance to escape, on the condition that it introduces itself in favorable circumstances in the face of this hopeless destiny and finally to resolve the old problem of survival. The Russian revolution is perceived as the producer of a new national society and of a credible method of development based on the doctrine of state control. Such an historical project seems really fascinating.

According to Rodinson, the *Stalinist synthesis* means the following:

Everything is there: the conception of a modern world, a universal sociology opening the doors for the same hope for all peoples of the world, an explanation of the imperialist phenomenon, a practical method of modernization and development, formulas for organization, strategies and tactics, making sacred the ethics of secular schemes which the situation finds pressing, and even an aesthetic theory. An apparently optimistic and militant philosophy headed up an encyclopedic science.

(Rodinson 1972: 302)

A dogmatic codification of Marxism relied on a mechanical conception of objective laws.

Fadl's adopted version is expressed in terms of social reform, salaries, the right to health care, housing, a practical equality and also access to education. Progress for him meant development, state control and industrialization with the conviction that the existence of special conditions in Egypt made a longer stage of transition necessary. The society had to rid itself of exploitation and misery, to build up a new community of free citizens where the Nubians would have a place of their own.

The fall of the U.S.S.R. does not seem to have provoked either disappointment or doubt or bitterness, although it can be termed "a catastrophe for all."

Fadl resolutely rebelled against the idea that a group gained ground by organizing the breakdown of the Soviet system. The collapse goes back further and has old roots. The problems go back to the time before Stalin. The periodization of the progressive descent towards this collapse is necessary. Imperialist forces dragged the U.S.S.R. into the arms race. Yet it was a longer process. Fadl is convinced that it is up to communists today to open the debate and study the question of the beginning of the deterioration in order to understand this failure so that the reconstruction of socialism can be contemplated.

Concerning Stalinism and its historic dimension in the U.S.S.R., Sheikh Moubarak distinguished two main things. Earlier, the communists tended to celebrate and sanctify Stalin. For example, they kept the memory of the day of his death alive as a real tragedy. The discovery of the errors, crimes and weaknesses of the Soviet CP created another situation. Consequently, it became necessary to return to this experience with a precise and profound analysis and without any sanctifications. It is impossible to grasp the breakdown of the U.S.S.R. without going back to the previous causes and their deep roots. With a party containing a million members, one cannot be satisfied with the explanation of submission (*khudu'*) to leadership. The experience had many positive sides but numerous and great errors created the present situation. Sheikh Moubarak refuses, however, to believe that socialism is dead, unlike many disillusioned people. He asserts his optimism without any doubt. The fall of the U.S.S.R. appears to him mainly economic.

Strategic Issues

The strategic implications of the Stalinist position meant self-limitation was central. The adoption of the revolution in stages meant that:

> in countries that are colonial or semi-colonial, the accomplishment of a bourgeois-democratic revolution by an alliance with the national bourgeoisie, is a preliminary historic stage to all future socialist revolutions.
>
> (Lowy 1987: 395)

This theoretical frame explains the support given to Nasserism. The non-capitalist road of development provided the keystone for their orientation. Sami Naïr underlined the harmful aspects of this theory pointing to three key issues. It harbors a confusion about the nature of imperialism which comes to overshadow local social relationships. It also supposes that the creation of the conditions of transition towards socialism can only be made via the "national" bourgeoisie. In fact, this does not lead to development but sets up the conditions for the reproduction of underdevelopment. Lastly, development is only understood in an economic way (Naïr 1984: 368).

Fadl's idea of revolution saw it as to an operation which combined the struggle against imperialism with class struggle. He had no understanding of phases, advance or retreat. The revolution had to be violent and bloody, with Russia as the example. For this young educated Nubian, Marxism "pushed the immediate movement into action following a program which will achieve the ideal" (Rodinson 1972: 249). The working class is the agent of universal emancipation with the mission of producing a complete new humanity out of this mosaic world.

Appraisal and Perspectives

Critical Statements

Fadl asserted to us that he would choose the same path today without the slightest hesitation. However, with experience and maturity, he would not have repeated certain acts or gestures. In 1948, after his action in Mahala al-Kubra, he found himself interned in Bulaq close to his family's home. He was 21 and did not try to contact his parents though he had neither food, covers nor even clothes in the middle of winter. He explains this gesture as springing from the excessive enthusiasm he felt in his youth. He remembers his father's visit to the Hackstep prison in about 1948-49. Despite their difficult relationship, his father brought him something. Steeped in ideology, he just tried to use his father to get into contact with foreign comrades. His dad was discovered, expelled and denied visitation.

On the political level, Sheikh Moubarak insists on the absence of any links between the Egyptian and the international Communist movement since the beginning of the thirties. He recalls the non-existence of regular contact or even integration with other existing structures. He insists that their politics consisted of an Egyptian nationalist element which is preoccupied primarily with the Egyptian question. He insistently recalls that the coup of July 1952 had the support of DMNL. The International Communist Movement, headed by the U.S.S.R., denounced it. Other Egyptian groups did the same. This position did not have any effect on him as he considered himself, first and foremost, an *Egyptian* activist. This lack of an organic link allowed them a better understanding of their 'Egyptianness' according to him.

Today he considers that they developed a rather negative attitude towards the national bourgeoisie. It is possible for him to cooperate with a sector of this class he considers to be progressive. His analysis follows the traditional developments of the pro-Moscow Communist trends. We consider that this development led the Marxists to a strategy of self-restraint in Third World Countries.

> The dramatic weakness in which, at present, we find the Marxist movement in the Arab social formations is a direct result of this: condemned to a strategy of alliance in relation to the so-called progressive States, the orthodox communist movement is paralyzed in the face of the considerably repressive policy exercised by these powers regarding popular claims. This is an admirable spirit and a praiseworthy abnegation trustworthy of the major holy preachers.
> (Naïr 1984: 367-68)

His approach remains within the framework of the Front. According to this concept, Marxists have to collaborate with all forces opposing imperialism.

Concerning the building of the organization, Fadl estimates that the theory was not always suited to local realities. They established the sector system. As an example of their organizational flexibility, he mentions the issue of regional affiliations. The feelings of belonging, of social bonds and solidarity of this kind are strong. In Kafr al Dawwar, workers were firstly organized in cells but rapidly the leaders realized that disagreements were based on regional or tribal lines. So they decided to rebuild on a regional basis.

On the Nasserist experience, he explains

the revolution was undertaken by the nationalist and patriotic forces in the army. Of course DMNL gave its support right from the beginning. We, however, remained opponents according to a political line that led us to call for the fall of the regime.

He considers this position was a mistake. Fadl still believes that the Nasserism regime was patriotic and anti-imperialist. His main critique focuses on its attitude towards other political forces, for which he sees no justification.

The 1965 self-dissolution of his group is his key self-criticism: this decision remains a mistake. His remarks followed the analysis of the first ECP congress in 1981 which condemned the dissolution as a "grave political mistake"[16] (*Bernamig al hizb al shuyu'i al masri*, op. cit.: 227, 237).

Fadl was surprised when I asked him if such a dissolution was a kind of political suicide or an abdication. For him, the dissolution was an extreme exaggeration of the situation. The idea of an alliance did not have any real basis, their evaluation was weak and faulty. The Cuban experience also had a considerable influence. Dissolution was never a resignation: They turned back to the path after they realized their error. The great majority of activists did not however return to political action. He believes that a lot of them lost the desire to remain activists in the context of secrecy and repression.

His assessment of Nasser is an interesting one. He described him as

a revolutionary man, a sincere and devoted patriot who had the capacity to accept new ideas. But he remained an oriental in the situation of a country where there was an absence of democracy or a genuine multi-party system. In addition, it was the military which reinforced his move towards authoritarianism and state interventionism. Purity and integrity characterize him, for he never profited from or used his position for his own personal ends or interests.

His perception of the Nasserists of the time is, by contrast, less flattering. If he recalls a number of honorable men, he cannot forget that "the majority played a negative role." Spontaneously, he mentions Zakareya Mohieddin whom he describes as a "dictator". Gamal Selim was not very political in his estimation. Marshal Amer appeared as a sincere patriot who did a lot to build up the army.

He views the existence of a Nasserist current today as positive, especially because the Nasserist party is led by progressive tendencies who envision cooperation with leftists. Nasserist and Marxist thought seems close to him despite disagreements over practice. Common work is the way to clarification. The failure of Nasserism makes it difficult to reclaim it, still it seems necessary to defend its gains.

The Present Meaning of a Struggle

Today he considers the main task is to benefit from negative situations internally and internationally. If secret action remains necessary, there is also a need for a public appearance through a spokesman. They must learn from the mistakes of the past and deepen the links with the *masses*. New conditions can expand their influence. He advocates a certain amount of flexibility on the subject of organization. They must allow much wider discussions. Every decision must be assessed, every member should contribute with critiques before applying.

The cooperation with Communists outside the ECP is an essential factor for him. Acting and debating would allow them to reinforce their position with these Marxist tendencies. They also have to work with other groups. For instance many doctors have progressive ideas but they only want to commit themselves on issues regarding health. The same situation exists with engineers or intellectuals. Today the basis for common action exists as a way of clarifying differences. He also insists on the necessity of joint platforms.

The junction with the new generations remains a sensitive problem:

if personal relationships do exist, the youth do not yet benefit from the heritage of those from the past, whether good or bad. There is no genuine study of international experiences. For a lot of young people, there is the risk of believing that there was not much good in what had happened in the past.

Today Communism retains for Fadl a meaning in term of general, political and economic objectives, which can however, differ from before. For instance, global nationalizations are no longer a condition. For him, it's a matter of advancing without forcing the pace and respecting individual freedoms. It is necessary to break off from the Stalinist experience by insuring the total political freedom through a true plurality of parties. Asked about other socialist experiences, he mentions China – "an interesting experience of progress, stages and progressions, especially after the death of Mao."

On the Arab level, he sees the situation as unbalanced with slowness and real difficulties. There has not been any progress in the realm of democracy. The economic and social situation continues to be bad and cooperation between leftists is not intense enough, "there is a sort of distance between us, in addition to the crisis of the different Arab communist parties."

For him, the question of Islamism must be dealt with through an analysis of the relevant period. In the 1940s, HADITU considered it possible and desirable to cooperate with the Muslim Brothers. This continued after the revolution. This position changed over time: today such cooperation is almost impossible except in very rare exceptions such as the Press Law.

Asked about the rise to power of the Islamists, he refuses to be pessimistic. This hypothesis does not seem possible even if the danger exists. For him, discussing this would be dangerous since it beguiles people and minimizes the gravity of the problem. Islamists cannot reach power if a real popular resistance exists. In such an eventuality, this will mean arrests, prison and assassinations. For Fadl the difference between the Muslim Brothers and the *Gama'at al Islameya* is not so clear.

Today the left is undergoing an acute crisis. The multiplicity of publications and debates on the U.S.S.R., the future of socialism, Marxism and the left are signs of the difficult situation (al-Sa'id 1994; Fathi 1994; Zahran 1992). The Nasserist experience also became subject to criticism. The Egyptian left seems to be more disconnected than ever from the popular milieu. It has also suffered from some serious setbacks among the workers (Posusney 1993; Beinin 1994: 247-70).

The relationships among the left are an important issue. Sheikh Moubarak explains the project of ECP to build a Socialist Alliance made up of Communists, the *Tagammu'* and the Nasserists. Disagreements exist, however, they have, from his point of view, the same line on defense of Nasserist gains. In Fadl's opinion, the *Tagammu'* is much closer to his own tendency than are the Nasserists. There are certainly some differences but the legal left party possesses a clarity of objectives and the key elements of the *Tagammu'* are closer in their backgrounds and actions (Ramsès 1997).

The Marxist movement today is characterized by weakness and splits (Strategic Report al-Ahram 1987: 363-77). Observers believe there exist around half a dozen groups. Though it is difficult to evaluate precisely, the ECP seems to be the most important organization despite several splits in the seventies and the late 1980s when a tendency around Michel Kamel (now deceased) gave birth to the Socialist People's Party (SPP) with the irregular bulletin *al-Badil*.

Our interlocutor considers that the ECP and SPP are the only parties with a significant amount of strength, the others being reduced to small propagandist activities. He speaks of the Worker's Party (*Hizb al-'Ummâl*) – a radical Marxist group which was influential in the seventies – in negative terms, describing them as 'Trotskyists' e.g. ultra leftists.[17] Still Fadl insists on the idea of the Communists' unity. Such a target can only be realized if some maturity concerning objectives and action is reached.

His main criticism is directed against the SPP, sign of their intense rivalry. Islamism is a central issue in their heated debate. While the ECP stands against the Islamists, the SPP considers it possible to cooperate with them against the regime.[18] For Fadl, Islamists represent a more significant danger which prompts dialogue with the state. Fadl considers that massacres could occur place if the Islamists were to reach power, like in Iran or Sudan. In May 1995, the ECP called for the building of a front made up of the Wafd, the *Tagammu'*, the Nasserists and other Marxist groups as well as the more enlightened or democratic Islamic elements[19] in order to combat Islamism.

Finally, we can say he developed a revised version of Communism, in direct line with the conceptions of the what was called the pro-Moscow currents. His analysis recaptured the developments of a national democratic revolution and the approach through stages in the post Soviet era.

Conclusion

Whatever is the evaluation of such commitment, one can only be fascinated by the richness of Sheikh Moubarak trajectory, the permanence and strength of his convictions. This activist knew lyrical illusions, the confrontation and transgressions before the revival. His confidence was never shaken.

The experience of time changes you and invites you to change again or even reinvigorate you into a new hope which will obliterate all trace of discouragement in spite of ... 'the ashes which strike my heart'.
(Tillon 1977: 13)

It can be asked if one cannot speak of several communist trends, with the stream of trends, groups and splits. This example shows the direction that brought about this type of position.

This adherence relies on the sincere conviction that the U.S.S.R. was the fatherland of socialism, the defense of which was an essential imperative; and that the national-democratic revolution opened the doors for the final butt of the labor movement: socialism.
(Lowy 1980: 32)

Sheikh Moubarak represents the specific engagement of a generation of young Nubians in the forties.[20] This is the trajectory of a leader of the DMNL.[21] An observer cannot be surprised by the *cruel destiny* they suffered under Nasserism. After a confrontation, the state introduced many reforms carried out in an authoritarian method. Their political line contributed to the blocking of any independent workers' voice, the corporatization of the labor movement and disbanding of any autonomous social expression. The present case can help us rethink Joel Beinin's thesis that insists on the key role played by the intellectuals in the elaboration of the Nasserist orientation (Beinin 1989: 87). It also questions Botman's approach that puts stress on a significant distinction between the workers'-popular elements and the middle class intellectuals who were granted important social positions in the regime through the party, the press or state institutions (Botman 1988: 146). Of course such elements played a role as well as did pressure from the Soviet or foreign Communist parties. Still the decisive factor was the political approach shaped by what we called the Stalinist matrix. Such an outlook was shared by most Communists at that time.

If this testimony rebuilds the uniqueness of an experience, it offers also an example

> to refer to the use of biography in order to explore the complex ways in which individuals find their way among social structures, processes and cultural interactions.
>
> (Burke 1993: 6)

It helps us improve our understanding and knowledge of society. Detailed biographical sketches allow us to continue research. Today, there exists a genuine stake in memory of a generation which is gradually disappearing. Preserving signs of such experiences is the work of the Committee for the Archives of the Egyptian Communist Movement.[22]

Such an example can be useful to break with the western distorting prism,

> at a time when the Middle East is often harshly caricatured in Western Society, these portraits of ordinary men and women and their struggles and attempts to survive in a context of great uncertainty and risk, serve to assert our common humanity.
>
> (Burke 1993: 3)

It can allow a more critical reexamination, and not only confined to the Middle East:

> Why, when we study other people's politics – especially people whose worldly power is less than ours – do we suddenly forget the frustrations and limitations of our own political life? Perhaps if we could see them and their struggles more clearly – and not just what we take to be their problems, their defects and their defeats – we might recover our capacity for openness to others and our willingness to learn from their most promising political experiments.
>
> (Baker 1990: 296)

Notes

Thanks to Maher Zaki for his generosity and decisive support, to Dr. Rifa'at al Sa'id, key historian of the left and to Sheikh Moubarak for his amiability and his constant good humour. This text benefited from the criticism of Elizabeth Longuenesse. It was translated from French by Rania Al-Malky.

1 This title was inspired by the thrilling book edited by Edmund Burke 1993.
2 Acronym of the Democratic Movement for National Liberation.
3 We interviewed Moubarak Abdu Fadl firstly at Maher Zaki's house, who introduced me to him, then in his own home and two times in the publishing house Dar al-Thaqafa al-Gedida in May and June, 1995.
4 See al-Sa'id (1989: 123-210, 365-370), Beinin (1987, 1989) and Botman (1988). Rifa'at al-Sa'id published interviews in 1989 (ibid.) and in July 1996.
5 See The British Archives Foreign Office: FO 371/vol 45916/J 311/3/16/telg Lord Killearn 147, 20.01.45.
6 Acronym for the Egyptian Movement for National Liberation.
7 FO 371/vol 62994/J 58/13/16/25.04.48, quoted in Botman 1988: 73.
8 FO 371/vol 69250/J 1890/1262/16/Sir R. Campbell to Mr. Bevin 134, 18.03.48.
9 A DMNL pamphlet in FO 371/vol 69250/J2953/1262/16/Sir R. Campbell, 25.04.48.
10 A Marxist group led by Ismail Sabri Abdallah, Fouad Mursi, Sa'd Zahran, Daoud ʿAziz in 1949; it was extremely hostile to the other leftist tendencies.
11 See al-Ghazali (1993). This version denounces the 'real' instigators of the trouble which provoked a confrontation between the army and the workers.
12 The debates held at the prison of *Qanater* were rapidly transmitted to the prisoners of the oasis.
13 See al-Mouslihi (1979), leader of the "Department of Anti-communist Struggle" who resigned because of the releases of 1964.
14 For such a meeting see al-Sa'id (1986: 270-271).

15 We are setting aside a small surrealist group Art and Freedom, who tried, unsuccessfully to promote an anti-Stalinist Marxism. See Gharib 1987; al-Siba'i 1988.
16 See how an ex-Communist explained this experience shaped by the Stalinist logic. See Sid Ahmed 1996: 67-75.
17 For a similar evocation see al-Said/Ismael 1988.
18 This organization recently opted for a resolute opposition to the Islamists.
19 See the statement of ECP published in *al-Yasar*, June 1995 (Bayan 1995).
20 See the meeting (24.05.96) at the Nubian club dedicated to the poet Mahmoud Shindi.
21 For other DMNL contributions, see al-Guindi (1996) or Hatata (1995); for other options see Sadeq Saad 1986.
22 See "waraqa ʿamal mashrou' tawthiq, tarikh al haraka al shou-you'ya al misrya [hatta 1965]", Cairo, 17.05.1995., and the bulletin "*al-dhakkira al-wataniya.*"

Selected Bibliography

Arabic Language

ʿAbdel Raziq, Hussayn (1984) *Misr fi 17 wa 18 yana'ir*, Cairo: Dar Shuhdy.
Abdu Fadl, Moubarak (1989) "al tadheya wa al boutoula wa al tawa-dou' al thawri". *Adab wa Naqd* 49, pp. 87-92.
────── /Nassar, Bahig (1992) "Qarar al magmou'a al ichtirakeya". *Qadaya Fikrya 11-12*, pp. 289-296.
Al-Ahali 11./18./25.03.1987, 29.11.1995.
al-Ahram Strategic Report (1987) Cairo: Al Taqrir al Istrategi Al Ahram (al-Ahram Center for Strategic and Political Studies), pp. 363-377.
Anis, ʿAbdel ʿAzim (1994) "Tamzim Abdel Nasser al sirri limdha?". *al-Yasar* 48, pp. 15-17.
Atteya, Shuhdi (1957) *Tattawur al Haraka al Watanya al Misrya 1882-1956*, Cairo: Dar al Fikr.
Barnamig al-hizb al-shuyu'i al-misry (1981) Beyrouth: Dar Ibn Khaldoun.

Bayan (statement of the ECP, May 1995), *al-Yasar*, June 1995.

Fathi, Ibrahim (1994) *Al markisya wa azmat al manhag,* Cairo: Dar al-Nahr.

Gharib, Samir (1987) *Al Sireyalya fi Misr,* Cairo: GEBO.

al-Ghazali, ʿAbdel Monem (1993) *Baʾd Arbaʾoun ʿaman biraʾa Khamis wa al Baqari,* Cairo: Dar al Sashat lil dirasat wa al nashr wa al tawziʾ.

al-Guindi, Mohammad (1996) *Al-Yasar wa al harakat al watanya,* Cairo: Dar al-Thaqafa al Gedida.

Hamrouche, Ahmed (1983) *Qissat Thawrat Yuliu, 2 and 4 Shuhud,* Cairo: Makatabat Madbouli.

Hatata, Sherif (1995) *al Mounafidha al Maftouha 2,* Cairo: Dar al Thaqafa al Gedida.

al-Hilali, Nabil (1989) *Houreya al fikr wa al ʿaqida, tilka heyya al qadaya,* Cairo: Dar il Masri al Gedid lil Nashr.

Ishaq, Sayyid (1996) *Al bahth ʿan al-Shamnadoura,* Cairo: Dar al-Thaqafa al-Gedida.

'Issa, Salah (1990-91) "Shuhdy Atteya". *al-Yasar,* August, September, November, January, May, June.

Khalil Qassem, Mohamad (1994) *Shamnadoura,* Cairo: Kitab Adab wa Naqd.

Labib, Fakri (1990) *Al Shuyu'youn wa Abdel Nasser 2,* Cairo: Dar Al Amal.

Mohieddin, Khaled (1993) *al ann attakalamu,* Cairo: Markaz al Ahram lil targama wa al nachr.

Morsi, Fou'ad (1990) *Al intikhabat al barlamania fi misr 1987,* Cairo: Dar Sina lil Nachr.

Mourad, Zaki (1979) *Rihlat al-hayat al-thawra,* Cairo: Dar Sina lil Nachr.

al-Mouslihi, Hassan (1979) *Qissati maʾa al shouyu'ya,* Cairo: Al Sharika al Moutahida lil-Nashr.

Qadaya Fikrya (1992) *Sabaʾoun ʿaman ʿala harakat al shouyu'ya al misrya* 11-12.

al-Rafiʾi, Ahmed/Shatla, ʿAbdel Mon'eim (1957) *Ayam al intisar,* Cairo: Dar al Fikr.

Ramadan, Abdel Azim (1976) *Abdel Nasser wa azmat maris 1954,* Cairo: Rose al Youssef.

Sadeq Saad, Ahmed (1986) "Qira'a thanya fi ahdath yana'ir 1977". *al-Raya al Arabeya 1*, pp. 80-135.

al-Sa'id, Rifa'at (1972) *Al yasar al misry 1925-40*, Beyrouth: Dar al Tali'a.

——— (1976) *Tarikh mounazamat al yasar al misri 1940-1950*, Cairo: Dar al Thaqafa al Gedida.

——— (1977) *Al sahafat al yasareya fi misr 1925-1948*, Cairo: Makatabat Madbouli.

——— (1984) *Al garima, watha'iq 'amalya ightiyal Shuhdi 'Ateya*, Cairo: Dar al Shuhdy.

——— (1986) *Tarikh al haraka al shuyu'ya al misrya 1957-65*, Cairo: Dar Al Amal.

——— (1989) *Hakadha takallamu al shuyu'yun*, Cairo: Dar al Amal.

——— (1992) "Mohammad Khalil Qasem, Hadret al Nazer". *al-Yasar* (February).

——— (1992) "Zaki Mourad, al moutafa'il dawman". *al-Yasar* (April).

——— (1993) "Dr. Moktar al Sayid, wa lil nidal achkal 'ida". *al-Yasar* (April).

——— (1994) *Markyssya al mustaqbal*, Cairo: Dar al-Amal.

——— (1994) "Abdu Dahad, Misr wa al Sudan al Kifah al Moushtarak". *al-Yasar* (March).

——— (1996) "Khidmat al gamahir ... badalan min khidmat al-aghneya". *al-Yasar* (July), pp. 66-68.

——— (1996) "Seif Sadeq, nubi kassar al qu'ida". *al-Yasar* (December).

Selim, Gamal (1982) *Al Tanzimat al sirrya li thawra 23 yuliu fi 'ahd Gamal Abdel Nasser*, Cairo: Madbouli.

al-Siba'i, Béchir (1986) *Miraya al mouthaqafin*, Alexandria: Dar al-Nil.

Tiba, Mustafa (1990) *Al haraka al chouyou'ya al misrya 1945-1965*, Cairo: Dar Sina lil Nachr.

unknown author (1996) *Rahil mounadil al sha'id Mahmoud Shindi 1927-1996*, Cairo.

Zahran, Sa'ad (1985) *Fi usul al siassa al misya*, Cairo: Dar al Mostaqbal al 'Arabi.

——— (1992) *Al harb al idiologya wa suqut al shuyu'ya al soufyetya*, Cairo: Dar al-'Arabi.

Western Languages

al-Amin, Mohammad (1995) "The Role of the Egyptian Communists in Introducing the Sudanese to Communism in the 1940s". *International Journal of Middle East Studies* 4, pp. 433-454.

Auzias, Claire (1994) "Générations politiques". *L'Homme et la Société* 111-112, pp. 77-87.

Baker, Raymond (1990) *Sadat and After*, Cambridge: Harvard University Press.

Beinin, Joel (1987) "The Communist Movement and Nationalist Political Discourse in Nasserist Egypt". *MEJ* 4, pp. 568-584.

—— (1989) "Labor, Capital and State in Nasserist Egypt 1952-1961". *IJMES* (February), pp. 71-90.

—— (1994) "Will the Real Egyptian Working Class Please Stand up?". In Zachary Lockman (ed.) *Workers and Working Classes in the Middle East*, New York/NY: State University of New York, pp. 247-270.

—— /Lockman, Zachary (eds.) (1987) *Workers on the Nile*, Princeton/NJ: Princeton University Press.

Botman, Selma (1986) "Egyptian Communists and the Free Officers". *Middle Eastern Studies* 3, pp. 357-367.

—— (1988) *The Rise of Egyptian Communism 1939-1970*, New York/NY: Syracuse University Press.

Boudarel, George/Brocheux, Pierre/Hémery, Daniel (1977) "L'insertion du communisme dans le national: la convergence vietnamienne". In Catherine Coquery-Vidrovitch (ed.) *Connaissance du Tiers Monde*, Paris: U.G.E., pp. 249-277.

Brossat, Alain (1991) *Le stalinisme entre mémoire et histoire*, Paris: Éditions de L'Aube.

Burke, Edmund (ed.) (1993) *Struggle and Survival in the Modern Middle East*, Berkeley/CA: University of California Press.

Dammame, Dominique (1994) "Grandes illusions et récits de vie". *Politix* 27, pp. 183-188.

Farrag, Fatemah (1993) *Third Stage of the Egyptian Communist Movement 1965-present*, Master's Thesis: The American University in Cairo.

Hémery, Daniel (1984) "Le communisme national: la contribution du Marxisme à la pensée nationaliste au Vietnam". In René Gallissot (ed.) *Les aventures du Marxisme*, Paris: Syros, pp. 287-317.

Hosseinzadeh, Esmail (1989) *Soviet Non-Capitalist Development, The Case of Nasser's Egypt,* New York/NY: Praeger.

Ismail, Tareq/al Sa'id, Rifa'at (1990) *The Communist Movement in Egypt 1920-1988,* New York/NY: Syracuse University Press.

Kriegel, Annie (1985) *Les communistes français*, Paris: Seuil.

La voie égyptienne vers le socialisme (1966), Cairo: Dar al Ma'aref.

Lazar, Marc (1995) "Après 1989, cet étrange communisme". *Autrement* 150-51 (January), pp. 243-253.

Lowy, Michael (1980) *Le Marxisme en Amérique Latine*, Paris: Maspero.

—— (1987) "Le stalinisme". In Pascal Ory (ed.) *Nouvelle histoire des idées politiques*, Paris: Hachette, pp. 392-400.

Mandel, Ernest (1986) "The Role of the Individual in History: The Case of W.W. II". *New Left Review* 157, pp. 61-77.

Morsy, Soheir/Nelson, Cynthia/Saad, Reem/Sholkamy, Hania (1991) "Anthropology and the Call for Indigenization of Social Science in the Arab World". In Earl T. Sullivan/Jacqueline S. Ismael (eds.) *The Contemporary Study of the Arab World*, Edmonton/AB: University of Alberta Press, pp. 88-111.

Naïr, Sami (1984) "Formations sociales, pouvoir, structures, idéologies: le cas du monde arabo-musulman". In René Gallissot (ed.) *L'aventure du marxisme*, Paris: Syros. pp. 357-382.

Neveu, Eric (1994) "Le Sceptre, les Masques et la Plume". *Mots* 32, pp. 9-13.

Peneff, Jean (1994) "Les grandes tendances de l'utilisation des biographies dans la sociologie française". *Politix* 27, pp. 25-31.

—— (1995) "Biographical Interviews and Class Relationships". *Current Sociology*, pp. 53-59.

Perrault, Gilles (1987) *A Man Apart*, London: Zed Press.

Pollak, Michael (1986) "L'entretien dans le cas de l'univers concentrationnaire". *Actes de la Recherche en Sciences Sociales* 62-63, pp. 10-14.

Posusney, Marsha P. (1993) "Irrational Workers: the Moral Economy of Labour Protest in Egypt". *World Politics* (October), pp. 280-320.

Pudal, Bernard (1991) "'Choice' of Method for a Historic Sociology of

PCF". In Denis Peschansky/Michael Pollak/Henry Rousso (eds.) *Political History and Social Sciences*, Bruxelles: Éditions Complexes, pp. 101-112.

Ramsès, Basel (1997) "Le Tagammu'". In Sandrine Gamblin (ed.) *Contours et détours du politique en Égypte. Les élections législatives de 1995*, Paris: L'Harmattan, pp. 165-195.

Rodinson, Maxime (1972) *Marxisme et Monde Musulman*, Paris: Le Seuil.

Shoukri, Ghali (1981) *Égypte la contre-révolution*, Paris: Le Sycomore.

Sid Ahmed, Mohammad (1996) "Autocritique du soutien inconditionnel à Nasser". *Peuple Méditerranéens* 74-75, pp. 67-75.

Soliman, Lotfallah (1987) "Les émeutes du 18 et 19 janvier 1977 en Égypte". *Sou'al* 6, pp. 45-78.

Tillon, Charles (1972) *La révolte vient de loin*, Paris: UGE 10/18.

—— (1977) *On chantait rouge*, Paris: Robert Laffont.

AL-DAGHT: PRESSURES OF MODERN LIFE IN CAIRO

MOHAMMED TABISHAT

In the last few decades there emerged an endemic sickness in Egypt which is a complaint that covers diverse social meanings which are linked, but hardly confined to the biomedical disease of high blood pressure.[1] From abstract medical treatises to newspaper reports to family debates and conversations, *al-daght* is a household term at all levels of society. Barely had I started my research in Cairo that this topic emerged in daily conversations about health and other related issues. Participants in those discussions were individuals and families who were not necessarily ill with high blood pressure, but who have developed a sense for the socio-economic and environmental conditions assumed to lead to such individual and social pain. Further, many among them have never tested for high blood pressure. Some have tested, but were diagnosed as having "normal" blood pressure. Nevertheless a large number of the latter claim they suffer from certain kinds of pressure.

For large numbers of the Cairene population *al-daght* is one concept that is readily communicable and an illness that is easy to contract. Initially it was found only in medical texts. Later, it took a history of its own reflecting social and cultural circumstances specific to the Egyptian context. I argue that the present concept of *al-daght* is only partly based on the concept of high blood pressure. More significant aspects are produced by processes of negotiating its meanings and embodying those, most crucially after attaching them to local social and physical circumstances which are assumed to engender the illness' incidence and its endemic spread.

The history and development of modern health categories have not been adequately studied in the context of contemporary Middle East societies. Concepts such as high blood pressure and *al-daght* are no exceptions. The present paper does not claim to cover this complex topic. It is an attempt to answer such questions as; how to identify *al-daght* and whether it is different from high blood pressure. What are the discourses involved in the interpretation and therapies for this category, conceptualized not as a disease but as a social problem? What specific meanings has the social category of *al-daght* acquired upon its insertion into Egyptian everyday life? Are these meanings the same for men and women, or for individuals occupying different socio-economic positions? How does *al-daght* shape, and consequently become shaped by individuals‹ bodily and socio-cultural circumstances, especially with regard to the relationship between the individual and social body?

These questions constitute part of a larger research on body perceptions in contemporary Egyptian culture that I conducted for my Ph.D. dissertation in medical anthropology in which I analyze specific illness experiences including *al-daght*. This present study is based on eighteen months of fieldwork in Cairo between the years 1995 and 1996. The principal method I used was participant observation in the homes of a number of people where I observed everyday life in depth and detail, and where I met and discussed individuals' and families' health experiences. Concurrently, I conducted similar research at a number of health facilities visited by my informants. I complemented this with a number of in-depth, structured interviews with a small number of individuals in their homes as well as in the health facilities they visited. These interviews were focused on the question of *al-daght* and upon which this paper is based.

This paper considers the above questions in light of five individual cases described in detail and in the context of individuals' specific socio-economic as well as cultural circumstances. The individuals included have been suffering from *al-daght* for varying periods of time and under different social and economic circumstances. In each case health experience is described within the context of the individual's family life. For the individuals included, the family is the best place to manage the majority of their practical and emotional problems including health-related ones. In many instances bodily pains were explained in terms of family relations and their contribution to the persistence or alleviation of those states of distress or discomfort; the importance of these factors are not the same in all cases.

Exemplifying processes of indigenization of knowledge the following interpretations of *al-daght* are instances where biomedical and other knowledges are re-presented through embodiment. But it has to be emphasized that biomedicine is embodied within a multiplicity of herbal and spiritual methods for healing. Within this complex structure of health practices it is rather misleading to describe different knowledges based on abstract definitions of medical practice. Therapeutic activities always involve mobilizing and using available medical resources to overcome pressing health conditions. Different medical knowledges take different positions and different meanings depending on the unique circumstances of individual cases. Therefore, the complex structure of medical knowledges does not exist in the same form across different classes and genders as will be discussed later in this paper. It is within such changing medical practices and not by theorizing about an abstract human body and medical knowledge that specific configurations of medical knowledges should be described.

Questioned about the prevalence of *al-daght* in the Egyptian capital, a well-known physician who is also associated with governmental health services, indicated his acute awareness of *al-daght* as a national health issue. In our conversations this physician noted that most likely many more people were "hypertensive" in Egypt beyond the numbers of those already diagnosed.[2] But he quickly lapsed into reciting the well-known standardized litany of "facts" about hypertension. It was a "disease of civilization", he continued, prevalence of which increased in "civilized" regions where stressful life-styles recognized as risks for high blood pressure could be found in abundance. This standard medical textbook explanation adds little insight to the particularities of the Egyptian experience.

It goes without saying that processes of health and healing are deeply embedded in structures of power and inequality. Economic exclusion is a central theme in the context of access to health care services. The question for a majority of Cairenes is not one of free choice among available possibilities, which they could choose according to cultural preferences, but is often a much more complex process of making the best of the available resources under economic and social structural constraints. Throughout this process people choose certain ways for interpreting, explaining, contextualizing and treating their states of health and sickness. These ways might coincide with, but need not necessarily conform to, any single model of health care. Physicians' observations and statements are but one among many statements in the larger debate of interpreting and treating *al-daght*. For many individuals the visit to a clinic is only one episode within a series of consultations, trials and home remedies which reduces physicians' advice to just one element within a vast field of practices, experiences and inherited wisdom.

Along similar lines a recent survey on hypertension conducted by the Egyptian Society for Hypertension states that physicians' concerns with the problem of hypertension does not go beyond standardized biomedical methods and variables (Ibrahim et al. 1995). The study which was designed and conducted in collaboration with an American team set out to further analyze sets of variables in their relationship to the occurrence of hypertension such as Bilharzia and "skin color" (Ashour et al. 1995: 884). The study recognizes the importance of including social variables such as education and income as parameters for social status. But it fails to grasp the circumstances of the majority of Egyptians in that it proposes to further look at "relevant variables unique to the Egyptian population (e.g. [sic] presence of electricity and air conditioning)" (ibid.). Air-conditioning, it needs to be mentioned is an irrelevant factor in most Egyptians' lives, but does play a more prominent role in the upper middle classes' imagination.

Outside the official and professional contexts the underlying causal factors of *al-daght* in Egypt are anger (*zaʿal*), tension (*tawattur*), nervousness (*ʿsabiyya*) and hard thinking (*tafkir*). Some physicians agree on such explanatory schemes although they don't offer precise explanations beyond their standard biochemical analysis. In the last few years there appeared in Egypt a group of small low-priced books or health pamphlets which contain a diverse collection of health and medical explanations and advice. People who author such books are physicians, herbalists, spiritual healers or lay persons who became experts on particular medical problems. Some of these books contain medical advices mixed with the moral and social views of the authors. One of these books is on high blood pressure and is written by a physician who studied at Al-Azhar Islamic University. Beside the standard biomedical explanation of *al-daght* the author argues that one main reason for raising blood pressure is competition for success which results in tension, impatience and sighing (*talahhuf*). The author condemns such behavior as he sees human competition as a fierce struggle between dogs over mundane gains (*takaalub ʿala 'umuri l-dunya*) (al-Hussaini 1993: 15-22).

Rather than engaging with abstract medical discussions and remote models of explanation this paper focuses on the narratives of a small number of people about their experiences with *al-daght*. The complexity of both their experiences and their narratives illustrates clearly that the conventional model of explanation – such as the physicians' encountered above – cannot even remotely capture the diverse aspects and elements of *al-daght*. Furthermore, these narratives touch upon layers of meanings that only a holistic approach in contrast to a purely biomedical analysis can adequately deal with. In the following analysis I am particularly concerned with patients who had *al-daght* for long periods of time and are currently under medication.

The Cases

Dr. Fawzi and Madam Farida (she likes to be called Madam for its taste of middle class cultural etiquette)[3] are a couple in their midsixties and have been married for more than 40 years. They live in a neighborhood on the fringes of Cairo that once was a fashionable winter and health vacation spot but has long since lost its former glory, and even its middle class aspirations of the more recent past. Over the past few decades the neighborhood became home to a number of severely polluting industrial enterprises including cement and asbestos manufacturing. In comparison to the majority of Cairene families, Dr. Fawzi's family is relatively well off. Dr. Fawzi, his wife and youngest 18-year-old daughter are living in a rented apartment. He has a doctorate in geology which he obtained in the 1960s in the United States. The social prestige attached to such a degree is considerable. Upon his return to Egypt he joined the government services and was eventually promoted to a high position in the Egyptian bureaucracy. Some years ago he retired from his public post but continues working as part time consultant for a ministry. Within his own reach and setting, Dr. Fawzi is not completely satisfied with his material conditions.

He feels he could have done better in terms of his bureaucratic career. He states with a certain bitterness: "The ladder up was too high and I was at some point simply pushed out."

Madam Farida has a high school diploma which is rather unusual in Cairo for women of her age and clearly indicates the family's deep middle class roots. She never worked outside the house. Her main job in life, as she explains, was to take care of her children and house. The couple have six children all of whom except for the youngest daughter are married and have left their parents' home. All of the five married children have university degrees. Dr. Fawzi, his wife and daughter live off his pension and earnings as a consultant. They do not receive support from their married children. Dr. Fawzi's semi-ironically remarked on his married children: "I just hope they will not ask me for help."

Both Dr. Fawzi and Madam Farida are currently taking medication for a variety of illnesses including *al-daght*. Dr. Fawzi was first diagnosed with *al-daght* some two decades ago when in his late forties. Ever since then he has been on medication. There were no special events or conditions relating to the onset of his illness. He merely recounts the day when he was walking down a street and all of a sudden felt the sensation of a strong headache and general weakness. He immediately consulted one of his doctor friends whose clinic was near-by the incident. The most serious encounter with disease in Dr. Fawzi's life was, however, clearly related to a special event: his heart disease which started with angina and was followed by a heart attack which occurred briefly after he had been denied promotion. He had at the time believed that he deserved this promotion and that it was his turn in line to be promoted. Shortly after this incidence of heart disease he also developed bell's palsy which Dr. Fawzi refers to as partial paralysis (*shalal nissfi*). Dr. Fawzi and his family and friends identify his diseases as a direct result of this denial of promotion.

Like many others in Cairo, Dr. Fawzi believes that disease in general and *al-daght* in particular are the results of *dughuuti lhayaah* (pressures of life). He identifies "economic pressure" as first and foremost among these. This type of pressure works as part of a vicious circle, as Dr. Fawzi notes: even the constantly rising prices of medication feed into the pressure that makes one sick. He further elaborates: "But it is all the demands of social life combined which made me sick." For him this is the particular result of his class position whereby he has to maintain class-based expectations with a budget that in actual reality no longer allows for that. Dr. Fawzi puts this pressure to reach for what is no longer possible for his family, in relation to his present physical condition. He uses the term *infiʿal* (best translated as agitation or provocation associated with irritation) and *tawattur* (tension) to describe his sense of being out of control of his social and economic conditions which he sees at the root of his physical suffering. His idea of how to deal with *infiʿal* is through *'iman* (faith) and *qanaʿah* (feeling content). He further explained that it is faith that enables him to live peacefully with disease and other hardships. Dr. Fawzi observes his prayers and a small dark spot on his forehead bears witness of this.

To my question how people in Cairo really managed to cope with all sorts of hardships, he offered this explanation: "It is simply *baraka* and *satr* and these two can never come except from Allah and our belief in Him." *Baraka*, an immensely rich term including the wider field of meaning related to blessing, also implies a very important notion of sharing. This notion holds that the goods of life can be increased if they are not strictly calculated; meaning, to give will engender blessing in itself and more so blessings of favors and goods returned. The notion of *baraka* further evokes the belief that all resources in the last instance come from Allah and hence carry an obligation for sharing. *Baraka* hence can come with sharing limited resources. For instance when small quantities of food are enough for many people it is believed that those foods have *baraka* in them. Similarly, *satr* (literally: a cover) is the practice of negating one's own needs, to "cover" them so to speak and also the practice of helping others in a hidden manner i.e. without showing off one's generosity. Such acts hold *baraka*.

In addition to biomedical treatment and his strong religious beliefs Dr. Fawzi also relies on herbal treatments recommended to him by friends. He regularly drinks *karkadieh* (hibiscus) which is widely used for its effect in reducing blood pressure. As he has also been diabetic for a long time, he starts his day by eating a mixture of fenugreek, coriander, and lupine, mixed with honey. He eats this mixture and drinks *karkadieh* along with the pills which the doctor prescribed for him. Dr. Fawzi is very disciplined in the routine of taking his medication and keeping to his prescribed diet. Both he and his wife follow the doctors' advices, which is reinforced by their son, who is a general practitioner, with regard to amounts of fats, salt, sugar, and other spices. As much as Dr. Fawzi defends these dietary rules, there remains a grain of doubt about them in his mind: "These pills are only preventive of further damage, they can never cure what has already changed in the body." Dr. Fawzi's doctor son keeps up with his parents' health. When need arises he refers them to various specialists who were his teachers at medical school. Unlike the majority of Cairenes Dr. Fawzi and his wife thus have access to some of the best of Cairo's facilities and practitioners. On the whole they have pieced together for themselves a rather unique and comprehensive system of treatments: faith, dietary rules and assistance of practitioners, and have found a way to live and cope with their health problems.

Regarding the effects of his various treatments Dr. Fawzi assigns clear priorities to his respective therapies. First comes the strict diet combined with the physician's medications. He respects herbal treatments especially if they are additionally recommended by a physician's advice. Fundamental for Dr. Fawzi is his coherent or inclusive larger structure of health and treatment as he sets it out by all his practices, rather than each one by itself. Dr. Fawzi, at moments, is critical of some of his family support both from within the nuclear family and beyond and he sounds like a physician when he states:

visits of relatives should be controlled and accepted at proper times only, but at the same time they can be very helpful if they involve material assistance too.

Madam Farida's initial encounter with *al-daght* differs from that of her husband's having begun when she was only 30 years of age. She has been taking medication ever since. She gave birth to three children after the onset of *al-daght* which has added further stress to her health. Madam Farida's treatment and rules, in particular her dietary rules are less strict than her husband's. She acknowledges the significance of controlling her diet but she usually breaks these regulations by taking more salt and spices on her food neglecting her son's instructions. Unlike her husband she believes that what counts in the case of *al-daght* is to live in a quiet and relaxed environment. Madam Farida largely believes in the medicines she takes and their remedying effects.

She highly values the pills that are prescribed for *al-daght* as the most effective means to guarantee a "comfortable" life with her illness. While she takes a number of herbs she refuses to confer any considerable healing effect to them. Madam Farida is not essentially in conflict with her husband's ideas. Her explanations of *al-daght* are connected to her feelings about economic needs as well as the tension associated with raising her children and making them succeed in their studies and lives. Dr. Fawzi interrupted his wife commenting: "Mothers are more emotional than fathers and that is why problems of children affect them more." It was clear that Madam Farida was most involved with the children's studies and other problems. She is keen to stress that she is still carrying on with her children:

We took good care of our children not only until they completed their studies. We also ensured that they have good college degrees, marriages and jobs.

Madam Farida perceives these sources of tension with relation to her children and family as directly connected to her poor health because she used to hide her feelings:

I had always learned to hide my feelings of unhappiness until I fell ill. Only after that, I started to 'scream' my discontent out which gave me relief.

On the whole, Dr. Fawzi and Madam Farida firmly assert that their sicknesses can never be ascribed to one single cause nor could be cured or even controlled through one single method. Living with their sicknesses becomes conceivable through the words of Dr. Fawzi:

My work, my wife and children, my everyday life problems, from the amount of salary I receive to the traffic jam I get caught up in when I drive to my work, are all full of situations which 'sets my nerves on fire' [*bitihra' 'a'ssabi*].

The experiences of Dr. Fawzi and Madam Farida stand in contrast to those of Um and Abu Ahmed who also have *al-daght* but whose life circumstances radically differ form the former. I learned about very different aspects of *al-daght* with Um and Abu Ahmed who are roughly of the same generation as Dr. Fawzi and his wife. Abu Ahmed is 70 and Um Ahmed 61 years old. They have been married for over 50 years and have eight living grown-up sons and daughters, four other children died in early childhood. The couple live in a small four bedroom apartment on the top floor of an old building in a heavily populated popular neighborhood located in an old commercial area which is densely occupied by small metal and car maintenance workshops. Most of the residential buildings (three to six stories) house workshops or even small industrial operations in their ground floors. A dusty patina covers the once nicely decorated facades and balconies. They bear witness to a prosperous past when the neighborhood was home to many successful merchants and manufacturers around the turn of the century. The buildings which are badly maintained are inhabited by low-income families. The Cairo earthquake of October 1992 further aggravated the already bad condition of the old buildings. Abu and Um Ahmed's apartment was seriously cracked.

In such physical surroundings the couple share their small apartment with three of their daughters and three of their sons ranging between the ages of 26 to 42 years. One son and one daughter are married and live with their families in other parts of the city. One of the daughters – living with Um and Abu Ahmed – is married and together with her husband and eight-year-old son occupies one bedroom in the apartment. The other daughter has been widowed a few years ago and subsequently moved back in with her parents. She, her 16-year-old son and the youngest unmarried sister share the second bedroom in the apartment. The three unmarried brothers occupy the third bedroom and the parents the fourth and biggest bedroom. A small and narrow entranceway or hall – with chairs and a narrow "couch" serve as a living room for this eleven-member family. The TV set occupies a prominent position in this hall. By the far end of this hall are a small kitchen and a bathroom with running water. Life happens in the "hall" space where eating, watching TV, discussions of everyday events, and negotiations of numerous and endless economic and other problems, take place. Many discussions take place with the background sounds of the TV.

Across from the entrance door to the other side of the stairs is an open space on the building's rooftop which the family use as their "living-room" throughout the hot summer months. They have nicely arranged a few pieces of old furniture and boxes to sit on and plants are in the corners and hanging from the walls. On hot summer nights this is a very pleasant space that also provides a beautiful view over the surrounding neighborhood. If it were not for this extra space summer nights would be unbearable in the dense space of the small apartment. In winter the house is too crowded because the family members hide from cold which they believe to be a serious cause of disease. Recently, the family added a small chicken coop to their rooftop "garden" to raise some poultry for their own consumption.

Abu Ahmed retired from his job as a bookbinder ten years ago and now lives on his pension. All three daughters work outside the house: one is a clerk for a public organization, one works as a helper in a restaurant/club, and the third is a trainee in a government department. Their salaries range between 40 and 120 pounds a month.[4] The three sons are only occasionally employed. They are what Cairenes call *'arza'i* (roughly temporary workers). As the saying goes in Cairo: somebody sits four days and works one. They get daily or temporary work and are constantly in search for permanent jobs. Each of the three brothers has some kind of expertise in the fields of electrical and metal work yet none of them has any school diploma or complete training in any of these fields. The days that they are able to secure work they tend to make good wages. Each one of them tries hard to save money for future marriages yet they still seem a long way from their dreams despite their ages (they are between their late twenties and late thirties).

All working family members give part of their earnings to Um Ahmed who manages the household. The son-in-law who lives with the family went into early retirement due to health problems. He has a pension and receives money from his brother who is a migrant worker in the Arab Gulf. He gives money to his wife who in turn contributes to the household expenses. The teenage grandson recently started working with a street vendor while still going to school. Each member of the household keeps small sums for themselves and also saves for various bigger or smaller items and dreams. The family share their food and the necessary expenses for the maintenance of the house.

Abu Ahmed has been ill for the last ten years. Beside *al-daght* he suffers from rheumatic arthritis (*rheumatism*), gout (*nuqrus*), and diabetes (*sukkar*). Around the time of his retirement he suffered from the first symptoms of *al-daght*. He remembers that at the time the family went through a severe economic crisis. He fell ill immediately after a major family fight, although he does not perceive this as the singular cause of the disease. Abu Ahmed's understanding of his illness illustrates the larger framework within which he understands his physical well being. Multiple frustrations and disappointments in life, economic instability, combined with heightened irritation resulting from spatial pressure (*di'ah*), bad or polluted food (*akli lkimaawiyyat*), noise (*dawsha*), pollution (*talawwus*) of the city, are factors as Abu Ahmed frequently points out, that cause people to fall sick. Such conditions and the feelings and impressions they engender can irritate the soul (*nafs*). All this is subsumed under the notion of *zaʿal*: anger, frustration, disappointment that, when it accumulates in the individual ultimately engenders poor health.

Abu Ahmed is a very quiet man. His is the image of the man withdrawn into himself amidst a large and noisy family, sitting in his white *gallabiya* on the small *kanab* in the hallway/living-room. He frequently expresses his general content and gratefulness for what he has in life by the gesture of kissing his hand inside and outside several times. It was only through observing a number of arguments and fights within the family that I understood what he meant by the notion of *zaʿal*. In and after arguments underlying issues of pressure and tension often remain ultimately unsolved which leads individuals to accumulate a growing sense of disappointment and unvoiced resentments. These build up to a pressing sense of *zaʿal* which thus constitutes a pervasive feeling in individuals' lives beyond limited instances of fighting and controversy. This feeling and its necessary oppression is closely connected to and can be explained by the notion of *katm* which means to suppress feelings of discontent and disappointment. When a person experiences *zaʿal* and has to suppress (*yiktim*) his/her feelings and hopes, *zaʿal* consequently can be transformed into physical symptoms. A person who is unhappy about the way he is treated by the others or by life in general is sometimes described as carrying unhappiness inside (*shayil gowwah*).

Feelings of *zaʿal* in Abu Ahmed's family largely originated in their economic crises which started in the early 1980s when Abu Ahmed and the eldest son, Ahmed, were holding more profitable and stable employment. The family owned a car, and a van which they rented out. Um Ahmed describes those good days with the remark that they used to have a picnic every other week. A few years later Abu

Ahmed retired from work, and Ahmed and his younger brothers one after the other lost their jobs. The short-term jobs which they had afterwards were much less rewarding compared to the ever-rising cost of living. It was at this point that Abu Ahmed fell ill for the first time. Around the same time the family had to accept a marriage proposal for one of the daughters where the future husband would move in with the family rather than provide a separate apartment for himself and his new wife as is the common custom. The other daughter was widowed in the same time period and her in-laws pushed her back to her father's house. It was at this point that spatial pressure was added to other pressures in the family's life. Nasser, the oldest son who still lives with his parents because he cannot afford to marry and set up his own household, once remarked:

This is exactly what caused my father to get sick, because many people pressured him to accept my sister back. It is not only my sister, we are all a pressure to my father in this house, look at how many we are and how many problems we created in his life.

Then, he added with a cynical laugh:

An entire government could get *al-daght* under such circumstances ... my father had a lot of *za'al* ... he could not do anything but hide it.

In a similar context looking dismayed yet maintaining his calm smile, Abu Ahmed noted: "The best thing in this case is to pray to Allah, and put even more trust in him."

Abu Ahmed is a very disciplined patient and shows great respect for his doctors' advice. When talking about his illness and treatment he always made a point to pronounce the foreign names of his medicines correctly as he had learned some English while working in a large oil company in the 1960s. He felt that he had in such ways acquired a basic familiarity with the workings of aspects of a different type of knowledge and he was thus partaking in the process of his treatment. Nevertheless, he regards these medicines as useless without his reading of the Quran which he does regularly. This, he feels, makes him calm and peaceful, as he notes: "That's what eventually counts, the refuge in Allah." Abu Ahmed rarely leaves the apartment and explains that, "my illness made it too difficult for me to go up and down the stairs." He even gave up attending the Friday prayers in the mosque. When he feels pain, family members call a physician neighbor to examine the father in his home. His sons and daughters buy his medication.

Um Ahmed also has *al-daght*, yet this is not her main problem. In general, she is more outspoken about her pains than her husband. Today, she carries most of the responsibility in the family and enjoys the authority that comes with that. Before Abu Ahmed fell ill, things were very different. Um Ahmed runs every detail of the household and aspects of the individual members' lives as well. Um Ahmed finished six years of elementary school and thus has basic reading and writing skills, though she rarely has a chance to use them. She is economically dependent on her husband and sons. The latter in turn are in a different sense socially dependent on her. She emphasizes that she "hosts" all her children in the house that she originally rented and furnished, which is true and none of them would argue against her about this. At the same time that they underline their wishes to be able to afford their own households they also acknowledge the benefits of sharing the expense. This allows each one to live cheaper and accumulate more for their individual futures, and even more so provides invaluable emotional support. The large sharing household, however, comes with its shadow of tension arising in the overcrowded space. Nevertheless, everyone agrees on the common saying reminiscent of Dr. Fawzi's notion of sharing: *"lu'ma haniyya tikaffi miyya"* (one enjoyable morsel is enough for a hundred).

Um Ahmed suffers from a possibly larger variety of illnesses and ailments than her husband. She would often jokingly say to me:

I am a moving hospital, why don't you write only about me ... they will give you a whole doctorate degree straight away when you tell them my story.

She has rheumatic arthritis, diabetes, gastric and colon ulcers in addition to *al-daght*. She keeps moaning with pain whenever she does or says something. Unlike her husband she can not afford the "sick role" in the house but runs frequent errands to secure food or other items on sale for the family or to make the obligatory visits to relatives to maintain valuable family ties. Despite all of this her husband and sons would maintain that *al-daght* is a male disease as it affects those who "think and work hard". They would argue that men are stronger than women, and for that reason they work harder. As I raised the issue of the immense strength required for multiple pregnancies Abu Ahmed said: "That is the strength of Allah, not women."

Um Ahmed is a disciplined patient of physicians' advice. She further commands a considerable knowledge about health and disease which she has accumulated from different sources such as herbalists, spiritual healers, doctors and relatives and friends. Furthermore, she is an ardent fan of TV where she always pays close attention to health related topics. Upon the advice of her doctor Um Ahmed worked hard to lose 15 kilograms but still thinks she remains somewhat overweight. She keeps a variety of herbs in the house, which she would readily recommend to me whenever I complained of some pain or cold. Nevertheless, she is always cautious to say that these herbs also need to be taken in ways that conform or harmonize with the doctor's advice.

Um Ahmed also attributes prominence to *za'al* with regard to her physical state. She describes *za'al* associated with the death of her younger sister about fifteen years ago as a starting point for some of her ailments. She recognizes a direct connection between *al-daght* and what she calls *'assabiyya* (nervousness) or *narfaza* (also a form of nervousness). Like *za'al*, *narfaza* generally means anger but denotes temporary and repetitive outbreaks of anger, high temper, in everyday life encounters. Um Ahmed is considered *'assabiyya* or nervous, by her family. She often gets angry and hurls, at times fierce, verbal abuse at family members. The latter for the most part avoid confrontations with her. In Um Ahmed's explanatory scheme *narfaza* is directly related to *za'al* especially with regard to poverty. She draws a correlation between the category of *il-ghalaaba*, or those poor people whose life is embittered by hardship and frustration and subsequently are susceptible to *za'al*. *Il-ghalaaba* in this sense is more often used to refer to those yet worse off than oneself, and only in more desperate situations would she refer to her own family as *il-ghalaaba*.

Um Ahmed's story of openly voiced anger is sharply contrasted by the gentle nature of Um Zaki, a widow in her late fifties who has four daughters and one son. Her youngest two daughters are unmarried and live with her. Both young women work to help out their mother and save money for their trousseaux. Um Zaki's older children are all married and live in their own households. Her husband who had been self-employed for most of his life left her no pension, she does however receive a small share of a pension of one of her brothers. Um Zaki and her daughters live in two neatly furnished rooms, they furthermore have a small kitchen, and a bathroom that they installed years ago in the old dwelling. For domestic consumption Um Zaki raises poultry on the roof of her building. Her two youngest daughters are by far the greatest source of material support for Um Zaki. Her only son is in her own words "a constant source of problems" and not much of a support to her. Some years ago he spent a period of time in an Arab country but was unable to accumulate a larger sum of money. At present he runs the family's small mechanic workshop where he also sells a variety of mechanical spare parts.

Um Zaki has for a number of years been suffering from *al-daght* and a number of other ailments. Her central discomfort is frequent numbness on her left side which as the doctors explained to her results from a clogged artery in her neck. Her main problem with *al-daght* is that when she has an attack of high pressure she cannot sleep. She is also frightened by the information she gathered about this illness and the possibility that it can kill people during their sleep. She directly relates both problems to an incidence a few years ago when her brother dealt with her unfairly and greatly insulted her. She explains: "right after I came back from his house my left hand started to feel numb for the first time." This ailment remained with her ever since. Shortly *al-daght* was added to it. Like in the other cases the reference to *zaʿal* is crucial in Um Zaki's narrative around the onset of her ailment. What makes her case somewhat different from the others is her comparatively more limited access to health care services both economically and physically. It is hard for Um Zaki – especially when she feels sick and weak – to go places by herself using public transportation. With her daughters at work and her son often unwilling to help she cannot always see a doctor when she needs to. The second obstacle, of course, is her limited financial resources. Um Zaki, who has excellent knowledge of the city and its multitude of resources, is never short of ideas of how to at least minimally improve her situation. When she finds somebody to accompany her she might take the tedious trip to the large governmental Qasr El-Aini hospital where many aspects of treatment are still for free or for a nominal fee. Furthermore, she is aware of the growing number of mosques that offer social and medical services and when possible she also consults doctors in one such clinic where she only has to pay a nominal fee. She also consults the private clinic of a doctor.

Repeated doctors' visits, watching television – the TV set stands opposite to her bed on which she also sits during the day when receiving guests – advice from friends and family, and most fundamentally and importantly a vast store of practical wisdom which she inherited from her mother and grandmother, form the basis of Um Zaki's vast repertoire of treatments and health advice.

Um Zaki's wisdom about life, people, health and disease and resources in the city is extraordinary and I never encountered another person like her in my fieldwork. Her superb ability to run a household, her own life and that of her daughters in financially adverse conditions is impressive. Despite her illness, she takes care of the house and her poultry on the roof, follows up the affairs of her married children and keeps up a large network of family ties. If her health allows her she tries to take a trip every few weeks to one of the larger weekly markets in the city to maintain a store of low-price food supplies and buy the occasional household items that the family needs.

Ever since she started to consult doctors regularly Um Zaki takes a number of medications which she keeps in a small plastic bag next to her pillow, one practice common in all the homes I visited in Cairo. As she is illiterate she cannot read the labels of her medications but nevertheless she knows exactly what pills are for which ailments and when and how to take them. She closely holds on to her little routine of taking the various pills before or after her meals. When the family is out of money, Um Zaki might go for days without her medication. On days like this when she feels an attack of *al-daght*, she resorts to her own treatments: "I simply drink water with a little bit of sugar. Sometimes I wash up with cold water which will 'cool' me down."

The meals of Um Zaki are representative of low-income Cairene families. A typical meal consists of, for example, cooked vegetables in tomato sauce, rice, bread, served with hot pickles. The food is prepared in low quality palm fat (*samna*). Um Zaki is aware of the possible adverse effects of some foods on her health condition. She very carefully recites some of the doctor's advice. One day in a conversation about food, health and disease, she ironically remarked:

Do we have so many foods to choose from? They [the doctors] say eating too many sweet things is no good, using hot spices is harmful, too much salt leads to death ... . I really don't know, I feel they should say, given what we are going through we are dying, what different does it make if death is by sweet or salty things?

Discussion

Al-daght then is not simply a physical problem resulting from one or a set of organic malfunctions. It is rather a complex of social and material relations conceptualized as engendering discomfort and thus illness. The distinction between disease, illness and sickness which Young (1982) and Frankenberg (1980) make is highly relevant here. This distinction rests upon the generally accepted premise that in each culture there are rules to interpret signs into symptoms, to link sets of symptoms to etiologies upon which socially recommended interventions are devised and undertaken (Young 1982: 270). In this connection, disease refers to what is recognized by medical people as a malfunction whether in the behavior or biology of the person concerned. Illness is about individuals' perceptions and complaints of socially disvalued states of being. These unfavorable states are not necessarily recognized by medical people as real. Most importantly to this paper is the concept of sickness which involves giving or denying these states of being socially recognizable meanings. In the words of Young, sickness is a *"process for socializing illness"* (ibid.: 270, emphasis in original). Furthermore, I argue that the process of socializing illness starts well before the onset of individual illness because the categories and methods devised for such recognition never exist outside the theme of the social. On the contrary, they are social products to begin with. During this process of socializing different meanings are allocated to different individuals occupying unequal position of social power. Consequently, people who enjoy less social power are assigned less valued therapeutic measures or resources.

Furthermore, this paper concerns individuals' subjective interpretations of their bodily pains and their speculations about the social origins of their sicknesses. As will be discussed below these interpretations and speculations are informed by biomedical understandings of a particular health problem. But they speak of social and economic problems as these are felt and embodied in the social and material surroundings, and not as abstractly stated in medical or other scientific constructions. They speak of social sickness and not of disease. The knowledge involved in the above interpretative and therapeutic activities is a mix between people's ideas and emotions about their bodies as well as their social relations. The body here is understood not in its biological, isolated form, but in its social existence. Specifically, collective as well as biological bodies are social statements about the human body and its various surroundings (cf. Lyon and Barbalet 1994). When Madam Farida for example speaks about her family's demands in response to a question about her illness, she reveals that she views her body as physically and emotionally merged into the body of her larger social unit.

This very aspect of analyzing illness experience in everyday life illustrates distinctive ways of perceiving the body. Morsy's (1980) insights on the beliefs about the body here gain support. Based on her research in the Egyptian Delta she concludes that among the members of the community "The proper functioning of the body is not independent of its surroundings" (ibid.: 92). Or as Lock/Scheper-Hughes (1987) argue, the patients' narratives not only transcend mere physical descriptions but also refer to larger social and political bodies. These references point to a significant underlying conceptual framework of the human body. In the cases above, the body is firmly interwoven with the social and economic environment through the mediating force of emotions of *zaʿal*.

In all the cases above the emotions listed collectively under *zaʿal* were seen as playing central role in mediating between one' own body and surrounding social relations. Individuals' narratives and explanations of encounters with *al-daght* display a rich pool of explanatory schemes yet most importantly they all point to a variety of social, economic and political pressures to which individuals are all exposed in different degrees and in various articulations. Each one of the case studies shows a different weighing of stresses in the patient's life. Aspects of pollution and low quality food were mentioned as much as complaints about the spatial crowdedness, social and emotional frustrations and economic hardships. The individual narratives explore the multi-layered stage of everyday experiences and *al-daght* where physician's schemes to test and follow up blood pressure play only one limited role. Medical procedures to curb *al-daght* often present mechanically predictable steps in the larger project of "modernization" with its central elements of urbanization and industrialization. In the narratives medical discourse is stripped of its self-assigned incontestable position. The simple prescription of pills helps but cannot do away with what patients' perceive to be the true roots of their suffering. Instead of emphasizing powerful but technically manageable physical processes, patients' narratives describe a very different scenario whereby life's pressing (or sickening) conditions stand center stage where individuals' control over them is extremely limited.

Common to all the above experiences is, environmental pollution which adds another dimension of outside pressures on each person's wellbeing. High degrees of air, water and food pollution are recurring themes in the narratives. The quality and rising prices of many food items are themes of endless debates in Cairo's households. The widespread use of pesticides, fertilizers and hormones (*kimawiyyat*) in agriculture and processed food causes fears among consumers and is directly related to physical well being. Older people endlessly reminiscence about the quality of food "in the old days" and how food gave people strength and health. None of this can be found, they note, in today's food. Abu Ahmed further added the element of noise as a problem both of the city at large and in his household in particular.

Closely related to pollution is the ubiquitous Cairene problem of crowdedness. Streets, buses, offices, apartments, and schools are crowded and people in many contexts refer to the suffocating density of human activities. *Zahma* (crowded) is a household term similar to *al-daght*; the two are often mentioned together. "*Zahma ya dunya zahma*" (crowded ... how crowded is the world) is the beginning of a popular Egyptian song. Armbrust (1996: 1) gives a very poignant analysis of the everyday cultural implications and sufferings related to experiences of crowdedness. I often heard references being made to Cairo's streets as suffocating (*makhnu'ah*). Once I told a taxi driver that I am doing research on *al-daght*, and he immediately said while pointing to the congested streets: "'*assli daghti l-bala 'aali 'awi*" (because the city's pressure is too high), "how," he continued, "could you then expect us not to have *al-daght*, '*assli lhagaat di bitihra'i dam* (such things sets one's blood on fire)." Clearly, crowdedness and spatial pressure are set in direct connection with individuals' own bodies and sense of health.

Frustration of social life are mentioned in all narratives. For Dr. Fawzi to refer to *al-daght* meant more than the mention of a physical ailment. He was rather evoking a whole social universe that by its combined stresses "sets his nerves on fire" as he put it. For his case the unfair treatment he received at work stands first in the inequitable social surrounding. Family life with its highly appreciated emotional support is accompanied by its backside of conflict and tension.

The frustrated dreams of Dr. Fawzi and Madame Farida and the struggle of the other two families are symptomatic of a larger issue of the political economic transformation of Egyptian economy during the last two decades. Dr. Fawzi's unrealized dreams and his children's unachieved economic stability are indications of non-rewarding investment in education for this middle class family. The scarcity of job opportunities for Abu and Um Ahmed's sons and daughters coupled with the ever-rising living cost which can never be met by their present individual incomes is an indication of larger structural problems originating in the free market or "open-door" economic policy which the government has initiated since the mid-seventies and after two decades of life under state centralized economic system.

All three narratives refer to these aspects as "pressures of life" most importantly the increasing economic pressure. These external pressures are reworked in the receiving person into *zaʿal*, as an emotional reaction/response. *Zaʿal*, in comparison to physicians' "stress", implies a much larger field of meanings and experiences. In Egyptian colloquial *'il-zaʿal* is opposed to content and relaxation, or what is called *bal raayi'* or *mizag raayi'* – calm mind or temper. Although it literally means anger, the term covers a wide variety of emotional states ranging from being upset after a minor dispute with friends or relatives, to being extremely dissatisfied and discontent with life in general. One modern standard Arabic dictionary postulates a connection between *zaʿal* (anger) and pain, as elements of a larger field of meaning (Majma' al-Lughah al-ʿarabiyya 1994).

But was *al-daght* understood and treated in the same way in the whole cases above? Was the notion of *zaʿal* for example and its consequent pain placed in the same way and given similar meanings by people coming from different social positions? The two men included perceived their bodies vis-à-vis their social surrounding differently. Abu Ahmed and Dr. Fawzi, although they come from different class backgrounds saw bodily problems in light of family problems and problems at the work place respectively. The *zaʿal* of the two male members sprang from unfair treatment and from extra demands by the family. But they sought similar interpretative and therapeutic methods, particularly those which rest upon viewing their illnesses as indirect result of general social and environmental problems taking place in public spheres of life: pollution, noise, crowdedness, traffic jams, etc. The therapies sought for such problems ranged from spiritual practices to herbal and biochemical medication. They both used prayers and reading Quran as means to alleviate their pains and retain their well being.

In contrast, women saw their bodies in direct connection with their family demands and pressures. The nervousness of Madam Farida and Um Ahmed was closely linked to supervision of children's performance at school and managing the material needs of the household respectively. Madam Farida comes from a social class different from that of Um Ahmed and Um Zaki. They were different in the way they used the notion of *zaʿal*. Madam Farida hid her feelings of anger while Um Ahmed and Um Zaki were always outspoken about them. The three women followed similar paths for treatment. They relied primarily on biochemical medication to control their physical well being which was always maintained in connection with spiritual activity. The latter activity was less conventional than that practiced by men. Women tended to use less praying and reading Quran than men. Further, when they relied on religious practices they chose to visit saint shrines instead of going to mosques. Madam Farida for example chose to go and visit one saint shrine in her home town outside Cairo and where she participated in a ceremony to celebrate the birthday of that saint. She did not mention that visit to me. It was her doctor son who complained to me at one occasion about his parents' "dated" healing practices. Um Zaki once remarked when her daughter had some severe stomach virus that if nothing helped they would go to the mosque of Sayyida Zeinab to pray for a cure there. The analysis of the narratives illustrates different ways for explaining and coping with *al-daght*. Healing strategies are more complex and require further research.

For women (here of the older generation) the additional element of having to conceive and give birth, preferably to sons, in order to achieve a relatively stable family and emotional life stands center-stage in the case of Madame Farida for example. Furthermore, being ill with *al-daght* was not enough reason to stop or regulate her pregnancies accordingly. Quite different from the "pressure" which men experience in their work place, this pressure is practiced within the close family surroundings. That it is essential for a woman to conceive and give birth to several children is taken for granted by Madame Farida as well as by other men and women in Egypt. Whether such a situation constitutes a source of additional stress and thus requires special bodily capacity is not particularly appreciated as in the case Abu Ahmed and his sons.

The narratives illustrate a number of other gender differences inherent in healing and coping strategies. High blood pressure as well as *al-daght* are often taken to be male diseases as mentioned above. Sickness is different from the concept of disease. It refers to differential social recognition of medically defined problems (Frankenberg 1980). In the case of the two couples *al-daght* gave Dr. Fawzi a legitimate reason to retire. It granted Abu Ahmed an excuse to stop worrying about family responsibilities. In contrast Madam Farida conceived four more children after the early onset of her illness. Um Ahmed's physical problems are more severe than her husband's, nevertheless, she carries the burden of housework and household responsibilities. These gender distinctions are part of dominant ways for explaining *al-daght*. It is eventually "a sickness of men who think harder" as one male physician explained to me. This statement is particularly ironic in the face of the recent survey of the disease which notes that high blood pressure was "slightly more common in women than men [26.9 percent versus 25.7 percent, respectively]" (Ibrahim 1995: 886).

Another factor which engenders *al-daght* according to all the individuals included is family tension and controversies. In general terms this factor is impossible to escape as obligation and ties are plentiful. Men and women are equally subjects to these tensions but not in the same manner. Family disputes and stress associated with raising children were mentioned by Madam Farida, Um Ahmed and Um Zaki in a much more direct way than in the case of Dr. Fawzi or Abu Ahmed. The three women included defined themselves as housewives, a factor which means that the time they spent at home with their children was longer than the husbands'. When family disputes were mentioned to men they expressed the problems they faced in managing the financial life of the family, a task which has to do with life outside their homes.

As with gender, so with class, the above two couples and one widowed women belong to two different and sharply distinguished economic classes of Cairo. The first couple above have direct and privileged access to the best health resources and references. They have room to choose among different options. Their contact with the modern health enterprise was enforced and promoted by the son doctor. The impact of this contact on Dr. Fawzi and Madame Farida was rather evident by the way the former set his priorities for therapies. He deliberately placed modern biomedicine and its categories for health at the top of every other option available. In contrast, Abu Ahmed's statement "that's what eventually counts, the refuge in Allah", and Um Zaki's almost complete reliance on her daughters emotional support, stand in sharp contrast to Dr. Fawzi's immense support for physician's control over family visits and his call for financial rather than emotional help.

Economic pressures in their different expressions are present in all three families. For Um and Abu Ahmed and Um Zaki it is the daily struggle of making ends meet, whereas Dr. Fawzi and Madame Farida feel the pressure of maintaining a middle class life style that is increasingly inaccessible to them. Their efforts at having what they for themselves perceive as adequate standards of living are frustrated again and again. In all families there is the implicit feeling that things are presently getting worse for the younger generation which is another worry of the parents generation who do not feel the calm reassurance of their children having found secure financial futures. Even Dr. Fawzi is worried that his college-educated children might ask him for help.

With regard to the role of *zaʿal* Dr. Fawzi and Madame Farida differ from the other two families in this regard. They used the modern Arabic terms of or *'infiʿal* and *tawattur* which have slightly different connotation than *zaʿal*. While *zaʿal* has largely negative connotations, *'infiʿal* and *tawattur* imply positive elements in that they are deemed necessary for success in life. They are the positive forces of ambition and willingness to struggle that can get people ahead in life. The positive value of ambition is deeply rooted in the middle class background of Dr. Fawzi and Madame Farida. This unrealized ambition is still the goal that the couple has set for their sons and daughters.

Whether *zaʿal* or *tawattur*, pollution or pressures or life, the above feelings and thoughts illustrate that *al-daght* has acquired a set of meanings specific to the social and cultural environment of Cairo. *Al-daght* is not equally distributed in all the city and neither are its meanings which differ from one social category to another and which constitute interesting examples for processes responsible for indigenizing knowledge not simply as abstract models of disease but as embodied categories and feelings about life struggles.

Notes

My research in Egypt was funded by a Karim Rida Said Scholarship of the Cambridge Overseas Trust, University of Cambridge, England, and an MEAward grant from the Population Council, Cairo. I am further grateful for the support provided through a Research Fellowship in the Anthropology Department at the American University in Cairo. Thanks go to Cynthia Nelson and Shahnaz Rouse for their helpful comments. I am grateful to Talal Asad for reading an earlier draft of this paper. Special thanks go to Petra Kuppinger for her support, inspiration and thoughtful comments.

1 High blood pressure is also known as hypertension. These are two technical terms and are used by practitioners of biomedicine. As a medical concept hypertension was first formulated by Franz Alexander in 1939. It was solely ascribed to a characteristic "psychodynamic structure" of the patients who suffer from it. Those patients where understood as having "very pronounced conflict between passive, dependent, feminine, receptive tendencies and over-compensatory, competitive, aggressive hostile impulses which lead to fear and increase a flight from competition towards the passive dependent attitude" (Alexander 1939 as cited in Dressler 1984: 267). More recently hypertension became a biomedical term whose cause might be unknown. Sometimes though it is ascribed to various physical factors such as aging, obesity, heart disease, kidney problems, etc. or to long-term psychological stress. Hypertension can turn into a chronic condition whose treatment depends mainly on long-term drug therapy to keep the blood pressure down. Unlike this biomedical individual-centered definition,

al-daght is a much more common term in Egypt and it has a wider scope of meaning which extends from high blood pressure to pressing social and economic conditions of life.

2 "Hypertensive" and "hypertensives" are terms used by many physicians in Egypt when they refer to individuals complaining from *al-dahgt*. For physicians hypertension can be of two types: essential and secondary. The essential type has no particular origin or cause. The secondary type is directly related to various conditions such as age, gender, obesity, kidney problems and substances such as dietary sodium. The Egyptian Society for Hypertension estimated the overall prevalence of hypertension in Egypt to be 26.3 percent (Ibrahim et al. 1995: 886). Only 37.5 percent of the hypertensive individuals were aware that they had high blood pressure. Hypertension can be asymptomatic. It is sometimes discovered accidentally during examinations for other complaints. Otherwise, blood pressure can rise and suddenly cause physical damages or result in death. Therefore, physicians and patients often refer to it as the "silent killer."

3 All the personal names are pseudonyms. I further changed a few details of people's lives and circumstances that are irrelevant to the present argument, in order to provide further anonymity.

4 During the period of my fieldwork each 3.34 Egyptian pounds had a purchase power equal to one American Dollar.

Selected Bibliography

Arabic Language

al-Hussaini, Ayman (1993) *Hal tuʿani min 'irtifaaʿ daghti ddam?: Dawaʿukal tabiʿ i minal 'aʿshaab wal-ghthaa'* (Do you suffer from high blood pressure?: your therapy is from herb and natural food), Al-Qahira: Makatabit Ibn Sina.

Majma' al-Lughah al-ʿarabiyya (1994) *Al-Muʿjam al-Wajiz*. Al-Qahira: Al-Hay'ah al-ʿammah li Sho'unil Mat abiʿ l-'amiriyya.

Western Languages

Armbrust, Walter (1996) *Mass Culture and Modernism in Egypt*, Cambridge: Cambridge University Press.

Ashour, Zainab et al. (1995) "The Egyptian National Hypertension Project (NHP): Design and Rational". *Hypertension* 26/1-1, pp. 880-885.

Dressler, William (1984) "Hypertension and Perceived Stress". *ETHOS* 13/3, pp. 265-283.

Frankenberg, Ronald (1980) "Medical Anthropology and Development: A Theoretical Perspective". *Social Science and Medicine* 14B, pp. 197-207.

Ibrahim, Muhsin et al. (1995) "Hypertension Prevalence, Awareness, Treatment, and Control in Egypt: Results from the Egyptian National Hypertension Project (NHP)". *Hypertension* 26/6-1, pp. 886-890.

Lyon, Margot L./Barbalet, Jack M. (1994) "Society's Body: Emotion and the 'Somatization' of Social Theory". In Thomas J. Csordas (ed.) *Embodiment and Experience: The Existential Ground of Culture and Self*, Cambridge: Cambridge University Press, pp. 48-66.

Morsy, Soheir (1980) "Body Concepts and Health Care: Illustration from an Egyptian Village". *Human Organization* 39/1, pp. 92-96.

Scheper-Hughes, Nancy/Lock, Margaret (1987) "The Mindful Body: A Prolegomenon to Future Work in Medical Anthropology". *Medical Anthropology Quarterly* 1/1, pp. 16-41.

Young, Allen (1982) "The Anthropology of Illness and Sickness". *Annual Review of Anthropology* 11, pp. 257-285.

Creating Bodies, Organizing Selves:
Planning the Family in Egypt

Kamran Asdar Ali

In a review article published in the late seventies on gender and women in the Middle East, Nikki Keddie ended her paper by suggesting that a future research agenda for the area should include the study of sexual habits of the people. She argued that the methodological problems posed by such studies should be overcome so that there could be a better understanding of gender relations in the Middle East (Keddie 1979: 239). This emphasis on understanding sexual relations would, according to the author, also aid our comprehension of peoples' attitude towards childbirth and their use of contraception. She claimed that only after knowing the intimate details of domestic life in the Middle East would researchers be able to gauge the success of the fertility control policy. This desire to learn about the private lives of the Arab family may be embedded in the liberal feminist political concerns of the seventies. Yet her position was also connected with a developmentalist agenda that seeks to change the private behavior of couples so that they can successfully use modern contraceptive methods. This concern with the private and sexual lives of the people continues in many forms in present day debates on health and reproduction in the Middle East.

Based on fieldwork in rural and urban Egypt this paper will present how such debates have historically sought to organize the female body through the rhetoric of good motherhood. I will show how in Egypt today the project of medicalization seeks to play a similar role through its arguments on reproductive health rights and family planning. Finally I shall argue that the historical and contemporary emphasis on the domestic and the private sphere in nationalist and developmental discourse are intrinsically linked to the construction of the modern Egyptian nation inhabited by a responsible citizenry.

The Focus Groups

I conducted a part of my field research in a village in the Nile Delta almost one hundred kilometers north-east of Cairo. My introduction into the village community was through a local family health center, staffed primarily by doctors from a research medical university in Cairo. The doctors provided services and conducted research in the area for their own post-graduate degrees. At this stage of my research I was primarily interested in getting to know the people who used the clinic. I was further looking forward to interviewing some women who came to the clinic to ascertain their response to the family planning project.

One of the doctors, who was a senior gynecologist and obstetrician attending in the clinic, suggested that conducting focus groups would aid the process of my introduction. He himself was working towards a degree in social demography from a British university and was interested in issues similar to my own. The participants were randomly selected through the network of other clinic staff members who lived in the area. The focus groups were primarily organized with selective groups of men of all ages and different professions (for example, peasants, local school teachers, public servants), community leaders (local sheikhs of mosques, members of cooperative council, people deemed important due to their wealth or connections to the state structure), *dayas* (midwives), religious leaders (instructors in religious schools) and two groups of peasant women who lived in nearby villages. As the participants were more familiar with the doctor and as I had no prior experience with this research methodology, a fact compounded by my still struggling local dialect, he moderated the sessions and I participated as his assistant. We would discuss the questions before the sessions and he would then conduct the focus groups asking a range of questions on family planning, domestic relationships, economic and social processes, etc. It took me a couple of sessions to realize that both my doctor colleague and I, were treated as authority figures by our informants. They ascribed this authority on me, even though I was non-Egyptian, primarily because I was introduced in the clinic as a physician and was working with one of the senior physicians of the clinic.

In the course of the interviews this authority was periodically challenged. Once in a session with young men my doctor friend probed the participants on their wives' use of contraceptives. Most men admitted preferring the IUD for their wives as they thought the IUD had fewer medical complications for women. When asked how the problem of breakthrough bleeding associated with IUDs was handled in their private lives, some men whose spouses were using IUDs responded that they treated it like menstrual blood and they did not have sex with their wives on such days. When we asked whether they engaged in foreplay on such occasions, a primary school teacher shot back, "Do you have foreplay before having sex or on days she menstruates?" The question caught us off guard, but made us aware of the boundaries between acceptable questions and those that would be resisted. Our response to the query was that we were the people who were asking questions and they did not have the right to ask us "personal" questions.

Such responses from the men somewhat subverted our authority. As researchers and doctors, we had assumed a right to probe the "private" lives of these men while at the same time assuming that they had no right to probe ours. We had definitely crossed the limits of acceptable questioning and from our position of authority sought to elicit information perhaps "crucial" to our project but arguably problematic for our respondents.

This episode and others like this did not stop my colleague from continuing on similar lines of questioning with other groups. Normally we would meet in the clinic with different groups of men and even the midwives. To show our sensitivity to local norms we met a group of peasant women in a villager's house near the clinic. The doctor was known to most of the women because they had consulted with him at the clinic. Our respondents were all married women between the ages of twenty five and fifty and only one among them had a high school diploma. After asking about their birthing history and questions about gender relations, the questions turned to body perceptions.

Q: 'What is the ovary and where is it?'
One woman replied, 'It is what carries the baby inside the mother.'

Another woman who had remained silent and was visibly uncomfortable with the questions, perhaps resenting our persistence, angrily replied, 'You are the doctor and should know more than us.'

We replied by explaining how we were interested in their perceptions of their bodies and what we knew was already present in health manuals and scientific literature. We hence continued and introduced questions about who teaches young women about sexual relationships before they are married. The women generally gave evasive replies but we persisted:

Q: 'So you think the girl should know something and not get married as a blind person (meaning uninformed)?'
One woman replied, 'We should tell them so that they do not get ill.'
Another argued, 'They know everything as the rate of education now is high.'
The third replied, 'The mother should tell her everything.'
And a fourth said, 'The mother or a friend should tell her.'

Q: 'Do you think we should tell the men more or the women?'
The woman who had replied third answered, 'The men as they know more.'

Q: 'If there were lessons arranged about how to sleep with men and how to get more pleasure would you be willing to attend such classes?'
Now the second woman said, 'No because all that is known here.'

Q: 'Do you agree or not that they should be taught how to have pleasure with their husbands?'
Again the second respondent answered, 'The girl is shy and may not like to attend.'

Q: 'Most women say that they do not get pleasure with their husbands so can we help them get more pleasure?'
The woman who spoke second continued to answer, 'The woman will not say whether she is pleased or not.'

Q: 'So if she gets pleasure or not it is not important?'
The same woman responded, 'She is free at home but she will not tell whether she gets pleasure or not.'

Q: 'If we teach women that there are sensitive places that if touched gives pleasure. Will the woman tell her husband to touch her in these places or not?'
The woman who had replied third, answered showing some irritation, 'No they will not.'
And the second woman said, 'It is impossible that women will go to these schools because the people will speak.'

Q: 'From your experience if he touches you some place and you felt pleasure will you ask him to touch again?'
The third woman answered, 'The man knows what makes his wife happy and comfortable.'

Q: 'But you would not ask him?'
The third woman, 'No!'

We perceived a hesitancy among the women in answering these questions. Should we have expected otherwise? We were two men, one a foreigner and the other a senior doctor, yet both strangers, prying into distinctly private aspects of their lives. These women were from the same village, at times related through marriage or blood. Talking about these issues could also implicate men all of them were familiar with. The evasiveness hence may have been linked to the role modesty, shame and respectability played in their daily lives. Moreover they may have thought the whole episode was insulting, prying and useless.

Questions on pleasure also exposed my own stereotypes about Egyptian rural and poor women and their passive role in sexual relationships. The agenda was at least two fold. One, an explicit argument was being made about how their sexual life could be more fulfilling if they asserted their individual desires to their husbands. The other implicit unspoken theme was of how circumcision may have affected the ability of these women to have pleasure. The hypothetical idea of lessons and arranging classes that was introduced into the conversation fit into a pedagogical exercise to grant these women consciousness of their bodies and sexuality. We had assumed, that these women possessed a certain universal core self, they only needed to be reminded of it. We were involved in a form of conversion. A conversion into modern sensibilities of self consciousness and of agency. We were also structuring new possibilities of interaction and seeking to destroy older ones. It is not that these women were not acting or were not agents in their own right. They were, however, according to our estimates, not choosing as individuals, not taking responsibility for their own improvement and hence were still tied up in "tradition". It should be mentioned, agency as a modern concept is not transcendental or universal; it is linked and regulated by specific historical structures of possibilities available to the agent (Asad 1996; Trouillot 1995). We were seeking to constitute specifically the modern choosing agent/subject. Our liberal humanist positioning made us forget that individuals are not free to choose the circumstances of their birth and their social membership in society. It led us to see their lives as an accident of "natural inequality" that social welfare policy, equal opportunity, or pedagogy could perhaps resolve (Chatterjee 1993: 232).

The women came to the focus groups because they were told that the doctors wanted to ask them some questions. The arrangements were done through the networks of social hierarchy present in the village. Our democratic posturing of a dialogue evidently was also not entirely dialogic. We were asking the questions, and they responded to the issues we raised. The parameters of discussion were not of their choosing. To initiate a conversation about where the ovary was or how they related to their husbands, was to draw them into arguments that were in this specific instance our concerns not theirs (see Comaroff/Comaroff 1992).

Whether *fellah* (peasant) women are more open about their personal lives or not, these focus groups became a part of a larger script of research on female reproductive and sexual habits being conducted in Egypt under the agenda of family planning research. The summary of my involvement is meant to emphasize the embeddedness of my own research in larger agendas beyond my own control. Also the intention here is not to accuse my colleague of insensitivity. His intervention was merely structured by the range of possibilities dictated by research questions raised by the international agencies and Egyptian researchers working on the fertility control program. Our masculine encounter with these rural women was an episode in a series of such sessions being performed all over Egypt at the time of my research.

Later, in Cairo, I observed several focus sessions being conducted by women's groups. The questions were very similar and the participants were poor urban women. Encounters like these, with the urban educated elite benevolently asking questions and the poor answering, are primarily embedded in the schema of traditional/modern dichotomy. The desire to understand is linked to an ambition to transform.

The need to change "traditional" customs has a long history in Egypt. In the following discussion I seek to show how the modern women sensitive developmental agenda is linked to the larger history of transformation of the "non-modern". In order to provide a historical understanding of this process of transformation I shall first briefly discuss how in late nineteenth century women's domestic sphere was sought to be regulated through the consolidation of modern medicine and the science of home economics.

The Colonial and the Nationalist Elite

Lord Cromer, the first Consul General of Egypt in his two volume treatise, *Modern Egypt*, attributes the low status of women in Egypt to Islam. He writes that the reason the social system of Islam is a total failure is because "first and foremost, Islam keeps women in position of marked inferiority" (Cromer 1908: 134). He then quotes the famous nineteenth century Orientalist Stanley Lane Poole to emphasize how "the degradation of women is a canker that begins its destructive work early in childhood and has eaten into the whole system of Islam" (Cromer 1908: 134 as quoted in Ahmed 1992: 152).

The modernizing Egyptian elite started replying to such writings by the end of the nineteenth century. Qasim Amin, a prosecutor in the Europeanized legal system and belonging to the Turko-Circassian landholding class, wrote several books on the issue of emancipation of women in this period. He agreed with colonial critics of Muslim social life regarding the backwardness of women. Yet he argued that this was not due to Islam but to the abandoning of the central traits of Islam. The future organization of society in which women would be liberated was conditioned on the premise of following new ideas of science and progress learnt from the European experience (Mitchell 1988: 113; Cole 1981).

In his most famous book, *Tahrir al Mar'ah* (The Liberation of Women), Amin concentrates on how customs of divorce, polygamy, female inheritance, lack of female education and the veiling of women in Egyptian society are detrimental to the progress of the nation as a whole. Reflecting the liberal and utilitarian influence of late nineteenth century European values, he reprimanded the ruling classes for their treatment of women and their retrogressive social mores. Juan Ricardo Cole (1981) argues that issues like veiling in late nineteenth century Egypt were not relevant to the multitude of poor and rural women who worked as domestic servants or as peasants. Amin's writings were primarily geared towards the reform of upper middle class women of his own social background. Taking on the themes invoked by Europeans, Amin created a national debate depicting native Turko-Circassian rulers as unjust, despotic and plunderers of national wealth (Cole 1981: 395). In contrast to this, the British and the Europeans were praised as benevolent and their rule as guaranteeing freedom and justice. His writings emphasized the virtues of the bourgeois European values as the epitome of civilization and argued for their adoption in Egyptian private and public life (Cole 1981: 396).

The salient feature of European thought that impressed Amin was modern science. In his view it was modern science that had attacked superstition, undermined the authority of the clerics, abolished slavery, created democratic constitutions, invented steam power and electricity. These changes Amin argued had an immense impact on the existing equality among European men and women (Cole 1981: 395).

However, for liberals like Amin, Egyptian men and women were never seen as equals in intellectual capacity. On the contrary, his books viciously attack the character of upper class Egyptian women. He portrays them as illiterate, shifty and manipulative in their dealings with men (Amin 1992 [1899]). This he attributes to their lack of education, improper upbringing and to their seclusion from public life. This belief in the lesser intelligence of women did not stop him from arguing for equal rights for women. He advocated female education and their right to work and support themselves. However, Amin complains in *Tahrir al Mar'ah* that men educated in the new schools found it difficult to find women who could be their true partners (Amin 1992 [1899]). Romantic love was supposed to be the basis of the relationship among spouses in the modern nuclear family and bourgeois household. Women's education was hence also linked to the fulfillment of the personal needs of upper class men like Amin who desired a cultured and educated life partner (Cole 1981: 400-401).[1]

Amin criticized upper class women for not taking care of their personal hygiene and appearance, thus not being able to influence the desires of their husbands. Similarly their lack of intellectual capabilities made them jealous and critical of their hardworking men. He demanded that women stop wasting their time in trivial pursuits and engage themselves in the vital aspects of organizing the household, dealing with the domestic budget, supervising the servants and busy themselves in the proper upbringing of children. Educated and domestically organized women could only become social equals of their men and guarantee a harmonious relationship based on true love and affection (Amin 1992 [1899]).

Ideas on the changes in domestic lives were also being presented among groups of women belonging to the upper classes (Baron 1994). Women writers published articles in the press arguing for a more equitable relationship between husbands and wives and also asserting the idea of marriage for love rather than economic consideration (Baron 1994: 165). Women like Malak Hifni Nasaf, who belonged to the upper middle class of Egyptian society who stood against unveiling nonetheless argued for a broad and professional education for women, and against the practice of polygamy (Cole 1981: 401). There was surely a diversity of opinion among women themselves on the issue of the emancipation of Egyptian women. However, there were also areas of shared agenda and agreement with liberal writers like Qasim Amin (Baron 1994; Cole 1981). One of these was the crucial interest in the process of motherhood. For Amin and other late nineteenth century modernist reformers, educating women was related to their responsibility in raising children. It was hoped that an educated motherhood would create a modern political order that would begin at their knees (Mitchell 1988: 113). Amin accuses the ignorance, non hygienic nature, and superstitious beliefs of women as detrimental to the prospects of a future modern Egyptian nation. For Amin the solution lay in training girls themselves on sound scientific basis enabling them to better raise the next generation. Similarly female writers concentrated on instructions of pre and post-partum health care for the mother and the child and showed extreme interest in the organization of childbirth on more scientific lines (Baron 1994: 159).

It is in this framework that we need to understand the focus on women's reproductive life and the private domain in late nineteenth century Egypt. The responsibility to raise children could not be left to women alone. The reproduction of the nation itself depended on the scientific reorganization of how and under what circumstances children would be born and raised.

At the turn of the century more than ninety percent of childbirth in Egypt were performed by midwives, some of these midwives were called *hakimas* and were graduates from the official midwifery schools. *Dayas*, the more traditional midwives were however, the mainstay of most maternity cases in urban and rural areas. The reorganization of women's healing and birthing practices meant the displacement of the *dayas* and other women healers by modern medicine. The *hakimas* were recruited and trained from the times of Mohammad Ali Pasha (1805-1848) in the basics of public health, surgical skills and gynecology and obstetrics to serve the female population of Egypt. By the turn of the century these practitioners were allowed to only practice midwifery and were being rapidly replaced by European nurses and male medical doctors. Moreover, the traditional midwife the *daya*, was increasingly blamed for infant deaths and unhygienic birthing practices by the colonial medical authorities and were under intense surveillance and attack by the early part of the twentieth century (Morsy 1993: 23-25).

Cromer argued that in the civilized world the rule was of attendance of patients by male doctors (Tucker 1985: 122). The male dominated medical system competed with the local midwife to seek dominance in controlling the health and well being of women. This meant an increasing interest by medical scholars in what were deemed as the traditional customs and beliefs of Egyptian women. An example of this concern was evident in the publication of *Tibb Al Rukka* or *Old Wives Medicine* in 1892 by an Egyptian physician Abd Al-Rahman Ismail.[2] In several volumes of this book, the author gave detailed accounts of the various health practices of the poor. The aim of the texts was to expose the negative and "foolish" aspects of these peoples' beliefs. His texts seek to display the falsity of the popular healing system and argue for the supremacy of scientific facts of medicine.

In a similar article published early in the twentieth century, Gorgy Sobhy, a graduate of the Kasr-el-Aini Medical College in Cairo, admonishes women for seeking treatment from a scientifically trained doctor only when their life was in danger (Sobhy 1904). The article goes on to present a study of the customs and superstitions of Egyptians on childbirth and pregnancy. Sobhy's detailed description of the traditional birthing method displayed the importance medical reformers in Egypt put in the context of indigenous beliefs. A knowledge of these beliefs would in turn help them to implement policies to transform these practices.

The history of public health and hygiene in most societies locates the body at the juncture of the public and private spheres of life (Chakrabarty 1992: 21). The emphasis on female practices in Egypt also speaks to the split between the modernizing elite and the yet to be modernized poor. Late nineteenth century reformers primarily concentrated on the improvement of their own class. However, they also saw themselves as representing the entire future Egyptian nation. Medicalized discourse on body and health helped them in incorporating other classes into their modernist agenda. The education of women, the organization of the household and the studying of female birthing practices hence created opportunities to ensure the future of the Egyptian nation to be different from the past. These processes continue even today in debates on the health and hygiene of Egyptian women. In the next section I shall focus on how women centered groups in Egypt are often involved in the process of acquiring knowledge from and prescribing changes for the Egyptian poor. Motivated by the rhetoric of social good linked to public health, these groups at times are embedded in the larger agenda of international development and its theories of modernization.

Women Groups and Their Politics

Secular women's/feminist groups in Egypt[3] to a large degree strive to change anti-women laws stipulated by the Egyptian State to control the private and public life of Egyptian women. They operate mostly through organizing seminars, lectures and other intellectual and cultural activities on women issues. These consciousness raising forums are meant for the interchange of ideas among the educated group of feminist women and men. In demanding the emancipation of women some groups link their politics to the larger political struggles in Egypt on social and economic rights, reforms in labor laws and the freedom of assembly and association. The agenda is to strive within the parameters of legality to increase the legal and political space of permissible democratic politics. However for the more politically active groups it is extremely difficult to survive as a legal entity. Under Egyptian law all not-for profit groups need to be registered with the government, specifically with the Ministry of Social affairs which retains the right to close down any organization that it deems subversive.

Afaf (not her real name) a member of a group that holds seminars on women issues and politically cooperates with other human rights and labor groups, argued that

We are caught between the state, the international funding agencies and the Islamic groups. We are not recognized by the state and need to register ourselves as commercial companies with tax paying status, where will we get the money when we do not generate anything.

This specific group had a policy of also not accepting international funds Afaf continued:

International funding is readily available in Egypt these days, but it binds us activists into certain kinds of priorities, discourses and engagements.

Like Afaf's group, some women's groups are critical of the internationally funded Egyptian family planning program on methodological grounds. They oppose the use of poor urban and rural women as objects of experimentation for new contraceptive technology by international donor agencies. A member of the National Council for Women, the women's wing of the left leaning *Tagammau* Party, clearly stated, "they use the bodies of poor Egyptian women to experiment their contraceptives." Others argue for a more comprehensive notion of rights that includes provision for the health of the mother and the social well-being of women. A larger agenda of reproductive rights, according to them, needs to be more inclusive and give equal opportunities to all classes of women. Through this critique and engagement they have been able to push the debate on reproductive rights beyond the mere providing of contraceptives, towards becoming more sensitive to the needs of women's health in general.

A number of women's groups act as NGOs or consultants and contribute to the developmental debate from a specific women centered and nationalistic point of view. They argue that their efforts can help in focussing the international funds to appropriate "targets", on issues of women and development. This guarantees a diminution of waste and corruption in the development process and sets priorities designated according to "real need".

An example of this endeavor is the study (1989-1990) on the sexual and reproductive health of women in the Giza governorate south of Cairo funded by the Population Council. A multi-disciplinary team consisting of a doctor who specializes in obstetrics and gynecology, an anthropologist and a social demographer among others was associated with this project. The research was focussed on the gynecological morbidities in the community under study. The youngest women in the study were less than twenty five years of age and the oldest were sixty. Most were uneducated and of poor social economic background. I shall discuss this project in some detail to show how feminist concerns for the health of poor women seek to influence policy on fertility issues.

In a series of papers published from the project data (Younis et al. 1993; Zurayk et al. 1994; Zurayk et al. 1995) the authors show a high rate of prevalence of reproductive tract diseases in the given population. They argue that most of these diseases go unnoticed because women do not complain about their problems and endure the disease in silence (Zurayk et al. 1994: 4). All women in the study, a total of 500, were given a clinical gynecological examination performed by female physicians. It was found that over fifty percent of women suffered from reproductive tract infections. More than fifty percent also had prolapse of the genital tract. Other diseases like cervical ectopy and premalignant cervical cell changes were present in almost a third of the women. There was incidence of high blood pressure, anemia and urinary tract infections in the community. The severity of the situation was underscored by the researchers' finding that many women had multiple diseases (Zurayk et al. 1994: 5).

Reproductive tract infection was reportedly higher among women who were sexually active. Current IUD use was also associated with high incidence of vaginal and cervical infections, anemia, prolapse and a predisposition to pelvic inflammatory disease. Women who, according to the researchers, had unhygienic practices during menstruation, were also susceptible to infections of the reproductive tract. In fact it was argued that only one-fourth of the women were regarded as having hygienic practices as they either boiled their menstrual protection or used disposable ones (Younis et al. 1993: 180-184).[4] An important aspect of the research was the attention given to women's own perception of their bodies and health status. Respondents were asked about vaginal discharge, for an assessment of genital tract infection. The researchers found that very few women ("only 13 percent") reported having a discharge other than ordinary. In contrast, the researchers own medical examination found that at least sixty four percent of all women had medically suspicious discharge. They presented this information to highlight how "women may not perceive certain symptoms as dangerous or abnormal, considering them part of their reproductive reality" (Zurayk et al. 1994: 11).

These studies sensitize us to the prevalent gynecological and health problems faced by the poor rural women in Egypt. The shift in the rhetorical emphasis of family planning services from merely providing contraceptives to the inclusion of broader health priorities of women are a welcome change in family planning policy and program. The studies have also advocated a sensitivity to women's needs in health delivery systems and asked for training of health care providers on cultural issues related to women. A recommendation was also made for the presence of female doctors in the clinics who could provide hygienic and safe reproductive tract examinations. These suggestions stem from hearing complaints by women about the available health delivery system. However, the policy solution advocated by these studies needs to be evaluated. For example, in face of the evidence that IUDs cause reproductive tract infection among most users, non-use of IUDs was never a recommendation. On the contrary, suggestions were made to improve insertion technique, to better train providers in the health facilities and to encourage women to have regular check up visits (Younis et al. 1994; Zurayk et al. 1993).

Following Soheir Morsy's excellent critique of maternal mortality discourse in Egypt (Morsy 1991, 1993), I argue that these interventions are basically meant to strengthen the family planning program itself. If women's health was the primary focus of these studies then the emphasis should not have been only on improving the health delivery system, but also on alleviation of poverty and social economic problems of the community, which were deemed to be responsible for most disease conditions. Also if IUDs were one of the major sources of infection, then why was there no suggestion to stop the use of IUDs for the poor and susceptible groups of women who have recurrent infections with its use? The training of providers and placing counselors in the community to aid women in their health problems (Zurayk et al. 1994: 20) are important steps. However, these interventions consolidate the health delivery system and make it more efficient and consistent with the larger international family planning policy goals of improving the state programs by making them more "sensitive" to the needs of the clients. The policy implications are more about streamlining the failures of the family planning program through an agenda of cultural sensitivity, counseling and persuasion.

The researchers also called for further studies on women's own perceptions of body health, sexuality and self. It was argued that such understanding would help providers in communicating with women and form a base for the health education campaigns. These campaigns were designed to raise women's awareness of their own reproductive health and guide them towards seeking health care in disease conditions (Zurayk et al. 1994: 18).

Not unlike the turn of the century arguments on the unhygienic and superstitious practices of women the researchers for the Giza study also blame the birth attendants (*dayas*) for obstetric trauma (Younis et al. 1993). They further label women's own personal habits as "unhygienic" and stress how women do not understand their own health system and need to be reminded of their "abnormal" discharges. The substitution of women's own understanding of their bodies by medicalized notions of female reproductive health exposes the somewhat elitist nature of these arguments. Hence the desire to learn more about women's own perception should be viewed in relation to researchers' aspirations to deal with the conflict between their own perception of health and that of women themselves. In the liberal language of equal partners in health and the relationship of provider and client is hidden a strange alliance, in which "one party avails itself of the other party in order to manipulate them all the more successfully" (Taussig 1980: 12).

I discussed this example not to make a blanket assessment of all women centered groups but to show how the international liberal agenda of development works itself into localized research. For example, NGOs with a women and development component are created by the donations and organizational skills of the larger international development program in Egypt. These groups as recognized NGOs generate debates within Egypt on internationally defined positions on women's reproductive rights. Under the auspices of the Population Council, Ford Foundation and the USAID, such groups organize seminars and write position papers on reproductive health related issues of women's individual rights and autonomy. Women centered literature on reproductive health supports the role of such NGOs as crucial in making governments accountable to comply with international treaties on the emancipation of women and also to the acts of discrimination that affect the status of women in different countries (Cook 1993: 83; Toubia/An-Naim n.d.: 18-24). Some women centered groups hence serve as a pressure group bridging the gap between international standards and its impact on the local situation within the state of Egypt. Of course the poorest women of Egypt do not have the critical voice in these debates that are led by Western feminists or educated upper class native "diasporics" (see Spivak 1996). Moreover, the argument on autonomy of women and choice in fertility control is made as welfare structures are being dismantled in Egypt leaving families, especially women and children economically and socially vulnerable.

In this process some secular women's groups speak in an universalized language of emancipation, thus invoking the authority to represent all Egyptian women and liberate them from their "misery". In such instances these formations remain within the parameters of the debate set by the larger neo-liberal agenda of international development. By speaking the language of liberal democracy they may become the interlocutors for the international agencies and representative of what is modern, what is communicable and what is within the framework of International capital. As Chakrabarty reminds us, the politics based on the agenda of "rights" and "consciousness raising" are historically linked with the effort of creating citizens and strengthening of the state along with its capacity of coercion, "the continual forgetting of which fact constitutes the kernel of the citizen's 'everyday life'" (Chakrabarty 1994a: 331).

Many women in these groups have suffered personally and collectively in their struggle for rights of women in Egypt. The politics based on the invocation of "rights" may be important in the sphere of local struggles against undemocratic structures. However, this discourse of rights reworked into formulation of reproductive rights and maternal morbidity/mortality studies, the new emphasis in family planning discourse in Egypt, retains the linkage of reproduction and fertility to women. This is not dissimilar to the notion of self control and discipline embedded in the rhetoric of "choice" for women propagated by the state sponsored family planning program. It is women who should choose; reproduction remains a female act. In doing this, liberal notions of individual agency[5] and gendered victimhood are reproduced to argue for women's emancipation.

Discussion and Conclusion

The history of the modern Egyptian nation-state is eminently linked with the transformation within its domestic sphere. As Dipesh Chakrabarty reminds us in the context of colonial Bengal "the public sphere could not be erected without reconstructing the private." (Chakrabarty 1994: 58). The internal ordering of the domestic was hence the key to the progress envisioned by turn of the century educated Egyptian elite. Here the issue of motherhood was crucial. Women were supposed to shed their unhygienic habits, superstitious beliefs and untidy lifestyles and get educated into becoming proper mothers. Qasim Amin's forceful admonishment to mothers is worth quoting:

Is it not a mother's ignorance that allows her to neglect her child's cleanliness so that he is dirty and left to wander in the streets and alleys, wallowing in the alleys in the dirt as baby animals do? Is it not her ignorance that allows him to be lazy, running away from work and wasting his precious time, which is his capital, lying around, sleeping and dallying, even though childhood years are the years of energy, work and action? ... Is it not a mother's ignorance that compels her to bring up her child through fear of *jinn* and evil spirits?

(Amin 1992 [1899]: 26-27)

The motherhood that guaranteed children would be well trained, ate proper diet, were regulated into work habits and had the correct moral values was crucial to the aims of Egyptian nationalist leaders. This not only meant a change in the lives of the women but a redefinition of what childhood would also mean from then onwards. Of course there were competing visions to this essentially upper class male discourse of creating citizen-subjects for the future nation. Other men sought to underplay the importance of women participating in the public sphere and criticized the unquestioning acceptance of European values. Similarly upper class women in late nineteenth century contested male centered representation of a good housewife, calling for more education, autonomy and independence for women (see Baron 1994; Badran 1995). In these terms the new disciplining power were not only repressive but created opportunities to challenge older forms of authority.

As new orders create new possibilities they also create new forms of governance. Where the discourse on motherhood was organized around modern notions of the domestic, there, new arguments incorporate the rhetoric of health risks and population control to again reorder female bodies. The crisis of the welfare state has given way to policies in which individuals need to shoulder responsibilities for their own ill health and the level of potential risk that they may pass onto the social. The discourse on permanent retraining, self-management and decentralized planning (Martin 1994; Donzelot 1991a) is distinctly different from the concerns of a welfare state that guarantees the eradication of poverty and provides a rhetoric of opportunity. Health becomes an issue of civic responsibility. As a list of unhealthy behavior is prepared that adversely affect the economy, public health campaigns seek to target the irresponsible social groups that are defined as the most pathological in terms of their cost to the collectivity (Donzelot 1991b: 271). Women who plan to have a third or a fourth child in Egypt are considered to be a part of this pathology.

The relationship between the social and the individual, between the responsibility of the state and those of its citizens are at times mitigated through NGOs. The celebration of civil society as a counterpoint to the oppressive state is a familiar refrain in the democratic politics of lesser developed nation-sates. In this paper I have however, argued that their role in Egypt may be linked to the neo-liberal international political agenda and in extension to the political history of the West. Moreover civil society cannot be thought outside the logic of the nation-state itself. The debate and contestation over reproductive rights and arguments for the privilege of labor to organize can only exist if there is a fundamental agreement on the language used by the democratic project of citizenship.

As new ideas create opportunities to rethink categories and reassemble possibilities, other rhetorics of community and the social may also co-exist with the larger developmental agenda of the modern nation-state. However, it is always a relationship of asymmetry and to label it as resistance or even a negotiation would be an injustice to the existing unequal relationship of power.

Notes

The field work in Egypt was supported by a doctoral grant by the Population Council and by the anthropology department at the Johns Hopkins University. Institutional support, while in Egypt, was provided by the American University in Cairo. I thank the editors of this volume, Cynthia Nelson and Shahnaz Rouse for their close readings and suggestions. I, however, remain responsible for the final shape of this article and any shortcomings herein.

1 Rather, Amin (Amin 1992 [1899] cited in Cole 1981: 400-401) complained that the seclusion of Upper Class women put them at a risk of being subservient to the male servants who walked along side them in the streets. Such women were the attention of impolite remarks on the streets which lower class women more often escaped. In the late nineteenth century narrative of nationalist liberation, servants and lower class populace were as important to be defended against as the aristocratic and conservative traditions.

2 It is interesting to note that the translator of these texts John Walker as late as 1934 explicitly declined to translate those portions that dealt with the condemnation of the foreign occupation of Egypt (Walker 1934: 9). Although European and modern Egyptians agreed on the primacy of medical science there was may have been a latent tension on the issue of occupation.

3 I interviewed members of different women groups. I occasionally attended seminars and presentations organized by them and also came across some of them individually in my research on Egyptian NGOs and while visiting offices of international development agencies. My focus in this paper is to represent the broader issues that unite their agenda rather than to do an ethnography of each group separately. However, it should be mentioned that the politi-

cal leanings of these groups range from Marxist nationalist to the mere liberal. The self expression of these groups as feminists is also a complicated issue and beyond the range of arguments presented here. For a more complex presentation of their views see Nadje Al-Ali in this volume.

4 The information on personal hygiene of women is also essential from a marketing point of view. As commodities enter the Egyptian market, manufacturers of sanitary products need this kind of information to create newer markets. Also a new sensibility towards cleanliness and hygiene is simultaneously introduced.

5 Talal Asad (1993, 1995), argues that the concept of agency linked to a consciousness is problematic as it obscures the fact that actions are occasionally not products of individual will, but structured by the range of possibilities available in a certain given situation.

Selected Bibliography

Ahmed, Leila (1992) *Woman and Gender in Islam*, New Haven/CT: Yale University Press.

Amin, Qasim (1992 [1898]) *The Liberation of Women*. Translated by Samiha Sidhom Peterson, Cairo: American University in Cairo Press.

Asad, Talal (1992) "Conscripts of Western Civilization". In Christine Ward Gailey (ed.) *Civilization in Crisis*, Gainsville/FL: University Press of Florida, pp. 333-352.

—— (1993) *Genealogies of Religion*, Baltimore/MD: John Hopkins University Press.

—— (1994) "Ethnographic Representation, Statistics and Modern Power". *Social Research* 61/1, pp. 55-88.

—— (1995) "Interview". By Saba Mahmood. Stanford Humanities Review. A special Issue on *Contested Politics* 5/1, pp. 1-16.

—— (1996) "Comments on Conversion". In Peter van der Veer (ed.) *Conversions to Modernities: The Globalization of Christianity*, London: Routledge, pp. 263-273.

Badran, Margot (1995) *Feminists, Islam, and Nation*, Princeton/NJ: Princeton University Press.

Baron, Beth (1991) "The Making and Breaking of Marital Bonds in Modern Egypt". In Nikki Keddie/Beth Baron (eds.) *Women in*

Middle Eastern History, New Haven/CT: Yale University Press, pp. 275-291.

—— (1994) *The Women's Awakening in Egypt*, New Haven/CT: Yale University Press.

Chakrabarty, Dipesh (1992) "Postcoloniality and the Artifice of History: Who Speaks for 'Indian' Pasts?". *Representations* 37, pp. 1-26.

—— (1994a) "Labor History and the Politics of Theory: An Indian Angle on the Middle East". In Zachary Lockman (ed.) *Workers and Working Classes in the Middle East*, Albany/NY: State University of New York Press, pp. 321-333.

—— (1994b) "The Difference-Deferral of a Colonial Modernity: Public Debates on Domesticity in British India". In David Arnold/David Hariman (eds.) *Subaltern Studies VIII*, Delhi: Oxford University Press, pp. 50-88.

—— (1994c) "Marx After Marxism: History, Subalternity, and Difference". *Positions* 2/2, pp. 446-463.

—— (1995) "Radical Histories and Question of Enlightenment Rationalism. Some Recent Critiques of Subaltern Studies". *Economic and Political Weekly*, 8 April, pp. 751-759.

Chatterjee, Partha (1989) "Colonialism, Nationalism, and Colonized Women: The Contest in India". *American Ethnologist* 16/4, pp. 622-633.

—— (1993) *The Nation and its Fragments*, Princeton/NJ: Princeton University Press.

Cole, Juan Ricardo (1981) "Feminism, Class and Islam in the Turn-of-the-Century Egypt". *International Journal of Middle East Studies* 13, pp. 387-407.

—— (1993) *Colonialism and Revolution in the Middle East*, Princeton/NJ: Princeton University Press.

Comaroff, John/Comaroff, Jean (1992) *Ethnography and the History of Imagination*, Boulder/CO: Westview Press.

Cromer, E., Lord (1908) *Modern Egypt*, London: Macmillan.

Cook, Rebecca (1993) "International Human Right and Women's Reproductive Health". *Studies in Family Planning* 24/2, pp. 73-86.

Donzelot, Jacques (1991a) "The Mobilization of Society". In Graham Burchell et al. (eds.) *The Foucault Effect*, Chicago/IL: The University of Chicago Press, pp. 169-180.

—— (1991b) "The Pleasure of Work". In Graham Burchell et al. (eds.) *The Foucault Effect*, Chicago/IL: The University of Chicago Press, pp. 251-280.

Freedman, Lynn P. (Undated) *Women Health and the Third World Debt: A Critique of the Public Health Response to Economic Crises.* Unpublished Manuscript.

Isaacs, Stephen/Freedman, Lynn (1992) "Reproductive Health/Reproductive Rights: Legal, Policy and Ethical Issues". Manuscript Prepared for Ford Foundation Reproductive Health Program Officers Meeting.

Keddie, Nikki (1979) "Problems in the Study of Middle Eastern Women". *International Journal of Middle East Studies* 10, pp. 225-240.

Martin, Emily (1994) *Flexible Bodies*, Boston/MA: Beacon Press.

Mitchell, Timothy (1988) *Colonizing Egypt*, Cambridge: Cambridge University Press.

—— (1995) "The Object of Development. America's Egypt". In Jonathan Crush (ed.) *Power of Development*, London: Routledge, pp. 129-157.

—— (1995) "The Space of Property and the Formation of the Nation". Paper presented at the symposium *Questions of Modernity*, 19-20 April, New York University.

Morsy, Soheir (1978) "Sex Roles, Power and Illness in an Egyptian Village". *American Ethnologist* 5/1, pp. 137-150.

—— (1991) "Maternal Mortality in Egypt: Selective Health Strategy and the Medicalization of Population Control". Paper Prepared for the Conference "The Politics of Reproduction", sponsored by Wenner Gren Foundation, Terespolis, Brazil.

—— (1993) *Gender, Sickness and Healing in Rural Egypt*, Boulder/CO: Westview Press.

Ong, Aihwa (1988) "The Production of Possession: Spirits and the Multinational Corporations in Malaysia". *American Ethnologist* 15/1, pp. 28-42.

Sobhy, Gorgy (1904) "Customs and Superstitions of the Modern Egyptians". In *Records of the Egyptian Government School of Medicine* 2, pp. 101-120.

Spivak, Gayatari Chakravorty (1996) "Woman as Theater". *Radical Philosophy* 75, pp. 2-4.

Taussig, Michael (1980) "Reification and the Consciousness of the Patient". *Social Science in Medicine* 14B, pp. 3-13.

Toubia, Nahid/An-Na'im, Abdullahi (n.d.) "Legal Dimensions of the Health of Women in Arab and Muslim Countries". Unpublished Working Manuscript for Population Council and Ford Foundation.

Trouillot, Michel-Rolph (1995) *Silencing the Past*, Boston/MA: Beacon Press.

Tucker, Judith (1985) *Women in Nineteenth Century Egypt*, Cambridge: Cambridge University Press.

―― (1993) "The Arab Family in History". In Judith Tucker (ed.) *The Arab Family in Egypt*, Bloomington/IN: Indiana University Press, pp. 195-207.

Walker, John (1934) *Folk Medicine in Modern Egypt*, London: Luzac and Co.

Younis, Nabil et al. (1993) "A Community Study of Gynecological and Related Morbidities in Rural Egypt". *Studies in Family Planning* 24/3, pp. 175-186.

Zurayk, Huda et al. (1994) *Rethinking Family Planning Policy in Light of Reproductive Health Research,* Cairo: The Population Council.

―― (1995) "Comparing Women's Report with Medical Diagnoses of Reproductive Morbidity Conditions in Rural Egypt". *Studies in Family Planning* 26/1, pp. 14-21.

DEATH OF A MIDWIFE

PETRA KUPPINGER

"*Shaifa al-awlad di kullaha?*" Um Ali all of a sudden asked me, "do you see all these children?"[1] We had been comfortably leaning out of Um Ali's first floor window in the community of El Tayibin, in Giza, the western part of metropolitan Cairo for the last fifteen minutes when Um Ali, immersed in watching some children in the alley had addressed me with this question.

"All these children that you see down there in the alley," she answered her own question, "I have brought them into this world. I know them all, their names and their mothers. This is what I have done for all my life," she added.

When I first met Um Ali in 1989 she was living and practicing midwifery in El Tayibin. In her late 50s, Um Ali lived alone in a room in her late husband's family's house. Her daughter was married and lived in Bulaq Al-Dakrour. The daughter, her husband and children frequently came to visit Um Ali. Her son had been working in an Arab country for many years and she only occasionally heard from him. Sometimes Um Ali hosted her nephews from a provincial town, when they came to Cairo to study, to look for work or for other purposes. Um Ali's days were busy: when not called for assistance in birth and matters related to her work, she was visiting her many neighbors, friends and relatives in El Tayibin (and sometimes beyond). She maintained an extensive and dynamic social network, and wherever we went together, she was received with the utmost of respect and friendship. In many social gatherings she was the center with her warm and humorous personality and sharp mind. Drawing on her experiences as a midwife she had many stories and anecdotes to tell.

The community of El Tayibin is one of the older villages in central

Giza that had been engulfed by and become part of the modern metropolis many decades ago. It shares features with many other low-income urban neighborhoods in Cairo where people work hard to make ends meet. El Tayibin is far from being internally homogenous, families of eight sharing one room in an old dwelling live next door to residents of small modern apartments in recently rebuilt concrete and brick buildings. Small scale street vendors, successful car workers, occasionally employed unskilled workers, migrant wives, small government employees and poor old widows live next to each other, and with each other in El Tayibin.

In decades of devoted midwife practice Um Ali had established an excellent reputation in El Tayibin and beyond. Sometimes she was called to attend births in the more prosperous and newer neighborhood of Sharia Al-Tawil, located at a close distance to El Tayibin. Similarly, she was asked for her services in the newer so-called informal neighborhoods around the old villages of Bulaq Al-Dakrour, Saft Al-Laban or Moatamdiya west of the Upper Egyptian Railways. Many of the younger generation – like Um Ali's daughter – from El Tayibin had moved there as space became scarce in the old community.

Residents of El Tayibin frequently praised the work of Um Ali, her expertise, and the special care and attention she gave to the women who sought her help[2]. In the early 1990s, however, Um Ali had to slowly withdraw from her work as her health increasingly failed her. For a while she only followed calls from people whom she knew particularly well, families with whom she had worked for decades, or those who simply lived nearby. Eventually she had to give up even those obligations. As she slowly retired there was nobody in the community to take over her position and women were forced to either go a much longer way to find a *daya* (midwife) like Um Ali, or to give birth in hospitals in the surrounding area, whether they liked those or not.[3] Um Ali died in 1994. Um Ali's death constituted a turning point for her community and those elsewhere who had relied on her services, as she left nobody to follow her and take over her work. Many women greatly regret the fact that there is no longer a *daya* like Um Ali close by to consult. The death of Um Ali and the end of *daya* practice in El Tayibin is not an isolated phenomena or an odd local coincidence but is representative of the larger trend of marginalizing and eliminating the practice of *dayas* and its larger context of time-honored popular female wisdom.[4]

Examining the experiences of Um Ali and other midwives in El Tayibin over the last century, I will illustrate aspects of midwife practices, and the slow disappearance of midwife services. I will analyze these developments within the context of transformations within a larger medical, social and cultural context. The work of a *daya*, the way Um Ali and many like her practiced it, was not merely a "professional" activity but was deeply embedded in a social and communal context. This, of course, was a very specifically female context. Um Ali's ways of work and times of work were immensely flexible and highly individualized in their social and economic aspects. Her scope of expertise and activities went far beyond pregnancy and childbirth and extended to a multitude of other aspects of reproductive, sexual and child health. Women and families who consulted and asked for her help knew her capabilities.

Hence not much needed to be said and she was discreetly called upon when need arose. This smooth and discrete practice of *dayas* created a perception that they stood outside the control of authorities, and hence were increasingly perceived as offensive to the rationalities of modern institutionalized medicine.

Starting from the early 19th century existing forms of midwifery in Egypt had come under attack from nascent western medical models and the emerging modern state. From the perspective of institutionalized modern medicine, existing forms of midwifery came to be viewed with contempt. Midwifery practices were labeled irrational, backward, ignorant and even dangerous. Taking the example of the midwives of El Tayibin, I will show that midwifery practices were none of the above. Instead, midwives were skilled practitioners who offered a large scope of physical treatments and social services.[5] In order to place the work of Um Ali and her predecessors, I will first introduce the community of El Tayibin.

El Tayibin

In the 1870s Princess Fatma Hanem, a daughter of Khedive Ismail, was endowed by her father with an estate in the lavish countryside on the western Nile bank opposite the city of Cairo. Surrounded by fields, the estate attracted or recruited a number of peasant families who settled in a cluster of houses outside the gates of Fatma Hanem's palace.

Um Ibrahim, a sixty-year-old residents of El Tayibin whose family has been settled in the community for three generations remembers accounts she heard about the early history of the community:

> The community of El Tayibin has not always been in the same place. A long time ago it was down by the main street, where the small mosque still is today. When Fatna Hanem was still alive, she used to live further down from there in her palace. When she was leaving or entering her estate with her carriage [*hantour*] she had to pass the old ‘*ezba* [village]. Driving by there, she was frequently bothered by village children. The children took great pleasure in running after the splendid royal carriage, which was drawn by eight beautiful horses, and was often announced and flanked by footmen dressed in white and red. The noisy and mischievous children annoyed Fatna. One day a child was hit by the carriage and injured. This incident convinced Fatna that it was better to move the community away from her driveway. Subsequently she selected forty families and gave them an entire feddan of land, divided into forty equal lots, at a short distance from the old ‘*ezba*. Forty houses were built in four identical alleys. Only the old mosque remained in the place where the ‘*ezba* had originally been.[6]

The resettlement of the forty workers and their families in the new community dates back to about 1915. From a cluster of houses the workers/peasants were moved into a modern model village. Contained in four alleys, each with ten one family dwellings, the peasants were to fulfil the new role of an orderly and productive peasantry in a modern nation. Fatma Hanem had joined the ranks of landowners who were entertaining and debating new ideas of workers' housing, productivity, order and hygiene, and were experimenting with the latter's implementation. Alleys should be regular and accessible, and the community as a whole orderly and conveniently supervisable. The forty houses were assigned to forty nuclear families.

Among those given a house in the model village were Sitt Khadiga, her husband Hassan Yunis and their five children, the youngest of whom was only one year old. Their oldest daughter, Um Soliman was already married or about to get married and together with her husband was assigned another one of the forty houses. Sitt Khadiga had been born in the early 1880s in a village in a rural province. There she had learned midwifery from her mother who had practiced in the village. Later Sitt Khadiga and her husband moved to Fatma Hanem's workers village. Sitt Khadiga took her skills to the new community and continued to practice there. In addition to working as a midwife, Khadiga also worked in Fatma Hanem's palace. Sitt Khadiga was immensely respected as a midwife in El Tayibin. Even today, fifty years after her death, older people fondly remember her and praise her excellent work.

In the 1920s residents from a small community further east, on the Nile front, had been removed from what had turned into prime real estate, and were assigned land adjacent to the forty houses of El Tayibin. At the time El Tayibin was an agricultural village surrounded by a lush landscape of fields and orchards.

The new neighbors had brought with them their own midwife, Um Ragab. As long as Um Ragab was alive she worked for her community, as one older man remembered: "She was ours, that's why we consulted her, but when she died we 'took' over Sitt Khadiga and those who came after her."

Over the next two decades the two communities grew together and shared life, experiences and increasingly a communal identity. Sitt Khadiga became the midwife of the new community which now was several times its original size.

In the 1920s most of the original families of El Tayibin engaged in agriculture. Yet, with the rapid expansion of modern Cairo to the west bank, agricultural land became scarce and some men started to work as guards, gardeners and helpers in the new neighborhoods and institutions. Others took up work across the Nile in Cairo. El Tayibin slowly integrated into metropolitan Cairo and by the 1950s the agricultural community became an urban low-income neighborhood.

Midwifery and the Midwives of El Tayibin

The skills and practices of *dayas* were extensive. They included anything related to pregnancy and childbirth, infant care and infant health, ear piercing, assistance in wedding nights, the administering of *subu's* (celebration of a birth after seven days), female circumcision and occasionally abortions. The *dayas'* expertise included herbal and other remedies. Some aspects of their practice were performed discreetly and behind closed doors. Um Zaki, a sixty-five year old resident of El Tayibin described details of the practice of *dayas* in the past:

> Sometimes a servant girl who worked in a rich household [*'and al-bashawat*] might have gotten in trouble with her employer. She could go to a *daya* who might get rid of the fetus. I remember a case in the village where my sister lived. Their *daya* took in a servant girl to whom such a thing had happened, and treated her. The girl had nowhere to go, so the *daya* pretended to the villagers that she was a distant cousin who had come to stay with her. Eventually the *daya* was even able to marry the girl to a decent man in the village.

The scope of *dayas'* practice was deeply embedded in female social ties and networks. A good *daya* could save the life of a girl or woman in more than one way.

Sitt Khadiga taught two of her daughters, Um Soliman and Um Hamid, the skills of midwifery. The three women practiced in El Tayibin and in the emerging modern neighborhoods in the vicinity of El Tayibin. In the 1930s, the neighborhood scheme of Sharia Al-Tawil was laid out. Yet, it took almost two decades to completely fill in with small apartment buildings. The neighborhood was largely inhabited by the new Egyptian middle classes of bureaucrats and professionals. Based on their excellent reputation, the clientele of Sitt Khadiga and her daughters expanded. Many women in the new middle class neighborhood preferred the established wisdom and all-female supportive environment that marked the practice of a *daya*. Despite their position in the new cityscape and the availability of modern hospitals, these middle class women maintained their faith in the practice of *dayas*. In the case of Sitt Khadiga and her daughters, ideas and practices radiated outward from El Tayibin appropriating momentary spaces in the modern city. Sitt Khadiga and her successors found open (front) doors in the new environment and moved in its streets as respected practitioners while some of their male neighbors, in contrast, were "conscripted" to the new cityscape as workers and helpers.

Despite efforts by the colonial state to formalize and control medical practice in general and midwifery in particular, Sitt Khadiga and her daughters continued practicing relatively undisturbed in El Tayibin and beyond, until the middle of the twentieth century. Um Ali and others recounted that around the middle of the century, an official decree was issued specifying that only licensed midwives were allowed to assist births, and, more importantly, to register births. Licensed midwives were equipped with a record book (*daftar*) where they officially registered births. Such measures to license and supervise *dayas* were elements of a long chain of developments that aimed at limiting or eliminating the practice of midwives. For an understanding of the course of events in the lives of Sitt Khadiga and her daughters, it is necessary to briefly review these developments.

Midwifery: Attacks and Reforms

Starting from the early 19th century, a rhetorical war was waged against *dayas* in Egypt by Dr. Clot Bey, the French physician who worked under Mohammed Ali starting from the 1820s on the establishment of a modern (military) medical system. Existing midwifery for Clot represented "'old-wives-medicine' with its magic potions, charms, and incantation, and he did everything in his power to undermine her persistent popularity" (Kuhnke 1992: 129).

In 19th century Europe, midwives were losing ground against the emerging dominance of a male bourgeois class of physicians and general practitioners. The integration of existing forms of midwifery into the new medical landscape was of little importance. Efforts to "license, regulate, and instruct midwives" had, for example, been defeated numerous times by the British Royal College of Physicians (ibid.: 220-221, note no. 45). These changes affected developments in places where European influence became increasingly dominant.

Clot Bey realized that if he wanted to include women into his new medical schemes he needed female practitioners. If he ever was to eliminate "old wives practices" he had to produce scientifically trained replacements. Subsequently, he established a school for midwifery.[7] The curriculum of the school aimed at educating *hakimas*, or "doctresses" whose field of expertise was to transcend midwifery to include basic medical tasks.[8] *Hakimas'* field of expertise was similar to the *dayas* yet they practiced under government supervision. The fact that *Hakimas* received their education at the new school, eliminated the continuity of older practices. Nevertheless, their practice, remained relatively independent and community-oriented. The majority of women, however, continued giving birth under the attendance of *dayas*. No attempts were made in the 19th century to integrate *dayas* into the new governmental health system.[9]

By the turn of the century colonial authorities made hygiene, health and medicine central – albeit ideological – elements on their agenda. Existing forms of midwifery continued being a target for attack and reform. At the same time, midwives were needed as handmaidens in the emerging modern state's efforts at ordering and counting its populace. Only through midwives could statistics about births be accumulated. In terms of medical reform, the colonial authorities did not invest significant sums in either health or health education for the colonized.[10] Women's health is conspicuously absent from the colonial agenda, except that colonizers insisted that it was their task to save women from the "barbaric" treatments suffered at the hands of local midwives (Arnold 1993: 257).[11]

While viewed with suspicion, midwives constituted an essential element in counting the colonized population, and hence needed to be incorporated into the governmental system of control and dominance. *The Egyptian Gazette*, the colonial newspaper, announced in 1906 that a test for midwives was being held at the central public hospital of Qasr Al-Aini (EG 1.6.1906) indicating testing and licensing practices with regard to (European) midwives. One month later, the Gazette published the authorization that was given to one Mme. Susanna Backman "to practice as midwife" (EG 19.7.1906). Midwifery was separated along existing ethnic and power lines with foreign midwives treating the colonizers and Egyptian midwives treating the colonized.[12]

Although the British built hospitals for the colonial population with such technical innovations as an "electric dynamo for lighting" and water pumps (EG 21.1.1904), "native" health remained a lesser concern. Efforts at improving women's or children's health were left to charitable ladies as the following notes illustrates:

> A free dispensary for sick children was opened in Boulac at the new house in Sharia Maatba al Ahlia, near the Cotton Mill, yesterday. Mothers with sick babies may bring them from 8 a.m. till 10 a.m. daily for treatment gratuitously.

This dispensary has been founded by Lady Cromer and is entirely supported by voluntary contributions.

(EG 21.2.1906)[13]

A year later a brief notice in the Gazette about the Boulac dispensary for mothers and children observed that the dispensary is attracting patients from as far as Shoubra, Maaroof and even from the other side of the Nile in Embaba and Giza which is an indicator of the scarcity of such facilities in other parts of the city and beyond (EG 28.5.1907).[14]

Starting from the turn of the century, the gynecologist Dr. Naguib Mahfouz worked on the integration of obstetrics into the structure of the modern hospital of Qasr Al-Aini. In 1904 he started a small gynecological outpatient clinic attached to the hospital (Mahfouz 1935: 77). Soon after "a ward of 10 beds was reserved for Gynecology and Obstetrics" (ibid.: 78). The surgical work was performed by two English doctors while Mahfouz himself was in charge of obstetrics. Dr. Mahfouz and his colleagues appropriated aspects of a field hitherto left to female practitioners.

Nonetheless, *dayas* continued to practice. They still performed most of the births and could not be ignored by the colonial authorities. Again, private initiative preceded official action. In 1912 a committee of British and Egyptian ladies headed by the Khedive's mother was formed to found a Maternity Training School with the goal of improving the standards of *dayas*. Two years later, the school closed for lack of funds (ibid.: 84-85). The Ladies Committee eventually handed over its work to the Sanitary Department which took on the task of opening maternity schools. "By the end of 1932 nine such schools were opened by the Provincial Councils and Municipalities under the supervision and inspection of the Department of Public Health" (ibid.: 85). Courses at the maternity schools for *dayas* lasted six months and the graduates were given "green permits" upon graduation (ibid.: 86). Mahfouz further mentions, but provides no details about the existence of courses for the "old type of daya" that lasted only two to six weeks at General Hospitals where "white permits" were granted upon sitting for exams. He notes, however, that "the Department of Public Health abolished this kind of training on January 1, 1928" (ibid.: 86). Dr. Clot

Bey's School of Midwifery continued to exist but had gone through a number of changes. By the 1930s the school was attached to the Faculty of Medicine. After graduating from the School of Nursing, students attended an eleven months course for the Diploma in Midwifery.[15]

The 1920s witnessed first steps toward the establishment of a larger network of maternal and child health institutions. A special "Child Welfare Section" was created in 1927 within the Public Health Administration which was to run

> a certain number of permanent and travelling Child Welfare Centres in various localities of Egypt and supervise the work of the Child Welfare Centres, the work of the Child Welfare Centres, Children Dispensaries and *Dayah's* schools belonging either to the Provincial Councils or Municipalities. Travelling Inspectresses in the Section are entrusted with the inspection of dayas and their work in the chief towns, towns and villages.
>
> (Ibid.: 88-89)

Some travelling centers were eventually transformed to be permanent ones.[16]

Sitt Khadiga and Her Daughters: Precarious Practice

Many of the political and institutional changes had little implications for the practice of Sitt Khadiga and her daughters. They were busy working and made a good living. Um Hamid had been divorced at a young age and left with four children to raise by herself. Her siblings supported her by giving her the right over a water tap in their parental house (the sole tap in the community) from which the family sold water to their neighbors before the community was given public water taps. Um Hamid's practice as a midwife and the (small) income from the water tap, helped her tremendously in raising her children. Her expertise as a midwife allowed her to escape the only other possibility that women of her generation had in term of work: to work as a domestic servant.

Based on their expertise and reputation, the services of Sitt Khadiga and her daughters were in high demand in El Tayibin and beyond. A decree which specified that only licensed midwives were allowed to perform births and more importantly to register births, however, did affect their practice. Only licensed midwives had a *daftar* (a big official account book) where they officially registered births. A *daya* in a neighboring village had both the license and the *daftar*. As Sitt Khadiga and her daughters practiced, they kept track of their activities and the *daftar* holding midwife came for occasional visits and entered all these birth into the *daftar* at once. The other midwife, of course, charged Sitt Khadiga and her daughters fees for her services.

Um Ali: Legitimate Practice

In the late 1940s, when Sitt Khadiga no longer practiced, Um Soliman and Um Hamid became increasingly annoyed with having to pay a fee to the licensed *daya*. Shorter courses at the maternity schools continued to exist. *Dayas*, usually those with years of practice already, could attend a six months to one year training program whereupon they received a license. The only prerequisites for the course were "good health and literacy" (Simon 1981: 33). After obtaining their licenses, the licensed *dayas* had to attend a refresher course at a Maternal and Child Health Clinic once a year. Yet, neither Um Soliman nor Um Hamid were willing – at midlife and after decades of practice – to sit for training, tests and licensing. Subsequently, they brought in their young niece, Um Ali, who had recently been divorced, to teach her midwifery skills, and, very importantly to send her to the six months training course at the famous Giza hospital of Um Al-Misriyin.[17]

Um Ali was the daughter of Sitt Khadiga's third daughter, whom Khadiga had never initiated into the world of midwifery. Um Ali's daughter was married to a relative from Sitt Khadiga's old village at a very young age and thus had left her mother's house a long time ago. As only a married woman could be trained in midwifery and attend birth, it was impossible for Um Ali's mother to learn these skills from her mother. Returning to El Tayibin a generation later, Um Ali obtained the long-term training provided by her aunts, passed down from her grandmother and great-grandmother, the hospital training, and the desired license. "I received the doctors' bag including even the white gloves," Um Ali insisted, when asked about details of her training.[18] The doctor's bag and the white glove were a symbol of her legitimate practice and they were frequently referred to by her relatives and neighbors.

Early in her career, Um Ali was working under the close supervision of her two aunts who controlled even parts of her income as their sense was that Um Ali owed everything she was to them. Meanwhile the aunts had escaped the control of the licensed *daya* from down the road and saved the fees they had been forced to pay for her registration services. Um Hamid taught one of her own daughters, Um Hani, midwifery but Um Hani never gained the expertise, nor the official license as Um Ali did. Um Hani did practice midwifery – more as a side line – but eventually moved away from El Tayibin. For many years Um Soliman, Um Hamid and Um Ali practiced side by side with Um Ali registering all their births. Um Soliman practiced well into the 1960s, as one of her granddaughters remembered:

My grandmother was always called to people's houses for her services. When she had a *subuʿ* to perform she would sometimes take me along. But she was a tough woman. Sometimes, the family that had the *subuʿ* was generous and gave me a small coin. On the way home, my grandmother would always check whether I had received a gift and would take it away form me. But I still liked to go out with her.

After Um Soliman and Um Hamid resigned and passed away, Um Ali was left to practice alone in El Tayibin. Her schedule was a busy one: checking on women in the last days of pregnancy, telling them to be patient and that they would still take a few days, spending long hours attending births, conducting wedding nights ("when I do the *dukhla*, it always bleeds nicely," Um Ali), checking on newborn babies and many more tasks. Her work surrounding birth was time-consuming and involved many trips back and forth to the house of the expectant mother, and long hours of sitting by the side of laboring women.

Um Ali charged her patients according to their ability to pay. Many of them she did not have to "charge" at all because they offered the appropriate sums of money or gifts without being asked. Furthermore, gifts of money came her way at the *subuʿ*, the celebration of a birth after seven days, which she would conduct for the new baby. Some of the poorer women she treated for free. The most unfortunate and miserable women, she occasionally even hosted in her own house after birth and fed them from her own supplies. Um Ibrahim, who is also a granddaughter of Sitt Khadiga, remembered:

Um Ali was not after money. Sometimes, if a woman was very poor, she might let her stay for a few days in her house. She would even slaughter a chicken from her own for the woman.

Um Ali: Precarious Practice

The late 1960s brought yet another round of changes in official policies with regard to *dayas*: in 1969 the Ministry of Health changed its policies once more, and all "licenses were revoked, and the practice of training the *dayas* was discontinued" (Simon 1981: 5). Underlying was "the conviction that *dayas* had become redundant" as large numbers of trained nurse-midwives (*hakimas*) had become available (ibid.: 5). However, the practice of the latter was set in the context of hospitals and mother-child centers and lacked the independence of *dayas*, and the first 19th century *hakimas*. In the early 1970s finally

the Ministry of Health declared *dayas* [sic] practice illegal, in a fresh move to staff MCH (Mother Child Health) units with assistant midwives and trained nurses … . Since then, older licensed *dayas* have been performing their trade informally, but no less actively.

(Ibid.: 34).

Women in El Tayibin continued giving birth with Um Ali in the 1960s and 1970s. Simultaneously, many women signed up at the new maternity centers, as Um Ibrahim remembers, but often only late in pregnancy. She recounted: "we signed up at the center because when the baby was born we would receive free milk powder and other things. But we delivered the babies with Um Soliman, Um Hamid and Um Ali."[19]

The centers were staffed with physicians, nurse-midwives or *hakimas*, nutritionists and a number of helpers and assistants (Simon 1981). The professionals all had received modern training. Simultaneously, however, as Simon observed in 1981 in the Maternal and Child Health

Clinic in Sayyida Zeinab *dayas* would often "cooperate actively with the MCH center" sending their patients there for supervision (ibid.: 4). Since physicians' at the centers knew that women delivered with the help of *dayas*, they often supported the work of those *dayas* who they felt were most experienced and reliable in their work. Simon noted that *dayas* felt protected in their (now illegal) practice through cooperation with the centers (ibid.: 43). Some of the helpers (*tamargiyas*) in the Sayyida Zeinab Center, Simon observed, were unlicensed *dayas* who occupied a central social position in the center as they were from the community and well-respected. Despite the professionalized set-up of the clinic, Simon found close and well-integrated cooperation between medical staff and *dayas*, often even united within one person's different fields of expertise and practice. Despite personal and meaningful cooperation on the level of the center, the fact remained that *dayas* practiced within a context of insecurity which required them to search for either the protection of the center, or to practice at a complete distance from the center. Their former independence and security was irretrievably lost.[20] Simultaneously, however, women's continued trust and respect for midwives' more individualized and socially oriented services allowed the continuity of midwives' practice. In many cases economic aspects also played a role in women's decisions about where or with whom to give birth. The work of *dayas* continued but behind closed doors. While on the one hand the *daya's* practice carried with it the uncomfortable sense of its own illegality, in its everyday reality this was of little relevance, as the following encounter illustrates.

In 1990, when Um Ali was still practicing regularly, I attended the initial phase of a delivery with her. Before we went for the actual birth, Um Ali had already been checking on Nabila, the expectant mother, several times (it was her first baby) and told her that it was still early and she would come back in due time. Nabila's mother, Um Abdel Rahman, was a good friend of Um Ali's, and together with Um Ali, I had frequently visited the household of Um Abdel Rahman and had gotten to know her and her daughter quite well. They did not object to my presence in the early stages of Nabila's labor. Um Ali and I arrived in Um Abdel Rahman's house late in the afternoon as Nabila's contractions had started to come more regularly. Nabila was half sitting half lying on plastic mats and a blanket on the floor, propped up against a number of pillows. Her mother and her mother's sister were also present. Um Ali immediately went to work. She slightly readjusted the pillows to make sure that Nabila would be as comfortable as possible. Covering Nabila's body with a thin cotton blanket, Um Ali did a vaginal exam to check on the progress of the birth. After she felt that Nabila still had quite some time to go, Um Ali started a conversation with Um Abdel Rahman and her sister that soon made everybody, including Nabila laugh. Um Ali and the other women continued their story telling and between painful contractions, Nabila joined them in their laughter and talk. Um Ali did not just provide the physical care but was also was in charge of the entertainment or distraction for the laboring mother. I only stayed for a half an hour and then left. The same night Nabila gave birth to a healthy girl. Nobody involved wasted a thought or note on the "illegal" context of this delivery.

Um Ibrahim, however, remembers an instance of how Um Ali's public role had become precarious:

Many years ago, Um Ali had commissioned a black sign with white writing on it, the kind doctors hang outside their buildings. The sign included her name, and stated that she was a midwife. Um Ali wanted to fix this sign to the wall of Sitt Khadiga's house, so that everybody who came into El Tayibin could see it. She was very happy about the sign. But then several of the relatives suggested that she not hang the sign as she was no longer officially allowed to practice and the sign might attract the eye of the authorities [al-hukuma]. In the end she never used the sign. She stored it away in my house. Years later, when we fixed the stairs, we used the board. It is still there on the side of the stairs. You can go and see it there.

Hospital Births

As long as Um Ali practiced, most of the women of El Tayibin continued using her services. A few women, however, started giving births in government hospitals. Initially for free, fees for various extra services and tips for nurses and attendants eventually added up to considerable sums. As one woman put it: "Every time the nurse brings you something, you have to pay a tip."

From the late 1970s prosperous labor migrants to the Arab Gulf started sending their wives back home in Egypt to more expensive private hospitals to deliver their babies. As a marker of prestige and concern of their husbands, some migrant wives will proudly mention the private hospital and the cost of their deliveries. Um Zaki noted: "My daughter delivered her first baby in a private hospital. Her husband send LE 800 from Qatar for this delivery."[21]

So long as Um Ali was practicing, government or private hospitals were a matter of choice, prestige and available funds. As she slowly gave up practicing, women had less of a choice and were forced to travel to hospitals. With limited funds, most women had no choice other then go to public hospitals whose facilities and services have been deteriorating over the past decades. Many woman were afraid of treatment and services in public hospitals. Um Kamal a friend and neighbor of Um Ali had given birth to four children with the help of Um Ali. In the early 1990s, years after her last birth, she became pregnant once more. When she was ready to give birth, Um Ali had fallen sick and had momentarily moved to her daughter's house and was unable to take the trip to El Tayibin. Left with no other choice, Um Kamal gave birth in a public hospital and afterwards noted:

I would much rather have given birth with Um Ali. She had delivered all my other children and everything had gone well with her help. But this time I had no choice, so I went to the hospital.

One of the most outstanding changes accompanying hospital births was and is the dramatically high rate of Cesarean births performed there.[22] From informal observations and conversations in El Tayibin it seems that almost one in three or four hospital births in recent years had been a Cesarean.[23] Um Ibrahim, complained about the fact that all three of her daughters had delivered their children in recent years with Cesareans in hospitals. Um Ibrahim recounted:

When Um Ali and before her Um Soliman and Um Hamid assisted women in birth, there were no Cesarean births and all the babies came out in the end. Um Ali was very patient, she would sit with a woman for hours, or go home and come back the next day if things were not ready yet. And if a baby was in the wrong position, Um Ali would carefully insert her hand and she could turn the baby around in the womb, so that it could be born head first. No woman ever died giving birth under Um Ali. She knew her work well, and she knew the women and she was very patient. In the hospital things are different.

Another neighbor recounted that only in very difficult cases Um Ali would advise a woman to go to a hospital. This neighbor attributed this to Um Ali's excellent knowledge and sense of responsibility, as he noted "she knew her work very well, and she had an official license." It is interesting to note that this male voice, more than the female ones, insisted on Um Ali's license as her basis of professional knowledge and legitimacy.

Um Hisham, a young woman in the neighborhood, just recently delivered her first baby in a public hospital by Caesarean. Upon my question why she needed a Caesarean she said the doctor had told her that the baby had been stuck in her pelvis. In the same conversation another neighbor offered an explanation for frequent Caesareans in general:

Look, when it is four o' clock or so in the afternoon the doctors want to go home, so they do Caesareans, that their day will be over. Also, remember a regular birth in a public hospital is for free, a Caesarean is a surgery and then they can charge the woman money for it. This is why they are so many Caesareans.

In the case of a Caesarean, like with other surgeries, patients have to supply the necessary materials themselves. Um Hisham recounted her recent delivery: "Then my husband had to run out of the hospital and buy the *bink* (anesthetic) and the cotton wool for the Caesarean." Older women, like Um Ibrahim, tend to be more critical about the Caesarean practices, she insisted: "I gave birth seven times with a *daya* and I was fine, there was no need ever to cut back then."

Frequent caesareans, bad services and high costs are the most frequent complaints about public hospitals. Neglect and indifference is another as the following incident illustrates. Um Zaki recounted the encounter of her niece who had given birth in a public hospital on the outskirts of Cairo:

My niece, Zeinab, was going into labor in her eighth month which is a dangerous time. Seven month babies have a good chance at living but eight months babies often die. So her husband rushed her to the public hospital. The baby was born but it was small and weak and died after a few hours.

When I asked Um Zaki whether the hospital had an incubator, she said, "yes, they did. But it costs more than 50 pounds a day and the doctors knew that my niece was poor and that she would not be able to pay for an incubator for a long time. So they did not bother."

Whether or not the story of Zeinab is representative, the underlying point remains, that women feel that even though advanced technologies might be generally available in hospitals, it might not be available for them in particular. Consequently, the argument that hospitals provide a better environment for complicated cases looses its credibility.

While in the practice of Um Ali, births were a social event with a few female relatives to distract and support the mother, hospital births and Caesarians in particular have turned into rather individualized and lonely procedures. Fear of mistreatment and suspicion often prevail. Um Hisham recounted her experiences and feelings:

After little Hisham was born, I had my husband and my mother take the baby to my mother's house the next morning. We were afraid that they would do something to the baby, steal him or exchange him for another child. My mother or my husband brought the baby at least once a day for nursing and apart from that they gave him water with sugar at home until I was released a week later.

Whereas the midwife would check on new mothers and their babies in the first days and weeks after birth, women who deliver in hospitals are left on their own in this initial period. As women in El Tayibin tend to return to their mothers' houses for births these circumstances are, however, greatly alleviated by the availability of a larger pool of advise from experienced older women. And it is in this context that female wisdom continues to flourish and dominate women's lives. As much as women consult physicians and hospitals, they also rely on available wisdom and remedies.

Replacing Um Ali?

Families in El Tayibin all have their stories about trips in the middle of the night to Cairo's renowned Abu Rish Children's Hospital because of sudden infant fevers and diarrheas. Abu Rish Hospital general practitioners and pediatricians are well-trusted and frequently consulted. But at the same time elements of older discourses of health and healing are also employed.

When infant Hisham was suffering from serious diarrhea his mother took him to Abu Rish Hospital but the next day her own mother took the baby to Um Abbas, an old woman in the neighborhood who gives therapeutic massages. I went with Um Hisham's mother to Um Abbas's room. Upon arriving there Um Abbas took a good look at the baby, then told me to fetch a small container with some cream from her kitchen cabinet in the hallway. Meanwhile she had undressed little Hisham and put the naked baby on her stretched out legs. First she gave him a tough massage from the back for some minutes, then turned him around and systematically rubbed his stomach. Hisham was screaming all the while. After about fifteen minutes she finished her work and wrapped a bandage-like piece of fabric that we had brought along around the baby so that it crossed over tightly both on his back and front. After he had been screaming throughout the treatment, little Hisham was surprisingly quiet afterwards. It needs to be noted that Um Abbas is not a midwife but a practitioner of particular types of beneficial massages. In this particular instance her field of expertise overlaps with aspects of the *dayas*. Yet, a similar question arises to her practice as with regard to Um Ali's practice: who will continue her work in the future?

The death of Um Ali, and the situation of El Tayibin devoid of such expertise does, however, not equal the end of a series of practices associated with older forms of midwifery. *Subuʿ*s, continue, but are now administered by grandmothers, or a few women in the community who are known for their verbal and other skills needed for a successful *subuʿ*.

Female circumcision, long ago outlawed by the Egyptian government, has been appropriated within the practices of general practitioners.[24] In the poorer quarters of Cairo, physicians will perform the operation for a fee starting between 20 to 30 LE, while the family of the girl supplies the cotton and sterilizing materials. In this context modern medicine's 19th century claim to a new medical universe has taken an ironic turn in its 20th century market oriented and male dominated universe: for a good fee modern physicians perform this highly controversial surgery.[25]

Wedding nights have largely become the private affair of the newly weds, or knowledgeable older women are brought in, should problems arise. Such women, however, are not always easy to find. In the mid-1990s a friend of one of Um Ibrahim's daughters got married in Bulaq Al-Dakrour. Problems arose for the young couple in the wedding night and the marriage could not be consummated. The next day they went looking for a midwife, but could not find one in their neighborhood. Two days passed and the wedding night was still not "happening" and the couple and their relatives frantically searched for a *daya*. Knowing that Um Ibrahim was the granddaughter of Sitt Khadiga and related to the midwives of El Tayibin, the friends also approached Um Ibrahim's daughter to ask her mother whether she could perform the wedding night (*dukhla*) for them. Um Ibrahim declined. Later she said:

I know how many of these things are done, because I watched my grandmother and my aunts in the past. But I don't want to get involved in these things.

Every great once in a while, she will however perform a *subu'* for people whom she highly appreciates.

One of Um Ali's young nieces, Samira, was interested in working in the medical field. A few years ago Samira went into nursing school – a three year vocational training after the completion of nine years of regular schooling – and hoped to specialize in obstetrics in line with the family tradition. Upon completing her nursing degree, she worked as a nurse in a hospital which is more of a helper's position and not even remotely comparable with the independent work and expertise of Um Ali. Back home in El Tayibin, Samira administers injections to diabetic neighbors which gives her neither the recognition, prestige nor financial rewards that Um Ali and the other midwives had once enjoyed. Since Samira was not doing too well at school, she could not continue her schooling and specialize in obstetrics.[26]

Reordering Dayas' Practices

With these few examples of the reassigning of earlier *daya* practices, it becomes clear that a large scale shift of bodily control from midwives to a male market-oriented medical establishment has been taking place, or in many aspects has already been completed. The practice of midwifery has been stripped of its social, female and communal aspects and has largely been allocated to male practitioners as 19th century European physicians had called for. Births have increasingly been assigned to hospitals where women are left alone in an unfamiliar environment faced with doctors' decisions which they have no means to challenge and oppose. The women of El Tayibin unequivocally agreed in their sentiments and opinions about public hospitals: Caesarians were many, services were bad and one should leave these places as fast as possible. In contrast, *dayas'* practices that demand less expertise (*subuʿas*, ear piercing, wedding nights) can be performed by experienced older women and are hence redistributed within female communities.

Only for a brief few decades, in the period between the early 20th century and 1969, attempts were made to upgrade midwives' expertise. This brief spell of interest in *dayas*, and giving them a recognized space in the medical system, in hindsight appears as a temporary make-shift solution within the larger flow of events surrounding politics of institutionalized medicine and obstetrics. Only institutionally trained nurse-midwives were integrated into the modern medical system at subordinate positions, enjoying nowhere near the prestige and independence as *dayas* did (and still do).

At the same time, similarities in tasks and expertise, and the continuing popularity of and respect for *dayas* among segments of Cairene society have allowed some *hakimas* to moonlight as independent midwives (Sourial 1969), as much as they enabled *dayas* to practice under the indirect protection of the more powerful institutional context, while yet other *dayas* chose to continue practicing at a safe distance from authorities. While the legal context and official picture are that of institutionalized obstetrics, at the level of everyday practices, circumstances are much more diverse and practices have been articulating in a multitude of ways. Despite these dynamic processes of articulation and negotiation of female wisdom, health, birthing and related practices, the fact remains that *dayas* and their knowledges have irreversibly been pushed to the margins, and indeed to "illegal" margins. Less and less young women are willing to enter a field that enjoys no official support and could easily get them into legal trouble. Without a government certificate, the practice of *dayas* has become a field that is looked at by young women as for those who are illiterate and "backward" and hence not worthy the consideration of a educated woman (Simon 1981). The more "appropriate" way is what Samira chose, which however left her as a helper in a large institution.

Debating or Ignoring Midwifery?

Debates about indigenization of knowledge, Islamization of knowledge, and the continuity of Islamic medical practices are conspicuously silent about forms of popular female wisdom, and most importantly the practices of *dayas*. The confrontation between various medical discourses is a male, abstract and supposedly rational one, and ultimately centers around the issue of which male (textual) discourse should have control over bodies, and for our case that would be female bodies. *Dayas* have no spokeswomen in such debates as their practice is based on long genealogies of female wisdom not written down in manuscripts, treatises and books. Male proponents of various discourses have little knowledge of *dayas*' practices as those have always been closely guarded among women. Moreover, these men have no interest in sharing their envisioned fields of medical (social and political) practices with possibly illiterate females.

The death of Um Ali symbolizes the slow death of age-old female wisdom and practices, as much as her life and work demonstrated the very feasible option of successfully inserting more recent knowledges into time-honored practices. Um Ali practiced within the female social context that had worked so well for midwives and women in the past, into which she integrated her new knowledge, while referring the few critical cases to hospitals. Some of her practices will be dispersed into the communities and kept alive by women, while others will completely disappear. The most important aspect, however, that of birthing and reproductive health has been taken over by the male medical establishment effectively stripping women and female communities of control of their bodies. In the context of hospital births women are isolated from the support of other women. While the *daya* was a well-known social equal, or at least member of the same community, poor women who give birth in hospitals are at the mercy of doctors who are socially distant from them in terms of gender, class, education and most importantly power. How could a poor uneducated woman speak up or enter into a debate about her body across such severe social dividing lines?

The statement that *dayas'* practices were irrational, superstitious and backward was never doubted or critically challenged in debates about medical practices. The possibility of upgrading older forms of midwifery was briefly practiced but eventually dropped in favor of institutionally trained and institutionally based nurse-midwives. Anti-colonial, national or Islamic movements have shown little interest in challenging the process of marginalization and elimination of midwifery set in motion 150 years ago. *Dayas* themselves have been too busy with the immediate demands of their challenging work to engage with authorities. Moreover, the structure of a modern society where only educational certificates, professional syndicates, written texts and treatises give legitimacy to one's projects and demands, from the start provided no space for *dayas*, who work in a different discursive universe, to voice their concerns and discontents.

The Future of Dayas?

The deep respect of women for *dayas* and the resilience of the latters' practices alone accounts for the continuity of *dayas* after 150 years of official onslaught and interference. How much longer *dayas* will practice, remains to be seen. Official disrespect, rhetorical war and decrees that made *dayas'* practices illegal, have rendered midwives' practices precarious. Few young women are willing to enter a field that is looked upon with contempt and is fraught with legal problems. Women like Um Kamal who gave birth with Um Ali and later were forced to use hospitals are the most outspoken at present for the case of midwives. Many younger women who from the beginning had no other choice than give birth in hospitals have little to compare other than the stories of their mothers and aunts. Taking hospital births as their only option, they accept them as a necessary "evil" but try to leave as fast as possible to escape the bad services and high costs.

Notes

I am grateful for funding by the German Research Foundation (Deutsche Forschungsgemeinschaft) administered through the Institute of Cultural Geography, Freiburg University, Germany. My work was further facilitated by a research fellowship in the Department of Anthropology at the American University in Cairo. My personal debts are to the people of El Tayibin. This paper is dedicated to the memory of the woman whom I have chosen to call Um Ali who has taught me a lot and opened up a new world for me. I want to thank Cynthia Nelson and Shahnaz Rouse for their helpful comments on this paper. Thanks for inspiration and support go to Mohammed Tabishat.

1. All the personal names and most of the place names are pseudonyms. To further guarantee the anonymity of individuals and their families I have slightly changed some of people's personal circumstances.
2. I am careful here not to use the term patient as it is not used in this context. "Women" is the straightforward term that Um Ali herself used to refer to those who seek her help and assistance.
3. I will use the term *daya* in English in order to distinguish between midwives who were trained (or mostly trained) by older experienced *dayas* and modern institutionally trained midwives, *hakimas* (see below). It will become clear in the course of my argument that lines between *dayas* and *hakimas* in actual practice are often blurred.
4. Needless to say here that the point of the following analysis is not to prove that one type of medical or health practice is better than the other, as Foucault noted in the preface to *The Birth of the Clinic* when he wrote that his book was not "written in favor of one kind of medicine, as against another kind of medicine, or against medicine and in favor of an absence of medicine. It is a structural study that sets out to disentangle the conditions of its history from the density of discourse." (1975: XIX)
5. I am using the past tense with reference to El Tayibin only. *Dayas* still practice in other parts of Cairo.
6. Um Ibrahim calls Fatma Hanem "Fatna Hanem" using the popular form of Fatma.

7   For details, see Mahfouz (1935).
8   The five year course at the school included: "(1) Arabic language. (2) Theory and Practice of Midwifery. (3) Ante-natal and post-natal care. (4) The treatment of simple diseases. (5) The principles of elementary surgery including bandaging, vaccination, dry and wet cupping. (6) Elementary dispensing." (Mahfouz 1935: 73).
9   In terms of attempts of integrating or using local practitioners, there was an interesting period when for lack of personnel, local barbers were trained to perform small pox vaccinations. These efforts were rather specific and relatively short-lived and never amounted to creating spaces for these practitioners in the emerging medical system which would be viable for the future (Kuhnke 1992: 111).
10 Arnold notes for the case of 19th century colonial India: "The diseases that preoccupied colonial medicine in the nineteenth century were epidemic diseases, the communicable diseases of the cantonment, civil lines, and plantations, the diseases that threatened European lives, military manpower, and male productive labor" (1993: 254).
11 Others rhetorically supported the campaign against midwives. For example, British anthropologist, Winifred Blackman, writing about Upper Egyptian peasants in the 1920s had little to say about actual *dayas'* work and skills, but emphasized that the various primitive medicinal remedies, well known to, and used by all villages matrons, are of such a nature that one wonders how any child manages to survive at all (1968: 42). Blackman complains that peasant women do not trust physicians' advice, and object to consulting physicians. She describes these women as hopelessly backward and superstitious (ibid.: 61). Blackman's narrative in the end does not leave much doubt that whatever it is that women practice, it is doomed to extinction in the face of the "brighter" scientific future looming on colonial horizons.
12 Statistics of births and deaths were frequently published in the Egyptian Gazette. Figures were neatly separated between "foreign/European" and "native" births. See, for example, "Vitality Statistics" (EG 19.6.1904 or 13.9.1904).
13 Already in 1898 Lady Cromer had initiated a foundling hospital, also by "public subscription" (Mahfouz 1935: 80).

14 Arnold describes similar circumstances in 19th century colonial India where a charitable fund, the Dufferin Fund, initiated by the "vicereine" Lady Dufferin at the urging of Queen Victoria was set up "to promote medical aid for India's women" (1993: 262).
15 The curriculum included "instruction in Obstetrics including Forensic Medicine in relation to Pregnancy and Midwifery, Gynecology, Pelvic Anatomy and Embryology" (Mahfouz 1935: 87).
16 For the case of the center in Sayyida Zeinab, opened in 1927, see Simon (1981: 16-17).
17 Um Ali mentioned Um El Misriyin to me as the place where she got her training. Simon, however, notes that these courses were held at a school by the name of Madrassat el Kabilat, which was also located in Giza. It remains to be found out whether the second was actually located within the premises of Um El Misriyin Hospital (Simon 1981: 33).
18 Simon also notes the importance of the bag: "At the end of the training course they were licensed, and provided with a simple midwifery kit with items needed for normal deliveries – scissors, dethol, gauze, a white *galabeya*. The licensed *dayas* that I observed still have their midwifery kit in perfect condition ..." (1981: 33-34).
19 Simon noted similar rationales of the women in Sayyida Zeinab for signing up at the Mother and Child Health Center (1981: 25).
20 In the meanwhile, *hakimas* were staffing the centers mentioned above and maternity wards of hospitals. A study about *hakimas* conducted in 1968 in the maternity ward of Qasr El-Aini hospital described the *hakimas*' education which had essentially remained as described by Mahfouz in the 1930s (Sourial 1969: 26). While their 19th century predecessors had been independent practitioners, Sourial observed in the hospital "that the *hakimas* participated in the delivery only to pass tools, gloves and antiseptics to the doctors when needed" (ibid.: 15-16). Similar to Simon's experience Sourial noted that one of the *hakimas* whom she had come to know in the hospital treated her own patients outside her place of work (ibid.: 8). In these examples Dr. Mahfouz's earlier policies have come full circle: *hakimas* (and some *dayas*) as subordinates within institutionalized medicine.
21 In 1997 LE 3.3 roughly equalled 1 U.S.-$. At the same time a

lower level government clerk earned about LE 100-150 per month. Young women in El Tayibin who worked in stores and factories earned between LE 65-100 per month.

22 Both public and private hospitals have high rates of Caesarean births.

23 These are only my informal observations based on a limited sample of women. No matter what the exact figures are, the fact remains that they are indeed very high.

24 As I am finishing this paper, in late June 1997 a decree was issued by an administrative court that "struck down a Health Ministry order that banned the ritual [female circumcision] from public and private hospitals and clinics" (Al Ahram Weekly 26.6.-2.7.1997). It is beyond the scope of this paper to trace the chain of events that fueled the recent debates and decisions, suffice to note that some of it goes back to heated debates around a film at the 1994 International Conference for Population and Development.

25 I will not enter the larger discussion of female circumcision in Egypt as it is an issue that is frequently debated both within and beyond Egypt. Western feminists' interference in this debate has for the most part been inappropriate and even more so detrimental. Some of it comes unfortunately close to earlier colonial interferences both in discourse and language.

26 Only the students with the best grades in nursing school are able to continue their training and specialize at a nursing institute or the *hakima* school.

Selected Bibliography

Arnold, David (1993) *Colonizing the Body*, Berkeley/CA: University of California Press.

Blackman, Winifred (1968, 1927) *The Fellahin of Upper Egypt*, London: Frank Cass.

Foucault, Michel (1975) *The Birth of the Clinic*, New York/NY: Vintage Books.

Gallagher, Nancy (1993) *Egypt's Other Wars*, Cairo: The American University in Cairo Press.

Kuhnke, LaVerne (1992) *Lives at Risk,* Cairo: The American University in Cairo Press.

Mahfouz, Naguib Bey (1935) *The History of Medical Education in Egypt*, Cairo: Government Press, Bulaq.

Simon, Dagmar (1981) *Dayas in Urban Health Care: Activities, Problems and Prospects for the Future*, unpublished M.A. Thesis, Department of Anthropology, American University in Cairo.

Sourial, Aida Fahmy (1969) *The Hakima. A Study on the Socialization of a Professional Role*, unpublished M.A. Thesis, Department of Anthropology, American University in Cairo.

Problematizing Marriage: Minding My Manners in My Husband's Community

Anita Häusermann Fábos

Introduction

As I edged myself towards my seat in the university auditorium, I recognized the Sudanese man sitting one seat over. ʿAdel and I had met more than a year ago during a social visit I made with my husband to celebrate the ʿAid al-Adha feast marking the end of Ramadan. We smiled as we greeted each other. The man immediately launched into a laundry list of my identifying characteristics – American doctoral student, right? In anthropology? At Boston University? Indeed, he remembered virtually everything about our meeting – except that I was married to a Sudanese businessman in Cairo. Working up to placing me by neighborhood and street, he announced that he had many friends nearby and that he would take my phone number, so that he could call me when he was in the neighborhood, and visit.

My understanding, prior to starting my research project on 'northern' Sudanese expatriate and exile networks in Cairo,[1] was that it was improper for a married woman in the Sudanese community to receive a male visitor without her husband present. I had discussed possible 'Sudanese' expectations about my behavior with my husband before starting fieldwork, naively assuming that there was an 'authentic' wifely role that I could try to play. I stared at the unfortunate man in disbelief: Doesn't he remember that I'm a married woman? I tried to communicate my disapproval of his 'transgression' through body language, turning away from him and giving his persistent questions curt,

283

one-word answers. Waves of embarrassment and anger rolled over me as I pondered the implications of his request. I abruptly excused myself and moved to another seat.

This incident emphasizes my ambiguous position as an anthropologist from the "Eurocenter" (Lavie/Swedenberg 1996) whose marriage to a member of her research community complicates the indigenization of knowledge debate. Compelled to understand a different set of subtleties about gender, ethnicity, and a host of other identity discourses as they are constructed through my home life as well as my fieldsite, as a married person I straddle a boundary that is much more blurred than the dichotomy 'native'/'non-native' connotes. Furthermore, my position as a 'Western' woman married into 'the Sudanese community' has been understood in different ways by various people from my fieldsite, my husband, and myself. These different readings of my position have shaped my own epistemological journey towards recognizing the importance of gender propriety – which I have glossed as 'manners' – as an identity discourse for displaced northern Sudanese communities in Cairo, a conclusion drawn from personal experience. Through the dual processes of negotiating my roles as 'spouse' and 'researcher', I learned much about the problems inherent in the use of labels and labeling, the epistemological process of 'making' gender (Ortner 1996), and the nature of 'authenticity' itself.

When I first embarked on my field research, I expected that I would have to deal with, and overcome, the various labels attached to my position in the global order, such as 'American', 'Westerner', and 'foreigner'. In this I thought I might be helped by the fact that I was the 'wife' of a 'Sudanese man', both labels that I assumed would enhance the process of socialization into my research community. My own assumptions about gender roles and relations in the Sudanese community, forged through a lengthy association with different segments of Egyptian, Sudanese, and other Arab and predominantly Muslim societies, were supported by my husband's understanding of gender ideals in his own community. By challenging my received knowledge, I learned a different, experiential set of norms that exposed the changing gender relations of Sudanese in Cairo.

Doing fieldwork in any research community necessarily muddles personal and professional identities. However, when the community under study penetrates the intimacy of marriage, the anthropologist has less room for misunderstanding in the complex process of grasping community mores, values, and taboos, since both husband and community may view her as someone who should know better. The complex dialectic that I must negotiate as a married female anthropologist – between my position as a researcher, on the one hand, and as a woman married to an 'insider', on the other – structures community expectations in light of the labels I wear. At the same time, negotiations within marriage structure my understanding of community ideals and demonstrate the link between various levels of power relations.

Feminist theorists have contributed an awareness of the differentials of power in gender relations to social science, while postmodern theorists have concentrated on the inequality inherent in its practice. The indigenization of knowledge discourse, with its emphasis on the prerogative of social scientists from the periphery to develop fields of study afresh from the perspective of non-Western knowledge traditions (e.g. Islam) is another attempt to turn relations of power around. But marriage in the context of the 'traditional' fieldwork encounter, symbolizing the intersection of these three critiques, might be seen as a site of negotiation for the complex interaction of gender, colonialism, and individual temperaments.

Marriage, as an institution and a process that interacts with the fieldwork experience, deserves to be problematized for the way it produces knowledge about self and other. The topic of spouses in the field has attracted interest particularly as it relates to anthropologist couples or the balancing of professional aspirations in an age of dual career families (Fluehr-Lobban/Lobban 1987). But just as the concept of the family as a universal social institution has been extensively rethought, particularly regarding alternatives to the mainstream 'family values' focus of certain dominant ideologies (Kennedy/Davis 1993; Lewin 1993; Stack 1983), marriage too needs to be theorized as a historically constituted institution with a multiplicity of forms (Borneman 1996). Once marriage is conceptualized as a process, rather than a status, we can move away from rigid categorizations of 'us' and 'them', perhaps creating a more fluid notion of authenticity.

Reflexivity, Boundaries, and the Insider/Outsider Debate

The boundaries between a researcher's private life and public work may be more or less ambiguous depending on her position, while perceptions of self and other, shaped by power relations and their ensuing stereotypes, may create new labels through which to construct identities. In my case, I was never quite sure whether to attribute being included in Sudanese community activities and categories to my position as a married woman or not. For example, a friend in Cairo asked for my participation in a protest against the editorial policy of the locally-published Sudanese newspaper on the grounds that I was a 'Sudanese woman'. This was an intensely flattering invitation, though ultimately I decided not to call the newspaper to complain about the way it portrayed women, concluding that the person on the other end of the line would have a different perception of my 'Sudaneseness'. Nevertheless, the suggestion that I was part of the Sudanese community spurred me to think about the meaning of my relationship with my husband and with my Sudanese colleagues from the perspective of the production of knowledge.

The recognition that anthropological knowledge is largely predicated upon the ethnographer's subjective understanding of issues brought up through interaction with their research community is not new. It has, however, been "rediscovered" by postmodern theorists (Marcus/Fisher 1986) grappling with the unequal power relations that characterize these interactions. The fact that theorizing on these power relations have largely ignored those between men and women has not gone unnoticed by feminist scholars, who have responded in part by highlighting the distinguished tradition of reflexive ethnographic writing produced almost solely by women (Behar/Gordon 1995). The fairly recent reflexive turn in mainstream anthropology, we are reminded, is predated by women writing about their personal triumphs and tragedies in the field in a way that blurred the boundary between their academic and emotional lives (Tedlock 1995; Bell et al. 1992).

Yet while the acceptance of ethnography as a joint project between an anthropologist and a research community has been widely recognized, there is still a reluctance to admit that crossing the line between 'us' and 'them' may lead to interactions on a more intimate level (Kulick/Willson 1995). Anthropologists are still averse to writing about their sexuality, let alone sexual relations with members of their field communities. The difficulties in simply bringing articles on sexuality and fieldwork together in a publication attest to the sensitivity of any sexual relations which may link anthropologists with their field sites (Kulick/Willson 1995).

Having a spouse from one's research community – a relationship overlooked, incidentally, in the section of an American Anthropological Association fieldwork report dealing with families in the field (Howell 1990) – also represents a different level of intimacy. Married anthropologists who study their own societies may also have to face the intrusions of research into personal life, but in the case where the researcher's spouse simultaneously embodies emotional marital closeness and cultural distance, the boundaries of intimacy become ambiguous. Inasmuch as marriage often legitimizes sexuality, such a relationship may be more acceptable to both colleagues in the country of origin and the community of the field than the erotic relationships so often entered into by anthropologists abroad. Nevertheless, the reactions to a marriage between an anthropologist and a person representing his or her field site may be met, in contrast, by muted hostility (Gearing 1995) on the part of friends and colleagues in the home country. Contradictory reactions from colleagues 'at home' to married intimacy in the field may reflect unspoken assumptions regarding the loss of the capacity for objectivity. But if other anthropologists have found that it is difficult, if not impossible, to separate the researcher and the researched into two neat categories (Karim 1992), could marriage signify the inevitability of interaction across the border?

The indigenization of knowledge debate (Morsy et al. 1991) with its roots in the call for decolonization of the social sciences in the 1970s, has suggested that blurring boundaries or crossing borders in anthropological fieldwork is more easily or legitimately done by the indigenous or 'halfie' (Abu-Lughod 1991) anthropologist. In this debate over what constitutes 'authentic' knowledge, the anthropologist who is linked to his or her research community by virtue of nationality, ethnicity, or even race, is seen as being able to tap a more 'authentic' vein of information about the society under study through perceived personal commitment to the community, and the community's acceptance of the anthropologist as 'one of them'. But while the 'nativeness' of the 'native' has been strongly challenged as a sign of eligibility for knowledge, his/her indigenous status still positions him/her methodologically, and epistemologically (Narayan 1993).

The anthropologists writing in *Arab Women in the Field* (Altorki/El-Solh 1988) examine the epistemological implications of being Arab or Arab-American women connected with their field sites in different ways. It becomes clear that whatever expectations were thrown up by being glossed as insiders, their personal relations with members of the community were equally powerful in mediating these expectations. In her response to a critique of her recent ethnography on Nubian gender relations (Shirazi 1996), Jennings writes that her expectations of being accepted by a Nubian community on the basis of her appearance as an African-American woman and her kinship bonds with them never fully occurred (Jennings 1996). I suspect that her feeling that her 'racial heritage' gave her quicker and more complete access to the community than she would have had were she an anthropologist with a different phenotype was predicated upon my similar hope and misconception that I held as a married woman expecting 'instant roots' in my husband's community. But to what extent does an anthropologist's position(ing) influence her personal relationship with people in the field? I propose that, through my position as an anthropologist blurring the boundaries of 'insider/outsider' status through marriage, I bear some of the same expectations that an indigenous anthropologist sustains despite being an outsider in terms of cultural knowledge.

Marriage As Position and Process

The fact of my marriage and the ongoing process of negotiation associated with it accords me an ambivalent position in the Sudanese community in Cairo. Other ethnographers have described their married status in the field as providing them a certain level of access and/or saddling them with constraints (but cf. Altorki/El-Solh 1988: 4-7), and most recognize its epistemological implications. Sayigh describes her life history research in the Palestinian refugee camps in Lebanon as greatly aided by the fact that she was the wife of a Palestinian and the mother of Palestinian children; her married status gave her credibility, while as a non-Palestinian she was not seen as partisan. Finally, as a woman she was less likely to face arrest than she would have as a male researcher (Sayigh 1994: 8). Fluehr-Lobban, writing on her fieldwork in Sudan, echoes the aphorism that women – and married women in particular – are more able than men to cross gender boundaries in segregated societies (Fluehr-Lobban 1984: 225), though she chose to emphasize her solidarity with Sudanese women. Freedman comes closer to the idea of marriage as a process in her narration of her fieldwork experience before and after her husband's death (Freedman 1986). The three 'roles' she played vis-à-vis her research community ("wife, widow, woman") and the three sets of relationships she developed according to her different positions were predicated upon change over time.

During my long-term relationships with the Sudanese community in Cairo and with my husband, I have experienced how the fact of my marriage has changed my understanding of cultural expectations regarding my behavior. While conducting field research, I was also a participant in the life of a Sudanese family, that of my husband, and I was responsible for comporting myself in a way that had implications far beyond my study. The process of learning to be a proper wife[2] contributed dramatically to the specific character taken by my research on gender and ethnicity, and my decision to study Sudanese norms of propriety within their immigrant identity discourse in turn sensitized me to the nuances of power in my marriage.

Marriage, Self, and Community

Marriage as a social category has long been represented by anthropologists as "the definitive ritual and universally translatable regulative ideal of human societies" (Borneman 1996: 215). But the rich body of scholarly work on marriage and the family encompassing kinship, gender, power, and political economy, among other units of analysis, has been criticized recently for its ahistorical view of marriage as a "privileged form that invariably produced gender as its effect" (Borneman 1996: 230). It is not the aim of this essay to contribute to the project of rethinking marriage as producing gender in terms of the inclusivity/exclusivity debate outlined by Borneman, but rather to demonstrate that marriage, in addition to endowing a person with a socially recognized status, is also a process shaped by discourses about gender and the specific circumstances of the relationship.

My fieldwork among northern Sudanese in Egypt centered around the changing content of gender relations, and the intersection of gender ideology with ethnic identity. The discourse of displacement as presented by Sudanese women and men in exile in Egypt suggested to me that morality and manners as ideal behavior patterns are a crucial part of defining Sudanese identity at the time of my fieldwork. Marriage is an important element of Sudanese morality, tied to female chastity, fertility, and division of labor, among other things (Boddy 1989; Mohamed-Salih/Mohamed-Salih 1987; Williams/Sobieszczyk 1996). However, the circumstances of exile do not support adherence to the ideal code (as expressed in the current context) of gender propriety, and Sudanese women's and men's actual behavior in Cairo has drawn my attention to this contradiction.

The influence of this discourse, however, has been powerfully illustrated for me in the context of my position as a married woman, and what that might mean for community expectations concerning my role. The behavior of ʿAdel, the Sudanese man who proposed visiting me, could be interpreted in several ways taking into account the circumstances of diaspora and desperation. His intent to visit could well be representative of a "new morality" in the community which blurs formerly clear-cut codes channeling male/female interactions into public space. Alternatively, his attempts to get to know me better could have been related to his reading my 'Americanness' as putting me in a possible position to help him leave Egypt for a chance at a new life in the U.S. Finally, his query could have been a test of my understanding of an ideal Sudanese code of propriety and a statement of his illicit intentions.

Killick notes that little is written regarding local expectations towards researchers as non-native men or women (Killick 1995: 88). Early on in my fieldwork, I had assumed that my marital status would demonstrate sexual unavailability in the way that the ethnographer Helen Morton's pregnancy warded off unwanted attention (Morton 1995: 177), since my own inability to see gender as a fluid process gave me a two-dimensional view of propriety. It took persistent questioning of my female informants for me to understand that the variety of possible explanations for ʿAbdel's behaviour had to do with how he might have seen me. The ambiguity of this encounter illustrates that marriage is a matrix of power relations that brings together a complex mix of personal and community expectations.

Marriage as a Site of Power Relations

The process of gender production within the framework of marriage can be analyzed in terms of relations of power that draw the female ethnographer into the complexities of the community's gender relations, as well as negotiations with her spouse. For an ethnographer married to someone from his/her field site, marriage becomes a site of knowledge production where several interconnected sets of power relations, including gender and sexuality, the legacy of colonialism, and ethnicity and race, converge and mingle. Karim has called the power relations of fieldwork "diabolical" for the troublesome research dynamic that places the anthropologist as ascendant in relation to the world 'outside', while the 'native' reigns supreme in the world the anthropologist is trying to comprehend (Karim 1992: 248). But the position of female anthropologists vis-à-vis these "opposing worlds" is more ambiguous, since their relations of power on both sides of the equation are complicated by gender (Kulick/Willson 1995; Morton 1995; Bell et al. 1992; Altorki/El-Solh 1988; Morsy et al. 1991). Furthermore, in deconstructing their experiences as the 'Other' within their own societies (Bell et al. 1992) it has been suggested that women are more sensitive to issues of domination (Fluehr-Lobban 1986; Dubisch 1995).

Other ethnographers writing about spouses in the field have described the confusion they caused by not adhering to community-defined gender roles in their marriage. Freedman discusses the doubts of Romanian villagers about her husband's masculinity, since he could not consume the quantities of alcohol expected of him without getting violently ill, and frequently performed household tasks such as laundry and carrying water which were, in this village, solely performed by women (Freedman 1986). Fluehr-Lobban and Lobban note that their dedication to sharing household tasks in northern Sudan raised eyebrows (Fluehr-Lobban 1987), while on the other hand Schrijvers suggests that the women in her Sri Lankan research community admired her husband for his participation in childcare (Schrijvers 1992). It is worth noting that none of these anthropologists' spouses were from their field site; although communities judged these individuals according to their own gender norms, the ethnographers did not note any ambivalence on the part of their spouses towards disregarding these norms.

Gender and power relations in the context of marriage to the 'Other' resonates more with the experiences of indigenous female researchers, who have discussed the conflicts they face in their own communities, or in communities which have adopted them (see, for example, Lila Abu-Lughod's mutually defined role as a 'dutiful daughter' in the Awlad 'Ali community [1988]). The assumption by both an indigenous ethnographer and her community is that, since boundaries demarcating researcher and researched are blurred, gender values and behavior should be shared. The tension produced by such an assumption lies in the contradiction that though the researcher and fieldsite are both gendered, relations are made ambiguous due to the differentials in power inherent in the research process.

The debate as to whether social science research can free itself of its Eurocentric heritage represents another set of power relations that is equally important in problematizing marriage in the field. As Dubisch points out,

[s]exual relations of women of the dominant cultures with men of the subordinate cultures ... confuse dominance relations, for gender hierarchy in such a relationship [from the point of view of the dominant Western society] contradicts the hierarchy of the cultural relationship by making the dominant women 'available' to subordinate men.

(Dubisch 1995: 34)

I do not believe that the dual status of a woman who is also a representative of her husband's colonial past suggests a neutral balance of power. Since marriage and fieldwork are both processes which call on the spouse/researcher to constantly renegotiate her relationship with both, it is through personal experience that 'authentic' knowledge based on the intersection of these sets of power relations is created.

Minding My Manners: Propriety, Marriage, and Knowledge Production

As a wife/researcher in the Sudanese community, my experiences have been transformed into certain types of knowledge through learning a culturally-mediated role. I had previously recognized that my access to information about my husband's community would be enhanced – and I quickly learned that some of my activities would be curtailed – because of my position. I had not realized that, in my conceptualization of my research, my partiality would lead me to structure my knowledge about Sudanese gender behavior in such specific ways. The process of negotiating my marriage brought me face to face with a very personal understanding of how Sudanese in Egypt were coping with their increasing disenfranchisement, both in their own country, and within their host society.

The historical entanglement of northern Sudanese with the Egyptian state and society is reflected in both the ambiguous status of Sudanese in Egypt, and their ambivalence over their ethnic identity. While Sudanese recognize long-standing ties of trade and marriage, cultural similarities, and the shared struggle against British colonial rule in the region, many resent patronizing Egyptian attitudes and ignorance of the problems facing Sudanese displaced in Egypt. The official Egyptian position, reflected in popular social discourse, maintains that Egyptians and Sudanese are one people, based on Egypt's historical claim to a 'united' Nile Valley. Northern Sudanese, in response, have asserted their identity as Sudanese through a discourse predicated on gender ideology, since other ethnic boundary markers such as language, religion, and dress are negated by Egyptian proclamations of unity.

During the period of my field research, my perception that Sudanese were using the idiom of 'manners' as a marker of ethnic difference coincided with my attempt to learn 'proper' behavior. Sudanese discourse on their identity increasingly took the form of disparaging comments about perceived lack of manners on the part of Egyptians, and on their own adherence to propriety. These were largely expressed in terms of gender norms. For example, one of my Sudanese colleagues regularly admonished her son for swearing, a habit she felt he had developed through his association with Egyptian schoolchildren. She told him, "Remember! You are a polite, Sudanese man!" Other associates from the Sudanese community described Egyptians as behaving immodestly compared to Sudanese, citing such 'impolite' characteristics as flirting across gender lines, or the alleged lack of generosity and hospitality that Sudanese believe sustains their masculinity. In addition, my husband and I had many conversations, prior to starting fieldwork, as to what behavior was 'appropriate' for the wife of a Sudanese man, and what behavior I should expect in response.

Taking my cue from these and other ideals, I initially limited my interactions with Sudanese men, keeping conversation on a more 'formal' level, giving out my office phone number rather than my home number, and leaving mixed gatherings on the early side so as not to excite comment about late-night fraternizing. I also mentioned the fact of my marriage to a Sudanese man frequently, believing that this connection would alert Sudanese to my understanding of the need to behave like a 'proper' Sudanese woman and thus creating the expectation that I ought to be treated in a 'respectable' and 'authentic' way – that is, like a 'native' and not a 'foreigner.' I must stress, however, that I experienced the adherence to these norms quite differently as a married woman. Thoughts of my husband's reputation usually ran parallel with worries about whether I was attracting negative attention as a woman.

Thus I was not prepared for my feelings of humiliation and anger when, for example, Sudanese men called our home asking for me late at night. I had internalized, it seems, certain norms of propriety that made me feel like I was behaving 'authentically.' However, over the course of fieldwork, I routinely noted the many contradictions to the stated ideals of Sudanese propriety, which led me to question the content of the labels that people in my research community attached to themselves and others. Despite my understanding that late-night calls from Sudanese men were improper, quite a few of my Sudanese women friends complained about 'inappropriately timed' phone calls as well. I came to recognize that many Sudanese, for whom it is nearly impossible to find work, do not start their day until noon and stay up late visiting friends or watching television, so for a significant segment of the population telephoning someone after midnight is not considered late, and therefore not improper.

Displacement has also affected other norms of gender propriety, such as women's freedom of movement. My research suggested that many Sudanese women in Cairo did not feel that they had to restrict their visits or errands to daytime or early evening, as was the stated norm as I understood it. Indeed, my husband and I were concerned that people would consider me an improper wife if I stayed out late during my field visits, only to realize that many married women were just starting their evening visits as I was getting ready to return home. Coping with the contradictions between ideal and real boundaries of propriety was stressful, since the constraints I had anticipated were still assumed by my husband to be part of Sudanese behavior, even as my research suggested otherwise.

Observing changing gender norms in the Sudanese community in Egypt through the lens of my marriage led me to a deeper understanding of the distress caused by displacement and the ways in which people cope. The fact that, through my marriage, I became a member of the moral community I was simultaneously studying served to heighten my perception of the gender subtext in the Sudanese discourse about identity. But my marriage, as a "processual encounter", conditioned my awareness of propriety as an idiom in a much more intimate way which involved both my husband and his community as participant-observers as well (Jenkins 1994: 452).

Conclusion

The full disclosure of the position of the researcher vis-à-vis the research community continues to be a vital tool of analysis for the anthropologist interested in how her own subjectivity influences the production of knowledge about the community. Different levels of insight are gained from doing rather than just watching, but comprehension of other societies can be enhanced by intimacy. Timothy Jenkins states that

> to understand is to acknowledge one's own participation, and therefore be changed since, in order to participate, one of the roles on offer has to be taken up and explored.

Becoming a partner in marriage within fieldwork is one such role. However, the concept of marriage is not a universal equivalent that translates across cultures, and it therefore produces different understandings of femininity and masculinity (Yanagisako/Collier 1996: 236). Rather than considering marriage as representing a role or a status, relations between husband and wife should be seen as producing knowledge specific to the confluence of power relations encompassed by the relationship. Through the process of negotiating this particular encounter I, as a married anthropologist, have come face to face with the challenge of authenticity and the ethical implications of social research.

Notes

I would like to thank Betsy Bishop and Muhammad Abd Al-Wadoud for planting the intellectual seed for this article. The comments of members of the Research Seminar for Visiting Fellows and Scholars, under the direction of Cynthia Nelson, were instrumental to developing the first draft. In particular, I am grateful to Nadje Al-Ali, Montasser Kamal, and Enid Hill for their contributions. Subsequent drafts were improved by the comments of Alison McGandy, Amira Abderahman, Steve Howard, Bettina Fabos, Nada Mustafa, Shahnaz Rouse and Cynthia Nelson. Final responsibility for all statements and interpretations included in this essay, however, rests on my shoulders.

1 Since the 1989 coup in Sudan several hundred thousand Sudanese nationals from northern central riverain Sudan have fled to Egypt where they joined a large settled community of 'northern' Sudanese. The label 'northern' refers to the handful of ethnic groups from the region who have dominated the political and economic stage of the Sudanese state, though this has been historically constructed and masks the cultural and political complexity of Sudan.
2 I note my debt to Lila Abu-Lughod's concept of the 'dutiful daughter' in her contribution to Altorki/El-Solh (1988).

Selected Bibliography

Abu-Lughod, Lila (1988) "Fieldwork of a Dutiful Daughter". In Soraya Altorki/Camillia Fawzy El-Solh (eds.) (1988) *Arab Women in the Field: Studying Your Own Society*, Cairo: American University in Cairo Press, pp. 139-161.
—— (1991) "Writing Against Culture". In Richard Fox (ed.) *Recapturing Anthropology*, Santa Fe/NM: School of American Research Press, pp. 137-162.
Altorki, Soraya/El-Solh, Camillia Fawzy (eds.) (1988) *Arab Women in*

the Field: Studying Your Own Society, Cairo: American University in Cairo Press.

Behar, Ruth/Gordon, Deborah (eds.) (1995) *Women Writing Culture,* Berkeley/CA: University of California Press.

Bell, Diane/Caplan, Pat/Karim, Wazir Jahan (eds.) (1992) *Gendered Fields: Women, Men, and Ethnography,* London, New York/NY: Routledge.

Boddy, Janice (1989) *Wombs and Alien Spirits: Women, Men, and the Zar Cult of Northern Sudan,* Madison/WI: University of Wisconsin Press.

Borneman, John (1996) "Until Death Do Us Part: Marriage/Death in Anthropological Discourse". *American Ethnologist* 23/2, pp. 215-238.

Dubisch, Jill (1995) "Lovers in the Field: Sex, Dominance, and the Female Anthropologist". In Don Kulick/Margaret Willson (eds.) *Taboo: Sex, Identity, and Erotic Subjectivity in Anthropological Fieldwork,* London, New York/NY: Routledge, pp. 29-50.

Fluehr-Lobban, Carolyn (1984) "Lessons from Fieldwork in the Sudan". In F. Hussain (ed.) *Muslim Women,* London, Sydney: Croom Helm, pp. 221-228.

—— /Lobban, Richard (1986) "Families, Gender, and Methodology in the Sudan". In T. Whitehead/Mary Ellen (eds.) *Self, Sex, and Gender in Cross-Cultural Fieldwork,* Urbana/IL: University of Illinois Press, pp. 182-195.

—— /Lobban, Richard (1987) "'Drink from the Nile and You Shall Return': Children and Fieldwork in Egypt and the Sudan". In J. Cassell (ed.) *Children in the Field: Anthropological Experiences,* Philadelphia/PA: Temple University Press, pp. 237-255.

Freedman, Diane (1986) "Wife, Widow, Woman: Roles of an Anthropologist in a Transylvanian Village". In P. Golde (ed.) *Women in the Field: Anthropological Experiences,* Berkeley/CA: University of California Press, pp. 333-358.

Gearing, Jean (1995) "Fear and Loving in the West Indies: Research from the Heart (as Well as the Head)". In Don Kulick/Margaret Willson (eds.) *Taboo: Sex, Identity, and Erotic Subjectivity in Anthropological Fieldwork,* London, New York/NY: Routledge, pp. 186-218.

Howell, Nancy (1990) *Surviving Fieldwork: A Report of the Advisory*

Panel on Health and Safety in Fieldwork, Washington/DC: American Anthropological Association.

Jenkins, Tim (1994) "Fieldwork and the Perception of Everyday Life". *Man* 29/2, pp. 433-455.

Jennings, Anne (1996) "Anne Jennings Responds to Faegheh Shirazi's Review of Nubians in West Aswan". *Middle East Women's Studies Review* 11/2, p. 14.

Karim, Wazir Jahan (1992a) "Epilogue: The 'Nativized' Self and the 'Native'". In Diane Bell/Pat Caplan/Wazir Jahan Karim (eds.) *Gendered Fields: Women, Men, and Ethnography,* London, New York/NY: Routledge, pp. 249-251.

—— (1992b) "With Moyang Melur in Carey Island: More Endangered, More Engendered". In Diane Bell/Pat Caplan/Wazir Jahan Karim (eds.) *Gendered Fields: Women, Men, and Ethnography,* London, New York/NY: Routledge, pp. 78-92.

Kennedy, Elizabeth/Davis, Madeline (1993) *Boots of Leather, Slippers of Gold,* New York/NY: Routledge.

Killick, Andrew P. (1995) "The Penetrating Intellect: On Being White, Straight, and Male in Korea". In Don Kulick/Margaret Willson (eds.) *Taboo: Sex, Identity, and Erotic Subjectivity in Anthropological Fieldwork,* London, New York/NY: Routledge, pp. 16-106.

Kulick, Don/Willson, Margaret (1995) *Taboo: Sex, Identity, and Erotic Subjectivity in Anthropological Fieldwork,* London, New York/NY: Routledge.

Lavie, Smadar/Swedenberg, Ted (1996) "Introduction: Displacement, Diaspora, and Geographies of Identity". In Smadar Lavie/Ted Swedenberg (eds.) *Displacement, Diaspora, and Geographies of Identity,* Durham/NC: Duke University Press, pp. 1-26.

Lewin, Ellen (1993) *Lesbian Mothers: Accounts of Gender in American Culture,* Ithaca/NY: Cornell University Press.

Marcus, George E./Fischer, Michael M.J. (1986) *Anthropology as Cultural Critique: An Experimental Moment in the Human Sciences,* Chicago/IL: University of Chicago Press.

Mohamed-Salih, Mohamed A./Mohamed-Salih, Margaret A. (1987) *Family Life in Sudan,* Khartoum: The Graduate College, University of Khartoum.

Morsy, Soheir/Nelson, Cynthia/Saad, Reem/Sholkamy, Hania (1991) "Anthropology and the Call for Indigenization of Social Science in the Arab World". In Earl T. Sullivan/Jacqueline S. Ismail (eds.) *Contemporary Studies of the Arab World*, Edmonton/AB: University of Alberta Press, pp. 81-111.

Morton, Helen (1995) "My 'Chastity Belt': Avoiding Seduction in Tonga". In Don Kulick/Margaret Willson (eds.) *Taboo: Sex, Identity, and Erotic Subjectivity in Anthropological Fieldwork.* London, New York/NY: Routledge, pp. 140-286.

Narayan, Kirin. (1993) "How Native is a 'Native' Anthropologist?". *American Anthropologist* 95, pp. 671-686.

Ortner, Sherry B. (1996) *Making Gender: The Politics and Erotics of Culture*, Boston/MA: Beacon Press.

Sayigh, Rosemary (1994) *Too Many Enemies: The Palestinian Experience in Lebanon*, London: Zed Books.

Schrijvers, Joke (1992) "Motherhood Experienced and Conceptualized: Changing Images in Sri Lanka and the Netherlands". In Diane Bell/Pat Caplan/Wazir Jahan Karim (eds.) *Gendered Fields: Women, Men, and Ethnography*, London, New York/NY: Routledge, pp. 143-167.

Shirazi, Faegheh (1996) "Africans as Kinsfolk? Anne Jennings' Nubians of West Aswan". *Middle East Women's Studies Review* 11/1, pp. 4-5.

Stack, Carol (1983) *All Our Kin: Strategies for Survival in a Black Community*, New York/NY: Harper Collins.

Tedlock, Barbara (1995) "Works and Wives: On the Sexual Division of Textual Labor". In Ruth Behar/Deborah Gordon (eds.) *Women Writing Culture*, Berkeley/CA: University of California Press, pp. 267-286.

Wade, Peter (1992) "Sexuality and Masculinity in Fieldwork Among Columbian Blacks". In Diane Bell/Pat Caplan/Wazir Jahan Karim (eds.) *Gendered Fields: Women, Men, and Ethnography*, London, New York/NY: Routledge, pp. 199-214.

Williams, Lindy/Sobieszczyk, Teresa (1996) "Attitudes Surrounding the Continuation of Female Circumcision in the Sudan: Passing the Tradition to the Next Generation". *PSC Research Report*, Ithaca/NY: Cornell University.

Yanagisako, Sylvia J./Collier, Jane F. (1996) "Comments on 'Until Death Do Us Part'". *American Ethnologist* 23/2, pp. 235-236.

A Tale of Two Contracts: Towards a Situated Understanding of "Women Interests" in Egypt

Heba El-Kholy

I am sitting on a plastic mat on the dirt floor of the largest room of a two story unpainted brick house, sharing a lunch meal of lentils, molasses, dry bread and green onions with Um Sayed and some members of her extended family, her daughter, Um Mahmoud, and her granddaughter Karima. As we casually talk about Karima's marriage, consummated four weeks ago, Um Mahmoud proudly recounts, for the third time, the particulars of the fight that took place over the value of Karima's marriage inventory, her *ayma*. Um Mahmoud explains how she insisted that the *ayma*[1] be valued at 4,000 pounds[2], citing in great detail its various items, whereas the groom's family, in particular his older sister, protested, insisting that the maximum her brother would agree to sign to was 2,000 pounds. Um Mahmoud stood firm on her demand and after several weeks of negotiations – during which the threat of canceling the wedding loomed – the groom, a semi-skilled worker, succumbed and both he and his uncle, as guarantor, signed on a 4,000 pound *ayma*. The groom's sister, Um Mahmoud reports in a victorious, self-congratulatory tone, was so angry she did not even come to the wedding.

Although I had heard this story for the third time, its importance to my research had not yet quite sunk in. I had heard about the *ayma* before, but had largely dismissed it as a formality. Munching on a piece of dry bread dipped in molasses, I casually asked the women whether the *ayma* was an important component of marriage negotiations in this community in general, or did it assume a significance in Karima's case for specific reasons. As I did not write an *ayma* myself when I got married eight years ago, I continued, I did not quite understand why Um Mahmoud made such a fuss about it, and I wondered if they could provide an explanation. The mixture of shock, pity and disbelief that my harmless question elicited from the three generations of women sitting around me was a turning point in my research. Um Mahmoud's reaction was the most severe:

What! You did not have an *ayma*? How is this possible? Are you living in another world? ... Do you not know your rights as a woman? The *ayma* is the only way to protect a woman from men and from time, *el ayma tedman ha' el sitt min el regalla w-el-zaman*. When you get old, who will feed you? Your husband will find himself a pretty, fair new bride and kick you out of the house, *yezátik*. Is there a house without an *ayma*? You were a fool, *moghaffala*, they sold you cheap ... If a woman does not have a *ayma* she is considered married for free, *itgawwizit bi balash*, and people would scorn/belittle/humiliate her, *yeaayrouha* ... It is not your fault, maybe you were young and naive. [Um Sayed was clearly desperately groping for explanations for my disgraceful behaviour, as in fact she knew from a previous discussion that I was married at 28, quite old by community standards.] But what about your parents, what is their excuse to throw you like that, *nasek mosh haram aleehom yermouki?* You must go and make a *ayma* immediately. Give your husbands some drugs, *birsham* [I presumed she meant to make him drowsy], and let him sign a *ayma* ... You must protect yourself by a *ayma*, a *ayma* ensures/secures a women's rights, *el ayma betsoon haq el horma*. Men are not to be trusted. A man is to be trusted as much as a sieve is to be trusted with water, *ya meamen lel rigal, yameamen lel maya fel ghorbal*.

Introduction

This paper is about the *ayma*, most closely translated as the marriage inventory. It is also about how poverty and gender intersect; how socio-economic location partly shapes one's perceptions of, and responses to, gender inequalities, and what this means for feminist activism. The data presented in this chapter is based on interviews and participation in the daily lives of 36 "poor" women in four low-income neighborhoods in Cairo[3]. The data suggest that the *ayma*, although ignored by both researchers and activists ("native" and foreign alike), is an essential aspect of marriage negotiations among the women I interviewed, and arguably in other low-income neighborhoods in Cairo as well.

By exploring this particular practice, the aims of the paper are three fold, all of which seek to contribute directly or indirectly to debates on gender and the indigenization of knowledge debate. First, I aim to describe an important practice in marriage negotiations, which has not been the subject of previous anthropological study, highlighting an indigenous local discourse surrounding it which reveals female discontent and attempts at curbing male power. Second I use the example of the *ayma* to raise theoretical questions regarding women's agency, consciousness and responses to gender inequalities. I specifically challenge universalist assumptions in feminist scholarship about women's acceptance of male dominance, their internalization of their relatively subordinate positions and their presumed passivity in the face of oppression. Despite emerging empirical evidence to the contrary, this view is quite entrenched and "continues to hold sway" in *both* western feminist discourse as well as in the work of some third world scholars writing about their own cultures (Agrawal 1994; Mohanty 1985). Thus, as has been suggested by some scholars, "indigenous" contributions to specificity may not necessarily contrast with "non indigenous" generalizations (Morsy el al. 1991: 92).

The *ayma* very vividly illustrates the mistrust and suspicions that characterize gender relations in the study community, specifically as they relate to marriage. It also illustrates the ways in which certain groups of women attempt to mitigate some of the acknowledged perils of men as husbands, and expand their options and bargaining power in their marriages. The practice of the *ayma* sheds light on how wives seek to secure themselves and their children financially in a specific socioeconomic and historical context where men are increasingly either unwilling or unable to provide for them. While a "culture of silence", and a "silent endurance" (see Khattab 1992), may accurately describe Egyptian women's responses in some contexts, a "culture of protest" may nonetheless prevail in other arenas and contexts. The practice of the *ayma* clearly demonstrates that not all categories of Egyptian women can be characterized, as they have been by some Egyptian feminist writers, as unaware that they are being oppressed in the first place ... as grooves in a wheel ... dolls that have learnt how to perform certain roles and who have neither the consciousness nor education that can enable them to begin to question and challenge their surroundings.

(Sahar el Mogy in Hagar 1994: 226, translated from Arabic)

Third, by contrasting the practice of the *ayma*, with the "new marriage contract" campaign, initiated by middle and upper class feminists in Egypt several years ago, I raise several theoretical and political questions about the role of the "feminist movement" in Egypt[4] in perpetuating unequal power relations between women. Juxtaposing two equally "indigenous" discourses and strategies related to marriage and gender relations raises questions about what constitutes "authentic" or "indigenous" knowledge and points to the need to de-construct both the concept of "indigenous" and that of "women". These questions lead me to argue for a more situated analysis of gender relations and "women's interests" in Egypt, as well as more concerted efforts at forging vertical coalitions amongst women across both class and educational lines.[5] Such efforts would contribute to both reformulating the existing body of knowledge and theory regarding gender relations and women's agency, as well as strengthen feminist activism in Egypt.

The "Study Community"

The paper is part of a broader anthropological study that investigates the ways in which women, at different points in their life cycle, perceive, talk about, experience and negotiate unfavorable relations in their daily life, both in the family and in the informal labor market. The study was carried out over 15 months between July 1995 and October 1996 in four low-income neighborhoods in Cairo. The broader study was based on interviews, informal discussions and participation in the daily lives of 87 women and 12 men in these neighborhoods. This "sample" was not selected to be representative of the neighborhoods, nor did I attempt to carry out a geographically focused study. Rather, the group of people on which the broader study is based constitute what may be termed a "purposeful" sample. I initially selected a few women to reflect particular patterns of female employment that I was interested in: waged work in the informal economy, and home-based sub-contracting. It is through the introductions of these few early key informants to their relatives, neighbors and members in their range of employment, market, and spirit possession networks that I ended up with this "sample". Although my interviewees resided in four different geographical neighborhoods, I refer to them as a "community" or a "study community" nonetheless, because they were all linked to each other through various informal networks.

This paper is based on interviews and participant observations among only 36 of the women in the larger sample, as well as some of their male relatives and several lawyers. "Low-income" is of course a general description that does not do justice to socio-economic differentiation and diversity of lifestyles within neighborhoods. However, the differences in family incomes and lifestyles did not vary significantly amongst the 36 women I interviewed. The majority of women were working in the informal economy[6] either as unskilled wage laborers in workshops, or as home-based sub-contractors. Depending on the type of piece work, and its regularity, a pieceworker can earn between 2-4 pounds for a ten hour working day.[7] An unskilled female wage laborer can earn between 3-6 pounds for a ten hour working day. There were also a few women who were self-employed as small-scale vendors. The occupations of their husbands varied, but most were closely tied to the informal economy, largely as unskilled, sometimes, casual labors. There were also a few skilled craftsmen whose incomes were higher. The irregular nature of employment, which meant that it was difficult to assure a fixed monthly income, however, was one of the main features of the economic lives of these families. Only three husbands were employed as lower level bureaucrats (guards and mailmen) in public sector companies, and thus had fixed and regular incomes.

The women ranged in age between 18 and 60. These were all Muslim and were mostly illiterate or had completed no more than primary school. Two had finished a high school diploma, and two had completed a preparatory degree. Most women lived in nuclear households with their children; only four women lived in an extended household with the parents of either the husband or wife. Twenty-eight of the women were renters and the rest owned their apartments. Those who were renting were typically renting two rooms in a larger building and shared a latrine with three or four other families. All households had access to electricity, but access to clean water was less universal. Ten of the women did not have a water tap in their rented rooms, and either used a public tap or bought water from neighbors.[8]

The Context: Marriage Transactions and Negotiations

My aim in this paper is not to provide a comprehensive account of marriage negotiations in the study community, capturing all the subtleties and complex dynamics of such relations, but rather, to focus on a specific practice directly related to my main theoretical concerns. More comprehensive accounts of marriage in low-income communities in Cairo, have been provided in several other studies, mainly generated by foreign researchers (see for example Singerman 1994; Rugh 1985). The role of marriage in the Middle East as an idiom for negotiating political and economic conflicts and expression of competition in the wider society has also been well illustrated by several studies (Rugh 1985; Tapper 1991; Eickelman/Piscatori 1996). Nonetheless the following brief description of marriage transactions among my interviewees provides a context for better understanding the practice of the *ayma*.

Marriage negotiations in the study community typically underwent four stages. The first stage, the formal declaration of intent, is signaled by both families getting together and reading the opening verse of the Koran, *irayet el fatha*. This is considered an informal engagement, and is usually referred to as *khutuba*, engagement. The reading of the *fatha*, which usually takes place usually in the bride's family's residence is often preceded by many negotiations, regarding the timing of the three following stages: the formal engagement party, *shabka*, the official religious ceremony, *katb el kitab*, and the consummation of the marriage, *el Dukhla*.[9] The financial commitments of both families are worked out, and agreed upon, at this stage, although they may remain the subjects of disagreements and renegotiations for many months afterwards.

The formal signature of the marriage contract and the religious ceremony, *katb el kitab*, sometimes takes place at the same time as the *shabka*, the formal engagement party, and sometimes at the time of the consummation of the wedding, *laylit el dukhla*. In situations, where an engagement is expected to be long which is becoming increasingly common, as when the families need time to amass the necessary "marriage capital", or because they want to wait for a girl to complete her education, there is a preference for signing the marriage contract at the time of the shabka, as this enables couples to associate more freely (see also Singerman 1995). The engagement party is usually paid for by the bride's family and the wedding party by the groom's family, although both families sometimes share the expenses of both events.

It is noteworthy that discussions between families take on straightforward financial overtones, from the very first stage of marriage negotiations, with terms like buying and selling, *bayi'ha* and *shariha* used to express degrees of commitment to a marriage. Typically a groom must provide the marital home, and a present of gold, referred to as a *shabka*, and the bedroom furnishings.[10] The average acceptable *Shabkha* in the community studied ranged between 500-1,000 pounds, and typically consisted of one or two 21 carat gold bracelets and a gold wedding band. A particularly expensive type of *shabkha*, the unattainable dream of all the women I talked to, was known as *shabka shabah*, literally "ghost shabkha", and consisted of two thick and elaborately decorated golden bracelets costing about 1,200 LE each. The name ghost, "shabah" is particularly interesting to note as it derives from the same nickname given by Egyptians to the top of the line Mercedes car in Egypt (costing about 600,000 pounds), the ultimate status, prestige and wealth symbol of the nouveau riche. While acquiring a "ghost" Mercedes may be a sign of social mobility and prestige for Egypt's upper classes, acquiring a "ghost" *shabka* is a marker of social mobility and status distinctions amongst lower class families.

In addition to the *shabka*, the groom is typically expected to provide an apartment, or more commonly a room or two. This is not always possible, however, given the high costs of housing in Cairo,[11] and new couples sometimes start the first years of their married lives in the parental household of the groom, or, more rarely, in the parental household of the bride. The groom is also expected to provide the bedroom furnishings, and cotton for upholstery of sofas and chairs, if there is a parlor or living room. The actual material for the upholstery, is usually the responsibility of the bride. The furniture for rooms other than the bedroom and kitchen equipment is open to negotiation between the bride and groom, but, is increasingly becoming the responsibility of the bride as part of her trousseau, *gihaz*.

The dower, *mahr*, whereby the groom's family pays the bride's family an agreed upon sum of money, has been documented as part of financial arrangements of marriage among Muslims in several other communities in Egypt (see Rugh 1985; Singerman 1995). However, it is noteworthy that the *mahr* was not prevalent in the community I studied, suggesting that it may be in fact a much more fluid and historically specific institution, *despite* it's religious basis, than is commonly assumed or suggested by anthropological studies in Egypt[12]. Only a few women, usually older ones who got married in rural areas, reported that they received a *mahr*. Many women explained that the *mahr* was part of the marriage negotiations of financially better off people, *el nas el mabsuta*, but it was not part of the negotiations of the very poor, *el nas el ghalaba*, like themselves. The more common arrangement in the study community was that the groom (and/or his family), would directly purchase some of the furnishing and equipment of the marital home, as well provide the *shabka*. No additional sum of money was normally provided for the bride.

The Marriage Inventory: "An Ayma Handcuffs a Man"

Within the context of marriage negotiations described above, the marital *ayma* emerged as a critical component. As the anecdote at the beginning of this chapter reveals, the *ayma* is an issue that I stumbled upon in my discussions and I was unprepared to deal with how emphatic women were about its value. Although my fieldwork demonstrates the centrality of the *ayma* in marriage negotiations, it has remained largely unexplored in depth in anthropological studies on the family by both indigenous and non-indigenous researchers (see for example El-Messiri 1978; Rugh 1981), including recent ones addressing marriage arrangements in Cairo in great detail, such as Singerman (1994).

The *ayma*, is used to specifically refer to a written document on which all items of furniture and supplies that a bride takes to her new home are recorded and itemized, stipulating that these are the sole property of the bride. These items include the goods she brings to the marriage, those her husband brings, and those items they receive jointly as gifts. The *shabka* is also sometimes included in it.

Mutually agreed upon in advance, often after tough negotiations, it is signed by the groom, before or on the day of the *katb el kitab*, as well as by two witnesses who act as guarantors, in case he defaults on any commitments. The negotiations center on the monetary value of the *ayma*, with the bride's family usually inflating it's value. By signing the *ayma*, a husband officially declares that he has received all these items for safe-keeping, *amana*. However, they remain the property of his wife which she can claim back anytime she wants during marriage or in the event of a conflict, a spouse's death or a divorce. This stipulation is enforceable both legally, as well by community arbitrations as will be discussed below. Once signed, the *ayma* is carefully guarded by women, and is usually in safekeeping with the bride's family, often the mother, to ensure that the husband does not have access to it.

There is some variation in how an *ayma* is formalized and the types of items that are included in it. Variations appeared to be based on either socio-economic standing or regional origin.

Most of the women in the community studied, tended to include equipment and furniture as well as the value of the gold of the *shabka*. Some women, particularly those who were relatively less well to do, included breakable and exhaustible items like glasses, china sets, and bed sheets, whereas others confined their *ayma* items to durable goods and furniture. Several women in the sample, who identify themselves as *masriyyin* (original dwellers of the city), not *fallahin* (migrants from lower Egypt), or *Sa'ayda* (migrants from Upper Egypt), emphasized, with a note of contempt, that they would never include the value of the *shabka* into the *ayma* and that it was only the *fallahin* who did that. In most *aymas*, each item is listed in detail and is assigned a monetary value, which is often inflated. The value of all the items are then added up to make up the total value of the *ayma*. A few families preferred not to assign a monetary value to each item, but simply described the item in detail, noting such things as the type of wood used and the brand of the implement, explaining that this protected them against inflation. Once the *ayma* is acted upon in case of a marital dispute, a monetary value can be assigned to the items, based on current market prices.

The value of *aymas* in the community varied tremendously, from a modest 50 Egyptian pounds, to 5,000 pounds. Some of this variation is, of course, a reflection of the date of marriage, since I interviewed women who were married within a span of 40 years. However, it is also important to note that the value of the *ayma* is not necessarily a good indicator of socio-economic status, as in many cases, some of the items included have not actually been provided, or their value has intentionally been inflated. For marriages occurring within the past two years, a typical *ayma*, which included a gold *shabka* of 40 grams of gold, was about 2-4,000 pounds.

The *ayma* is usually negotiated formally by men, generally fathers, uncles or older brothers of the bride, but informally it is the women, generally mothers, aunts or older sisters of the bride who decide on the items to be included and on their value. As Um Nasra put it, "When it comes to negotiations over an *ayma*, it is the women who needle and prompt, and the men who do the formal talking: *el-sittat bt wiz w-el rigalla bitithakim.*"

The *ayma* is not an Islamic convention, and although it has legal standing as will be discussed later, it has no explicit basis in state legislation, but is based on customary law, *'urf*. The history of the *ayma*, when and how it was actually introduced is difficult to trace.[13] Although women were not aware of the history of the *ayma*, many, but not all, of the older women I interviewed (in their 60s) recalled having a *ayma* in their marriages, but were not sure whether their own mothers also had one. Although the importance of the *ayma* was uncontested by all the women I interviewed, as an item of negotiation, it appears to have taken on a new significance in more recent marriages in the community.

The *ayma* appears to be used in various ways and gains different meanings in specific marriage negotiations. Discussions surrounding the *ayma* were sometimes in effect being used to screen potential grooms, or to improve a family's social status by showing off the "value" of their daughter. The greater the value of the *ayma* that a husband signs on, which is always publicly declared, the greater the status of the bride and her family in the community. Negotiations regarding the *ayma* thus partly serve to create or reinforce rankings and distinctions amongst families. The *ayma*, however, also appears to play an important role as a form of insurance against women's vulnerability in marriage, which is the aspect most relevant for my interests in this paper. The next section will elaborate this argument.

Marriage negotiations, of which the *ayma* was an essential component, operate within the framework of specific rights and obligations conferred by prevalent gender ideologies. Moore (1994) terms these local, customary and standard understandings of the rights and needs of different types of people, "local theories of entitlement". She argues that these are fluid, always subject to contestation, as well as "resources which are drawn on in the process of negotiation" (Moore 1994: 104). Moore's argument is well illustrated by the practice of the *ayma*. The *ayma* appears to have gained a particular importance in more recent marriage negotiations in the study community, particularly over the past decade. Discussions with several generations of women suggest that their strategies for pressing claims and gaining entitlement from men are changing.

'Local theories of entitlements' within marriage in the community studied, appear to be changing – and thus giving more centrality to the practice of the *ayma*, partly in response to broader socio-economic changes in society and family structures. Some of these changes relate to the dramatic rise in the cost of living over the past decade which has been unmatched by male wages.

Partly as a result, there are indications that female-supported families are increasing. Conservative estimates suggest that at least 18 percent of households are mainly financed by a woman (Fergany 1994). In-depth research in urban communities indicate that these may reach 30 percent (EQI 1987; El-Kholy 1996). These developments pose a challenge to one of the material basis of patriarchal ideology in Egypt.

Woman and men's relationships to marriage thus appear to be changing. Women are realizing that men may no longer provide the financial security needed. The increased emphasis on the *ayma* in recent marriages may be an indication that women are both conscious of these developments and actively seek to mitigate their options. In a context of poverty, divorce also poses a financial burden on the wife's family as a divorced woman is expected to go back to her parents and becomes once more their financial responsibility. The insistence on the *ayma* is thus strongly supported by a social and family structure that is trying to rescind the cost of divorce.

My data suggest that women in the study community realize that they are disadvantaged in the marital union. These feelings are exacerbated in the current context where male wages are generally not enough to sustain a family. As men lose one of their main markers of masculinity as defined by prevalent gender ideologies, my fieldwork suggests that they respond in different ways. Some men simply withdraw completely from any financial responsibilities in the household, *el rigalla khal'a*, was how some women expressed it, and retain their limited income for their own purposes, such as drinking or smoking. Alternatively, women reported that men often asserted themselves through being more violent during the common disagreements and conflicts over finances, as well as more sexually demanding and abusive.[14]

Some studies in other parts of the world have suggested a link between increased domestic violence and women's lack of access to cash due to rising poverty. In her study of a low-income district in Ecuador over a ten-year period (1978-1988), Moser shows that 48 percent of her sub-sample of women reported an increase in domestic violence during this period. Her interviewees made an explicit link between increases in prices and their lack of assess to cash, reporting being physically or emotionally abused by their husbands when forced to ask for more money.

Personal status laws in Egypt grant men a range of rights over women in marriage which expose wives to various sorts of vulnerabilities. These include men's rights for unilateral divorce, the right to marry up to four wives, and the right to forcefully return a wife to a marital home, the home of obedience law, *bayt el ta'a* (see NGO Platform 1994, 1995; Egypt's Report 1995; Zulficar 1994).

These rights and obligations, however, gain specific meanings and are contested differently in different socio-economic and historical contexts.

Women in the study community appear to be taking explicit measures to "up the stakes" of being abandoned, unprovided for, or mistreated in their marriages. Some of the powers of men that a *ayma* aims at restricting are the threat of divorce, the threat of being thrown penniless out of the house, and the threat of a second wife. The *ayma* was also used to pressure a husband to take marital conflicts more seriously and attempt to resolve them, as well as to increase a wife's ability to demand a divorce should she so desire. The *ayma* seems to be a powerful mechanism for negotiation partly because men are particularly susceptible in an economic context where it would be difficult to replace the items on the *ayma*, and so a husband's economic situation could deteriorate markedly should a woman reclaim her *ayma*.

The strong words that women used to express why and how the *ayma* works to control and check male power, reveals that the *ayma* provides a local *discourse* of male disempowerment and female power. It reveals quite clearly some of women's perceptions about marriage, and the need to reduce men's control within it. Amal, newly married, talks with great pride about her *ayma*.

My *ayma* was large, it was for 7,000 pounds. I have *hand cuffed/tied up* my husband with it, *kattiftu biha*. We put things in it that were not even there, like the television and a video. And he signed on them. This way he is *restricted/controlled/condemned, mahkoum*, he cannot play with his tail, *yil'ab bi-dayluh*. [This is an Arabic idiom generally implying illicit extra-marital affairs, or get married and get *dura* (co-wife) to live with me.]

Karima, 32, married to a grocery shop owner and with three preschool children, generates income through sewing shoes at home. She explains why her *ayma*, which she is guarding carefully since her marriage five years ago, is important:

It is important so that he does not throw me out to my father's house after he takes what he wants from me, *ghiyyitu* [meaning sexual pleasure]. I have *a hold on him* with an *ayma*, but without an *ayma* there is no rope with which I can tie him, *mafish habl rabtah bih*. Any time he can tell me go out with your *galabiyya* [traditional dress for some women in low-income areas]. A *ayma protects a woman's rights, bitihfaz ha' el sitt*. Otherwise how can a woman ensure her rights, *tidman ha' aha izay*? Men, as a kind, cannot be trusted, *sanf el riggala malush aman*.

Shocked that I could even ask whether she had an *ayma*, Laila, whose parents migrated to Cairo from lower Egypt when she was a few months old, confirms that she wrote an *ayma*, emphasizes its role in protecting women's rights in marriage, and details some of it's items. Her comments highlight the link between the *ayma* and a very common form of female protest, referred to as *ghadab, ghidbit*, which literally means angry but refers also to a woman deserting the marital home and going to her parents home until some form of reconciliation takes place. This practice of *ghadab* was frequently used by women to publicly express their grievances and demand that relatives and neighbours intervene to resolve a conflict. The homes of parents were often nearby in the community, so this form of temporary desertion of a marital home caused minor disruptions to work schedules or child care.[15] The existence of an *ayma*, however, increased a woman's ability to engage in this type of contestary behaviour. Laila explains:

How can a girl marry without an *ayma*, if she does, she can be told goodbye by her husband [i.e. be kicked out of the house] any second. He would have no incentive to try and get her back from her parents house when there is a conflict and she is upset, *ghidbit*. The *ayma* is much more important than the deferred dower *Mo'akhkhar*[16] for safeguarding/ensuring a woman's rights, *daman ha' el sit*, to restrict/control a man, *'alashan el ragil yeb'a mahkum*. On my *ayma*, which was for 3,500, I wrote all the things that both he and I got, from the bedroom, to the aluminum sets to the spice rack …

Emphasizing the importance of the *ayma* in ensuring that your husband does not throw you out and sell your belongings, Laila then told me the story of her neighbor, Um Mohammed, whose husband divorced her without informing her, *ghiyabi*, when she was in the village visiting her family. When she came back, she found that he had sold most of the furniture, had married someone else, and was now living with her in another community. She issued a complaint and her husband was arrested. He returned some of the furniture, but was not able to provide the rest or to pay the remaining value of the 4,000 LE *ayma*, on which he had signed. He received a three-month prison term. While this only partly helped Um Mohammed, it nonetheless sent a strong message to other men in the community, argued Laila emphatically, about what they should treat their wives.

As I talked to more women and observed discussions about marriage arrangements, I began to realize that the *ayma* was indeed a critical component of marriage negotiations, and an important tool for women to secure their marriage, ward off the looming threat of divorce, and secure themselves financially. Reducing the husband's options in terms of taking on a second co-habitating wife was mentioned several times as one of the situations where an *ayma* can be invoked. On the surface, this was singled out as the main source of resentment: not that a husband could take another wife, but that the co-wife could be made to share the house. Um Samir explains:

> I do not care if he married someone else as long as he does not bring her here to use my *gihaz*, the things on my *ayma*, and as long as my husband is making my life comfortable [meaning largely financially], *mi'ayyishni 'isha Hilwa*. With an *ayma*, it is more difficult for a man to remarry, because he can find himself penniless, *'ala el balata*, if he has to get the furniture and equipment for another house.

On probing further, however, it became clear that in fact, the *ayma* is used as a strategy to realize women's desire to deter a husband from taking a second wife, co-habitating or otherwise. Women realize that finding another apartment or room and furnishing it is so expensive, that a man can rarely marry a second wife unless his first wife accepts co-habitation, hence they stress on this issue. Women clearly believe the *ayma* serves as an important deterrent against polygamy. Although polygamy is legally allowed, in practice its prevalence rate is lower than 2 percent in Egypt.

In the study community, there was only one polygamous marriage. Could these strategies be working? The significance of the *ayma*, however, goes beyond attempting to get a better deal if divorce occurs, providing economic security for the future, or warding off the threat of a divorce or a co-wife. Perhaps just as importantly, it is used as a *bargaining chip*, throughout the marriage. It enables women to monitor their husband's behaviour, and ensure that they do not default on their main responsibilities as economic providers. Mayada's grandmother, a woman in her seventies, explains,

> the *ayma* is important not just to ensure a woman's rights if there is a divorce or a dispute, but it is also important *to correct a man if he becomes deviant, etawag* [literally bent], or *mosh mashi 'alatul*, not walking straight.

On probing what *it'awag* meant, it became clear that it centered on the man's responsibility to provide for his household, *yekafey el bit*.

Mayada's husband's behavior was pointed out as an example of inappropriate behavior that reference to the *ayma* was able to address. Even though Mayada is recently married and is pregnant with her first child, her husband, Ragab, has stopped providing for her and spends a lot of his time gambling and drinking. Mayada and her husband had a fight last month, during which he told her that if she did not like his behavior she could leave. Mayada's entire extended family intervened, insisting that Mayada be divorced, because her husband's behavior was unacceptable, and demanding that he pay them the value of the *ayma*, estimated at 10,000 LE, almost double the real value of the furniture and equipment listed on it. After a few days of negotiations and discussions, Mayada's husband came to his senses, *'i'il*. He now gives Mayada money regularly and no longer spends all his wages on drinking. The family knew that Ragab had a reputation as a gambler, which is one of the reasons they had insisted on a large *ayma*.

It is noteworthy however, that part of the reason why the *ayma* was effective in the above account is partly because Mayada and her husband were living with her extended family of 14 other people, and that the entire family was united in its decision. The *ayma* is not always as effective. Clearly the *ayma* is not an effective tool for all women. The structure of the family was one of the factors that determined the relative power of the *ayma*. Other factors, such as the nature of the relationship between the two families, as well as the personal attributes of a wife (such as beauty, or a good reputation) were also important factors in determining how successfully an *ayma* could be invoked.

Reda, originally from Tanta in Lower Egypt, expressed deep sorrow for me because I did not have an *ayma*, and thus no security in my marriage. I was living *barakawi* (from *baraka*, meaning as a fatalist relying on good luck, with no strategies or plans for the future), and this is the worst situation a woman can be in, she emphasized. Reda views the *ayma* as a way to wear a man out, make his throat dry, *tinashif ri' elragil*, so that divorce is not that easy for him. She was married two years ago and her *ayma* was valued at 2,500 LE. Although she has had no disputes with her husband so far, so that the question of the *ayma* never arose between them, she explained that it was important to her sister Somayya who got married 6 years ago, and whose husband divorced her last year because they were unable to conceive. She took back much of the furniture and equipment, most of which he had provided.

Amal, 27 years old, and divorced last year, also recounts how the *ayma* enabled her to pressure her husband into divorcing her. She had signed her marriage contract 2 years ago, but the actual consummation of the marriage, the *dukhla* was scheduled for a year later to give her husband time to accumulate the necessary financial resources for the marriage. Her husband, however, had accepted to sign on a large *ayma*, when they signed the marriage contract, although they had not yet provided most of the items listed. Although he was a skilled carpenter, he had been out of work for a few months and was in the process of looking for a new job. He assured them that he would provide Amal with a full *gihaz* as soon as he starts working. Amal explained that her mother insisted that he nonetheless sign an inflated *ayma* so as to secure Amal's future, particularly since her groom was not previously known to them; he was a Cairene, not an upper Egyptian like themselves and they did not know his origins. He had seen Amal briefly while she was visiting one of her relatives, when he was fixing some window shutters for them. Amal's relative explained to me in private that his proposal for marriage was accepted quickly by both Amal and her family, because she was already 25, and was not only unengaged, but she was also not getting many suitors.

Six months after signing the marriage contract and *ayma*, Amal's husband began going out with another woman in public, no longer gave Amal any presents, and began maltreating her and hitting her. After various attempts at reconciliation, Amal's parents insisted that he divorce Amal, but he refused unless he was paid 1,000 pounds in return. It was at this point that Amal and her mother went to the lawyer and issued a complaint in court, presented a copy of Amal's original *ayma*, and accused her husband of selling the items on it, a criminal offense known in the legal system as *tabdid manqulat*. Um Amal recalls:

When he was unable to produce the items on the *ayma*, the judge sentenced him to 6 months imprisonment. He then entered into negotiations with us, and we struck a deal, whereby we agreed to give up our rights, *nitnazel*, if he divorces Amal immediately. This process took about six months and we paid 200 pounds for the lawyer. If it was not for the *ayma*, we would have never been able to make him divorce Amal, and she would have remained at his mercy and miserable, *missa"ha el dabab*.

Although of utility as a bargaining chip within marriage, a woman has to choose her battles carefully so as to decide strategically *when* the *ayma* should invoked or used. Once the *ayma* is presented to the court, the original document must be submitted (as will be discussed later), and once a settlement takes place, a woman loses recourse to her *ayma* for use in future marital negotiations, should she decide to continue with the marriage. Some women thus prefer to settle out of court by means of *taradi*, without giving up their *ayma*. As an insurance policy for securing women's rights in the conjugal union, clearly conceived of as an essential part of life, but nonetheless as a high risk proposition, the *ayma* thus has some inherent limitations.

The *ayma* was only practiced among Muslim women. I was told that Copts did not have an *ayma*, partly perhaps because divorce is generally not allowed by the Coptic church and marriage is considered a sacrament, rather than a contractual arrangement as is the case in Islam. Another reason may be that the underlying property regime in Coptic marriages is that of a joint property of spouses, whereas in an Islamic marriage, separation of property/goods, known legally as a *dhimma maliyya munfasila*, is the underlying principle. This difference adds a layer of complexity to understanding women's options and reveals how, even within similar socio-economic locations, there are some variations in men's and women's negotiating mechanisms due to variations in the marriage practices of different religious communities. Since the *ayma*'s value, however, goes far beyond the fear of divorce and is used more broadly to contest certain actions by husbands throughout a marriage, more research is needed to investigate more carefully Coptic women's marital strategies.

The narratives and accounts related above suggest that the *ayma* may play an important role for ensuring that a wife is not thrown out of the house penniless, deterring a husband from taking a second wife and enabling a woman to terminate an abusive marriage. Its stipulations are enforceable through both informal and formal mechanisms. In order to better understand how the *ayma* is enforced legally, I conducted interviews with two lawyers from the community, who had personally arbitrated several cases related to the *ayma*. I also spent several afternoons in one law office in the community and was able to observe several women who came in to get legal assistance on issues related to the *ayma*. Interestingly, the discussions with lawyers revealed that the *ayma* falls under commercial transactions and contracts and is part of the criminal law, rather than the personal status law which regulates marriage and divorce. Mr. Mahmoud explains:

Ayma cases fall under the same category as defaulting on a commercial transaction such as writing an invalid cheque. Thus it is treated as both a criminal offense, which can result in imprisonment, as well as a civil offense which results in a fine. This is unlike the deferred dower, *mu'akhkhar*, which is only a civil offence and thus does not entail imprisonment.

Women can raise a complaint through two mechanisms: either issuing a written complaint at the police station, or a direct appeal in court. It is considered a "*Gunha*", "*khiyana*" or "*tabdid amana*". As a legal document, the *ayma* falls under safekeeping contracts, *'uqud al amana*, stipulated under clauses 340 and 341, in the criminal laws, and is thus considered a direct criminal offense, *gunha mubashra*.

The legal enforceability of the *ayma*, through resort to civil, not criminal law is crucial to note as it highlights some of the institutional basis of gender discrimination as manifested in the various laws, and women's pragmatic attempts to cope with such institutional biases. Unlike other elements of the marriage contract, such as the *mahr* and *mu'akhkhar*, which are also enforceable but only through the judicial system as they are items of personal status laws (and thus entails a drawn out, and complicated process of court proceedings) the *ayma*, as an item of civil law, can be settled much faster at the level of the police.

The other lawyer I interviewed confirmed the legality of the *ayma*, as a commercial transaction, and, revealingly, expressed his sympathy for men as he saw the *ayma* as a sword, *sayf*, which married women dangle over their husbands' necks:

I see many court cases related to *ayma* complaints. If problems occur in a marriage, it is common for a wife to say that her husband has destroyed – *baddid* – the furniture, and a lot of times, what is written on the *ayma* is not actually there. Usually the courts respond by issuing a sentence for imprisonment [from 6 months to three years] if the husband does not produce the furniture or its value. The legal procedures are usually quick, and do not take more than two to three months. I usually sympathize with the men, however. If I was asked, I would say, ban the *ayma*, it is not a good *'urf*. I usually sympathize with the men, because I know that many of the complaints raised by women are not real, they are fictitious, driven by ulterior motives, *kaydiyya*.

This view was echoed, but in more subtle terms and couched in academic language, in the November 1996 issue of a widely read middle class social magazine published in Arabic, *Nuss el Dunya*. In an article titled: *"The ayma is a useless piece of paper and the law is clear"*, the writer, a man, probes into the legality of the *ayma*, from an Islamic *fiqh* point of view, and from a legal point of view, using sophisticated legal language and resorting to examples from Islamic history and the Koran.

After his extensive review, the writer concludes that the *ayma* has no basis in either Islamic *fiqh* or in civil or criminal codes, and calls upon the courts to rethink its legality. He argues that it creates a lot of problems in marriages and is a burden on the court system. Although he does not articulate it outright, the writer was clearly arguing for rejecting the *ayma*'s legal enforceability. His conclusions and recommendations are quite dangerous from the point of view of the women I talked to for whom the *ayma* was indispensable both as an insurance policy and as a negotiating lever.

It is interesting to note, however, that this article did not elicit any reaction from women's rights activists in Egypt. This contrasts with another recent newspaper article questioning the right of female professors to supervise academic dissertations by male students, on the presumed grounds that in Islam women have no right of supervision or guardianship, *wilaya*, over men. This latter article was the subject of several published responses by feminists, and the source of public debate amongst women's groups, some of whom are academics or are in supervisory positions themselves, so that they were also directly threatened by the article. The article on the *ayma*, however, which is potentially more threatening to lower-class women, went unnoticed. The practice of the *ayma* is more limited among the middle and upper classes – it is not part of our daily realities as relatively well off professional women with an independent income, so that the issues surrounding it were invisible to us.[17] In fact, had I read that same article two years ago, before my fieldwork, I suspect the article on the *ayma* would not have attracted my attention either. This type of myopia is noteworthy, has important implications for the success of feminist activism, and raises important questions about who sets the feminist agenda, and whose discourses are hegemonic? The question raised by Nelson (1985) in the context of development discourses in Egypt, "Whose Knowledge Counts?" remains salient with regards to feminist discourses as well.

As suggested earlier, the stipulations of the *ayma* are enforceable through both legal measures, and informal community arbitration, negotiations, and, sometimes intimidation. I am not trying to suggest that the *ayma* is always an effective deterrent for abuse in marriage, nor that it works well for all women. However, even in cases where a husband uses force, family pressure or intimidation to avoid enforcement of the stipulations of the *ayma*, or in cases where a woman cannot afford to pay for legal assistance or for whom a divorce is a much worse option than remaining in an abusive marriage, the *ayma* still offers a significant "indigenous" discourse of female discontent regarding marriage arrangements. Although indigenous, it is a discourse that does not derive its basis from either Islamic laws nor from other, equally indigenous, discourses put forth by upper class feminists in Egypt.

Both legal and community mechanisms for enforcing an *ayma* appear to be currently working well for some of the women in the study community. There are possible limitations to the *ayma* as a deterrent or form of insurance, however, which must be considered. These are partly related to the possible breakdown and fragmentation of the normative pressures and moral community needed for its, as well as the possible challenges of its legal basis by emerging conservative forces.

Although set in an urban context, most of my sample consisted of first or second generation migrants to the city, who still maintained close knit relationships with relatives and had brought with them to Cairo many of their customary forms of conflict resolution. As families disperse into more distant communities in search of employment or housing over the years, some of these relationships and structures may become more fragmented and forms of customary pressure by family elders may break down. The possible erosion of the social and legal basis of the *ayma* offers a concrete basis, arguably affecting the perceived interests of a broad segment of Egyptian women, around which participatory politicization and mobilization of women can take place.

Women's presentation of the rationale for the *ayma* using the seemingly unambiguous term for rights, *ha'*, which is the same term used by women activists in Egypt and internationally, is significant, as it illustrates how conceptions of rights are socially and historically situated and are linked to both discursive elements as well as to constructions of meanings and identities (Fraser 1989; Moore 1994; Nicholson 1994; Molyneux 1998). The use of the same terminology of rights and interests between different groups of women does not imply the same content and understandings of such interests. The following section elaborates on this point by illustrating the contrasting agendas and tactics of different female constituencies in Egypt.

"The Ayma Is Like a Contract": Contrasting "Indigenous" Tactics

"The *ayma* is like a contract, it regulates/has a hold on a groom" (*El ayma zay el á'd, bitimsik el áris*) was a phrase I heard repeatedly during my fieldwork. Since the *ayma* was clearly seen and presented by women as a "contract", whose aim is to safeguard and ensure "woman's rights", *haq el marraa* (including the right to request a divorce, ward off the threat of an unwanted divorce or ensure that a man does not default on his responsibilities, *yit'wig*), it is interesting to juxtapose it with the "marriage contract" campaign.

The marriage contract campaign was initiated by a prominent feminist lawyer during the International Conference on Population and Development (ICPD) in 1994. An example of organized action by several women's groups in Egypt, the campaign aimed at increasing women's leverage within their marriages, by promoting the concept of marriage as a contractual arrangement, and emphasizing that as a contract between two parties, its terms, conditions, rights and obligations should thus be specified and agreed upon in advance.

A draft of an "ideal" marriage contract was drawn up and was discussed extensively in public fora, with a view to achieving its acceptance by the Ministry of Justice as the basis of future marriage legislation for Muslims. The terms of the "new contract" reflected the legitimate priorities, and anxieties of middle and upper class Muslim women in Egypt, and included new issues such as: the right for married women to travel out of the country without the husband's approval (which currently is not allowed by law), the right of a woman to divorce herself, the right to work and the right to continue a higher education after marriage. The contract stipulations may also be used to limit a husband's rights, as recognized by *sharia* laws. For example one could stipulate no polygamy as one of the conditions.

The new contract was eventually rejected by the government, critiqued by the religious establishment, and failed to receive much support from the public, both men and women. The reasons varied, from charges that it "legitimizes the forbidden and forbids the legitimate", is contrary to *sharia*, to arguments that some of it's stipulations, such as women's rights to work or travel abroad are harmful for the family, or not necessary since they are not questioned, such as the right to education (see Karam 1996). Other reasons voiced in public seminars I attended were that such a contract has overly materialistic undertones, which threatens the harmony and symbolic meaning of marriage.

What is germane to my purposes here, however, is that despite some obvious links between the marriage contract and the *ayma*, there was no reference to, or discussion of, the *ayma* at all during the campaign. Attempts to justify the "new marriage contract" to the public were largely based on excellent historical research. The research demonstrated that the idea of a contract with detailed stipulations of rights and duties of husband and wife was not an alien concept and that it had historical precedent in the practices of Islamic dynasties in Turkey and Egypt. There was no attempt, however, to link the proposed contract with current practices and marriage arrangements among the majority of women and men in Egypt, which have a clearly contractual and financial nature. In retrospect, I can now recognize that this made our campaign much weaker and prevented us from recognizing *both* similarities and differences across class boundaries, which could have strengthened the campaign by mobilizing a broader constituency of women.

A survey was conducted among low-income women to elicit their responses to the suggested contract, hoping to increase the campaigns' base of support. However, none of the survey questions addressed what lower income women's actual concerns were nor what their marriage negotiations actually entailed, so as to build on them, and take them into account. The campaign, and the research on which it was based, had undoubtedly laudable aims and was a worthwhile effort. Nonetheless, its approach was a top down and myopic one that did not allow for an understanding or appreciation of the diversity of lower-income women's perceptions of their rights within marriage, their own ways of articulating these rights, or their strategies for promoting their perceived interests. This suggests that the national identity of a researcher (or activist) is not automatically linked to the production of more "authentic" or "indigenous" knowledge. As Morsy et al. argue emphasizing the impact of colonial domination and intellectual dependency, the production of knowledge,

> is the output of people whose thought patterns reflect the 'truths' of their social millieux. To the extent that indigenous anthropologists [and I would add women's rights' activists] social millieux are not simply and purely, 'indigenous', neither are our thought patterns nor the 'truths' of our scientific productions.
>
> (1991: 92)

As mentioned earlier, the language used in marriage negotiations in my sample, was openly contractual and based on material calculations. Literally the terms selling, *bay'ha* and buying, *sharia*, were used to describe relationships in which a groom is serious about wanting a particular bride/family, versus one who is not serious/committed. This language is not commonly used outside this context and is considered quite "improper" among more upper class Egyptians. In fact, in one of the many public discussions of the new marriage contract at a posh hotel in the center of Cairo at which I was present, one of the major criticisms voiced was that the contract was based on "western", "materialistic" notions, and that it took out all the "love" and "emotion" out of marriage, reducing instead to the domain of cold calculations, and market transactions, which is not at all what marriage is about in "traditional" Egyptian culture.[18]

An effective response of course, but one which was not voiced, would have been to point out the class bias inherent in this particular view of Egyptian marriage, by highlighting the largely material considerations and dispositions which characterize the marriage negotiations of, arguably, a large percentage of families in Egypt. It would have been worth noting that the *ayma*, is so overtly a financial arrangement, that its stipulations fall under commercial laws. Clearly, marriage gains different meanings among different classes. There is not one "indigenous" meaning of marriage, but several distinct, possibly overlapping ones.

Azza Karam (1996), in her excellent recent study of middle and upper class women activists in Egypt, notes how the new marriage campaign was discredited, arguing that this was partly due to the lack of dialogue and alliance building between different groups of indigenous "feminists" (which she categorizes as "secularist", "Islamists", and "Muslim feminists") to safeguard women's rights. While I agree with Karam's call for horizontal coalition building, my data suggests, that it may not be enough. Given the class/educational disparities in Egyptian society, which as seen above generate different, but possibly overlapping perceptions of gender needs, rights and interests, it would seem crucial to strengthen activist campaigns not only through cultivating horizontal links, but also through forging more *vertical* coalitions, alliances and linkages, *across* class and educational lines. (N.B.: I am not underestimating the difficulty of such an effort since low-income women may not always have their own organizations and representatives to facilitate such linkages.) Such efforts would significantly enrich the current debates about women's rights and priorities for change. By taking a "grounded" approach to theoretical production, such efforts would also contribute to broader theoretical debates on women's consciousness, agency and the dynamics of gender relations in different contexts.

Politically, efforts to forge vertical coalitions may also increase the chances for the success of some campaigns by rallying more public support, could result in the politicization and mobilization of a broader and more diverse constituency of women and men, and more importantly, carries the promise of encouraging the emergence of local leadership in different low-income communities, who can begin to articulate their own concerns more vocally and publicly. It seems to me that actively seeking to establish such shared platforms may be the only way that we could move from the "gender activisms" (see Badran 1993, 1995) of today, to a social *movement* with a strong mass base that can challenge the many forces and mechanisms contributing to not only patriarchy but social inequality more generally in Egyptian society.

Bourdieu's stinging analysis of the possibilities of social change and his cynical view of the potential of organized resistance, while uncomfortable for many feminists, is nonetheless relevant in this context. Bourdieu "stresses the struggle among the privileged themselves and the relative inability of the oppressed even to enter into the 'dialogue' among more privileged groups" (Risseew 1991: 77). This was clearly the case with the marriage contract that we were promoting presumably on behalf of all Egyptian women. What this suggests is, as middle/upper class feminists in Egypt with "orthodox" qualities of class and education, we need to seriously rethink the possibility that we may be ourselves perpetuating power inequalities. Our power as activists trying to improve the situation of women and challenge gender inequalities, over the women on whose behalf we often speak, can perhaps be captured by Lukes' three dimensional view of power as a "latent" force, one which is exercised by the fact that we are

controlling the agenda, mobilizing the bias of the system, determining which issues are key issues, indeed which issues come up for decision and excluding those which threaten the interests of the powerful.
(Lukes 1986: 9-10)[19]

It seems to me without necessarily intending it, we may be implicated in reproducing inequalities between women by privileging our own voices, forms of knowledge and discourses and by deciding which issues to include and which issues to exclude. By doing so we may be not just marginalizing the knowledge, priorities and discourses of other groups of women in Egypt and weakening the impact of our campaigns, but we may also be blinded to understanding what shapes these alternative discourses. In the case of the *ayma*, it is partly a context of general impoverishment for both men and women, as well as a context in which women have relatively less opportunities for financial security and ownership of economic assets. For most of the women in the study community, the items on the *ayma*, were the *only* property or economic asset that they owned, or would ever hope of owning in the future. Incorporating these broader issues of poverty and economic vulnerability into our feminist practice and theories is one way forward to make social theory more relevant and address one of the identified sources of the "crisis" of social science in the Arab world, that is "the missing link between societal problems and intellectual production" (Morsy et al. 1991: 85).

Conclusions

A detailed and sensitive examination of the *ayma,* paying particular attention to the local idioms underlying it, through which women express ideas like resentment, discontent, the need to curb male power, and rightful entitlements, and the lines of argumentation through which they make claims over men, has revealed a striking awareness amongst women of certain aspects of gender-based oppression. The literature on gender relations in Egypt is still so influenced by the image of the "corporate" family, where "male dominance is matched by female accommodation, male authority by female obedience" (Rugh 1985: 75), and undifferentiated "family strategies" (Ibrahim 1980), that highlighting a local, historically specific, and arguably also class bound discourse about women's rights, entitlements, and perceived self-interests, is an important finding. It is a finding that seriously questions the ahistoric usage of the concept of patriarchy and the common assumptions about women's passivity, which as discussed earlier, are reflected in the writings of both Egyptian and non Egyptian researchers and activists.

Arguing for a more nuanced and situated understanding of gender relations and women's interests, this paper shows how, although women in the studied community used the same terms for women's rights, *haq el maraa,* that more upper class and intellectually inclined feminists use, they often attached different meanings to this term. This finding touches upon one of the main tenets of the post-modernist critiques to feminist scholarship whose theoretical and political foundation was based on an essential and universal category of Woman. Butler argues that the term women "designates an undesignatable field of differences, one that cannot be totalized or summarized by a descriptive identity category" (Butler 1992: 16). I do not subscribe to the notion of "undesignatable differences", as it implies that all differences amongst women have equal weight for their identities and their ability to achieve their "human capabilities" (see Nussuwbaum 1995). I do, concur, however, with the need for some deconstruction of the universal "woman" in order to identify the most salient differences, *and* similarities, amongst women in different contexts. My particular concern, given the Egyptian reality where the majority of women and men belong to lower income groups, is in differences along *socio-economic* lines. As analytical constructs, both the category of "women" and "indigenous" needs to be deconstructed along these lines.

The paper has demonstrated that a common sex does not imply common interests, *even* when similar terminologies for expressing these interests are used by different groups of women. Any claims about women's interests thus need to be conceptualized very carefully. As Molyneux argues, women's interests are historically and culturally constituted, as well as related to specific socio-economic locations.

Claims about women's interests need to be framed within specific historical contexts since processes of interest formation and articulation are clearly subject to cultural, historical and political variance and cannot be known in advance.

(Molyneux 1998: 10)

Or, as Nicholson, arguing for more nuanced "coalition politics" within the feminist movement elegantly puts it:

Maybe it is time that we explicitly acknowledge that our claims about women are not based on some given reality but emerge from our own places within history and culture; they are political acts that reflect the contexts we emerge out of and the futures we would like to see.

(1994: 103)

Furthering our understanding of the complexity of gender relations and women's responses to gender inequalities in various contexts, requires a conscious effort to abandon abstract notions of "universalism", without abandoning a basic commitment to values of justice, equity and human freedom (Kandiyotti 1994). In-depth, contextualized research which is both self-reflective as well as sensitive to the perceptions, thought categories, language and local idioms used by women and men in various settings presents an opportunity for generating knowledge about gender that can escape the traps of both western ethnocentrism and indigenous elitism.

The point is not to expropriate other people's issues, or use research results to speak on behalf of others, for that is never an innocent act as it serves to strengthen the position of the speaker, and can create a backlash for those on whose behalf she speaks. The point is to start a process, a broad-based movement that moves beyond identifying particular products and using those to advance certain positions, to creating a critical consciousness about gender inequality.

Notes

I am deeply indebted to Magda Al-Nowaihi for her careful review of the transliteration. I am also grateful to Hania Shalkany and Nadia Wassef for their comments on an earlier draft.

1 The word *ayma* is derived from the classical Arabic word *qa'ima*, which means list or inventory.
2 One U.S.$ is equivalent to 3.4 Egyptian Pounds.
3 The diversity and heterogeneity of Cairo's low-income residents, based partly on their geographic origin was captured in my "sample" as will be explained later.
4 For a description of the various women's groups and "gender activisms" in Egypt see NGO platform of action documents 1994, 1995; Badran 1993; Ilbaz 1997; Al-Ali 1997; Karam 1996.
5 I write this paper as a researcher as well as an active feminist and a development practitioner in Egypt. I thus consider myself fully implicated in any questions that I raise about feminist activism in Egypt.
6 The concept, measurement and role of the informal sector has been the subject of much debate in Egypt and internationally. Despite it's inadequacies, I adopt the definition of the informal sector as consisting of those workshops employing less than 10 employees and which are generally not subject to formal laws or regulations (see Rizk 1990). Recent research suggests that depictions of the informal economy as a source of high earning, skilled

jobs with possibilities for upward mobility may be an accurate depiction of some male occupations, but may be seriously misleading picture of female employment in the sector, see El-Kholy 1996.

7 For a detailed analysis of the social organization of piecework, see El-Kholy 1996.

8 If one were to take into account local ranking and socio-economic classification systems, the women in my sample would predominantly be considered by others in the neighborhoods, and would consider themselves, as *nas ghalaba*. *Ghalaba* (sing. *ghalban*) comes from the Arabic term *gholb*, which connotes fatigue as a result of daily struggles for survival as well as endurance despite difficult circumstances. As used by community members, however, *ghalban* implies two important characteristics. On the one hand, it denotes toiling to make ends meet, and on the other, it implies certain favorable moral qualities such as kindness, lack of greed, and lack of deviousness and corruption. This double meaning of the term is interesting and suggests a belief that despite their poverty, *el nas el ghalaba* are still honest. Deprivation has not driven them to corruption, cheating or stealing. Many times, I heard people use the term *ghalban* with pride. *El ghalaba* was often used to denote the *working poor*, that is those who may have steady jobs but whose incomes are meager and/or whose job conditions are difficult. Some of those who were considered *ghalaba*, also worked as casual irregular labourers, *urzu'i*. Derived from the Arabic work *ris'*, god given livelihood, the term connotes lack of security, precariousness of livelihoods and a certain degree of fatalism. *Urzu'i* is a more specific occupational category which refers to a wide range of jobs in which employment is of a casual nature with no assurance of a regular or future income.

Some of the better off interviewees considered themselves as *masturin*, literally "covered" but implying that what comes in as income goes out in expenses and that there are no extras to cover any emergency situation, such as a sick child. It also implies lack of security for the future, or the ability to engage in the prestigious and status providing act of giving charity to others. This term contrasts sharply with *mabsut*, literally happy, which is used to refer to those who are financially well off, often skilled craftsmen, *sanay'iyya*, or wholesalers/merchants, *tuggar*. In addition to wealth, the term also indicates security due to a regular income and lack of vulnerability. Existence of substantial savings or investments, often in the form of real estate, as well as public displays of charity, are an important distinguishing characteristic of this category in the community. None of my interviewees would be considered *mabsutin* in the local sense. The women I interviewed and spend extended periods of time with were engaged in daily struggles to cloth, feed, educate, and seek medical care for their families. In many ways, their livelihoods reflected a general state of poverty as a result of the overall deterioration in the conditions of life in Egypt over the past decade. Most were recent (first or second generation) migrants to the city.

Fergany (1997) comparing national income and expenditures surveys between 1990 and 1995, shows that conditions of life have deteriorated at a alarming rate during this period. Real family incomes have fallen on average by 14 percent in urban areas and 20 percent in rural areas, prices have increased by 170 percent in rural areas and 160 percent in urban areas, and malnutrition among five year old children (as measured by stunted growth) has increased by 5 percent during this period.

9 Sometimes these stages are condensed into three, with the *shabka* merged with either the *fatha*, or with the *katb el kitab*.

10 These arrangements relate to first time marriages, "virgin" marriages. Particularly if a woman is divorced, the arrangements are often quite different. She is likely to be denied a *shabka,* and the financial expectations of the groom are usually less.

11 By the early eighties rents on newly constructed apartments had skyrocketed. One estimate suggests that by the early eighties, 30 percent of the income of couples within the lowest quartile of income distribution in Egypt went into rent (Abt Associates 1981). Moreover, the strategy of "key money", whereby landlords ask new tenants for exorbant amounts of money before renting out a flat has become a rampant practice. One study shows that both the occurrences and the amount of key money have increased at a rate of 30 percent annually (Abt Associates 1981).

12 The *mahr* is an Islamic convention with a fixed meaning according to *sharia* laws, stipulating that the whole *mahr* should go from a groom's father to the bride herself. Marriage transactions in the

Middle East have thus been rigidly conceptualized as a form of "dower" in comparative anthropological theory (Goody/Tambiah). In practice, however, the *mahr* appears to gain different meanings in different settings suggesting that it is not a fixed institution, but one that is historically specific and fluid. Depending on the specific context, marriage payments in the Middle East may incorporate aspects of both dower and bride price. Moors (1991) illustrates this argument based on her comparison of the changing meanings of marriage and the *mahr* in a village in Palestine in the 1930s and the 1980s.

13 On possibility is to go back to court records and see when the first cases of the *ayma* were arbitrated.

14 For a discussion of how some women may be articulating their protest and grievances against what they perceive to be unjustified demands on their sexual services, see El-Kholy 1997.

15 Based on research in a low-income neighborhood in Cairo, Watson (1992) provides some detailed examples of the process of women's temporary desertion of the marital home as a conflict resolution between husband and wife. See also, El-Kholy (1997) for a discussion of the strategy of *ghadab* in the context of women pressing for the education of their daughters.

16 The deferred dower, is a sum of money that is written into the Muslim marriage contract and which the bride is entitled to incase of divorce.

17 Another study is needed to determine the prevalence of the *ayma* among the middle and upper classes in Egypt. However, none of the women from this background whom I knew, either socially or professionally, had written a *ayma*. The 6 key Egyptian activists and researchers who led the marriage contract campaign were all married except for one, but none had written an *ayma* (Personal communication with Iman Bibars, and Hoda El-Sadda, two of the six activists).

18 This particular view of marriage in itself raises interesting questions about the middle class "domestication" of women and about the dependency of middle class women on men and the naturalization or "euphemization" of that dependency as "romantic love."

19 Lukes builds on the view advanced by Peter Bachrach and Morton Baratz (1970).

Selected Bibliography

Arabic Language

El-Mogy, Sohar, Book Review in Hagar (1994) *On Women's Issues*. Book 2, Cairo: Dar Sinai Publishing House.
NGO Platform of Action (1994) International Conference for Population and Development, Cairo.
El-Rehimy, Osama (1996) "The Ayma Is of No Value and the Law Is Clear". *Nos El Donia Magazine* 4/339, 11 August 1996.

Western Languages

Agrawal, Bina (1994) *A Field of One's Own: Gender and Land Rights in South Asia*, Cambridge, New York/NY: Cambridge University Press.
Bachrach, Peter/Baratz, Morton (1970) *Power and Poverty: Theory and Practice*, Oxford, New York/NY: Oxford University Press.
Bourdieu, Pierre (1990) *The Logic of Practice*, Cambridge: Polity Press.
Butler, Judith (1992) "Contingent Foundations: Feminism and the Question of Postmodernism". In Judith Butler/Joan Scott (eds.) *Feminists Theorize the Political*, London: Routledge, pp. 3-21.
Davis, Kathy/Leijenaar, Monique/Oldersma, Jantine (eds.) (1992) *The Gender of Power*, London: Sage Publications.
Eickelman, Dale F./Piscatori, J. (1996) *Muslim Politics*, Princeton/NJ: Princeton University Press.
Ibrahim, Barbara (1985) "Family Strategies: A Perspective on Women's Entry to the Labour Force in Egypt". In Saad Eldin Ibrahim/Nicholas Hopkins (eds.) *Arab Society: Social Science Perspectives*, Cairo: American University in Cairo Press, pp. 257-268.
Karam, Azza (1996) "An Apostate, a Proposed New Marriage Contract and Egyptian Women: Where to Now?". *Women Against Fundamentalism* 8, pp. 29-31.
Khattab, Hind (1992) *The Silent Endurance*, Amman, Cairo: UNICEF and the Population Council.
El-Kholy, Heba (1996) "The Alliance Between Gender and Kinship Ideologies: Female Sub-Contractors in Cairo's 'Informal Econo-

my'". Proceedings of the Regional Arab Conference on Population and Development, Cairo, Brussels, December 1996.

—— (1997) "The Education of a Girl Is a Treasure: Gender Politics in Low Income Egypt". The Population Council's Regional Office for the Middle East and North Africa, Cairo.

—— (Forthcoming) "Spirit Possession as a Discourse of Protest among Low-Income Women in Cairo" Paper presented on a panel: "Feminist Discourse and the Indigenization of Knowledge Debate" at the 6th Congress of IAMES held at Bayl al-Ayn University, Imafrag, Gordon, April 10-14, 1996.

Lukes, Steven (ed.) (1986) *Power*, Oxford: Basil Blackwell.

Molyneux, Maxine (1998) "Analyzing Women's Movements". In R. Pearson/C. Sacks (eds.) *Divided We Stand: Gender Analysis and Development Issues*.

Moore, Henrietta (1994) *A Passion for Difference*, Cambridge: Polity Press.

Morsy, Soheir/Nelson, Cynthia/Saad, R./Sholkamy, H. (1991) "Anthropology and the Call for the Indigenization of Social Science in the Arab World". In Earl T. Sullivan/Jacqueline S. Ismael (eds.) *Contemporary Studies of the Arab World*, Edmonton/AB: University of Alberta Press, pp. 81-111.

Nicholson, Linda (1994) "Interpreting Gender". *Signs* 20/1, pp. 79-105.

Risseew, Carla (1992) "Bourdieu, Power and Resistance: Gender Transformation in Sri-Lanka". In Kathy Davis/Monique Leijenaar/Jantine Oldersma (eds.) *The Gender of Power*, London: Sage Publications.

Rugh, Andrea (1984) *The Family in Contemparay Egypt*, Syracuse/NY: Syracuse University Press.

Singerman, Diane (1995) *Avenues of Participation: Family, Politics and Networks in Urban Quarters of Cairo*, Princeton/NJ: Princeton University Press.

El-Solh, Camilia Fawzi/Mabro, Judy (eds.) (1994) *Muslim Women's Choices: Religious Belief and Social Reality*, Berg Publishers.

Tapper, Nancy (1991) *Bartered Brides: Politics, Gender and Marriage in an Afghan Society*. Cambridge Studies in Social and Cultural Anthropology, Cambridge, New York/NY: Cambridge University Press.

Watson, Helen (1994) "Separation and Reconciliation: Marital Conflict among the Muslim Poor in Cairo". In Camilia El-Solh/Judy Mabro (eds.) *Muslim Women's Choices: Religious Beliefs and Social Reality,* Berg Publishers, pp. 33-54.

"We Are Not Feminists!"

Egyptian Women Activists on Feminism[1]

Nadje Al-Ali

Introduction

Experimental and post-colonial anthropology has increasingly problematized the "pursuit of the other" (Visweswaran 1994: 20), power relations between researcher and informant as well as representation. Attempts to decolonize anthropology have been particularly notable with regard to feminist scholarship, which, by its very definition, needs to continually challenge the very notion of the canon. Nevertheless, not every feminist scholar doing research in the Arab world is as conscious of power relationships between cultures (colonizer/colonized) as s/he might be of power relations within culture (male/female). Therefore, an analysis of "positioning" is a key to understanding how many feminist ethnographers theorize.

A new kind of feminist scholarship related to the "wind of cultural decolonization" (Morsy/Nelson/Saad/Sholkamy 1991) has taken different directions. One manifestation of this kind of research is marked by the various ways in which female ethnographers confront their biases as western women, feminists, or belonging to a particular class, religion, etc. Many anthropologists have pointed out that fieldwork is situated between autobiography and anthropology (Hastrup 1992) and that it connects a personal experience with a general field of knowledge. Fieldwork is not the unmediated world of "others", but the world between ourselves and the others. The concept of "intersubjectivity" – the relationship between the researcher and the research community, the politico-cultural worlds to which each belong, and the ultimate purpose of the research project (Sayigh 1996: 2) – is addressed by many feminist researchers.

The move to decolonize anthropology also induced more and more "indigenous" female scholars to do "home-work", or "anthropology in reverse" (Visweswaran 1994: 102). While "home-work" is still largely unaccepted by the mainstream canon, it is becoming very clear that the cultural insights, language-skills and motivation of many indigenous female anthropologists subvert some of the cultural stereotypes, generalizations and misconceptions brought forth by earlier conventional Western scholarship.

At the same time as indigenous researchers have increasingly entered and contested the field of anthropological knowledge production, a growing number of "hyphenated" researchers, "hybrids" or "halfies" have not only challenged the canon but also notions of "Western" vs. "indigenous" scholarship. The term "halfie" has been coined by Lila Abu-Lughod to categorize "people whose national or cultural heritage is mixed by virtue of migration, overseas education, or parentage" (Abu-Lughod 1991: 140). While I refuse to be labeled "halfie", I am certainly facing the dilemmas that Abu-Lughod associates with being "halfie" and feminist:

> Halfies' dilemmas are ... extreme. As anthropologists, they write for other anthropologists, mostly Western. Identified also with communities outside the West, or subcultures within it, they are called to account by educated members of these communities. More importantly, not just because they position themselves with respect to two communities, but because when they present the Other they are presenting themselves, they speak with a complex awareness of and investment in reception.
>
> (1991: 142)

In previous research, I experienced the shifting boundaries between "self" and "other", between my own identity and the identities of the people I studied: what had started out as an endeavor to understand what it means to be a woman in Egypt and in the Arab world became a project where I learned as much about myself. However, more often than being a source of "self-knowledge", "mediation" and "bridging", the experience of being "here and there" poses great dilemmas and conflicts for the researcher (see El-Kkoly/Al-Ali 1999).

Hyphenated identities enact an often violent struggle between two or more worlds. Nasser Hussein's description of post-colonial identities certainly rings a bell:

> Hyphens are radically ambivalent signifiers, for they simultaneously connect and set apart; they simultaneously represent both belonging and not belonging. What is even more curious about a hyphenated pair of words is that meaning cannot reside in one word or the other, but can only be understood in movement.
>
> (1990: 10)

The attempt to negotiate the terms between shifting alliances results in the feeling of being "born over and over again as a hyphen rather than a fixed entity" (Trinh 1991: 159). Being an Iraqi-German doing research in the Arab world suggests more than an accidental academic trajectory, since the very subject matter of my Ph.D. dissertation is related to this "hybrid subject position" (Visweswaran 1994). In my research among secular-oriented[2] Egyptian women activists, I have been particularly interested in exploring the intersections and contentions of gender and national identity. Because the Egyptian women's movement is often accused of being "westernized", women activists are constantly challenged to reassert their "authenticity" without giving up their struggles and visions, as well as their links to regional and international organizations.

The issue of "hybridity" is problematized by Sayigh who questions the effects of prolonged exposure to a specific culture:

> While culturally enriching, hybridity perhaps induces a half-conscious adoption of the research community's ethos; and this, while enhancing rapport, may block off certain questions and inquiries.
>
> (Ibid. 1996: 2-3)

In my view, it is not only important to acknowledge our "positionality", that is the different components of our identities, presuppositions and political orientations that we bring from our home(s), but as

Lindisfarne (1997) and Sayigh (1996) point out, we must also recognize that our research community will have an impact on the ways we see and think about the world. Lindisfarne, for example, explains how her fieldwork in Syria shaped her "political voice" and identity (Lindisfarne 1997), which in many ways parallels my experiences in Cairo. My political commitment to feminism and my attempts to counter dehumanizing depictions of "Arabs" in the western media developed and grew while living and doing research in Cairo. Only later, throughout my recent fieldwork, did I also become sensitive to sweeping generalizations concerning "the West" which have become part of my battles and research agenda.

Feminism as the Other

Imagine a woman who does not correspond to common ideals of beauty and does not even make an effort to hide her unattractiveness with make-up. Aside from her physical shortcomings, she has a personality problem. She is loud, shrill and terribly aggressive. She goes around fighting everything and everyone, especially men. She hates them. All of them. Most likely she is a lesbian. In any case, she is obsessed with sex.

You are not wrong in guessing that I am describing a feminist – to be precise, a western feminist. Cliches and stereotypes of this sort are prevalent among men and women all over the world. You might ask yourselves why I would invoke such a crude image of a western feminist when writing a supposedly academic paper about indigenous knowledge and feminism in Egypt. I suggest that there is a relation between the stereotype described and the way many Egyptian women activists define feminism.

Egyptian feminists, whose activism has been historically rooted in nationalism, have always run the risk of being stigmatized as anti-religious and anti-nationalist. In recent years, women activists have been increasingly accused – particularly by Islamists and conservatives, but also by leftist-nationalist voices – of collaborating with "western imperialism" by importing alien ideas and practices and circulating them throughout society. In light of these very intimidating charges, it is not surprising that many women activists internalized these accusations, and themselves equate feminism with a Western concept, alien and alienating to their social, cultural and political context (Al-Ali 2000: 47).

The resistance of many Egyptian women to identifying themselves with feminism is not only related to its negative image in society, but is also linked to the conviction that it detracts from such "larger issues" as imperialism, class struggle and Zionism. In this view, feminism is perceived to divide women and men in their common struggle against these forces. Nevertheless, many women activists in Egypt are engaged in producing knowledge of and attitudes towards "feminism". My chapter does not simply focus on the widespread construction of feminism as a western phenomenon or even conspiracy, but addresses other current interpretations among Egyptian women activists. In particular, I would like to share with you some insights of women who attempt to overcome the devastating rhetoric of "us and them" that dominates issues of both knowledge and identity formation in contemporary Egypt.

Experience and Knowledge

Another reason for starting my paper with a cliche is my interest in debates about the origins of knowledge, and especially the relationship between knowledge, experience and identity. We all know about stereotypes and their effectiveness, which resides in the way they invoke consensus, reproduce certain power relations, and create difference. The consensus invoked by stereotypes is generally accompanied with negative evaluations, which in turn relate to the disposition of power within society.

Stereotypes – whether about "the Orient" and "Muslim women" or "the Occident" and "western feminists" – do not only invoke people who do not belong and map out the boundaries of acceptable and legitimate behavior, but they also insist on boundaries exactly at those points where "in reality" there are none. Furthermore, the dichotomies of East vs. West, indigenous vs. alien, etc. which are often linked to particular cliches, actually reproduce the hegemonic discourse of Orientalism instead of subverting it.

The line between ordering our complex reality in terms of stereotypes and what we call common-sense is often very thin and blurry. Both are an effect of hegemony which defines the boundaries of the thinkable and, therefore, limits discursive possibilities. However, what is "common knowledge" among some people might not be taken for granted by others, and vice versa. This problem becomes evident when we meet each other in everyday situations and talk about ordinary things. It often occurs that the most controversial issues are related to some vague feelings and reactions deeply rooted in the specificity of our historical and cultural experiences – such as those triggered by the word "feminism".

The relation between experience and knowledge has been central to various academic critiques towards the notion of universal, objective and rational knowledge. Whether articulated in terms of phenomenology, postmodernism, feminism or postcolonialism – and I do recognize the differences among and within these schools of thought – knowledge has been separated from "the truth". Subjectivity, partiality and relativity are catch words which were coined to destabilize eurocentric and androcentric mainstream thinking in the humanities and in the social and natural sciences. Implicit in these various epistemological debates is the recognition of the social and cultural construction of reality and the political nature of all knowledge (Smith 1987; Haraway 1988; Liz/Wise 1990; Longino 1993; Dominguez 1994; Charles/Hughes-Freeland 1996). Associated with this view is the idea that "knowledge is produced by social agents who occupy particular social locations and it is shaped by the conditions of its production" (Charles/Hughes-Freeland 1996: 25).

Feminist Standpoint Theory

Among the various contributions of contemporary feminist thought to epistemological debates, "feminist standpoint theory" has been one of the most distinct and controversial approaches (Longino 1993: 201). This particular theory revolves around the privileging of the knowledge of women as a social group. It rests on the premise that "oppressed groups are epistemologically privileged in that they have more direct access to accurate knowledge about the conditions of their subordination" (Griffin 1996: 180). In other words, knowledge is given directly by experience and, to put it bluntly: if you do not have the experience, your knowledge is less valid. However, another supposition of feminist standpoint theory is that the very knowledge of women has been systematically ignored or invalidated by the dominant institutions of knowledge re/production (Smith 1987; Hill Collins 1991). For feminist politics, this both challenges the distinction between abstract theory and concrete praxis, and implies that women's experiences form an important part of feminist analysis (Lather 1990).

During the past decade, much of feminist theorizing has paid considerable attention to differences within the concept "woman" and to the problem of constructing an identity as women. While Dorothy Smith[3] seems to assume the existence of a common universal woman's standpoint, other feminist standpoint theorists, like Sandra Harding and Liz Stanley, argue that universalization is not intrinsic to the theory (Longino 1993: 205). Since differences among women with regard to class, race, culture, etc. have been generally acknowledged, I do not want to belabor the dangers of essentialism. What is most significant here is the problematic conceptualization of experience as "authentic truth" that provides evidence for identity, difference and agency. Implicit in this approach is the epistemological position that "reality" is immediately knowable, without the mediation of concepts or theory since experience produces knowledge directly (Charles 1996: 6).

Recently, some feminist scholars pointed to the dangers of ignoring the constructed nature of experience. Joan W. Scott (1992: 25), for example, argues that "experience" has to be problematized by asking how subjects are constituted in the first place, how one's vision is structured, and what roles language and history play. In other words, Scott suggests that the concept of experience has often been used in a way that resulted in essentializing identity and reifying the subject. Her project, in contrast, is to analyze the ways in which experience itself is constructed through discourse.

My research attempts to examine how the discourses to which particular women have access influence their experience of the women's rights struggle in Egypt. While not representing easily separable and identifiable strands, the dominant discourses of social change in Egypt have generally been labeled nationalist, modernist, socialist, developmental and Islamist. Since the context of this paper is my larger research project on gender and national identities among secular-oriented women activists, I have chosen to leave out the various Islamist discourses concerning feminism.

"Feminisms", according to Deniz Kandiyoti (1996), "are never autonomous but bound to the signifying networks of the contexts which produce them." In this sense, I will attempt to outline the discursive context of secular-oriented women activists in Egypt today. However, as Dorothy Smith argues, feminist researchers "should never lose sight of women as actively constructing, as well as interpreting, the social processes and social relations which constitute their everyday realities" (Stanley/Wise 1990: 34). It is important to stress that the activists do not just mobilize pre-existing discourses to make sense of their experiences, but also develop new concepts, discourses, approaches and visions throughout their struggles.

Al-Haraka Al-Nissa'iyah or Al-Nassa'wiyah?

Identifying localized knowledge and problematizing "experience" involves a consideration of language, that is, the specific words available to articulate what I broadly define as "feminism"[4]. The actual Arabic terminology used when the women's rights struggle is addressed varies according to ideological outlook and political affiliation. All terms seem to carry "heavy baggage", and I would like to start this part of my paper by quoting Marlyn Tadros, a feminist and human rights activist who expresses the difficulty of choosing the "right" words:

> There exist different words for feminism in Egypt. This is problematic. '*Tahrir al-mar'a* [women's liberation] has a horrible connotation to many people. They associate it with promiscuity: she has to go out until midnight to be a free woman. The term was used in the past. ... *Al-haraka al-nissa'wiyah*" [the feminist movement] is very elitist. Very few people would understand it. It is only used with educated leftist people. ... There is a book by the Tagammu called 'Naqd Al-Haraka Al-Nisswaniyah.' Usually *nisswaniyah* [women's] has a rude connotation. Men use '*niswan*' to undermine women. ... Whether '*nissa'iyah* or *nassa'wiyah*': even the '*haraka*' puts people of guard: '*eh, da, sitat fi haraka?*' [what's that, women in movement?] It tends to be exclusive. Men get very offended. ... Normally I use '*qadaya al-mar'a* [women's issues]. But all of these terms have horrible connotations. If you say '*qadaya al-mar'a*, of course you get all kinds of comments. If you use '*wada' al-mar'a* [situation or

status of women] you are actually just making people feel safe. This is the status of women and it has a less threatening connotation. *'Wada' al-mar'a* is also more narrowly defined. It mainly addresses women's legal rights.

This particular quote reflects a very sad reality: women activists constantly have to be on the defensive against a vast number of charges ranging from being "loose women" to paying lip service to "the West". The attempt to legitimize and justify their outlooks and activism is at the center of many debates and can be detected in the various trends I am going to present. Moreover, the diverse terminologies used have roots in historical discourses, but are also shaped by ongoing activities and debates (Al-Ali 2000:47-48).

The term "*al-haraka al-nissa'iyah al-misriyyah*" (the Egyptian women's movement)[5] is generally evoked concerning the past. As a member of the radical leftist women's center *Ma'an* (Together) put it:

Historically, the women always used '*al-haraka al-nisai'yah al-misriyah*' [the Egyptian women's movement]. It was a politicized women's movement from the 20s to the 50s. It represented the nationalist's women's point of view. From Huda Sha'rawi to Inji Aflatoun, women were interested in how to develop the law, how to create new social, economic and political relations. In all of this, they were trying to see how changes for women were going to improve the whole situation and all of society.

Implicit in this seemingly historical account of the Egyptian women's movement is a whole range of information concerning this particular activist's positioning within the contemporary context. Stressing the close link between the beginning of the women's movement and "the nationalist view", this activist alludes to an attitude, in which "*tahrir al-mar'a*" (women's liberation) is part and parcel of anti-colonial and anti-imperialist struggle.

This perspective can be traced back to what has been called the "national liberation discourse", in which women are dealt with as part of the struggle for economic and political decolonization (Hatem 1993: 42). Many women I interviewed agree with the writer and activist Latifa Zayyad, who holds the view that every important feminist movement, or feminist, reached certain rights only in collaboration with the nationalist movement: "the woman who binds herself to a national movement requires rights and requires influences; the one who does not is easily excluded."

While early feminists like Huda Sha'rawi struggled with "a West" perceived to be outside the Egyptian nation (British colonialism), contemporary struggles with *"al-hagma al-thaqafiyya"* (the cultural attack) and *"imberiliyya"* (imperialism) are of a far more complex nature. When asked about the actual meaning of imperialism, women activists affiliated with leftist organizations often allude to U.S.' policies which are seen to promote both Egypt's dependence and capitalist expansion. Many women mentioned the IMF and USAID, as well as multi-national companies and enforced privatization in relation to capitalist expansion. Zionism and normalization with Israel are also perceived to be part of "imperialist hegemony" (Al-Ali 2000: 48).

Several women referred to "western culture" and its attempt to undermine local cultures as posing a threat to Egypt. Mass consumption, "McDonaldization", disrespect for the family, promiscuity, the AIDS epidemic, and drug addiction are reported to represent the characteristics of "western civilization". It became obvious to me that, in this context, discussions about "the West" often revealed and concealed discourses about social classes and malaise within Egyptian society. Some consider the "nouveau riche" and "westernized Egyptians" *khawagas* (foreigners) just like the tourists who roam the country (ibid.).

In response to my question of what is unique about Egyptian culture, Latifa Zayyad said:

There are so many things that are unique about Egyptian culture. The answer to your question is: what is so beautiful about American culture that you want to make it the only culture? Racism? Loneliness? Absence of human relations? Technologies?

Other women were more cautious with their generalizations about "the West" and differentiated between government politics and people. Many women stressed that they refer to the United States and not Europe when talking about imperialism.

Coming back to the activist I quoted with regard to the historical women's movement, it is obvious that, aside from her nationalist leaning, she also subordinates women's rights to a wider struggle for social justice. She describes the women's movement from the 20s to the 50s as a politicized movement concerned with the liberation of the whole society. Here, this activist differs with the majority of – who, for lack of a better term, I would call – "leftist nationalist women". Most women I talked to distinguish between the beginning of the movement associated with Huda Sha'rawi, which they consider elitist and bourgeois, and the period of the 40s and 50s, which is generally seen to involve radical middle-class women. According to Latifa Zayyad:

In the 40s there were new forces which came into play. This part of the story is usually dismissed, because it denoted a radical change and gave the national fight also a social level. What we fought for was not only national independence but also social justice.

In most of my interviews with the members of the *Ittihad Al-Nisa'i Al-Taqadummi* (The Progressive Women's Union), the Nasserite party, and the leftist women's center *Ma'an* (together), the term "*al-haraka al-nissa'iyah*" (the women's movement) links the struggle for women's rights to the general political struggle for social justice – sometimes explicitly expressed as class struggle – and democratic rights. These women distinguish "*al-haraka al-nissa'iyah*" from the recently coined term "*al-haraka al-nassa'wiyah*" (the feminist movement) which they perceive as reducing women's issues to the struggle between men and women.

The Marxist-feminist 'Arab Loutfi told me:

We mainly use '*al-haraka al-nissa'iyah*' [the women's movement] as a terminology in our analysis, because '*nassa'wiyah*' [feminism] rings different bells. As a word we use '*nissa'iyah*', because we think definitely that the social and class struggle is very important in seeing women's oppression. We see it in the context of a complex social, historical and economic struggle. This is not related to the relation between women and men.

Many members of development-oriented NGOs, like *Rabtat Al-Mar'a Al-'Arabiyah* (the Alliance of Arab Women), share a similar outlook concerning "*al-haraka al-nassa'wiyah*". According to Fatema

Khafagi: "it merely addresses the patriarchal system and does not address economic and political issues."

Egyptian women activists who opted to consider themselves *"nassa'wiyat"* (feminists) – like members of the group *Markaz Dirasat Al-Mar'a Al-Gedida* (the New Woman's Research Centre) – stress that they initially entered the struggle for women's rights as political activists in a wider sense. All the founding members of *Al-Mar'a Al-Gedida* were involved in the student movement of the 70s and were members of the political left. When they originally came together in the 80s, they were united by vague notions regarding the importance of "women's issues" and the women's movement in Egypt. After more than a decade of internal debate, research, campaigning and activism all these women moved away from their initial position of considering the women's rights struggle as secondary to the wider struggle.

However, all *Al-Mar'a Al-Gedida's* members emphasize their concern with issues such as poverty, illiteracy, democracy and human rights. They reject the routine and traditional accusation of merely being engaged in a struggle against men. Amal Abdel-Hadi, a member of *Al-Mar'a Al-Gedida* explained:

Feminism is a perspective: a man can be a feminist. There are women in the women's movement who are very reactionary. They only do charity work and are not embracing a holistic perspective. There are men who are advocates of women's rights.

Another widespread perception is the "foreignness" and linked "corruption" of the concept of feminism. The majority of both development-oriented NGO members and leftist women perceive *"nassa'wiyah"* (feminism) as a western concept. In their view, feminism imposes certain issues, like sexual freedom, abortion, circumcision or wife battering, for example, which are perceived to be insignificant in the Egyptian context. One activist told me that she, like others, would generalize about western feminists, because

this is how things have reached us. The only attempt in the feminist line was taken by Nawal El-Saadawi who was not very popular.

The idea of feminism being western is vehemently rejected by those activists who chose "*al-haraka al-nassa'wiyah*" as the most appropriate term for themselves. Hala Shoukrallah, one of the founding members of the women's group *Al-Mar'a Al-Gedida* explains:

> The whole notion of feminism being Western reflects the lack of basic concepts, which is related to the general crisis of intellectuals. There is a lack of understanding that feminism is a way to look at power structures. Feminism is often considered to be a bourgeois concept, linked to foreign funding. We are perceived to be a women's organization that works only on abortion and wife battering. It is disturbing for others if we work on labor laws, for example.

While some Egyptian "*nassawiyat*" reject the notion of feminism as a western movement and approach, a number of other feminists distance themselves from "western feminism", by making claims to authenticity and rootedness in Egyptian culture. Some women told me, that, while they are seen as too radical in the Egyptian context, they would be considered as too conservative by western feminists. "Our struggle is not about hating men, nor is lesbianism an issue for us". In this sense, even some Egyptian women activists who consider themselves feminists appear to have appropriated the stereotype I evoked earlier. Only very few stress the existence of different tendencies and schools of "western feminism". Nevertheless, most feminists feel compelled, especially in public, to not totally break with "nationalist discourse" as this would totally delegitimize their activities in Egypt today. Those who dare are a minority. Mary Assad, a feminist who has been active since the 50s told me:

> I work on women's issues, because I happened to be the 4th girl in the family and I was unwanted. Since I was a little girl I always felt the oppression. I felt very vulnerable. My real experience with oppression started from there. But I got an idea about feminism through my contacts with western feminists. One thing we have in common is that we women have always been defined by men. I still get very angry if anyone tries to define me. A sense of identity is very important for any human being. I am struggling so that women define themselves. Gender oppression is as bad as racial oppression, if not worse. Of course, I can dialogue with western feminists. Anyhow, it is not very clear what is Western feminism. It is certainly not one thing. In 1975, I attended the

women's conference in Mexico. There were lots of radical feminists who would not even listen to the Mariachi, because they were all men. Since then they have mellowed down a lot. And there are many different trends.

This voice represents an exception among the 80 women I have interviewed. Nevertheless, I have sensed that the more recent experiences related to international conferences had a constructive impact on many women activists. A number of women told me that they have gained strength and confidence throughout the preparations for the ICPD and Beijing. Despite the many criticisms towards the preparations and actual conference proceedings, most women also perceived both the ICPD and Beijing as turning points in their personal and political development. Encounters with feminists from all over the world, in some cases, led to an increased awareness that, worldwide, there exist many different movements with distinct approaches and agendas. Some women revealed to me their surprise that, despite all the differences, similarities and solidarities can be found across cultural borders (Al-Ali 2000: 50).

The experiences related to the international feminist community also resulted in the questioning and reconceptualization of the traditional public versus private dichotomy. Despite obvious differences between liberal pro-government and leftist opposition women, a common discursive universe exists. The apparent common ground concerning the public versus private sphere has its roots in the historical male-created modernist discourses and the more recent development discourse.

According to Mervat Hatem (1993: 42), both nationalist and liberal-modernist discourses only focused on women's rights in the public sphere as part of the process of creating new societies. They accepted "women's public space, where they were expected to pursue public activities like education, work, and some form of political participation, especially suffrage" (ibid.: 40). In both cases, women's rights within the "private", family sphere were not only ignored, but also considered as standing outside the legitimate struggle for women's rights.[6]

Personal forms of subordination, patriarchal domination and oppression within the home still remain "taboo issues" among the majority of women activists in Egypt today. However, those women who bring up such issues as women's reproductive rights and domestic violence have succeeded in raising awareness about the existence of previously disregarded forms of oppression.

A tremendous amount of work remains in order to convince the majority of the urgency and significance of certain issues. If nothing else, these issues have been put on the public agenda and can no longer be completely ignored. Even if most activists perceive the issue of "women and violence", for instance, as secondary to problems of poverty and illiteracy, they have been forced to seriously consider it and take a position. This increased awareness of domestic violence has changed the way many activists experience their own and other women's situations in Egypt which, in turn, has increased their knowledge about *"qadaya al-mar'a"* (women's issues) as well as what their own struggle entails.

While many activists still hold on to established discourses of social change, there is a tendency to question former certainties. The original modernist discourse of social change promotes women's liberation as a direct consequence of modernization, that is technological progress and the development of socio-economic and educational arenas. On the other hand, socialist discourse in its initial form views women's liberation as a direct consequence of the abolishment of economic exploitation. Today, most women express their shift in outlook concerning the links between both modernization, socialism, and women's liberation.

Farida Naqash, a prominent literary critic and member of the *Ittihad Al-Nissa'i*, told me:

Ten years ago I rejected the concept of feminism totally. Human socialist struggle, I thought, would emancipate women. However, it has been proven that even within a socialist system, there still are cultural ideologies marginalizing women. Now I am a feminist in this sense: it is not enough that women take part in struggle against imperialism and economic exploitation, there has to be another struggle for improving women's image and role in society.

Some activists mentioned the marginalization of women in international political struggles like in Algeria, Palestine and the former Soviet Union as the main reason for reconsidering their original approach. Others declared that the crisis in socialist ideology after the breakup of the Soviet Union provoked them to be more concerned with women's issues. Sometimes, this crisis of ideology results in a degree of confusion concerning the particular meanings attached to various concepts:

We see that *abawiyah* [patriarchy] is a by-product of the economic system. But it is so dominant and domineering, so powerful in the superstructure that it even effects the infrastructure. So when we discuss items we use *'haraka nissa'iyah'*, but we call ourselves *'nassawiyat Marxiat'*; we are Marxist women fighting patriarchy; the point is that sometimes when we discuss with Europeans, it mixes them up; there are differences of definition.

Disappointment in the actual implementation of socialist values and the general crisis of socialist ideology are not the only reasons for questioning the earlier certainties. Many women confessed that their personal life painfully showed them that "there is something called 'women's issues'," which has to be tackled independently of the general struggle for social justice. The awareness that even "progressive" men oppress women – either within the context of party politics or within the institution of the family – is a turning point in the lives of many activists.

"Reality is stronger than all theories," is how a member of the *Tagammu* party and the *Ittihad Al'Nissa'i Al-Taqadummi* started her personal account of disillusionment:

I will give you an example of my life: I was married for twelve years. My husband was a progressive political activist and we were together in the Tagammu party. Then I decided to get a divorce. If he had wanted to divorce me he could have done it without my knowledge for five pounds and then sent me a paper. However, my wanting a divorce was a struggle. I got it after three months. Actually I got it after five years and three months, because when I first told him he traveled away and did not return until five years later. He told me that I must be kidding when I asked for the divorce. He said that I was psychologically disturbed and needed therapy. Then he left. When he came back after five years, I did not want to live with him anymore. After three months I got a divorce, but I had to give up all my rights and property. He took everything: the apartment, the furniture, even the gifts I had received from my friends.

Accounts of personal hardship, struggle and challenge constitute an prominent element in my interviews. Instead of the slogan "the personal is political", most respondents formulated the relationship between their personal lives and their political outlooks and activism as a dialectic. In this dialectic, women tended to start out their political activism by viewing men as partners, as comrades. They rarely questioned their secondary roles within political organizations as well traditional roles within the family. The accumulation of discrimination and humiliation over the years provoked many women to search for new explanations, visions and solidarities. New concepts entered their discourses, such as *abawiyah* (patriarchy), which allowed for ways to explain many of the contradictions which were previously ignored. Whether conceptualized as *nissa'i* or *nassa'wi*, the particular experiences of what it means to be a women activist in Egypt have changed considerably during the last decade.

The category "woman" allows activists to explain their exclusion from and subordination within the leftist political movement as a consequence of their gender. Although acknowledging differences among women concerning class, religious and political affiliations, etc. womanhood becomes significant as a method of distinguishing women from men in political struggle. Thus women activists counter criticisms that leftist men raise by replacing an objective understanding of oppression with a subjective one rooted in experience.

Conclusion

Standing in front of the bookshelves of "Silvermoon", my favorite feminist bookstore in London, I am always reminded that I cannot just lump together tendencies and approaches as different as radical feminism, liberal feminism, Marxist feminism, existentialist feminism, psychoanalytic feminism, postmodern feminism, and other assorted hybrids which are produced by women all over the world. Without doubt, there were times when North-American and European feminists appropriated the term "feminism". This, however, never negated that no other women's liberation movements emerged in various societies and cultures. Today, the existence and diversity of feminisms worldwide can no longer be ignored. In feminist scholarship, the acknowledgment of and engagement with a multiplicity of feminist activisms and perspectives indicates a process of flowering and maturing.

The homogeneous category "western feminism" raises many questions. An interrogation of its content – like the content of any cliche – shows that its "reality" is invented anew every time it is deployed for this or that purpose. I have tried to show how stereotypical representations of "man-hating lesbians" have not only become "common knowledge", but have also entered the discourses of identity and difference of many Egyptian women activists. As I have pointed out earlier, the role of stereotypes is to create boundaries and to make firm and separate what is, in reality, fluid and much closer to the norm than the dominant value system cares to admit. This holds true for both Egyptian men and women who stereotype women activists in order to show their "otherness" and "marginality," as well as Egyptian feminists who use stereotypes to distance themselves from "western feminists".

It has become clearer since Edward Said's "Orientalism" that stereotyping is actually part of a political ploy: it uses available cultural categories to gain symbolic advantages for the self and to handicap the "other". Occidentalism, like its orientalist counterpart, is shaped by political contingencies which seek power and influence (Carrier 1995). Historically, so-called "westerners" have been more powerful – and hence more able than people elsewhere – to construct and impose images of alien societies. Nevertheless, essentialist definitions of "the West", and categories such as "western feminism", are actually manifestations of the very same process, that, in Said's words almost two decades ago, seeks "to intensify its own sense of itself by dramatizing the distance and difference between what is closer to it and what is far away" (Said 1978: 55).

Epistemological debates about the specificity of knowledge, whether gendered or localized, have been the theoretical frame of this paper. Feminist standpoint theory has sought to provide an account of knowledge rooted in women's concrete experience. But, experiences are rooted, at least to a certain extent, in *a priori* knowledge. Thus, the jump from knowledge to "truth" will always be partial and exclusionary. However, Egyptian women activists do not just mobilize pre-existing discourses to make sense of their experiences. Discourses are produced by actors, and are at the same time productive of those actors. Some activists are engaged in developing new discourses, which either reconstruct experience or make knowable experience which was previously unknowable.

While academic approaches to knowledge constitute one of the less accessible debates for feminist activists, they are crucial to feminist politics and greater efforts should be made to bridge the gap between feminist philosophizing and activism. Another task for all researchers – not only halfies – is to overcome long-established binary oppositions between "indigenous" and "western" bodies of knowledge. Knowledge, theories and concepts are being produced in Latin America, South-East Asia and Africa and not only in Europe and Northern America. At a time of interpenetrating communities and power relations (Narayan 1997) "the West" has far from ceased to pose concrete threats and encroachments. However, notions of "indigenous" or "authentic" knowledge remain meaningless and narrow-minded as long as they do not self-critically tackle the relative lack of actual theory building from within the Arab world and persist to be locked into "what the other is."

Notes

1 This chapter ist based on a larger research project about the Egyptian women's movement and the political culture it is embedded in. See Al-Ali 2000.
2 A "secular-oriented" tendency refers to the belief in the separation between religion and politics, but does not necessarily denote anti-religious or anti-Islamic positions. Secular-oriented women do not support *shari'a* as the main or sole source of legislation; rather they also refer to civil law and human rights conventions, as stipulated by the United Nations, as frames of reference for their struggle. See Al-Ali (2000) for more detailed discussion.
3 One of the original standpoint theorists, the sociologist Dorothy Smith advocates an alternate sociology that begins with "insiders knowledge", that is, personal knowledge of one's own lived experience. She tries to show how sociological concepts are expressions of social relations, that are coined by men who, since its beginning, have been dominating the discipline of sociology.
4 For the purpose of my analysis I have chosen to use "feminism"

as a conceptual framework in its broadest possible sense: it denotes both a consciousness and a social movement. It is based on the awareness that women suffer discrimination because of their gender. Awareness of injustice, however, is not sufficient. The other aspect of "feminism" is found in the actual attempts to change these inequalities and remove constraints placed upon women in favor of a more equitable gender system. I perceive any groups or individuals who try to alleviate the position of – or change ideas about – women as "feminist".

5 My research findings diverge from Margot Badran's conceptualization of *Nissa'iyah* in her recent work *Feminists, Islam, and Nation* (1995). She states that with the creation of the Egyptian Feminist Union in 1924 "women for the first time in a highly public and unequivocal way used the adjective *nisa'i/yah* to signify feminist instead of the ambiguous 'women's'." All my respondents translated *nissa'i/yah* as "women's" and referred to the new term of nassawi/yah as feminist.

6 In this respect, modernist and socialist discourses parallel Islamist discourses of women's liberation. While I am focusing on "secular-oriented" women in my research, both in my readings and in the few interviews with Islamist women, like Zeinab Radwan, I detected a similar approach of restricting women's rights to what is perceived to be the "public sphere".

Selected Bibliography

Abu-Lughod, Lila (1991) "Writing Against Culture". In Richard Fox (ed.) *Recapturing Anthropology*, Santa Fee/NM: SAR Press, pp. 137-162.

Al-Ali, Nadje (2000) *Secularism, Gender and the State: The Egyptian Women's Movement*, Cambridge Middle East Studies 14, Cambridge: Cambridge University Press.

Badran, Margot (1995) *Feminists, Islam, and the Nation: Gender and the Making of Modern Egypt*, Princeton/NJ: Princeton University Press.

Carrier, James G. (ed.) (1995) *Occidentalism: Images of the West*, Oxford: Clarendon Press.

Charles, Nickie/Hughes-Freeland, Felicia (eds.) (1996) *Practising*

Feminism: Identity, Difference, Power, London, New York/NY: Routledge.
Dominguez, Virginia R. (1994) "Differentiating Women/Bodies of Knowledge". *American Anthropologist 1*, pp. 127-130.
Griffin, Christine (1996) "Experiencing Power: Dimensions of Gender, 'Race' and Class". In Nickie Charles/Felicia Hughes-Freeland (eds.) *Practising Feminism*, London, New York/NY: Routledge, pp. 180-201.
Haraway, Donna (1988) "Situated Knowledges: the Science Question in Feminism and the Privilege of the Partial Perspective". *Feminist Studies* 14, pp. 575-99.
Harding, Sandra (1991) *Whose Science? Whose Knowledge? Thinking from Women's Lives*, Ithaca/NY: Cornell University Press.
Hastrup, Kirsten (1992) "Writing Ethnography: State of the Art". In Judith Okeley/Helen Callaway (eds.) *Anthropology and Autobiography*, London, New York/NY: Routledge, pp. 116-133.
Hatem, Mervat (1993) "Toward the Development of Post-Islamist and Post-Nationalist Discourses in the Middle East". In Judith Tucker (ed.) *Arab Women: Old Boundaries, New Frontiers*, Bloomington/IN: Indiana University Press, pp. 29-48.
Hill Collins, Patricia (1991) *Black Feminist Thought: Knowledge, Consciousness and the Politics of Empowerment*, Boston/MA: Hyman.
Hussein, Nasser (1989) "Hyphenated Identity: Nationalist Discourse, History, and the Anxiety of Criticism in Salman Rushdie's Shame". *Qui Parle?*, 3/2 fall 1989, pp.1-18.
Kandiyoti, Deniz (1996) "Contemporary Feminist Scholarship and Middle East Studies". In Deniz Kandiyoti (ed.) *Gendering the Middle East: Emerging Perspectives*, London, New York/NY: I.B. Tauris Publishers.
El-Kholy, Heba/Al-Ali, Nadje (1999) "Inside/Out: The 'Native' and the 'Halfie' Unsettled". In Shami Seteney/Linda Herrera (eds.) *Between Field and Text: Emerging Voices in Egyptian Social Science*, Cairo Papers in Social Science 22/2, Cairo: The American University in Cairo Press, pp. 14-40.
Lather, Paula (1990) "Review of 'Critical Pedagogy and Cultural Power' by David Livingstone et al.". *International Journal of Qualitative Studies in Education* 3, pp. 90-94.
Lindisfarne, Nancy (1997) "Local Voices and Responsible Anthropo-

logy". In Verena Stolcke (ed.) *Reassessing Anthropological Responsibility*, London, New York/NY: Routledge.

Longino, Helen (1993) "Feminist Standpoint Theory and the Problems of Knowledge". *Signs* 19, pp. 201-212.

Morsy, Soheir/Nelson, Cynthia/Saad, Reem/Sholkamy, Hania (1991) "Anthropology and the Call for Indigenization of Social Science in the Arab World". In Earl T. Sullivan/Jacqueline S. Ismael (eds.) *Contemporary Studies of the Arab World*, Edmonton/AB: University of Alberta Press. pp. 88-111.

Narayan, Uma (1997) *Dislocating Cultures: Identities, Traditions and Third World Feminism*, London, New York/NY: Routledge.

Said, Edward W. (1978) *Orientalism*, New York/NY: Random Books.

Sayigh, Rosemary (1996) "Researching Gender in a Palestinian Camp: Political, Theoretical and Methodological Questions". In Deniz Kandiyoti (ed.) *Gendering the Middle East: Emerging Perspectives*, London, New York/NY: I.B. Tauris Publishers, pp. 145-167.

Scott, Joan W. (1992) "Experience". In Judith Butler/Joan W. Scott (eds.) *Feminists Theorize the Political*, New York/NY: Routledge.

Smith, Dorothy (1987) *The Everyday World as Problematic: A Feminist Sociology*, Boston/MA: Northeastern University Press.

—— (1990) *Texts, Facts, Femininity: Exploring the Relations of Ruling*, London: Routledge.

Stanley, Liz (ed.) (1990) *Feminist Praxis: Research, Theory and Epistemology in Feminist Sociology*, London: Routledge.

Stanley, Liz/Wise, Sue (1990) "Method, Methodology and Epistemology in Feminist Research Processes". In Liz Stanley (ed.) *Feminist Praxis*, London: Routledge, pp. 20-62.

Trinh, T. Minh-ha (1991) *When the Moon Waxes Red*, New York/NY: Routledge.

Visweswaran, Kamala (1994) *Fictions of Feminist Ethnography*, London, Minneapolis/MN: Weidenfeld and Nicholson.

The Contributors

Mona Abaza has undertaken field research in Egypt, Indonesia, Malaysia and Singapore. She published numerous articles on gender, intellectuals and Islam in Southeast Asia. Her books are: *Islamic Education: Perceptions and Exchanges. Indonesian Students in Cairo* (Cahier d'Archipel 23, Paris: EHESS, 1994). It was translated into Indonesian language. *The Changing Image of Women in Rural Egypt* (Cairo Papers in Social Science 10/Fall, The American University in Cairo, 1987). Her forthcoming work is *Shifting Worlds; Two Intellectual Islamic Milieus, Debates on Islam and Knowledge in Malaysia and Egypt*. She is currently an Assistant Professor at the American University in Cairo.

Nadje Al-Ali is a lecturer in social anthropology at the Institute of Arab and Islamic Studies at the University of Exeter. Her publications include *Secularism, Gender and the State in the Middle East: The Egyptian Women's Movement* (Cambridge: Cambridge University Press, 2000). She is a feminist activist with Women in Black and the movement to lift sanctions in Iraq.

Kamran Asdar Ali teaches anthropology at the University of Rochester, U.S.A.

Anita Häusermann Fábos is Assistant Professor in the Department of Sociology, Anthropology, Psychology and Egyptology at the American University in Cairo, Egypt. She received her Ph.D. from Boston University in Anthropology in 1999. Her areas of interest include ethnicity, citizenship, and gender in the context of migration and forced migration. She has conducted extensive fieldwork among Sudanese communities in Egypt.

The Contributors

Heba El-Kholy has a Ph.D. in Social Anthropology from the University of London. She has published several articles related to gender and poverty and women's everyday forms of resistance. She is currently Senior Regional Officer at the United Nations Development Programme (UNDP) in New York.

Petra Kuppinger is Assistant Professor of Anthropology at Monmouth College in Monmouth/IL. She has an M.A. in Anthropology from the American University in Cairo and a Ph.D. in Anthropology from the New School for Social Research. Her research interests include questions of space and power, space and culture, colonial urban histories and popular culture. She has spent many years in Cairo doing research on a small low-income urban community and its transformations in the context of larger urban developments. She is married and has one daughter.

Philip Marfleet is Director of the Refugee Studies Pogramme at the University of East London, England. He has worked at universities in the Middle East and in Britain, and has published widely on religious activism, globalization, migration and refugee affairs. Among recent publications is (with Ray Kiely) *Globalisation and the Third World* (London: Routledge, 1998).

Didier Monciaud, Associate Researcher of the GREMAMO (Research Group on the Maghreb and Machrek), Denis Diderot University, Paris; Member of the Editorial Board of the review *Les Cahiers d'Histoire*, Paris. Currently Ph.D. candidate in History *Individual Trajectory and Social Movement in Modern Egypt: The Case of Taha Sa'd 'Uthman (1916-1998)*, National Institute for Oriental Languages and Civilizations, Paris, under the supervision of Dr. Henry Laurens. Research interests: Modern history of Egypt and Sudan; social and national movement; political mobilization; Egyptian historiography and contemporary historical debates.

Cynthia Nelson is Professor of Anthropology and Dean of the School of Humanities and Social Sciences of the American University in Cairo. Author of *Doria Shafik, Egyptian Feminist: A Woman Apart* (Gainesville: University Press of Florida, 1996). Fields of academic teaching and research: Sociology of knowledge, Women's Movements in the Middle East, discourses on gender, globalization, development and medical anthropology.

Shahnaz Rouse, Sociology Faculty, Sarah Lawrence College, New York. Research interests and publications in agrarian transformation; social movements; the state, religion and identity; gender and nationalism; globalization; the politics of representation; and social/spatial constructions and transformations.

Mohammed Tabishat is a Ph.D. candidate in social anthropology at the University of Cambridge (United Kingdom). He also holds an M.A. in social anthropology and B.Sc. in medical technology, both from Yarmouk University (Jordan). His training and research are focused on medical anthropology, and power relations in contexts of modern technology and science. His dissertation focuses on contemporary perceptions of the body in illness in Cairo.